"In this clear and convincing book, Richar[d] beliefs and practices of ten popular 'cults' short of God's unchanging standard of truth. If you are interested in cult-proofing your family, this is the book to read and study. Armed with God's truth, you and your family will be better prepared for the spiritual battle that rages around us."

RICK WARREN,
Pastor, Saddleback Valley Community Church
Author of *The Purpose-driven Church*

"Carefully researched and thoroughly documented, this book is an indispensable resource on major cults and new religious movements. It is the most up-to-date source of information on these kinds of groups that I know of. This invaluable, easy-to-use resource is both informative and challenging. It will be helpful to families and anyone needing information about cults and new religions. It is current, readable, yet informed by scholarship. Required reading for anyone concerned about the spiritual supermarket that's out there."

RONALD M. ENROTH, PH.D.
Professor of Sociology, Westmont College
Author of *Churches That Abuse* and *Recovering from Churches That Abuse*

"In this helpful and enlightening volume, Abanes discusses some of the most important false religious systems confronting our society. He represents their views fairly and accurately. I especially appreciate his biblically informed, theologically astute critique of each group's doctrinal beliefs."

DR. ALAN GOMES
Associate Professor and Chair,
Department of Theology,
Talbot School of Theology

OTHER BOOKS BY
RICHARD ABANES

Journey into the Light: Exploring Near Death Experiences

American Militias: Rebellion, Racism, and Religion

Defending the Faith: A Beginner's Guide to Cults and New Religions

Embraced by the Light and the Bible

End-Time Visions: The Road to Armageddon?

CULTS,
NEW RELIGIOUS MOVEMENTS,
AND YOUR FAMILY

A Guide to Ten Non-Christian Groups
Out to Convert Your Loved Ones

RICHARD ABANES

CROSSWAY BOOKS • WHEATON, ILLINOIS
A DIVISION OF GOOD NEWS PUBLISHERS

Cults, New Religious Movements, and Your Family

Copyright © 1998 by Richard Abanes

Published by Crossway Books
    a division of Good News Publishers
    1300 Crescent Street
    Wheaton, Illinois 60187

All rights reserved. No part of this publication may be reproduced, stored in a retrieval system or transmitted in any form by any means, electronic, mechanical, photocopy, recording, or otherwise, without the prior permission of the publisher, except as provided by USA copyright law.

Cover design: Left Coast

First printing, 1998

Printed in the United States of America

All Scripture quotations in this book except those noted otherwise are from the *New American Standard Bible.*® Copyright © 1960, 1962, 1963, 1968, 1971, 1972, 1973, 1975, 1977 by the Lockman Foundation and are used by permission.

Library of Congress Cataloging-in-Publication Data
Abanes, Richard.
    Cults, new religious movements, and your family : a guide to ten
    non-Christian groups out to convert your loved ones / Richard
    Abanes.
        p.   cm.
    Includes bibliographical references and index.
    ISBN 0-89107-981-5
    1. Cults—United States. 2. New Age movement—United States.
    3. Sects—United States.   I. Title.
    BL2525.A33   1998
    239'.9—dc21   97-35599

11	10	09	08	07	06	05	04	03	02	01	00	99	98
15	14	13	12	11	10	9	8	7	6	5	4	3	2	1

To my nephew Lee Gale—
a terrific kid who grew up to be a terrific young man

CONCORDIA UNIVERSITY LIBRARY
PORTLAND, OR 97211

CONTENTS

Foreword   7

Introduction   9

1 Behind the New Age Craze   13

2 World of the Occult   35

3 The Devil Made Me Do It   47

4 Hollywood's Favorite Religion   67

5 Christian Identity: White Makes Right   93

6 Nation of Islam: Allah's Black Supremacists   107

7 Moon's Moonies   135

8 All in "The Family"   161

9 Mormonism Through the Looking Glass   185

10 Jehovah's False Witnesses   225

Appendix A: 265
Blessed Trinity

Appendix B: 269
Recommended Ministries

Notes   271

Index   309

FOREWORD

Alan Gomes

News media in the last few years have done their part to raise public consciousness about "cults" and "fringe" religious movements. The inferno at the Branch Davidian compound and the mass suicide of the Heaven's Gate cult are but two poignant examples. The events surrounding these two groups were certainly newsworthy by any standard. Nevertheless, while the incessant and graphic coverage made these groups appear larger than life, it is easy to forget that they had but a handful of followers and therefore posed little risk to the public at large. Furthermore, the secular media, placing no credence in biblical truth, could not evaluate the true *spiritual danger* of these and other such groups, however wide or narrow their sphere of influence.

In this well-researched and lucidly written book, Abanes deals with ten groups that readers are much more likely to encounter and that certainly pose at least as grave a spiritual threat. Some are sociologically mainstream (e.g., Mormonism), while others would be considered behaviorally odd and potentially even dangerous (e.g., "The Family" and Christian Identity). Yet, as Abanes demonstrates clearly, all lead people away from the true God of Scripture, in whom alone is eternal life (John 17:3).

Abanes begins each chapter with a vignette, in which a former member of the group talks about how he/she came to join it, what life was like inside it, and how the Gospel's transforming power led the person out.

These stories are valuable because they give flesh and bones, as it were, to the analysis that follows. Abanes is careful to document his stories, giving real names of real people, not a fictionalized composite that defies validation. He draws on previously published case histories that can be evaluated independently, if someone wished to do so. Abanes also avoids the fallacy of hasty generalization and does not suggest that these stories characterize everyone's or even most people's experiences in the group. Rather, he has chosen his case histories judiciously with a view toward demonstrating that Christ can liberate those ensnared by each of these false religious systems.

Next, Abanes provides an engaging history of the group, containing the pertinent information about its founder(s) and its development. Most important, in my view, is his detailed analysis of each group's belief system. He is fair in representing each group's position. Rather than relying on hearsay, he quotes from the group's own publications; each group is allowed to speak for itself. Abanes covers the standard and essential doctrinal categories, such as God, Christ, sin, and salvation. He scrutinizes each belief in light of the Bible and demonstrates clearly the deviations from historic Christian orthodoxy. Because the spiritual damage of false religions is by far their most insidious aspect, Abanes has done well to dispel the darkness with the spotlight of God's truth, which alone can liberate (John 8:32).

Finally, Abanes ends each chapter with a brief discussion of the group's psychological enticement. This will be helpful to parents, relatives, and concerned friends as they seek to understand why some are attracted and what they might do to draw their loved one out or, even better, to prevent the destructive involvement in the first place.

INTRODUCTION

*Many teenagers and young adults are relatively free of serious
responsibilities and commitments such as having a family or a full
time job. Their lack of experience in the world is often accompanied
by naiveté and idealism, leaving them open to the inflated promises
and simplistic answers offered by cults.*

JOAN ROSS, ED.M. AND MICHAEL D. LANGONE, PH.D.,
THE AMERICAN FAMILY FOUNDATION[1]

The year 1982 saw a number of memorable achievements. On the aero-
nautical frontier, the shuttle *Columbia* completed its first operational flight
through space. In the field of medicine, sixty-one-year-old Barney Clark
became the first recipient of a permanent artificial heart. At the box office,
Gandhi won the Academy Award for Best Picture, beating out the sci-fi
thriller *Blade Runner* and the now-classic *Conan the Barbarian*, starring
Arnold Schwarzenegger. But the most momentous event for me took place
in New York City: I turned twenty-one. *Finally* I was an "adult" in every
state of the union!

Spiritually, though, I was still a babe, having become a born-again
Christian barely three years earlier. Not only did I rarely read the Bible, but
my ambitious, career-oriented lifestyle had prevented me from meeting
older believers who could disciple me in the faith. As a result, I knew precious little about Christian living and even less about *why* I believed *what*
I believed. But by God's grace, I soon realized my need to mature in Christ
(2 Tim. 2:22; 2 Peter 3:18).

Within a year of deciding to make a concerted effort to grow spiritually, I met Randy. He knew Scripture far better than I did and prayed with
a sincerity I had never heard before. Each week he even attended a "Bible
Study," which he described as an informal gathering of fellow believers
who wanted to plumb the depths of God's Word. Randy was everything I

wanted to be. Little did I realize that he was also a cultist, a member of The Way International, founded by Victor Paul Wierwille.

Only after attending several Bible study sessions did I find out from a friend living in another state about The Way's true identity. I couldn't believe it. Randy and the other people I had met in The Way were wonderfully kind and extremely intelligent. They were not spaced-out weirdos. All of them were good-natured, friendly, funny, and always available for counseling. They visited me when I was sick and prayed with me when I was troubled. They seemed so "Christian."

In order to see if the allegations against The Way were true, I looked up the address of a nearby Christian bookstore and paid it a visit. I had never been in such a store before and had no idea what to look for. Fortunately, I managed to find the "Cults" section and ended up buying two books: *The New Cults* by Dr. Walter Martin and *Answers to Cultists at Your Door* by Bob and Gretchen Passantino. Through these two volumes I discovered that The Way International rejects the deity of Christ, denies Jesus' virgin birth, repudiates the doctrine of the Trinity, and eschews Christianity's affirmation of the personality and deity of the Holy Spirit. Members of The Way also maintain that Christendom is an apostate empire under the spiritual control of Satan. Consequently, members of The Way believe that only in their organization can one experience New Testament Christianity.

I can still remember my shock in subsequent weeks as I gradually learned more about The Way's cultic belief system. I had always thought cults were limited to two types of sinister groups: 1) those that consisted of members who shaved their heads and danced around with tambourines in airports; and 2) those that gathered together in isolated locations á la The People's Temple under Jim Jones. I found out, to my great surprise, that most cults—or new religious movements, as some sociologists prefer to call them—can be very attractive to seekers of spiritual fulfillment. Eventually, however, such alternatives to Christianity always lead to destruction—if not physical, mental, or emotional, then spiritual (Prov. 16:25).

Interestingly, a significant number of these religious belief systems either claim to be Christian or claim to be compatible with Christianity. This is perhaps the most common mark of a theological cult. Note the following definitions of a cult given by leading experts in this particular area of religion:

- "[C]ults contain major deviations from historic Christianity. Yet, paradoxically, they continue to insist that they are entitled to be classified as Christians."[2]
- "[A]ny religious movement which claims the backing of Christ or the Bible, but distorts the central message of Christianity by 1) an additional revelation, and 2) by displacing a fundamental tenet of the faith with a secondary matter."[3]
- "[A group adhering to] . . . doctrines which are pointedly contradictory to orthodox Christianity and which yet claim the distinction of either tracing their origin to orthodox sources or of being in essential harmony with those sources."[4]
- "A cult of Christianity is a group of people, which claiming to be Christian, embraces a particular doctrinal system taught by an individual leader, group of leaders, or organization, which (system) denies (either explicitly or implicitly) one or more of the central doctrines of the Christian faith as taught in the sixty-six books of the Bible."[5]
- [A] group of persons polarized around a heretical interpretation of religious truth. Such groups typically cite the Bible and claim to be in harmony with Christianity, but deny such basic doctrines of the Christian faith as the Trinity, the unique deity of Jesus Christ, salvation by grace alone, and justification by faith."[6]

Solid, biblical information showed me that I *had* to leave The Way. Sadly, I ended up losing some good friends. On the other hand, the experience brought me closer to God. My prayer to "grow in the grace and knowledge" of Jesus Christ was indeed answered, albeit not in the way that I thought it would be answered. That period in my life also marked the birth of an interest in cults that remains with me to this day and continues to be used by God for His glory (Rom. 8:28), which leads me to the purpose of this book.

Cults, New Religious Movements, and Your Family, although it can be used by seasoned Christians wanting a good introduction to cults and new religious movements, is written primarily for young adults and the parents of young adults. In a simple, easy-to-understand style, I catalog some of the religious groups that a young person is most likely to encounter in the early twenty-first century as they venture out into the adult world. I also discuss the occult, which includes countless rituals, ceremonies, and trendy practices (e.g., channeling) that serve as a means of spiritual expression in the lives of millions of individuals. This particular form of spirituality has become extremely popular in our day.

Each of the following chapters explores a particular religious group or movement from four perspectives: 1) experiential; 2) historical; 3) doctrinal/biblical; and 4) psychological/emotional. For persons who want to go beyond a beginner's level to look more deeply at a particular cult or religious movement, a short list of recommended reading concludes each chapter. My hope is to provide a useful tool that can be used by persons who want to obtain a significant degree of spiritual protection for both themselves and the people about whom they care.

As a result, we are no longer to be children, tossed here and there by waves, and carried about by every wind of doctrine, by the trickery of men, by craftiness in deceitful scheming; but speaking the truth in love, we are to grow up in all aspects into Him, who is the head, even Christ.

EPHESIANS 4:14–15

BEHIND THE
NEW AGE CRAZE

Between 1987 and 1991, there was an explosion of awareness that occurred on the planet. The New Age Movement rapidly began to lose its reputation as a "circus sideshow of psychic hucksters" and emerged as a major force for reclaiming personal power and knowledge of who we are.

DANIEL JACOB, NEW AGER[1]

Brad Scott grew up in a two-parent home marked by rigid discipline and little emotional warmth. The family's degree of spirituality was nil. Mrs. Scott, a lapsed Roman Catholic, had abandoned her faith years earlier. Brad's father—a spiritual free-thinker—believed in reincarnation and had an interest in psychic phenomena. Nevertheless, Brad, along with his younger brother and sister, was sent to Sunday school each week for four years, until Brad was twelve years old.

Mr. and Mrs. Scott were not necessarily interested in having their children become Christians, but they did want to sleep late at least one day a week, and church seemed like a way of getting their kids out of the house. During these early years Brad grew to love Jesus Christ very much. Unfortunately, his love turned cold when a change in his family's living arrangements prevented him from attending church.

At the age of fourteen, Brad's father introduced him to the writings of New Age writers such as spirit medium Ruth Montgomery and psychic Edgar Cayce, known as the sleeping prophet because of his focus on dream interpretation. Although these subjects intrigued Brad, he did not pursue them until after turning twenty in 1969, the year his high school sweetheart, whom he had married, left him. Brad was heartbroken and soon found himself in the occult section of a nearby bookstore in hopes of finding something that would ease his emotional pain. He walked away with thirty dollars worth of astrology books.

A year later Brad befriended a woman claiming to be a "New Age" Christian. He subsequently attended one of her prayer meetings where he met a number of ex-Roman Catholics who had turned to the same type of literature he had been reading. But these "Christians" introduced Brad to even more occult/metaphysical sources, including those produced by Rudolf Steiner (1861–1925), founder of the Anthroposophical Society; occultist Levi Dowling (1844–1911), author of *The Aquarian Gospel of Jesus the Christ*; and Pierre Teilhard de Chardin (1881–1955), a Jesuit paleogeologist who theorized that humanity is evolving not only physically but spiritually and that one day we will reach our "Omega Point," a time when "everything—material, spiritual, energy, love, etc.—will become synthesized in a final 'super-totalization,' which will be God."[2]

Within a year Brad met his first spirit medium. Through this contact he learned of Eastern mysticism and proceeded to look for enlightenment in the world of gurus. Brad turned to the East for spiritual truth because in college he had been told by professors and fellow students alike that Christianity was a simplistic, backward religion that held no solutions to modern problems, especially those that involve suffering. Christians, he believed, were out of touch with reality. Eastern mystics had all the answers.

Brad soon traveled to India in search of truth from that country's famed "miracle"-worker Sai Baba. He remained there for a month but was sadly disappointed. He had been denied an audience with Sai Baba because of the guru's distrust of Americans. This, however, did not dissuade Brad in the least. He returned to America and met Swami Shraddhananda, with whom he ended up studying for almost seven years.

Shraddhananda was an intelligent man who had an earned Master's degree in chemistry. He also had lectured extensively in both the United States and abroad. Most appealing, however, was this guru's air of spirituality. He glowed with a kind of self-confidence and authority that Brad thought could only come from great inner wisdom. Shraddhananda seemed to possess tremendous power. Of course, this perception was reinforced over and over again by older devotees who taught Brad that their master knew everything about them. Accordingly, Shraddhananda's followers literally worshiped him, bowing before him to touch his feet in adoration.

Brad quickly progressed in Shraddhananda's ranks. In fact, after several years he was informed that he would be his guru's successor. It was an honor that Brad never dreamed his master would bestow upon him. But at the same time, Brad began noticing a number of negative aspects to his chosen path of enlightenment. For example, a high degree of conformity was being demanded of him. He could not think, feel, say, or teach anything contrary to his guru.

There were also inconsistencies in the behavior of Shraddhananda, who touted himself as being compassionate, loving, and genuinely concerned for the welfare of his devotees. At one of the group's special functions, for instance, the venerated master became irritated with a woman who was not serving him properly and resorted to calling her a "dumb bunny," telling her to move more quickly. This was certainly not in line with the popular image of a guru.

Gradually, Brad started seeing that all of his self-effort at achieving enlightenment was not going to work. Time and again he failed to kill the ego, overcome desires, and make his mind pure. He soon realized that these goals would remain out of reach forever. They were *impossible* to obtain through self-effort. This realization led to an intense crisis of faith and a deep depression. Brad could not bear knowing that he would one day have to take over for Shraddhananda. Meditation became hopeless. Every morning Brad would simply rock back and forth while weeping, praying to Ramakrishna for some kind of insight or relief; but it never came. This spiritual, emotional, and mental torment continued unabated for nearly two years.

Fortunately, Brad was miraculously delivered from his ordeal just prior to Christmas 1979. He, like every other follower of Shraddhananda, was busily putting up holiday decorations in celebration of Jesus' birth. Within the Ramakrishna Order such celebrations are allowed because it is taught that all paths are true: "As there are many faiths, so there are many paths." Buddha's birthday was celebrated, as was Krishna's birthday, Ramakrishna's birthday, and of course, Christ's birthday. Holiday carols would even be sung in the temple in front of a beautiful Christmas tree.

During this particular Christmas, though, Brad went one step further. He decided to read a little bit of the New Testament. He happened to come across the story of the sinful woman who bathed Jesus' feet with her tears and wiped them with her hair (Luke 7:37–50). Brad was at the end of his rope and could identify completely with the woman. He then read Jesus' response: "Your sins have been forgiven. . . . Your faith has saved you; go in peace." These loving words cut deep into Brad's heart. Immediately he felt something in him melt away, sensing "a presence of light and love" (i.e., the Holy Spirit) pour into his soul and over his troubled heart. This "presence" reached down into the deepest parts of Brad's being and surged back up again, as if it were washing every part of him. He remembers that moment as if it happened yesterday:

> I felt that I was unconditionally loved as a person. It wasn't an impersonal abstraction calling me. It was Jesus Christ who had loved me since before creation. He just melted all of those structures of fear, frustration, and worry that I had built up inside through my path of self-effort.

Brad had been delivered from the spiritual bondage of his guru and transposed from the kingdom of the New Age Movement to the kingdom of God. He has since become an adjunct associate professor at California's Golden Gate College and a Christian author.[3]

HOW IT ALL BEGAN

The New Age Movement (NAM) is extremely difficult to define. It has no founder, primary leader, central headquarters, organizational structure, or definitive statement of beliefs. It does not meet in any one place or at any one particular time. It is not even limited to a single group. As a result, varying descriptions for the NAM have been proposed. Cult expert Elliot Miller calls the NAM "an extremely large, *loosely* structured network of organizations and individuals bound together by common values (based in mysticism and monism—the world view that 'all is one') and a common vision (a coming 'new age' of peace and mass enlightenment, the 'Age of Aquarius')."[4]

Award-winning journalist Russell Chandler characterizes it as "a hybrid mix of spiritual, social, and political forces" that encompasses sociology, theology, the physical sciences, medicine, anthropology, history, the human potential movement, sports, and science fiction.[5] J. Gordon Melton, a nationally recognized chronicler of religions, calls the NAM an international social and religious movement that has "showed itself to be an important new force in the development of the ever-changing Western culture."[6]

The NAM is quite literally a *movement* of spirituality, health, politics, education, and business that encompasses countless groups seeking to direct the path of society. These groups, while sharing many beliefs in common, often hold numerous distinctive doctrines and at times even disagree with each other on significant issues. The term "New Age" is applied to this collection of groups because persons involved in it (i.e., New Agers) believe that humanity is currently standing on the brink of something very significant—an evolutionary leap of man's spiritual nature that will eventually bring about the "emergence of a new cycle of human consciousness and experience."[7]

Unlike previous ages, the coming *new* age will be marked by global peace, mass enlightenment, and unparalleled spiritual advancement. Major New Age spokespersons David Spangler and Marilyn Ferguson explain:

> The New Age is a concept that proclaims a new opportunity, a new level of growth attained, a new power released and at work in human affairs, a new manifestation of that evolutionary tide of events which, taken at the flood, does indeed lead on to greater things, in this case to a new heaven, a new earth and a new humanity.[8]

> [We have] come upon the control panel of change—an understanding of how transformation occurs. We are living in *the change of change*, the time in which we can intentionally align ourselves with nature for rapid remaking of ourselves and our collapsing institutions.[9]

To understand the NAM, one must first realize that much of it is not really "new." Even *Time* magazine has called the New Age "a combination of spirituality and superstition, fad and farce, about which the only thing certain is that it is not new."[10] Behind all of its twentieth-century packaging, terminology, and sociopolitical agendas, the nuts and bolts of the NAM's worldview is a mix of ancient occultism, Eastern religious philosophy, and in some segments of the NAM, pseudo-Christian ideas.

Unlike most cults, however, the NAM did not spring from one source at a specific moment in time. Instead, it gradually took shape as several strains of nineteenth- and twentieth-century religious thought and social change merged into a unified, social-religious-political movement. This coalescing of spiritual philosophies within the rapidly evolving world of the twentieth century has been compared to the formation of a river fed by many tributaries "now all aswirl, one virtually indistinguishable from the next, and all drawing on one another."[11] Some of the most influential groups, religious personalities, and spiritual movements to contribute to the NAM's development include, but are certainly not limited, to the following.

1700s–1800s: Mesmer and Quimby

Foreshadowings of the NAM can be seen as far back as the inner/mental healing movement of the early nineteenth century. It was initiated by Austrian physician Franz Anton Mesmer (1733–1815), whose teachings about the alleged existence of an invisible "universal fluid" ultimately led to today's widespread belief in psychic energy and the popularity of hypnotic/mediumistic trances,[12] and by Phineas P. Quimby (1802–1866), who taught that all disease is a product of "wrong thinking." Quimby's ideas eventually produced a new religious movement known as New Thought,[13] which in time would become a major force behind the formation of the NAM.

1836–1870: The Transcendentalists

It was the transcendentalists—the inspirational writer Ralph Waldo Emerson (1803–1882), author Henry David Thoreau (1817–1862), and renowned poet Walt Whitman (1819–1892)—who first introduced Eastern religious ideas, especially those associated with Hinduism, into mainstream American society. Their endorsements of, and reflections upon, oriental philosophies and holy books (e.g., Bhagavad Gita and Upanishads) created "a uniquely American form of mysticism . . . the first substantial religious movement in North America with a prominent Asian component."[14]

Although this new belief system never actually evolved into a fully organized religion, it did draw together a set of religious/philosophical principles and beliefs that played a prominent role in the birth of the NAM. Transcendentalism taught: 1) beyond the material world there are other modes of existence (i.e., the spirit realm); 2) all creation is a unified whole, everything is ultimately "one" in essence; 3) humanity is inherently good; 4) intuition must reign supreme over logic and reason in one's search for spiritual knowledge; 5) all authority—whether religious, scientific, or political—is secondary to the preeminence of one's own insight.

With regard to the formation of the NAM, one of the most influential ideas to come out of Transcendentalism involved the nature of truth itself. Transcendentalists, like modern-day New Agers, saw truth as entirely subjective. There is no objective truth per se. That which is true is limited to what is true *for you*, even though your truth may contradict someone else's truth.

1848: Spiritualism

Nineteenth-century spiritualism contributed a great deal to the NAM's theological fabric. Early spiritualists claimed to have obtained scientific evidence of survival after death. According to the National Spiritualist Association of the United States of America, the assertion was based on their alleged ability to communicate with persons living in the spirit world.[15] Such communication was usually achieved through seances (i.e., gatherings at which a person entered a trance to speak with spirits of the dead).

This practice, also known as necromancy, has a long history going back thousands of years. Its modern form in America, however, dates back no further than 1848, the year in which an outbreak of "spirit communications" in the form of mysterious knockings and raps occurred in the home of John Fox and his family at Hydesville in upstate New York. The written testimony of John Fox, signed four days after the knockings began, stated: "I do not know of any way to account for those noises, as being caused by any natural means."[16] His wife Margaret, in her written statement, said: "On the night of the first disturbance we all got up. . . . The noises were heard in all parts of the house. . . . We heard footsteps in the pantry, and walking downstairs. . . . I then concluded that the house must be haunted by some unhappy restless spirit."[17]

As word of the phenomenon spread, the popularity of attempting to contact the deceased also spread. By 1851, there were 100 mediums in New York and fifty to sixty private seance circles in Philadelphia. By 1855 there were nearly two million spiritualists in America.[18] Interestingly, in later years two of the Fox sisters—Kate and Margaretta—confessed that as children they had actually produced the "supernatural" noises by cracking the joints of their toes, knees, and ankles.[19]

1875: Theosophy

Theosophy, founded by Helena Petrovna Blavatsky (1831–1891) in 1875, blended metaphysical thought, spiritualism, science, Transcendentalism, and Quimby's concepts of mental healing power into one vast worldview that allegedly explained the nature of the entire cosmos. Its key addition to the aforementioned beliefs was the claim that there exist many spiritually advanced beings in the universe, a "ruling spiritual elite" who actually control all that exists.[20] Moreover, it was asserted that these beings can regularly take possession of various persons and, through them, communicate messages containing spiritual truths. Blavatsky was one of the first persons associated with this practice, which is now referred to as "channeling" in the NAM.

Like Transcendentalism, Theosophy helped spread Eastern spirituality in America. In fact, the first English-language Hindu book designed to actually "convert" readers (*Nature's Finer Forces* by Rama Prasad) was published by the Theosophical Society in 1890.[21] Even before popularizing Hinduism, though, Theosophy had already done much to spread Buddhism. Furthermore, it was Blavatsky who standardized usage of the term *reincarnation*, which refers to "the cyclical evolution of a person's soul as it repeatedly passes from one body to another at death. This process continues until the soul reaches a state of perfection."[22] After Blavatsky's death, high-ranking Theosophical Society member Annie Besant (1847–1933) became the movement's prominent personality. She eventually achieved even more success than Blavatsky in spreading Eastern beliefs throughout the United States.

1879: Eddy's Ideas

Christian Science, founded by Mary Baker Eddy (1821–1910) in 1879, combined the concepts expressed by transcendentalists and spiritualists with some of the inner healing notions expressed by her early mentor, Phineas Quimby. Unlike Quimby, however, who taught that there was actually a healing agent (i.e., mind power, Mesmer's universal fluid, etc.) that needed to be mentally tapped into for the healing of real diseases, Eddy believed that all disease was an illusion. Healing, according to her, would occur if one mentally refused to accept as real the illusion of illness. According to

Eddy, in fact, everything material was unreal. Consequently, all negative aspects of one's life could be removed by focusing on the unreality of those negative things.

To these views she added overtly Christian terminology, often referring to Jesus Christ and appealing regularly to the Bible in support of her contentions. The result was a metaphysical "Christian" science geared toward the eradication of poor health through the use of positive thinking and mental conditioning against the "illusory" nature of the entire world and everything in it, including death, an "illusion" to which Eddy herself succumbed in 1910.

1886: New Thought

Another independent tributary of spiritual teaching that has fed the NAM is New Thought. Although its seeds were planted by Quimby's teachings, they did not reach full maturity until expressed in the views of Emma Curtis Hopkins (1853–1925), a student of Mary Baker Eddy who disassociated herself from Eddy in 1885. A year later Hopkins opened her own religious school in Chicago, the Emma Hopkins College of Metaphysical Science. She taught a modified version of Eddy's views that came to be known as New Thought. Hopkins's courses quickly gained popularity throughout both the West and Midwest. Eventually all of the major mind science cults were founded by students of Hopkins: Nona Brooks (Divine Science), Myrtle and Charles Fillmore (Unity School of Christianity), and Ernest Holmes (Religious Science).

Although similar to Christian Science, New Thought departed in a number of ways from Eddy's declarations. Like Christian Science, it "placed its major emphasis on spiritual healing, was organized around practitioners, and trained its students through the Christian Science 'class' structure."[23] Contrary to Eddy, however, New Thought placed a heavy emphasis on prosperity. Poverty, to New Thought adherents, was just as much of an illusion as sickness and disease. Consequently, the cure for poverty was the same as the cure for sickness: positive thinking.

New Thought teachings on the divinity of man, the "oneness" of all creation, the sacredness of all religions, the impersonal nature of "the Christ," and the possibility of limitless prosperity and health can be seen in every corner of the NAM. According to religion scholar J. Gordon Melton, the influence of New Thought has been so great that a number of leading Christian ministers have adopted some of its doctrines relating to the power of positive thinking and positive confession for health and wealth—namely, Norman Vincent Peale, Robert Schuller, Kenneth Hagin, Kenneth Copeland, Frederick Price, and Rex Humbard.[24]

1923: Arcane

The Arcane School—an offshoot of Theosophy—was founded in 1923 by Alice Bailey (1880–1949), who, like Blavatsky, channeled a number of spirit entities. Out of the Arcane school emerged two very prominent features of the NAM: 1) all humanity must unite in the goal of achieving a new world civilization or world religion combining the East with the West; and 2) at some point in the future there will be a reappearance of "the Christ" (not Jesus, but someone uniquely imbued with cosmic, impersonal Christ Consciousness).[25]

1932: "I AM"

The "I AM" sects, also spawned by Theosophy, reached significance in 1932 with the founding of the St. Germain Foundation and the Saint Germain Press. These groups followed both the Arcane School and Theosophy in the practice of interaction with higher spiritual beings, adding to that an emphasis on the importance of "light" (a common element in mystical experiences) and the spiritual (occult) significance of "color." According to the *New Age Encyclopedia*, this attention paid to color, "especially as experienced in the light of gems, underlies the love of crystals in recent decades."[26]

1944: Huxley's Philosophy

The Perennial Philosophy, an indispensable part of the NAM worldview, was first presented to Americans by British novelist Aldous Huxley (1894–1963) in his 1944 book *The Perennial Philosophy*. According to Huxley, all religions at their core teach the same three things: 1) the existence of a divine Reality; 2) a belief that the soul is either similar or identical to this divine Reality; and 3) a life ethic that places man's ultimate meaning in the discovery of the divine Reality.[27] Huxley identified these alleged components of every religion as the *Philosophia Perennis* or Perennial Philosophy.

From Huxley's perspective, it mattered little if one were a Buddhist, Hindu, or Christian. The presence of the Perennial Philosophy indicated to him that all religions (when properly understood) were ultimately teaching the same thing. Consequently, all religions lead to God. Theologian David Clark, in his insightful work *The Pantheism of Alan Watts*, relates a famous Eastern parable that illustrates Huxley's view quite well:

> Four men decide to climb a mountain, but they approach it from four different directions. This fact causes no problems for the climbers, however, for all the paths up the mountain eventually lead to the top of the peak. Thus it is with religions: "The Paths are many but their End is One."[28]

1950s–1970s: Enter Zen

Zen Buddhism, popularized in America by Japanese scholar D. T. Suzuki (1870–1966) and one-time Anglican priest Alan Watts (1915–1973), was perhaps the most significant twentieth-century contribution to the formation of the NAM. Suzuki's role in spreading Zen not only stems from his many books, but also from the countless lectures he gave at Columbia University between 1950 and 1958.

As with Suzuki, the vehicles through which Watts influenced America included many lectures over several years (Harvard, Yale, Cambridge, Cornell) and numerous books. Most notable was his 1957 work *The Way of Zen*, which was billed as "The first comprehensive explanation of Zen Buddhism, the unique Oriental philosophy which shows how to live with serenity and fulfillment in a frustrating and confusing world."[29]

Zen seemed tailor-made for some of America's most tumultuous decades. First, it stressed self-reliance, self-effort, and rugged individualism, three hallmarks of America's collective consciousness. Zen was yet one more way to plunge deeper into the self.[30] Second, Zen's experience-oriented philosophy fit perfectly into the sexual/drug culture revolution of the 1960s that made "experience" the god of spiritual/mental/emotional enlightenment. Third, there is a "nonattachment" aspect to Zen that boasts freedom from suffering at a very low cost: simple detachment from that which is causing pain. As Christian scholar J. Isamu Yamamoto notes, "[P]eople in our society would prefer to cut themselves off from the causes of their suffering rather than face them and allow suffering to chisel them into better persons."[31]

Furthermore, Zen promised to deliver enlightenment not from thinking or from precise doctrine (a decidedly Christian approach), but from *not* thinking and *no* doctrine. Anyone could use Zen to spiritually accomplish whatever it was they wanted to accomplish. Suzuki wrote: "Zen is neither monotheistic nor pantheistic. Zen defies all such designations. Hence there is no object in Zen upon which to fix the thought. Zen is a wafting cloud in the sky. No screw fastens it, no string holds it."[32]

Also, Zen could be fashioned into a completely amoral philosophy of living. As Suzuki once remarked: "[A]s long as its intuitive teaching is not interfered with [Zen may be] wedded to anarchism or fascism, communism or democracy, atheism or idealism, or any political or economic dogmatism."[33] Zen provided a means by which the beatnik-hippie-psychedelic generation of the 1950s–1970s could maintain a sense of "spirituality" in the absence of any objective moral standard or rigid set of ethical rights and wrongs. This attraction would also be found in the Eastern spirituality promoted by yet another group of NAM builders: gurus.

1900s–1990s: World of the Gurus

Numerous gurus form the capstone to the NAM's overall structure. Their influence in the formation of the NAM cannot be overstated. The most famous gurus include:

Swami Vivekananda (1863–1902), the first guru to travel to the West. He marked his appearance at the 1893 World's Parliament of Religions in Chicago with a dynamic presentation of Hinduism "as a viable religious option for the modern world. . . . The audience accepted his faith as on a par with their own Western religious beliefs. In so doing they implicitly abandoned the traditional view that Hinduism is a primitive religion that Christian missionaries should seek to supplant with Christianity. This attitude marked a change in attitude of historic significance."[34] One year later he founded the Vedanta Society in America.

Swami Paramahansa Yogananda (1893–1952), founder of the Self-

Realization Fellowship in 1925/35. He is perhaps best known for his extremely influential book *Autobiography of a Yogi*.

Meher Baba (1894–1969), the "silent" guru who, after revealing that he was God, stopped speaking in 1925 and communicated only through hand gestures and writing.

Swami Muktananda Paramahansa (1908–1982), advisor to many of the entertainment industry's biggest stars.

Maharishi Mahesh Yogi (c. 1918–), father of Transcendental Meditation.

Sathya Sai Baba (1926–), an Indian "miracle"-worker who, as of 1997, had a following of approximately twenty million in India.

Sri Chinmoy (1931–), famed marathon runner/weight lifter, and spiritual advisor to the United Nations.

These men, along with a host of other gurus (e.g., Bhagwan Shree Rajneesh, Maharaj Ji, and A. C. Bhaktivedanta Prabhupada) repackaged Hinduism in such a way as to make it not just palatable, but actually appealing to Americans. Such gurus, despite their various idiosyncratic ways of expressing themselves, have essentially taught the same doctrines, especially with regard to the nature of self:

Muktananda: "The Guru is God Himself."[35] "Muktananda . . . is the God of the universe."[36] "God dwells within you as you; worship your Self."[37]

Maharishi Mahesh Yogi: "God-realization is possible . . . it is a matter of perception."[38]

Sai Baba: "You are the God of this universe."[39] "You are God in reality."[40] "You are not a man, you are God."[41]

Many celebrities have looked to these gurus for spiritual enlightenment. For example, Muktananda's followers have included California governor Jerry Brown, singer Diana Ross, the late recording artist John Denver, and actresses Marsha Mason and Olivia Hussey. Those seeking guidance from the Maharishi Mahesh Yogi have included actresses Elizabeth Taylor and Mia Farrow, sports superstar Joe Namath, clothes designer Calvin Klein, and four musicians from Liverpool named John, Paul, George, and Ringo—The Beatles. Although some of these high-profile personalities have drifted away from their respective gurus, the media attention given to them introduced countless Americans to what has since become the theological foundation of the entire NAM: Hinduism.

The last several decades have seen what can only be described as a spiritual marriage of the East and the West. America's many gurus are but one more part of the complex system of theological/philosophical streams of thought that have merged together to form the NAM, as the following chart illustrates.

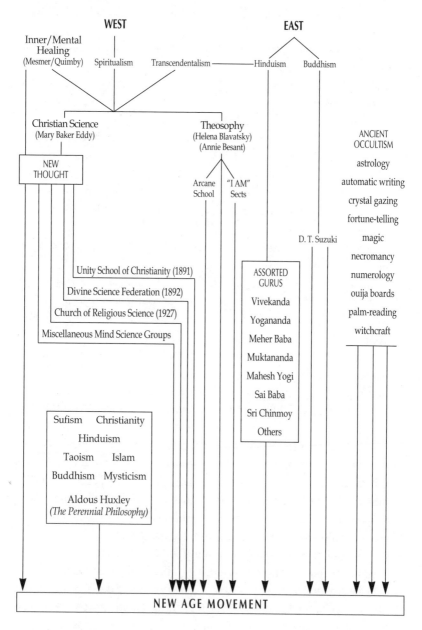

ACCORDING TO THE BIBLE

Obviously, the God of the New Age Movement is not the God of the Bible. Marilyn Ferguson admits that in "the emergent spiritual tradition God is not the personage of our Sunday-school mentality."[42] New Agers usually define "God" as an impersonal force pervading all creation. This view is a natural by-product of the NAM's most basic belief—monism, which literally means "one." It teaches that "all reality may be reduced to a single, unifying principle partaking of the same essence and reality."[43] The diversity we perceive is actually an illusion. "Oneness is the only reality and diversity is its apparent manifestation," says New Age advocate David Spangler.[44]

In other words, people only *think* that a rock lying in a field is something entirely separate from the field in which it is lying. Reality is that the rock *is* the field, and the field *is* the rock. Similarly, we only *think* we are individual entities. But the "Reality" is that there is no "you-me" distinction. There is only one big "I." This "I" includes not just every person, but every *thing* (e.g., soil, trees, raindrops). All are part of the One that New Agers usually refer to as the Reality, Power, All, Mind, Force, Absolute, Principle, or Universal Energy. Hence, the pantheism that is embraced by nearly every New Ager. After all, if all that exists is one, then "God" must also be one with everything. New Age personality Benjamin Creme puts it in these terms:

> [I]n a sense there is no such thing as God, God does not exist. And in another sense, there is nothing else but God—only God exists. . . . This microphone is God. This table is God. All is God. And because all is God, there is no God. . . . God is everything that you have ever known or could ever know—and everything beyond your level of knowing.[45]

Contrary to the Hinduistic philosophy of the NAM, God is not all and all is not God. Genesis 1:1 clearly establishes God as being distinct from the universe. The entire first chapter of Genesis portrays God not as part of all that exists, but as the Creator of all that exists. Other passages supporting this are Psalm 33:13–14, Isaiah 42:5, 44:24, and Acts 17:24–25. Paul the apostle further demonstrates that God and creation are separate when he mentions those persons who exchange the truth of God for a lie so that they worship and serve the creature rather than the Creator (Rom. 1:18–25). In *The New Age Is Lying to You*, Eldon Winker points out that worship of the creature is possible only if the creature is separate from the Creator.[46]

God is also not an impersonal Substance or Cosmic Force. In Exodus 3:14-15, the Lord applies to Himself the divine name "I [first person singular] Am [the verb to be]." Only a reflective, cognizant ego/mind can say, "I Am." Consequently, God must be a person. Additionally, God performs acts that are only possible for a personal being. In Jeremiah 29:11, for example, He declares that He knows the thoughts He thinks toward His people. How can an impersonal force know or think? God hears (Ex. 2:24), sees (Heb. 4:13), speaks (Lev. 19:1), is omniscient (1 John 3:20), judges (Ps. 50:6), loves (Prov. 3:12; Jer. 31:3) and has a will (1 John 2:17).

In sharp contrast to the impersonal God of the New Age Movement, the God of Christianity is an intelligent, compassionate, and personal being. He is the living and true God (2 Chron. 15:3; Jer. 10:10; Dan. 6:20; 1 Thess. 1:9; 1 Tim. 3:15; 4:10; Heb. 10:31). As such, God is also the quintessential enemy of New Agers, whose most cherished belief is that they are God, another doctrine that Scripture refutes.

Numerous biblical passages contrast God and man (Psalm 113:5–6; Ecc. 5:2; Isa. 43:7; Jer. 27:5; 1 Tim. 2:5). The Lord Himself has declared that He alone is God (Isa. 45:21–22). Even demons recognize there is only one God (James 2:19). Some New Agers, however, contend that it is this concept of a personal, transcendent God that has actually caused most of the world's problems: "[T]wo-thirds of evil (for humanity) comes from false God concepts, promoted by clever minds to enslave humanity. There is no God, no one intelligent entity outside His creation."[47]

In reality, the root of the world's problems is sin, a reality that the NAM has conveniently labeled as illusory. This mind-set has led New Agers to abandon a concrete moral standard. Their behavior is not governed by God, the Bible, or His eternal law, and they want nothing to do with an objective code of righteousness. New Agers claim that they can decide for themselves what is right because they are god:

> God is everything—He is every *thing*. So *any* thing you do, you have an inner action in divinity. Remember that, and do what you want to do.[48]

> [C]ontemplate the love of God; how great this Entity-Self is, that is all encompassing, that will allow you to be and do anything you wish and hold you judgeless. God has never judged you or anyone. If He has then He has judged Himself, for who be *you* but He.[49]

We can take all the scriptures and all the teachings, and all the tablets, and all the laws, and all the marshmallows and have a jolly good bonfire . . . because that's all they are worth. Once you are the law, once you are the truth, you do not need it externally represented for you.[50]

New Agers are characteristically inconsistent on this point. For example, they will say there is no objective right or wrong and yet at the same time contend that some things are indeed inherently "good" (e.g., ecology, natural health, brotherhood). Such a position is irreconcilable with their overall belief system that claims there is no objective right or wrong. More consistent is the pattern of morality found in Scripture.

The prophet Jeremiah observed that the heart of man is *desperately wicked* (Jer. 17:9). All have sinned and fallen short of the glory of God (Rom. 3:9–12, 23) and stand justly condemned as sinners before the righteous God of the universe (Rom. 5:18–19) who judges according to His eternal law (Rom. 7:7; James 2:10–11; 1 John 3:4), which is itself holy, just, and good (Rom. 7:12). Such a concept is especially distasteful to New Agers who believe that human nature "is neither good nor bad but open to continuous transformation and transcendence."[51] Christianity is the epitome of all that belongs to the unenlightened, discardable, and patently offensive "old" age that must pass away:

[F]or two thousand years, we have been called *sinful creatures*. That stigma automatically takes away our ability to remind ourselves that we are great, or that we are equal with God or Christ or Buddha, or whoever.[52]

The classroom must and will become an arena of conflict between the old and the new—the rotting corpse of Christianity, together with all its adjacent evils and misery, and the new faith of humanism.[53]

Predictably, the NAM also rejects the Christian doctrine of one's need for salvation. The New Age brand of "salvation" is basically freedom from ignorance of one's godhood. Seeing one's own divinity—an event described in the NAM as "god-realization," "enlightenment," "attunement," or "at-one-ment [with God]"—comes only through what is termed "personal transformation." Denver Theological Seminary professor Doug Groothuis writes: "To gain this type of transformation, the three ideas that all is one, all is god, and we are god, must be more than intellectual propositions; they must be awakened at the core of our being."[54] This transformation is achieved by looking "within" where all reality and truth allegedly exists. When "god-realization" is achieved, salvation is obtained.

> We already know everything. The knowingness of our divinity is the highest intelligence. And to *be* what we already know is the free will. Free will is simply the enactment of the realization that you are God, a realization that you are divine.[55]

> The aim of *A Course in Miracles* is to lead us from duality to oneness—to the realization of our At-one-ment with God, our Self and all people— our brothers. In this healing is our Salvation—we are *saved* from our misperceptions of ourselves as separated individuals. When our perception is corrected we remember our true or higher Self. . . . Salvation is really enlightenment.[56]

Here is where the significance of reincarnation and karma come into play. Reincarnation refers to "the cyclical evolution of a person's soul as it repeatedly passes from one body to another at death. This process continues until the soul reaches a state of perfection."[57] Karma refers to "the 'debt' accumulated against a soul as a result of [perceived] good or bad actions committed during one's life (or lives)."[58] Doug Groothuis, who has closely studied New Age teachings, explains how these very complex and sometimes confusing doctrines work together:

> [M]any lives are required to reach oneness with the One; salvation is a multi-lifetime process of progression or digression. If one accumulates good karma, positive benefits accrue in later lives. Bad karma produces future punishments. Eventually one may leave the cycle of birth and rebirth entirely through the experience of enlightenment. Redemption, if it could be called that, is a process of realizing the true self throughout many lifetimes.[59]

New Agers teach that at the moment you recognize your own godhood, you can pick up the threads of your karma, find out where you were in your past reincarnations, correct the mistakes you made there, and go on to live a better life. After countless lives you will *finally* be perfected and re-absorbed back into the great All from which you originally emanated. You will have reached Nirvana, a state of absolute peace. This will eventually happen for everyone. All will be saved by their own works coupled with reincarnation. David Spangler asserts, "None are lost."[60] New Age author Benjamin Creme writes, "The path to God is broad enough to take in all men."[61]

But Jesus said that the way to God is narrow. The broad way is the way "that leads to destruction, and many are those who enter by it" (Matt. 7:13). Jesus prophesied that on the day of judgment many individuals will be told to depart from his presence (Matt. 7:23; 25:1–41). Revelation 21:8 reveals that they will not be reincarnated: "[F]or the cowardly and unbelieving and abominable and murderers and immoral persons and sorcerers and idolaters and all liars, their part will be in the lake that burns with fire and brimstone, which is the second death."

New Agers desperately need help seeing the narrow way that has been hidden from them by the god of this world (2 Cor. 4:3–4). No amount of meditation, yoga, chanting, or astral projecting is going to produce salvation, which is a free gift from God through the person and work of Jesus Christ, who bore in his own body our sins (Eph. 2:10; 1 Peter 2:24). New Agers, however, maintain that the "Christian Church's concept of a vicarious atonement is a misunderstanding of the Christ's function."[62]

This is not surprising, since the Jesus of the NAM is very different from the Jesus of the Bible. New Agers see Jesus as only one avatar (or great teacher) among many other men, who were also "saviors" in their own right. They were "way-show-ers." All of them, including Jesus, had been prepared for their mission by living and working through countless reincarnations. Jesus was unique among these avatars only in that he had an incredible grasp of his deity.

> Jesus differed but little from other children only that in past lives he had overcome carnal propensities. . . . Jesus was a remarkable child, for by ages of strenuous preparation he was qualified to be an avatar, a saviour of the world.[63]

> In every age Teachers have come forth from this spiritual centre to enable mankind to take its next evolutionary step; we know them, among others, as Hercules, Hermes, Rama, Mithra, Vyasa, Sankaracharya, Krishna, Buddha, and the Christ. All perfect men in their time, all sons of men who became Sons of God, for having revealed their innate Divinity.[64]

To New Agers, Jesus' unique place in history is based "upon his unprecedented realization of the higher intelligence, the divinity, the Ground of Being incarnated in him."[65] He was divine "in exactly the sense that we are divine; only we have it in potential while He has manifested it, perfected Himself and *achieved* that divinity."[66] The idea of multiple avatars is but another Hindu tenet adopted by the NAM.

The New Testament, however, explicitly declares that Jesus Christ is the "one of a kind" (*monogenes*, John 1:18) Son of God who in the fullness of time came to reconcile mankind back to the Lord of the universe (Gal. 4:4; Col. 1:20). John 1:18 additionally tells us that Christ came to declare God to us. He was also sent to accomplish that which no one else could do—to die for the sins of the ungodly (Rom. 5:6; 14:15).

This concept, too, is rejected by NAM followers, who feel every religion is perfectly acceptable because each one teaches essentially the same thing. There is no personal Savior, Redeemer, or atonement for sins. All religious leaders are equal: Buddha, Mohammed, Zoroaster, Confucius, Krishna, Jesus, whoever. But Scripture declares that Jesus alone is the way, the truth, and the life (John 14:6) and that there is "salvation in no one else; for there is no other name under heaven that has been given among men, by which we must be saved" (Acts 4:12).

New Agers make yet another error concerning Jesus' identity: they divide him from what they term "the Christ." New Agers believe that "the Christ" is a form of the great One comprising all things. This "Christ Consciousness" came upon Jesus at some point during his life, just as it may come upon *anyone*.[67] (A minority of New Agers maintain that "the Christ" is an *office* now being held by another great avatar.)

The apostle Peter thought differently. He exclaimed to Jesus, "You are the Christ, the Son of the living God" (Matt. 16:16). He did not say, "You are a great avatar upon whom rests the Christ." Luke, too, identified Jesus as the Christ: "[T]oday in the city of David there has been born for you a Savior, who is Christ the Lord" (Luke 2:11). Passages identifying Jesus as the Christ fill the New Testament from Matthew to Revelation (Matt. 1:16; Luke 24:46; Acts 9:22; 18:28; Eph. 5:25; Heb. 3:6; 1 John 5:1; Rev. 11:15). In fact, the entire New Testament was expressly written so that those reading it would realize that Jesus was "the Christ" (John 20:31).

WHAT'S THE ATTRACTION?

As spiritually destructive as the NAM is, it can be extremely attractive to some individuals because of its optimistic view of a future wherein everyone dwells in harmony, peace, and prosperity. It envisions military disarmament and ecological preservation of the planet. Basically, the NAM offers a version of heaven on earth.

Another attraction of the NAM is the intense commitment of its adherents, which appears admirable to many onlookers. Most New Agers are zealous activists who feel that the arrival of their era of harmony is dependent upon the dissemination and mass acceptance of New Age doctrines. Consequently, they have instituted an ardent belief-spreading campaign using organized rallies, huge conventions, free literature, and high-profile personalities of the NAM, such as actress Shirley MacLaine. The success of this spiritual onslaught is undeniable. In 1994 Americans bought one billion dollars worth of New Age books and products.[68] As of 1997, New Age teachings had been integrated into the entertainment world, the food industry, public school curricula, health care services, politics, numerous international businesses, and even the U.S. military. The NAM has been called "the fastest growing alternate belief system in the country."[69]

The NAM's doctrine of personal godhood has also contributed to its success. Groothuis notes: "The underlying theme of the New Age is that as self-realized gods, we inherit the supernatural. New Age disciplines teach that as lords of our own universe, we create our own reality by the power of our thoughts.... The prerogatives of the Godhead are ours for the taking."[70]

For some people, the NAM is simply a place where they can, in a religious sense, "lighten up." Several elements make spirituality in the NAM nothing short of fun: New Age music, unicorn statues, rainbow stickers, and beautiful crystals. To New Agers, these aspects of their quest for truth radically divide it from the seemingly dead, boring, and drab character of "organized religion." New Agers tend to feel they are on an exciting adventure rather than on an oppressive road of religiosity paved by do's and don'ts.

Finally, the NAM offers answers to some of life's most pressing questions in an age where nothing seems to make sense. As Hedda Lark, spokesperson for a New Age publishing company, comments: "'I think people are searching for a sense of security in a world that's gone pretty mad, and they have the feeling that there must be more to life than this craziness.'"[71] There is indeed something more to life than just the "craziness" surrounding us. As Christians, it is our job to tell New Agers that the sense of security for which they are looking can be found in the free gift of salvation that is offered to them through Jesus Christ by a personal God who loves and cherishes them.

RECOMMENDED READING

Abanes, Richard. *Embraced by the Light and the Bible* (Camp Hill, PA: Horizon Books, 1994).

_____. *Journey into the Light: Exploring Near Death Experiences* (Grand Rapids, MI: Baker, 1996).

Ankerberg, John and Craig Branch. *Thieves of Innocence* (Eugene, OR: Harvest House, 1993).

Ankerberg, John and John Weldon. *Encyclopedia of New Age Beliefs* (Eugene, OR: Harvest House, 1996).

Chandler, Russell. *Understanding the New Age* (Grand Rapids, MI: Zondervan, 1993 edition).

Geisler, Norman L. and David K. Clark. *Apologetics in the New Age* (Grand Rapids, MI: Baker, 1990; 1992 edition).

Geisler, Norman L. and J. Yutaka Amano. *The Reincarnation Sensation* (Wheaton, IL: Tyndale House, 1986).

Groothuis, Douglas. *Jesus in an Age of Controversy* (Eugene, OR: Harvest House, 1996).

Mangalwadi, Vishal. *The World of the Gurus* (Chicago: Cornerstone Press, 1992).

McConnell, D. R. *A Different Gospel* (Peabody, MA: Hendrickson, 1996).

McRoberts, Kerry D. *New Age or Old Lie?* (Peabody, MA: Hendrickson, 1989).

Miller, Elliot. *A Crash Course on the New Age Movement* (Grand Rapids, MI: Baker, 1989).

Rhodes, Ron. *The Counterfeit Christ of the New Age Movement* (Grand Rapids, MI: Baker, 1991 edition).

Scott, Brad. *Embraced by the Darkness* (Wheaton, IL: Crossway Books, 1996).

Winker, Eldon K. *The New Age Is Lying to You* (St. Louis: Concordia, 1994).

WORLD OF
THE OCCULT

Magick is the Science and Art of causing Change to occur in conformity with Will.

ALEISTER CROWLEY
(1875-1947), OCCULTIST[1]

For many years Karen Winterburn considered herself a Christian. In her mid-twenties, however, she rejected Christianity, soon after becoming a Roman Catholic nun. Her convent was extremely liberal, and its teachings crushed all of her cherished beliefs about God, Jesus, and the Bible. Karen subsequently pursued Marxism, hedonism, and humanism. But these worldviews did not fill her spiritual void.

Her sister, an occultist, then provided what seemed to be the answer: astrology. This ancient practice appealed to Karen because although it suggested spirituality, it had an air of secularism about it. Astrology, it seemed, was more scientific and psychological than "plain old religion." This was especially attractive to Karen because by this time she was a practicing sociologist.

Astrology led Karen to other forms of divination: numerology, psychometry, I Ching, Tarot cards, visualization, the Kabbalah, Eastern yoga, and spirit-guided meditations, to name a few. Although these techniques proved to be adequate methods of obtaining supernatural knowledge, Karen still felt an emptiness inside. She not only wished to contact whatever higher spiritual entities existed but wanted access to the power—the spiritual reality—behind astrology and the other occult practices.

Consequently, Karen purchased a Ouija board and became a trance medium. Daily use of the board quickly brought her to a place where she finally utilized one of the most popular tools of modern occultism: channeling. She periodically allowed "Ithursis," a spiritual entity of unknown origin, to inhabit her body and speak forth messages. Karen eventually found herself in the Church Universal and Triumphant (C.U.T.), founded by Elizabeth Clare Prophet, who is herself a renowned channeler.

Finally, after twelve years of occultism, Karen began doubting the value of her spiritual path. The change in her outlook began after she heard C.U.T.'s leader make a dreadful historical error. Elizabeth Clare Prophet stated that one of the main messages of the Old Testament was that people should be friends with pagan gods. Karen knew immediately that Scripture did not say such a thing. Karen was not particularly interested in accepting the Bible, but it occurred to her that if Elizabeth Clare Prophet was wrong on this issue, maybe she was wrong about many other things also.

Suddenly all of the beliefs that Karen had accepted throughout her spiritual journey were suspect. Her mind was filled with penetrating questions about the lifestyle she had been leading: *Am I really god? What kind of person am I? Have I been truthful with people? Have I been faithful? Have I been responsible with my children? Have I been doing the right things as a mother, as a wife?*

After months of examining her actions and attitudes, Karen reached a startling conclusion: "This must be what sin is." Karen also realized that God, whom she had been pursuing for years, was far away, and she could not get to Him on her own strength. She felt completely helpless. Then, seemingly out of nowhere, various Scriptures started coming back to Karen's mind, including, "[T]here is salvation in no one else; for there is no other name under heaven that has been given among men, by which we must be saved" (Acts 4:12). One day Christ met her in a very personal way, as she explains:

> It was as though a grandfather whom you really loved had died and you thought you'd never see them [sic] again. Then suddenly there's a knock on the window and he's there—alive! And you're in shock. That's the way it was. I knew this was real, so I grabbed on to him.

Karen was ready to re-commit her life to Jesus Christ and sought counseling from several places, eventually landing on the steps of Trinity

Evangelical Divinity School. There she met professor John Feinberg, who at last provided Karen with a solid theological base. Today she is the director of the Chicago branch of Mt. Carmel Outreach, a ministry dedicated to reaching people in the cults for Christ.[2]

HOW IT ALL BEGAN

The occult is a vast system of religious studies, theories, practices, and beliefs that allegedly enable participants to obtain supernatural knowledge, which can then be used to control or at least in some way influence their environment (e.g., change the future, bring harm to an enemy, make someone fall in love, or secure sudden wealth). The word *occultism* derives from the Latin *occulere* ("to hide"), a term originally used in reference to the knowledge held by initiates of various "mystery religions" and secret societies. Modern occultism's link to this Latin term can be seen in its ultimate goal, which is to gain "secret powers" of the mind and spirit.[3]

Occult practices can be traced back thousands of years to an era when people believed that "apparent deviations from natural law involved mysterious and miraculous 'supernatural' or occult laws, deriving from gods, invisible entities or the souls of the dead."[4] Hoping to access the power behind these supernatural forces, various individuals and cultures developed *magick* rituals, which in turn gave rise to witch doctors and shamans, persons who claimed a heightened ability to perform magick. (Adding the letter *k* to the word *magic* was popularized by occultist Aleister Crowley in an effort to differentiate occult rituals from sleight-of-hand tricks performed by stage magicians.)

Thus began humanity's quest to control an uncontrollable world through the defiance, alteration, or suspension of natural laws. The Babylonian, Egyptian, and Chaldean civilizations were some of the earliest cultures to embrace an occultic belief system. Today the occult label is applicable to numerous practices including astrology, alchemy, automatic writing, channeling, crystal gazing, dowsing, dream interpretation, extrasensory perception (ESP), fortune-telling, magick, necromancy (communication with the dead), numerology, Ouija boards, out-of-body travel (astral projection), palm-reading, psychic healing, psychokinesis, pyramidology, Satanism, shamanism, Tarot cards, telekinesis, voodoo, and witchcraft. Occultism additionally encompasses various abnormal or unusual phenomena such as UFO abductions, hauntings, and reports of unexplained creatures (e.g., Bigfoot, the Loch Ness Monster, and Mexico's *Chupacabra* [a vampire-like creature]). Paranormal events that seem to contradict natural explanation (psychic visions, premonitions, etc.) also fall within occultism. The modern world of the occult basically involves "anything from the conjuror's [sic] hat-trick to the dark ceremonies of the witches' sabbat."[5] This, of course, has made discussion of the occult a daunting task, as Julien Tondriau's landmark book *The Occult: Secrets of the Hidden World* explains:

> Occult belief comprises traditions both of immense antiquity and great complexity in which it is nearly impossible to find any degree of uniformity and consistency, and the followers of occultism are themselves notoriously given to mystification so that their own accounts of an [sic] subject are full of strange pseudo-scientific jargon and merely add to the confusion.[6]

As far back as 1977, 114 million Americans were either directly or indirectly involved in the occult.[7] A rising number, in fact, continue to dabble in occultism:

- A 1987 survey by SRI International—an opinion research organization in Menlo Park, California—revealed that at least 42% of American adults feel they have been in contact with someone who has died (up from 27% in 1976).[8]
- A 1990 Gallup Poll found that 75% of Americans at least occasionally read their horoscopes, and 25% actually believe the tenets of astrology. This same poll revealed that 49% of Americans believed in ESP, 17% felt they had been in touch with someone who had died, and 14% had consulted a fortune-teller.[9]
- In 1993 various surveys revealed that one out of three adults believed fortune-tellers could foresee the future,[10] 43% of all teens believed in ESP,[11] and 70% of baby boomers (individuals born between the end of World War II to the early/mid-1960s) believed in psychic powers.[12]
- By 1994 65% of Americans were claiming to have had their own ESP experience, 28% thought they had experienced a clairvoyant episode (ability to predict the future), and 67% were saying they had contacted the dead.[13]

America's apparent fascination with occultism has manifested itself in many ways. Several occult television programs enjoy immense popularity: *PSI Factor: Chronicles of the Paranormal* (CBS); *Poltergeist: The Legacy* (KTTV—Fox); *Millennium* (KTTV); *The X-Files* (KTTV); *Profiler* (NBC); and *Sabrina, the Teenage Witch* (ABC). Moreover, since the late 1960s, Hollywood has produced a steady stream of occultic pictures such as *Rosemary's Baby* (1968), *The Exorcist* (1973), *The Omen* (1976), *The Shining* (1980), *The Witches of Eastwick* (1987), *Ghost* (1990), and *Phenomenon* (1996).[14] Some occult films have specifically targeted young audiences. Columbia Pictures' 1996 film *The Craft*, for example, tells the tale of four attractive high school girls who mischievously use witchcraft. The *Baltimore Sun* reviewed this low-budget production as "wicked fun."

Psychic hot lines appear to be the latest rage thanks to the endorsements of celebrities such as singer Dion Warwick and actor Billy Dee Williams.[15] The Internet, too, is being used to advocate occultic involvement. In early 1997, for instance, I signed on to America Online only to be met with an official AOL "TAROT TO GO" button accompanied by the promise: "Your future is available today." The selections at this AOL-advertised site included "1997 Predictions" and "Your Weekly Horoscope."

Even the U.S. government has had its hand in the occult cookie jar. Documents de-classified in the 1990s revealed that during the last twenty years of America's cold war with the Soviet Union, America spent $20 million investigating ESP and other psychic phenomena "in an effort to determine whether these forces of the paranormal world could somehow be put to use by espionage experts in the natural world."[16] This is not to say that everyone interested in occultism is involved in it in the same way or to the same degree. In fact, sociologists have divided occultists into three separate categories:

> At the first level are people whose involvement in the occult is minimal who do not see themselves as occultists per se but as concerned individuals interested in explaining such strange occurrences as flying saucers, assorted land and sea monsters, and various parapsychological phenomena. Typically their activities are characterized by an absence of mysticism, supernaturalism, and anti-scientific thought; in fact, scientific support for their beliefs is highly valued. . . . [On the] second level of occultism are people who seek to understand mysterious causal rela-

tionships between events—who express an interest, for example, in numerology, sun-sign astrology, and palmistry. Knowledge gained at this level is more likely to be ascientific or extra-scientific rather than anti-scientific. . . . [The] third level of occultism is concerned with those complex belief systems—witchcraft, Satanism, ritual magic, and other mystical traditions—that combine elements from the first two levels. Third-level believers often question or contradict scientific validation of an event or relationship, and thus may see themselves as competitors to science. . . . [A]lthough some occult believers exist in "pure form," most are a combination of all three types.[17]

Interestingly, there has recently been an attempt on the part of some avowed scientists to prove the existence of supernatural forces. This pseudoscientific field of study has been dubbed parapsychology. Its origin dates back to the 1930s and Duke University professor Joseph Banks Rhine, who began "looking for evidence of a strange and remarkable capability that he called extrasensory perception, or simply ESP."[18] Rhine's search included at least four "senses" that science had supposedly missed:

- *Telepathy,* or mind-reading ("direct mental communication between two persons").
- *Clairvoyance,* or second-sight ("specific perception of an event or object through means that do not involve the known senses").
- *Precognition,* or telling the future ("perceiving of future events without deducing their occurrence from existing knowledge").
- *Psychokinesis,* or use of one's mind power to "effect change in external matter."[19]

These four areas of investigation are commonly referred to as "psi," a word corresponding to the twenty-third letter of the Greek alphabet, which is sometimes used in scientific equations for an unknown quantity. The emergence of parapsychology has opened up yet another avenue for occult involvement and obsession.

ACCORDING TO THE BIBLE

Scripture explicitly forbids involvement in the occult. Astrologers, for instance, are condemned in Isaiah 47:13–15. Similarly, Jeremiah instructs

God's people to reject astrology: "Do not learn the way of the nations, and do not be terrified by the signs of the heavens although the nations are terrified by them" (Jer. 10:2). The clearest reason for avoiding astrology is found in Deuteronomy 4:19: "[B]eware, lest you lift up your eyes to heaven and see the sun and the moon and the stars, all the host of heaven, and be drawn away and worship them and serve them."

Astrology, of course, is not the only occult practice God condemns (Isa. 44:25; Gal. 5:20; Rev. 21:8). The Israelites were to shun all forms of divination (Lev. 19:26). In fact, anyone who turned to occultism instantly became God's enemy (Lev. 20:6) and was "defiled" (Lev. 19:31). Witchcraft, divination, spiritism, and the use of mediums were activities that God's people considered nothing less than "evil" (2 Kings 21:6). The Lord spoke in the clearest of terms about occultism in Deuteronomy 18:10–12:

> *There shall not be found among you anyone . . . who uses divination, one who practices witchcraft, or one who interprets omens, or a sorcerer, or one who casts a spell, or a medium, or a spiritist, or one who calls up the dead. For whoever does these things is detestable to the* LORD; *and because of these detestable things the* LORD *your God will drive them out before you.*

Necromancy (speaking with the dead), an extremely popular occult activity, receives especially harsh criticism in the Bible. God commanded that all sorcerers, mediums, and spiritists in Israel were to be executed (Ex. 22:18; Lev. 20:27). Fortune-tellers also fell under the Lord's condemnation (Mic. 5:12). Why would God make such strong prohibitions against occultism? There are several reasons.

First, God is not a God of the dead but of the living (Matt. 22:31–32). Isaiah 8:19 asks, "[S]hould not a people consult their God? Should they consult the dead on behalf of the living?" The answer to the former question is obviously yes. The answer to the latter is undeniably no. The realm of the dead is not where individuals will find the answers to life that they seek. Nor will they find eternal life in that domain. Jesus, in whom life itself resides (John 5:26), came that He might give life to others (John 10:10, 28). It is to Christ that spiritual truth-seekers must look. Occultism presents nothing but a distraction. God wants individuals to seek after Him, not spirits of the dead.

Second, the occult provides access to certain powers that are demonic in nature and as such are spiritually deadly and ultimately ineffectual (Ex.

7—8). The powers of darkness are no match for God's omnipotence (Ex. 8:19). They are inferior spiritual forces. Consequently, there is no reason to waste one's time on them.

Third, information obtained through occult methods is unreliable. Like the power that occultism presents, the vast storehouse of "knowledge" available through occultism is a poor substitute for what God offers: absolute truth. The source of true "light," or trustworthy information, is the Lord (Isa. 8:19–20). This fact is evident from the confrontation between the prophet Daniel and the Babylonian astrologers (Dan. 1:20; 2:13, 18–19; 5:7–17).

Fourth, practically every form of occultism, when boiled down to its irreducible minimum, is merely a different vehicle through which one may practice magick.[20] This, too, is condemned by God (Acts 13:6–12; 19:19). Magick—defined as any spiritual technique designed to harness either supernatural forces or the secret power of nature in order to influence events for one's own purposes[21]—is a direct affront to God's sovereignty. It is to the personal Creator-God of the universe that individuals are to look for assistance in this life. Attempting to control one's own destiny and the environment through occultic means is the equivalent of making oneself into a god, which interestingly is one of the main tenets promoted in occultism: man is god.

Fifth, most occult practices involve entering an altered state of consciousness (ASC) wherein one's normal everyday awareness (or consciousness) is replaced by an alternate (or altered) awareness. An ASC is induced when anything interrupts or brings to a halt "the normal patterns of conceptual thought without extinguishing or diminishing consciousness itself."[22] A hypnotic trance, for example, is an ASC.

While experiencing an ASC, persons cannot separate fact from fiction. They function under a confused sense of reality. This in turn opens a doorway to the mind through which demonic forces may funnel information in hopes of leading someone away from God. Demonic entities might even take the form of deceased relatives, friends, or religious figures in order to add credibility to their messages. Consider the following report from occultist Robert Monroe concerning one of his "out-of-body" excursions that he claims enabled him to spiritually travel to higher realms of existence:

> I started out carefully—and felt something climb on my back! I remembered the little fellow from before, and certainly didn't want to try to go

somewhere with him hanging on my back. I let the vibrations continue, and reached down my side to get hold of his leg. . . . I was quite surprised when my hands did touch something! The consistency felt much like flesh, normally body warm, and somewhat rubbery; it seemed to stretch. . . . I finally pulled what I thought was all of it off my back. . . . It got to be quite a struggle . . . and I was getting a little panicky . . . as I was trying to hold off the first, a second climbed on my back! Holding the first off with one hand, I reached back and yanked the second off me, and floated over into the center of the office, holding one in each hand, screaming for help. I got a good look at each, and as I looked, *each turned into a good facsimile of one of my two daughters.* . . . I seemed to know immediately that this was a deliberate camouflage on their parts to create emotional confusion in me and call on my love for my daughters to prevent my doing anything more to them. The moment I realized the trick, the two no longer appeared to be my daughters [emphasis added].[23]

Finally, the various theological doctrines and overall worldview normally associated with occult practices are decidedly unbiblical. Consider how astrology can influence an unsuspecting person:

[T]he client, in a state of heightened receptivity, is being exposed to a new way to look at himself, his situation and concerns. and the world around him. New categories, explanations, and solutions are being offered: reincarnation, karma, rhythm or cycle adjustments, archetypes, synchronicity, symbol. . . . The client talks about himself and his world. The astrologer gives it all back to him within a new perspective, and with a promise that as this perspective is internalized, the flawed microcosm of his character and experience will begin to reflect the perfect harmony of the macrocosm—"as above, so below." The client's worldview is changing. He is learning to look to his own effort and metaphysical enlightenment for a "new birth." He is learning to put his trust in whatever can help him internalize this new perspective. He is learning that such internalization will put him into a right relationship with the impersonal cosmos—not in whose image he was "made," but of which substance he is composed [pantheism, see chapter 1].

Some people argue that occult practices such as Tarot card reading, palmistry, and astrology are at best harmless amusements and at worst, scams that can be used by scrupulous individuals to bilk trusting customers out of hard-earned cash. But as we have seen, occultic involvement does have serious, negative spiritual ramifications.

WHAT'S THE ATTRACTION?

What kind of people are being drawn toward occultic beliefs? Christian writer W. Elwyn Davies, in *Principalities and Powers*, identifies the various types of individuals who are consistently interested in occult phenomena:

- *The curious*, who experiment with demonic forces without having a fully formed system of religious beliefs. A number of teenagers, for example, get involved in the occult due to nothing more than curiosity.
- *The dissatisfied*, "whose religious experience has left him unfulfilled and skeptical."
- *The sad*, "whose bereavement inclines him towards anything that offers knowledge of the dead."
- *The psychically inclined*, "who wants to develop suspected latent powers."
- *The rebellious*, "who recoils from the status quo in the church and in society, and seeks a viable alternative elsewhere."
- *The credulous*, who are ready to believe just about anything and everything.
- *The children of practicing occultists*, "who are conditioned from childhood."
- *The conformist*, who looks around at his or her peers and says, "'Everyone does it,'" and then decides "to be another who 'does it.'"[24]

Christian counselor Russ Parker, who has worked with many victims of the occult, lists six major reasons why people get involved in occultism:

[1] Fear of the Future . . . Superstition and occult practices are attractive because they appear to meet a need for security regarding the future. [2] The Desire for Power . . . [3] Fascination with the Supernatural: Some people seem to be attracted by the unusual. . . . The various phenomena of occult meetings provide such people with a degree of meaning and fulfillment. . . . [4] A Spiritually Impotent Church: Many . . . have looked for a real spiritual experience within the church but have been disillusioned by its liberalism and unbelief. They begin to search elsewhere and

are attracted to the occult with its demonstrations of spiritual power. . . . [5] The Bankruptcy of Materialism . . . For many . . . the pace of such [materialistic] living offers no fulfillment, and so they start to look for a spiritual center for their lives. This need for a spiritual center is clearly the force behind the rise in "new age" religions. . . . [6] Occult Power and Deception: Many people have found that, for them, the occult works. . . . [M]any discover its power to be real.[25]

The media's positive portrayal of occultism has also had a profound effect on people. According to Ken Myers, a Christian producer at Mars Hill Productions in Charlottesville, Virginia, the broader public has been desensitized to the very real dangers of occultism, especially when it comes to such fashionable religious belief systems as witchcraft:

A lot of sympathy for occult ideas with baby boomers was prepared for by decades of Disney films that innocuously presented those kinds of magic powers. . . . They were regarded as innocent because there was not a serious occult movement in the country. There weren't covens meeting in Central Park at the time. Occult thinking was not considered as a serious option before, but now it's an imaginable reality.[26]

Tragically, the children of baby-boomers are being introduced to occultism at an alarming rate thanks to occult-promoting cartoons, movies, and books for young audiences such as *The War of the Wizards* (Dial Books) by Stephen Wyllie, which displays an occultic five-sided pentagram inside its front cover, *Wizard's Hall* (Scholastic) by Jane Yolen, which tells the story of a young apprentice wizard, and *The Witches' Christmas* (Scholastic) by Norman Bridwell. The *Christian Research Journal* described this latter volume as "a bizarre mixture of religious and profane symbols, even having 'a good witch [saving] Santa with a neat piece of magic.'"[27]

Because there is a certain degree of satanic power within the world of the occult, Christians must be careful as well as prayerful when confronting persons lost within its enticing rituals and symbols. At the same time, however, believers in the biblical Jesus must never forget that there is nothing to fear: God, who is in us, is greater than he who is in the world (1 John 4:4). Furthermore, our Lord said to His followers, "Behold, I have given you authority . . . over all the power of the enemy, and nothing shall injure you"

(Luke 10:19; cf. 9:1). This promise assures us that a Christian's safety and authority rests in nothing less than the power of the risen Jesus Christ.

Such a promise is especially important for individuals, both Christians and non-Christians, who have been involved in occultism and now seek deliverance from its influence. The path to freedom is not a difficult one to follow: "If we confess our sins, He is faithful and righteous to forgive us our sins and to cleanse us from all unrighteousness" (1 John 1:9).

RECOMMENDED READING

Abanes, Richard. *Embraced by the Light and the Bible* (Camp Hill, PA: Horizon Books, 1994).

_____. *Journey into the Light: Exploring Near Death Experiences* (Grand Rapids, MI: Baker, 1996).

Ankerberg, John and Craig Branch. *Thieves of Innocence* (Eugene, OR: Harvest House, 1993).

Ankerberg, John and John Weldon. *Encyclopedia of New Age Beliefs* (Eugene, OR: Harvest House, 1996).

Groothuis, Douglas. *Jesus in an Age of Controversy* (Eugene, OR: Harvest House, 1996).

Hawkins, Craig. *Goddess Worship, Witchcraft and Other Neo-Pagan Movements* (Grand Rapids, MI: Zondervan, 1998).

_____. *Witchcraft: Exploring the World of Wicca* (Grand Rapids, MI: Baker, 1996).

Kjos, Berit. *Under the Spell of Mother Earth* (Wheaton, IL: Victor Books, 1992).

_____. *Your Child and the New Age* (Wheaton, IL: Victor Books, 1990).

Kole, André and Terry Holley. *Astrology and Psychic Phenomena* (Grand Rapids, MI: Zondervan, 1998).

Passantino, Bob and Gretchen. *When the Devil Dares Your Kids* (Ann Arbor, MI: Servant Publications, 1991).

Rhodes, Ron. *The Counterfeit Christ of the New Age Movement* (Grand Rapids, MI: Baker, 1991 edition).

Spencer, Aída Desançon with Donna F. G. Hailson, Catherine Clark Kroeger, and William David Spencer. *The Goddess Revival* (Grand Rapids, MI: Baker, 1995).

Strohmer, Charles. *What Your Horoscope Doesn't Tell You* (Wheaton, IL: Tyndale, 1988).

THE DEVIL
MADE ME DO IT

Hate your enemies with a whole heart, and if a man smite you on one cheek, smash him on the other!; smite him hip and thigh, for self-preservation is the highest law! . . . Stop the way of them that would persecute you. . . . Let them be as chaff before the cyclone and after they have fallen rejoice in thine own salvation. . . . Cursed are the weak, for they shall inherit the yoke. . . . Cursed are the righteously humble, for they shall be trodden under cloven hoofs. . . . Cursed are the god-adorers, for they shall be shorn sheep. . . . Cursed are the "lambs of God," for they shall be bled whiter than snow! . . . i am a satanist! bow down, for i am the highest embodiment of human life!

THE SATANIC BIBLE[1]

Death by lethal injection. Thus ended the 1986 trial of seventeen-year-old Sean Sellers, the youngest person ever to be placed on death row at the Oklahoma State Penitentiary. It seemed a predictable ending to a life marked by nothing but anger, bitterness, frustration, and hatred. Sean had been a lonely child whose mother and stepfather spent most of their time on cross-country trucking runs, leaving him to be raised in Greeley, Colorado, by a succession of relatives. The emotional void he felt led him to where many of today's youths find themselves: the world of the occult.

Sean's occult-driven life began with his involvement at the age of thirteen in a local Dungeons & Dragons (D&D) fantasy role-playing group. It provided an ideal distraction from the pain of the real world. He excelled at the game and soon became Dungeon Master. His new position as game leader prompted the attention-starved teen to scrutinize every book on witchcraft, Satanism, wizards, and black magic that he could get his hands on. Eventually he found his way into a satanic coven, complete with animal sacrifices, worship rituals, and baptismal ceremonies:

> The leaders would be in black robes, but the new person would be in a white robe. We would stand in front of an altar that had black candles and a silver chalice on it. They made the new person strip, kneel before the altar; then we'd cut his hand and let the blood drip into the chalice. Then we would pass the cup around, drinking the blood and dedicating ourselves to Satan.[2]

During Sean's sophomore year (1984) he moved with his parents to Oklahoma City, where he fell into yet another satanic cult. His obsession with the black arts increased dramatically after a fifteen-year-old female witch gave him his own incantation, claiming that it was a powerful prayer to the Devil. When Sean recited it during a ceremony at his homemade altar, he was not disappointed:

> I felt a power there. The temperature in the room dropped about ten degrees. I got a shot of adrenaline and I felt my blood pressure go up. There was an erotic sensation, a lifting sensation in my whole body. And sharp claws—fingers—touched me. I opened my eyes and saw bright spots dancing around the room. There was this mist, and I saw demons flying. And then there was this voice. A whisper. It said, "I love you." I knew that God didn't love me; but Satan did.[3]

Not long after having this experience Sean formed his own coven—the "Eliminators Club"—based on D&D's multi-level system of advancement. He was anything but secretive about its existence or his role as leading devil-worshiper. In fact, Sean went out of his way to appear bizarre in front of classmates. He grew his left pinkie fingernail extremely long and painted it black. He carried vials of his own blood, which he would drink in front of horrified students in the school cafeteria.

But the attention Sean received only made him more of an outcast. This in turn caused him to pursue with even greater fervor the one whom he considered the King of Outcasts, the one who would be his source of strength—Satan.[4] Before reaching this point of no return, however, Sean tried to get help. He mentioned to several adults that he might be going insane and sought counseling from a priest, a teacher, and various

Christian ministries. He even tried to make friends with some born-again believers at school. The results were devastating to his already disturbed psyche:

> Satan was really fouling things up. My mom was always crying, my dad was wanting to kill me. I'd open my eyes and think, "This is not what I want to be doing; this is not what I want to be like. I want out of this mess." And I called different Christian ministries and talked with them and they didn't tell me anything. I went to a priest; and he told my mom to give me back my satanic books. She'd taken them away and he says, "They're not your books; they're his books. Give them back to him." And so that didn't work. I went to a prayer group thing and they quoted a lot of Scripture to me but they didn't tell me what I now know I needed to hear, which was, "You don't have to be involved in the occult to be somebody. You don't have to be like that. . . ." The Christians at my school didn't say anything about the way Jesus loves me; it was just: "That's the guy that drinks blood; that's the guy that ate a live frog over there. Don't mess with him." I'd go "Hi" and they'd go "Bye." My mom walked in on me one time while I was calling a counseling hotline from a Christian ministry and she didn't like the fact that I was doing it. . . . [P]arents feel threatened by the fact that their kids need help because it might suggest they're not doing a good job as parents. . . . I remember asking [my mom] a couple of times, hinting around that, "I think I'd really like to talk to someone. . . . I think I'm going crazy." But she'd say, "Well, if you think you're going crazy, that's a good sign you're not." . . . I think I was really reaching out but there just didn't seem to be anybody there. . . . So it felt like no one was ever there. And I got so mad, I got so frustrated with all these "good" people around me that I said, "Fine. Forget it. I can't get out." And that's what I was always told: Once you're involved in Satanism you can't get out. So that's when I really got into it. I dove into it with everything I had. Because I figured, "Well, if I can't get out of it, then I'm going to do the best I can in it." That's when I jumped in with both feet and got in over my head and started drowning.[5]

By the time Sean reached his junior year, he was fascinated with death and murder, especially the kind displayed in horror films. Moreover, the line between fantasy and reality was rapidly blurring. In a school essay he wrote: "I can kill without remorse and I feel no regret or sorrow."[6] Meanwhile, Sean's abuse of amphetamines, alcohol, and marijuana was taking its toll. He started suffering from prolonged periods of sleeplessness and occasional blackouts.

Just after beginning his junior year in 1985, Sean decided it was time for a sacrifice. His first offering to Lucifer was the life of a convenience store clerk who had refused to sell him beer. This same individual had also made the mistake of flirting with Sean's girlfriend. Vengeance was taken when Sean took his stepfather's .44-caliber handgun, walked into the store, and shot the clerk at close range.

The homicide went unsolved for six months as Sean spiraled into a living hell. He now believed he was actually possessed by a demon named Ezurate. It was this entity that allegedly prompted Sean to make the ultimate sacrifice: his parents. On the night of March 4, 1986, Sean dressed in black underwear and a black cape, knelt down by the satanic altar in his bedroom, and invoked demonic help for what he was about to do. He then grabbed the .44-caliber gun used on the convenience store clerk, walked into the room where his parents were sleeping, and shot his stepfather in the head. His mother bolted up and looked at Sean just long enough for him to aim at her forehead and fire.

> When I killed my parents I stood over their bodies. I watched blood pour from the hole in my mother's face and I laughed. . . . It haunts me that I could have been the person that did that.[7]

Sean spent the rest of the night with a friend. When he returned home the next day, he pretended to be a "shocked and innocent son, horrified by his parents' brutal deaths."[8] All of the evidence, however, pointed to Sean, and he was arrested. Satan had betrayed him. His life was ruined.

Amazingly, Sean no longer lives in torment. He found deliverance in prison while reading a Bible. He learned that even he could be forgiven by God through the life, death, and resurrection of Jesus Christ. Shortly after realizing this glorious truth, he became a Christian and started using the collect-calls-only phone in his cellblock to counsel troubled teens dabbling in Satanism.

> If there's anything to say about getting involved in Satanism, it's: "Don't!" Don't get involved. Get out of it. It's not worth it 'cause it's

going to destroy your life. That's all there is to it: It will destroy your life. And I'm living proof that it's true.[9]

Exactly how long Sean will be able to continue assisting troubled youths across America remains uncertain. As of 1997 he was still on death row awaiting the outcome of an appeal that would commute his death sentence to life in prison. Whatever happens, though, Sean knows that beyond this world the King of kings and Lord of lords awaits him with open arms. He will never again have to fear the Prince of Darkness, whose power was broken by Sean's new master, Jesus of Nazareth.

HOW IT ALL BEGAN

The developmental history of Satanism is a long and twisting path that winds back through centuries of witchcraft, superstition, religious folklore, and ancient paganism. It was a blending of these elements by persons seeking to fight Christianity's growing theological and moral influence (c. A.D. 400s–1600s) that led to the birth of Satanism, which has since come to represent the ultimate expression of rebellion against God. Although this blasphemous system of religious beliefs technically falls into the world of occultism, it is unique for a number of reasons.

First, Satanism "is not a monolithic, unified whole in its organizational structure, beliefs, and practices."[10] The components of Satanism are as diverse as the personalities of those involved. According to Satanism experts Bob and Gretchen Passantino, this is because all Satanists are characterized by a self-serving attitude. Consequently, "it is to be expected that Satanism could have almost as many definitions as practitioners."[11]

Second, Satanists have no universal definition for their object of worship and service (i.e., Satan). Journalist Arthur Lyons, in his investigation of contemporary American Satanism, found that a Satanist is "anyone who sincerely describes himself as a worshiper of the Christian Devil, *whatever he perceives that to mean*."[12] Satan is variously identified as "a supernatural person, a deity, a devil, a supernatural force, a natural force, an innate human force, or, most commonly, the self."[13]

Third, Satanism is a deliberate reversal, or inversion, of an established world religion: Christianity. It is literally *anti*-Christian in all that it teaches. For example, Christian vices such as pride, greed, and lust are viewed by

Satanists as virtues to be enjoyed. Christian virtues such as humility, self-control, and sacrificial love are seen by Satanists as utterly abhorrent and worthy of destruction. Even satanic rituals, when initially formulated, were designed to mirror Christian rituals, but in a mocking fashion.

Religion scholar J. Gordon Melton categorizes all Satanists into two main groups. On the one hand are "public groups which take Satanism as a religion seriously and have developed articulate theologies which do not resemble in many ways what one might expect"[14] Individuals involved in such groups—sometimes called "religious" Satanists—rarely commit occult-related criminal acts and frown upon those who do. Church of Satan founder Anton LaVey (1930-1997), for instance, states: "Satanism has nothing to do with kidnapping, drug abuse, child molestation, animal or child sacrifice, or any number of their acts that idiots, hysterics or opportunists would like to credit us with."[15]

On the other hand, there are those Satanists who constitute the many "disconnected groups of occultists who employ Satan worship to cover a variety of sexual, sado-masochistic, clandestine, psychopathetic, and illegal activities. These groups typically engage in grave-robberies, sexual assaults and bloodletting (both animal and human) . . . [and] are characterized by a lack of theology, an informality of gatherings, ephemeral life, and disconnectedness from other similar groups."[16] Participants in this latter group are commonly referred to as "self-styled" Satanists. They invent their own brand of Satanism based on an eclectic collection of beliefs/rituals that they have been exposed to through satanic literature, sensationalized accounts of Satanism, occult movies, rumors about Satanism, and occult music.

In his book *Satan Wants You*, journalist Arthur Lyons splits Satan-worshipers into three separate groups: 1) solitary Satanists; 2) "outlaw" cults; and 3) neo-Satanic churches.[17] He describes these in the following manner:

> Solitary Satanists belong to no cult and employ their own made-up brand, which they usually procure from books on the subject. . . . [T]hese Satanists are alienated teenagers who have a difficult time socializing, and the rituals they perform usually involve some sort of wish fulfillment, such as the acquisition of money, popularity, romance, or sex. Often the practices of these individuals are tied to drug use and a fanatical devotion to rock music—particularly heavy metal rock—and their Satanic "rituals" consist of little more than getting stoned, lighting can-

dles, and reading a passage aloud from Anton LaVey's *The Satanic Bible*, to the accompaniment of an Ozzy Osbourne tape. . . . "Outlaw" groups worship Satan as the Evil One of the New Testament, and their practices reflect that orientation. . . . [T]he focus of such groups has tended to be more on drugs, music, and vandalism than sex. The members are usually young (fifteen to twenty-five), socially alienated, and held together by a charismatic leader. Meetings are generally sporadic and lack any coherent theology; the rituals, like those of solitary Satanists, tend to be slapped together from movies and books on black magic. . . . [T]he rituals often include socially deviant, and sometimes violent, acts. . . . [Then there] are the neo-Satanic churches. . . . These groups—which constitute the overwhelming bulk of the current Satanic membership—strictly prohibit the ritualistic harming of any living thing, and enjoin members from participating in illegal activities. . . . They advocate egotism, indulgence, and the acquisition and use of personal and political power, have well-defined theologies and authority structures, and recruit members openly. . . . [T]wo such groups, the Church of Satan and the Temple of Set, maintain listings in the San Francisco yellow pages.[18]

To these categories may be added "dabblers" (which Lyons includes among "solitary" Satanists) and so-called "traditional" Satanists (also known as "generational" Satanists). The former category includes people who only have a light association with Satanism. Their involvement usually goes no further than the most superficial traits held in common by Satanists: fascination with satanic literature (e.g., *The Satanic Bible*), love of horror/satanic movies and fantasy role-playing games containing satanic elements, and "heavy-metal" music that relies on satanic lyrics and symbols.

Most dabblers are teenagers going through that difficult period of transition from childhood to adulthood. During this time many teens try to assert their own independence by breaking connection with family and parents through deliberate use of anything that marks them as unique, such as odd hairstyles or strange clothes. Some young people gravitate toward satanic symbols, music, movies, and games because such elements reek of nonconformity.

Traditional/generational Satanists are allegedly born into Satan-worshiping families and continue in the depraved tradition of their relatives. Such persons have repeatedly been accused of gruesome killings, kidnappings, and ritualistic abuse/murder of children and babies. When reports detailing this kind of horrific activity began surfacing in the mid-1980s, near-panic broke out in the Christian community.

More stories soon began coming from "adult survivors" who, although brutalized as children, had "forgotten" their terrible experiences until a psychotherapist helped them "recover" the lost memories. These accounts were almost immediately followed by additional allegations that generational Satanists had formed a widespread network of like-minded believers that reached into the highest levels of our government—a network used to abduct, torture, and sacrifice countless babies and children.

Fortunately, investigations made by police and Christian journalists have conclusively proven that such lurid tales have no basis in fact. They exist only in the minds of the "adult survivors" and those who believe them. Apparently, a number of psychotherapists have inadvertently (some say deliberately) implanted "false memories" of satanic ritual abuse (SRA) into the impressionable minds of their clients. Some SRA "victims" have even had their "memories" implanted simply by watching sensationalistic talk shows on the issue, reading SRA-related literature, and talking to other "survivors" associated with various "support groups" for SRA victims.

According to psychologist Elizabeth Loftus, this would be possible because about 25 percent of all individuals "can be easily induced to remember events that never happened to them—false memories that feel absolutely real."[19] Such "memories" have resulted in numerous church scandals, lawsuits, suicides, splintered families, murders, and "endless fodder for talk shows."[20] To date, none of these recollections have ever been validated. Many of them, in fact, have actually been proven false. A few cases were exposed as episodes of outright fraud, and a majority of those who originally recalled SRA "memories" retracted their stories.[21]

This is not to say that all satanic crimes are a figment of someone's imagination. Many rapes, kidnappings, and murders have been perpetrated in the name of Satan. Unlike the rumors surrounding generational Satanists, however, these crimes—which were typically committed by either "self-styled" Satanists or "outlaw" groups—left ample evidence of the crimes and were easily uncovered. Although neo-Satanic churches take great pains to distance themselves from such acts, the whole structure of Satanism, as diverse as it is, lends itself to violation of the law and the harm of other human beings. A brief look at the beliefs held by *most* Satanists bears this out.

The God of Self

The most common element in all forms of Satanism involves the promotion of oneself above all else—complete indulgence of personal desires. Pressure to conform to cultural, societal, or religious standards is the antithesis of Satanism, according to Anton LaVey:

> My brand of Satanism is the ultimate conscious alternative to herd mentality and institutionalized thought. It is a studied and contrived set of principles and exercises designed to liberate individuals from a contagion of mindlessness that destroys innovation.[22]

In other words, what *you* want takes precedence over what anyone else wants. *Your* needs are of primary importance. And the more you strive to go against the grain of society, the better off you are. Nonconformity "is Satanism's strength."[23] A Satanist "should not allow himself to be programmed by others. . . . [T]hat is the greatest enemy to his freedom of spirit. It is the very denial of life itself, which was given to him for a wondrous unique experience—not for imitation of the colorless existence of others."[24]

The term *Satanism* could just as easily be replaced by the term *you-ism*. Why, then, does LaVey bother calling his belief system Satanism? One reason, he states, is "because it's fun."[25] Another reason stems from the emotional punch held by the word *Satan*, as well as its inherent link to rebellion: "I have termed my thought 'Satanism' because it is most stimulating under that name. Self-discipline and motivation are effected more easily under stimulating conditions. Satanism means 'the opposition' and epitomizes all symbols of nonconformity."[26] LaVey additionally feels that use of the term *Satanism* better identifies his worldview as a legitimate religion complete with ceremonies and rituals, which he feels can fill the emotional needs of his unholy flock.[27]

Satanists view their approach to life as the fullest expression of living, even though others might perceive their actions as evil: "'Evil' is still 'Live' spelled backwards, and if evil we be, live we will! Living well is still the best revenge against all adversity. Love, laugh, fancy, create, innovate, reap, and revel—as Satanists—in this best of all worlds, World without end."[28] A Satanist's obsession with the self is epitomized in "The

Nine Satanic Statements" of LaVey's Church of Satan, as listed in *The Satanic Bible*:

1. Satan represents indulgence, instead of abstinence!
2. Satan represents vital existence, instead of spiritual pipe dreams!
3. Satan represents undefiled wisdom, instead of hypocritical self-deceit!
4. Satan represents kindness to those who deserve it, instead of love wasted on ingrates!
5. Satan represents vengeance, instead of turning the other cheek!
6. Satan represents responsibility to the responsible, instead of concern for psychic vampires!
7. Satan represents man as just another animal, sometimes better, more often worse than those that walk on all-fours, who, because of his "divine spiritual and intellectual development," has become the most vicious animal of all!
8. Satan represents all of the so-called sins, as they all lead to physical, mental, or emotional gratification!
9. Satan has been the best friend the church has ever had, as he has kept it in business all these years![29]

This list reveals yet another hallmark of Satanism: a virulent hatred of Christianity. Satanists hold that "the morality put about by the Christian Church, which is based on guilt and self denial, is a load of hogwash."[30] This is but one of the many attacks made by Satanists against Christians and their faith.

Down with Christ

Satanists see followers of Jesus as hypocritical, narrow-minded, ignorant fools. LaVey writes: "Christian doctrine has become outmoded and unbelievable, even to the most feebleminded. One wonders, 'How is it possible for people to be so stupid as to believe the lies they are taught by ministers and priests?'"[31] One reason Satanists find Christianity so detestable is that they feel the Christian church has historically been concerned with nothing but controlling the populace through dreary lists of don'ts:

> The squealing Christian creep is correct in assuming Satanism is dangerous. . . . Satanism is dangerous because it encourages originality

over herd mentality. Large masses or people who all act and think within a prescribed set of options are much easier to control. And exploit.[32]

Given the stress placed on self-indulgence by Satanists, it is only natural that they would view Christianity—a religion marked by an objective of righteousness, self-control, and love of others—as a loathsome belief system. In response, they do all they can to demonstrate a reversal of Christianity. For example, Satanists have been known to recite the Lord's Prayer backwards during their ceremonies and to use an inverted cross to mock Christ's crucifixion.[33]

It must be stressed that in rejecting Christianity, *most* Satanists are not necessarily pledging allegiance to the personal spirit-being whom Christians identify as Satan. The majority of Satanists denounce all forms of spirituality and hold to a philosophy that is basically materialistic and atheistic. Satan, whom they "worship," is merely a symbol for the self. In LaVey's words, "We don't worship Satan, we worship ourselves using the metaphorical representation of the qualities of Satan."[34]

Magick

Today's occult understanding of magick was popularized by infamous occultist Aleister Crowley (1875–1947), who stated: "Magick is the Science and Art of causing Change to occur in conformity with Will."[35] Both witches and Satanists accept this definition of magick and employ it to change situations that would, using normally accepted methods, be unchangeable. Unlike witches, however, who claim that there is "white" magick (used for good and others) and "black" magick (used for self-serving purposes), Satanists maintain that *all* magick is the same. LaVey, in fact, takes great exception to what he sees as a ludicrous distinction made by "white" witches:

> There is no difference between "White" and "Black" magic, except in the smug hypocrisy, guilt-ridden righteousness, and self-deceit of the "White" magician himself. . . . No one on earth has ever pursued occult studies . . . without ego gratification and personal power as the goal.[36]

A distinction should also be noted between the way witches view magick's power and the manner in which Satanists view magick's power. Satanic magick usually draws upon the natural inner forces resident in one's ego rather than on external forces or entities from a spiritual dimension.[37] As a result, witches see their magick as a way of accessing supernatural powers, whereas Satanists perceive magick "not as supernatural (i.e., forever scientifically inexplicable), but simply as supernormal (i.e., not yet fully understood by science but amenable to eventual scientific explanation)."[38]

Magick, as practiced by both witches and Satanists, is accomplished through the use of spells or incantations. These often consist of highly evocative imagery, repetitive phrases, and/or power words designed to bring forth supernatural forces (as in witchcraft) or the inner forces of the self (as in Satanism). Of course, *some* self-styled Satanists feel they are indeed speaking to the Devil as defined by Christians—i.e., an external, personal, spiritual entity known as Lucifer.

The *Encyclopedia of Occultism and Parapsychology* defines a spell as a "written or spoken formula of words supposed to be capable of magical effects."[39] The theory behind spells seems to have come from the idea that there is a natural and intimate connection between words and whatever objects or persons they signify. It is believed that under the right circumstances a magician can cause an event to occur by either chanting about or describing the event desired, while at the same time describing the actions of the objects/people/spirits that the magician wants involved in the event.[40] Such a spell was discovered in the personal diary of Sean Sellers:

> O great desolate one, spawn of the abyss, enemy to the weak, send forth your most glorious blessing and heal the wounds of one of your children. Send forth the dire powers of darkness so that we may do your will. Send to us a burning flare of change so that we may place ourselves to help you. Cast down the cowardly lies of suppression with a clap of earth-shattering thunder! Let your presence be known, for you are among your most talented. Upon this night, send the soul of mortality to your newfound child and grasp him/her as you would a lover. We unite to strengthen through the true power of darkness an abandoned god, in all the black glory and richness of truth. Unite among us

the powerful force of freedom, and through our power rise, to some-day be free. Allegiance to your power shall be sworn, as eternity revolves without end.[41]

Ritual Sacrifices

Sacrifices are an indispensable part of satanic rituals. The four basic kinds of sacrifices are self, pain, parts from once living animals or humans, and living animals or humans. Each brings about different effects "in accordance with one's will." Like most formal religious ceremonies, satanic sacrifices help to "concentrate the mind through symbols and words and suggested altered states."[42] The sacrifice of self is a perverted analogy of the Christian's submission to God as expressed by the apostle Paul: "[P]resent your bodies a living and holy sacrifice, acceptable to God, which is your reasonable service of worship" (Rom. 12:1). These satanic sacrifices often involve such practices as masturbation, sexual intercourse, homosexual acts, and oral copulation. They signify the supremacy of self-indulgence and self-pleasure.

Pain sacrifices are closely aligned to self sacrifices because the physiological responses and emotional reactions to pain are allegedly similar to those associated with sexual ecstasy. Professor John Cooper of Eastern Kentucky University, who specializes in the study of Satanism, explains the most common methods of pain sacrifice:

> Satanists are prone to . . . slashing themselves with razors or sharp knives, generally on the arms (usually the tops of the forearms, to avoid striking an artery), the upper sides of the thighs, or the buttocks. Shallow slashes across the chest or breasts are not unknown, but care is taken not to cause dangerous bleeding; this rite aims not so much at shedding blood but at causing pain. Some criminally involved Satanists, under the influence of alcohol and drugs, have reportedly cut off the joints of their fingers. The cultist starts with the first joint of the little finger at the first ritual and goes on to the second joint of the same finger at the next one. Satanists seek mutilation as an in-group sign, like tattoos in some cultures; but pain offered to Satan is the overarching point of this terrible practice.[43]

The use of animal and/or human body parts occurs quite frequently in all forms of Satanism. This is common because animal parts are easily obtainable either from mail order occult supply companies or animal carcasses on the road. Human body parts, of course, cannot be obtained legally. Such a barrier to magical rites, however, is overcome by some Satanists ("self-styled") through grave-robbing.

Finally, there is the unfortunate occurrence of sacrifices involving live animals or humans. The victim is "slaughtered at the height of the ritual to augment the Satanist's own psychic energy . . . thus increasing the Satanists' chances for success in obtaining the purpose of the ritual."[44] Most of the time, Satanists will capture whatever kind of animal is easiest to acquire. Suburban Satanists often use cats and dogs, while rural Satanists turn their sacrificial attention to squirrels, rabbits, and small farm animals. In *Magick in Theory and Practice*, influential occultist Aleister Crowley outlines the perfect sacrifice: "for nearly all purposes the human sacrifice is the best."[45]

[T]he method of killing is practically uniform. The animal should be stabbed to the heart, or its throat severed, in either case by the knife. All other methods of killing are less efficacious; even in the case of crucifixion, death is given by stabbing.[46]

It should be noted that every satanically-related human/animal sacrifice in America has been perpetrated by either a self-styled Satanist or a group of self-styled Satanists. Religious Satanists such as Anton LaVey denounce such actions in the strongest terms. One Church of Satan publication reads: "The Church of Satan is in no way affiliated with these despicable criminals who pretend to be members of the church in order to carry out their foul deeds. The Church of Satan stands firmly for law and order, and is violently opposed to ritual murder . . . animal sacrifices, etc."[47] LaVey himself writes: "Under no circumstance would a Satanist sacrifice any animal or baby!"[48]

At the same time, LaVey leaves open a dangerous door: "The only time a Satanist would perform a human sacrifice would be if it were to serve a two-fold purpose; that being to release the magician's wrath in the throwing of a curse, and more important, to dispose of a totally obnoxious and deserving individual."[49] He has also proclaimed: "The Satanist, being a magician, should have the ability to decide what is just, and then apply the powers of magic to obtain their goals."[50] It is through this open door that far too many individuals, especially teenagers, have walked in an effort to reach a state wherein they could produce change in accordance with their will.

In May 1996, for example, residents of San Luis Obispo, California, were shocked when seventeen-year-old Royce Casey, sixteen-year-old Jacob Delashmutt, and fifteen-year-old Joseph Fiorella were arrested and charged with the kidnap, rape, torture, and murder of fifteen-year-old Elyse Pahler. Police say the three youths "drugged Pahler to lessen her resistance, raped her and cinched a belt around her neck to make it easier to stab her."[51] Prior to the killing, the boys had formed a musical rock band to "glorify Satan." This led to discussions about the need for a human sacrifice in order to enhance their musical ability to worship Satan. The end result was the death of Pahler, a girl described by family and friends as being gifted in painting, acting, music, and dance.

According to Deputy District Attorney Dan Bouchard, the boys "selected and stalked her, believing that the blonde, blue-eyed girl was a virgin and that her sacrifice would earn them a 'ticket to hell.'"[52] Pahler's disappearance, which took place on June 22, might have gone unresolved had it not been for the guilty conscience of Royce Casey. Eight months after the murder, Casey led deputies to Pahler's decomposed body.

In an interview with KNBC/TV (Los Angeles), Pahler's mother described her anguish: "Something is wrenched from you, a piece of your heart. . . . The pain, it's so great, it's as great as any physical pain, anything you can imagine. . . . [T]he worst thing to think about [is] the torture."[53] If tried as adults and convicted, the three Satanists face a maximum penalty of life in prison without the possibility of parole.

ACCORDING TO THE BIBLE

The amoral, nearly sociopathic philosophy promoted in Satanism stands in stark contrast to the Lord's well-defined standards of righteousness. While lying, cheating, stealing, homosexuality, fornication, adultery, drunkenness, drug use, violence, murder, rape, and incest are justified in Satanism as acceptable forms of self-gratification, Scripture teaches that all those who practice such things will be condemned to hell on the day of judgment (1 Cor. 6:9-10; Gal. 5:19–21; Heb. 13:4). The most obvious negative aspect of Satanism, however, is its denial of *every* theological doctrine of Christianity.

THE BIBLE

Satanism

Scripture

"Why [profanity deleted] didn't writers mean what they said or say what they meant when they wrote that stupid book of fables, the Bible."[54] "If one is to believe this theological accusation that the Devil represents falsehood, then it surely must be concurred that it was he, not god, that established all spiritual religions and who wrote all of the holy bibles!"[55]

"The Word of God is living and powerful. Sharper than any two-edged sword, it penetrates even to dividing soul and spirit, joints and marrow; it judges the thoughts and attitudes of the heart" (Heb. 4:12).

"I have given them Thy word. . . . Sanctify them in the truth. Thy word is truth" (John 17:17).

GOD

Satanism

Scripture

"There is no God . . . no supreme, all-powerful deity in the heavens that cares about the lives of human beings. There is nobody up there who gives a [profanity deleted]. Man is the only god. Man must be taught to answer to himself and other men for his actions."[56] "It is a popular mis-conception that the Satanist does not believe in God. The concept of 'God,' as interpreted by man, has been so varied throughout the ages, that the Satanist simply accepts the definition which suits him best. Man has always created his gods, rather than his gods creating him. God is, to some, benign—to others, terrifying. To the Satanist 'God'—by whatever name he is called, or by no name at all—is seen as the balancing factor in nature, and not as being concerned with suffering. This powerful force which permeates and balances the universe is far too impersonal to care about the happiness or misery of flesh-and-blood creatures on this ball of dirt upon which we live."[57]

"The fool has said in his heart, 'There is no God.' They are corrupt, they have committed abominable deeds" (Ps. 14:1). "The wrath of God is being revealed from heaven against all the godlessness and wickedness of men who suppress the truth by their wickedness, since what may be known about God is plain to them, because God has made it plain to them. . . . God's invisible qualities—his eternal power and divine nature—have been clearly seen, being understood from what has been made, so that men are without excuse" (Rom. 1:18-20). "Now then, listen, you wanton creature, lounging in your security and saying to yourself, 'I am and there is none besides me.' . . . You have trusted in your wickedness and have said, 'No one sees me.' Your wisdom and knowledge mislead you when you say to yourself, 'I am, and there is none besides me.' Disaster will come upon you, and you will not know how to conjure it away" (Isa. 47:8-11).

JESUS CHRIST

Satanism

"I think, in short, that Christ has failed in all his engagements as both savior and deity."[58] "I dip my finger in the watery blood of your impotent mad redeemer, and write over his thorn-torn brow: The true prince of evil—the king of the slaves!...Say unto thine own heart, 'I am mine own redeemer.'"[59]

Scripture

"We did not follow cleverly invented stories when we told you about the power and coming of our Lord Jesus Christ, but we were eyewitnesses of his majesty" (2 Peter 1:16). "At the name of Jesus every knee will bow in heaven and on earth and under the earth, and every tongue confess that Jesus Christ is Lord, to the glory of God the Father" (Phil. 2:10–11).

SATAN

Satanism

"[The devil is] the dark forces in nature that human beings are just beginning to fathom."[60] "Satan is, therefore, an extension of one's psyche or volitional essence."[61]

Scripture

"[The devil] was a murderer from the beginning and does not stand in truth, because there is no truth in him. Whenever he speaks a lie, he speaks from his own nature, for he is a liar, and the father of lies" (John 8:44). "The devil, who deceived them, was thrown into the lake of burning sulfur, where the beast and the false prophet had been thrown. They will be tormented day and night for ever and ever" (Rev. 20:10).

SIN & SALVATION

Satanism

"Behold the crucifix; what does it symbolize? Pallid incompetence hanging on a tree.... There is no heaven of glory bright, and no hell where sinners roast. Here and now is our day of torment! . . . Here and now is our day of joy! Here and . . . now is our day of opportunity! Choose ye this day, this hour, for no redeemer liveth![62]

Scripture

"[A]ll have sinned and fall short of the glory of God, being justified as a gift by His grace through redemption which is in Christ Jesus.... God was in Christ reconciling the world to Himself, not counting their trespasses . . . against them . . . we beg you on behalf of Christ, be reconciled to God. He made Him who knew no sin to be sin on our behalf, that we might become the righteousness of God in Him" (Rom. 3:23–24; 2 Cor. 5:19–21).

WHAT'S THE ATTRACTION?

Satanism's primary attraction is its promise of absolute power, which can be especially enticing to teenagers, as the following comments from Sean

Sellers and two other two teenaged Satanists, James and Phil, clearly reveal:

> Key words [are] "power" and "control." All Satanists want to have control of their lives and they all want power.... Whether they believe Satan to be a force of nature or a fallen angel, they all seek to petition the "Darklord" for power in their lives.[63]

> What I like about Satanism is the power that it gives me. The people at school know I'm into it, and they don't mess with me.... It also gives me the feeling that I can do anything I put my mind to.... Why should I love anyone else? All people want is to get as much as they can. That's the way life is. Satanism has taught me about life. It helps you grow.[64]

> If you know anything about satanism, you know it's about one thing—power. Power over yourself, power over others, power over your surroundings.[65]

Another aspect of Satanism that makes it so appealing to some individuals lies in its extremely Machiavellian (completely self-serving) approach toward life. In catering to every human lust, Satanism allows participants to revel in utter self-indulgence and sinful depravity, often at the expense of others. Consider the counsel of Anton LaVey:

> A pest shows little responsibility where you are concerned, yet expects it in return. Cut him off [on the phone] with, "I must attend to something—I'll be right back." Leave him and don't return. In other words, lie. Your conscience shouldn't bother you a bit.[66]

> If a Wrong is gotten away with, and someone else repeats it and also gets away with it, Right is birthed into existence. The Wrong becomes Righter each time it succeeds. . . . There is no such thing as "moral" Right. . . . Morality is a human invention conferred by the self-serving interests of the sensually impoverished. . . . I apply my own rule, which is: "There are no rules."[67]

Finally, a cynical realism permeates Satanism. As LaVey declares, "[T]he world is not simply a stage, but a Barnum and Bailey world, just as phony as it can be."[68] Satanists typically call things as they see them, regardless of who is listening, who may be hurt, or whether they are right. This often results in gross exaggerations and inaccurate generalizations. Occasionally, however, Satanists make insightful observations, which can make them appear more honest and intellectually astute than others.

In order to effectively witness to Satanists, a Christian must be able to demonstrate that followers in Jesus Christ have a logical, well-reasoned faith that is more fulfilling than Satanism's God-denying worldview. Additionally, Christians must remain calm when confronted by the blasphemy and mockery they will undoubtedly encounter when dialoguing with Satanists. If a Satanist is willing to listen and enter into a discussion with a Christian, then self-control, gentleness, and love must consistently be shown by the believer (Gal. 5:22–23; 2 Tim. 2:24–26). Only in this way can such attributes be proven as more powerful than mockery, hate, anger, and other satanic "virtues."

The logical contradictions within Satanism might also be brought up in an effort to show why that philosophy is inconsistent. For example, Anton LaVey declares that a Satanist can be utterly self-indulgent. Each person decides what he or she wants to do and then does it. Nevertheless, LaVey provides his own set of "moral" rules, which include a prohibition against vandalism and senseless killing.[69]

LaVey is simply creating his own standard of righteousness that he expects Satanists to adhere to or else they are not a "true" Satanist. But why should these rules exist? What makes LaVey qualified to judge what can and cannot be done? Is there any reason not to sacrifice the last surviving Giant Panda should the opportunity arise? Why shouldn't a Satanist vandalize and inflict harm on animals and humans if that is what brings the most gratification? After all, self-gratification is what Satanism is all about. Ultimately, LaVey's promises of total self-indulgence through Satanism are "lost under a welter of pseudo amoral posturing. . . . [O]ne set of mores and laws is merely being replaced with another."[70]

Christians can point out how Satanists, at least "religious" Satanists embracing LaVey's philosophy, have simply placed themselves into a religion established by a man no more qualified to set up a religion than anyone else. This argument might then be followed with a discussion of how Christianity is different from any other world religion since it is founded upon the actual life, death, and resurrection of the most loving individual ever to live on our planet—Jesus Christ, God in human form.

Prayer is the most important aspect of witnessing to Satanists. Believers in the satanic way of life, especially older teens and young adults, can be dangerous. Caution, discernment, and common sense must always be used in ministering to *anyone* who poses a physical threat. On the other hand, it must also be remembered that our struggle is not against flesh and blood, but against spiritual forces of wickedness in heavenly places. Consequently, Christians must be "strong in the Lord," having put on the full armor of God in order to "stand firm against the schemes of the devil" (Eph. 6:10–17).

RECOMMENDED READING

Cooper, John Charles. *The Black Mask: Satanism in America Today* (Old Tappan, NJ: Fleming H. Revell, 1990).

Gross, Edward N. *Miracles, Demons, and Spiritual Warfare* (Grand Rapids, MI: Baker, 1990).

Mayhue, Richard. *Unmasking Satan* (Wheaton, IL: Victor Books, 1988).

Passantino, Bob and Gretchen. *Satanism* (Grand Rapids, MI: Zondervan, 1995).

_____. *When the Devil Dares Your Kids* (Ann Arbor, MI: Servant Publications, 1991).

HOLLYWOOD'S FAVORITE RELIGION

The whole agonized future of this planet, every Man, Woman, and Child on it, and your own destiny for the next endless trillions of years, depend on what you do here and now with and in Scientology. This is a deadly serious activity.

L. RON HUBBARD, SCIENTOLOGY FOUNDER[1]

Shawn stared at the Scientology recruitment poster: "You shall know the truth. And the truth shall set you free." Intrigued by these words, she entered the church offices for a free "personality test." It went so well that Shawn inquired about the organization's various courses. Although the course costs were prohibitive, she was offered a way of taking them for free: a five-year contract working seven days a week at the church.

During her training, Shawn learned a new language based on the group's terminology that sounded like gibberish to outsiders: she became a "tresec," one small cog in the Scientology machine; new recruits were "raw meat" to be processed by "auditors" (counselors); an "overt" was a harmful deed; and a "misunderstood" was an unintentional blunder regarding policy or procedure. The list of unique terms seemed endless. It was wonderfully different from anything else she had ever known.

Eventually, however, Shawn began feeling troubled by a long-ignored commitment she had made as a youth to Jesus Christ. Spiritually confused, she sought the advice of her auditor. "I understand why you would feel that way," he sympathized. "Jesus is just an 'implant,' an 'engram' that has been fed to all of us. We need to run the engram out." In Scientology terms, Shawn's counselor was telling her that the concept of Christ as a Savior was false. It was an unreal perception in her mind that had been implanted there by evil spiritual entities. Although this new assessment of Christ took

Shawn by surprise, it did not prompt her to leave the church because she had fallen in love with a fellow Scientologist named Keith, the executive secretary to the branch manager.

Both Keith and Shawn soon experienced one of the most difficult times in their lives. It began when church officials charged Keith and five other staff members with "ineptitude" that slowed down income generation. Keith was sentenced to the Rehabilitation Project Force (RPF), which he would later describe as "slave labor." He was allowed no visitors, no reading material, no TV, and no radio. He worked on the grounds from 7:00 A.M. to 8:00 P.M., then studied Scientology lessons for two hours. Food was so scarce that a friend had to smuggle in a jar of peanut butter.

Meanwhile, Shawn was going through her own problems. She had hired a cashier who ended up stealing money from the organization. Shawn's punishment for her "lack of discernment" in dealing with the dishonest employee was washing and spackling walls. She was also forced to assume a loan to replace the money. "I felt like a degraded being," she remembers. "I was afraid Keith would stop loving me." But Keith did not stop loving her, and the two were eventually married.

Keith, however, was still in RPF, which made things very difficult. They were only allowed to spend Saturday nights together. Moreover, Shawn's harassment at work did not cease. Although Shawn often felt like she was losing her mind she never spoke to Keith about it because she thought it might jeopardize his progress in the church. The final blow came when Scientology's founder, L. Ron Hubbard, sent out an intolerable directive: all visitation rights between Scientologists in RPF and their spouses would immediately be stopped because the spouses had become a distraction.

This was too much for Keith, who went to his supervisors and stated, "Don't waste your time rehabilitating me. In three months, when my five year commitment is up, I'm gone." By the time he left, he had spent twenty-six months in RPF. Shawn ended up being expelled for leaving her office for about an hour without permission. After a lengthy period of time, the expulsion was overturned. But by then it was too late. She had given her life to Christ, whom she learned was actually the One who said, "You shall know the truth, and the truth shall make you free" (John 8:32). At first Keith was unreceptive to Christianity, but he gradually saw the light of Christ through positive changes in Shawn. Today the Scotts direct Cults

Awareness Ministry and conduct seminars on the doctrinal conflicts between Scientology and Christianity.[2]

HOW IT ALL BEGAN

Some individuals assert that Scientology is little more than a money-making business cleverly disguised in religious garb by corporate leaders with one desire: to exploit the 501(c)3 tax-exempt status that the U.S. government offers to religions. But such a criticism does not take into account the fact that Scientology bears all the marks of a religious organization, including its own set of scriptures, a worldview that recognizes the existence of a supreme deity and other spiritual beings, and various techniques designed to help members obtain what might best be thought of as Scientology's version of "spiritual enlightenment." It is, therefore, quite proper to refer to Scientology as a religion entitled to all of the rights and privileges protected by the U.S. Constitution.

Of course, *defining* Scientology as a religion does mean *endorsing* it as a religion. In fact, it is the opinion of this author that Scientology—although a religion—is a false religion because its teachings depart from the biblical God and His plan of salvation as understood and proclaimed in historic, orthodox Christianity. Herein lies one of the great blessings that the U.S. Constitution provides American citizens: all of us are not only free to embrace and practice religion according to our conscience (freedom of religion), but we are free to present our reasons for rejecting the religions we believe to be false (freedom of speech). As "The Creed of The Church of Scientology" states:

> We of the Church believe . . . That all men have inalienable rights to conceive, choose, assist or support their own organizations, churches and governments; That all men have inalienable rights to think freely, to talk freely, to write freely their own opinions and to counter or utter or write upon the opinions of others.[3]

This aspect of religion in America is especially important for Christians to understand when publicly criticizing any religious group. Applying a "false religion" label to any organization such as Scientology must never be confused with seeking to deny that group their constitutional right to exist. Even Jesus, although he sharply rebuked the religious leaders of his day, never denied their freedom of belief (Matt. 23:13–29). Like Jesus, Christians should freely speak out against what they perceive as false religions without denying the rights of persons in those religions.

We must categorically separate seeking to deny someone's rights from simply pointing out that their religion is false according to Scripture, the standard of truth that for 2,000 years has helped Christians discern spiritual truth from error. This chapter will attempt to do the latter with Scientology, which is only one of the many new religious movements to be born in America during the twentieth century.

According to its alleged 8,000,000 members,[4] the church's founder— Lafayette Ron Hubbard (1911–1986)—was a man of "stellar accomplishment unequaled in the world today."[5] In his church's eyes, he was "the world's single most influential author, educator, humanitarian and philosopher."[6] Others, however, describe Hubbard as little more than "part storyteller, part flimflam man."[7] Some say he was "the greatest con man of the century."[8] In 1984, a Los Angeles Superior Court judge presiding over one of the numerous Scientology-related lawsuits went so far as to call him "virtually a pathological liar."[9] But most people, no matter what they believe, would agree that Hubbard was an interesting fellow who led a colorful life.

Hubbard first achieved notoriety in the 1930s by writing for various pulp fiction magazines. His specialties included adventure, Westerns, mystery, war stories, and science fiction.[10] He was a prolific author and churned out lengthy yarns under his own name as well as under several pseudonyms such as Winchester Remington Colt and Rene Lafayette. But just before Hubbard reached widespread fame and fortune, World War II struck. It landed him in the Navy and placed his budding career on indefinite hold.

The post-war years were not kind to Hubbard. Instead of being back on the civilian fast-track to literary success, he found himself broke, in debt, and having serious troubles with his first wife, Louise Grubb.[11] These circumstances only aggravated the mental instability he had begun to experience while in the Navy. Finally, in 1947, he sent a letter to the Veterans Administration requesting psychiatric help:

> I avoided out of pride any mental examinations, hoping that time would balance a mind which I had every reason to suppose was seriously affected. I cannot account for nor rise above long periods of moroseness

and suicidal inclinations, and have newly come to realize that I must first triumph above this before I can hope to rehabilitate myself at all.[12]

It was during this time that Hubbard began writing bizarre messages to himself in private journals. Once he noted: "All men are your slaves." He also wrote: "You can be merciless whenever your will is crossed and you have the right to be merciless."[13] Because of his inner turmoil, Hubbard developed a deep interest in mental health, a subject that would later form the backbone of Scientology.

This is not to say that Hubbard's areas of study were limited to mental health. As early as 1946, he had struck up a friendship with renowned rocket fuel scientist John Whiteside Parsons, a protége of the British occultist Aleister Crowley, who proudly billed himself as "The Beast" (666).[14] Eventually Hubbard actually lived with Parsons in Pasadena, California, at an aging mansion that served as home to "an odd mix of Bohemian artists, writers, scientists and occultists."[15] It seems that Crowley—best known for his perverse "sex magick" rituals—also had close contact with Hubbard, who in 1952 referred to the infamous occultist as "my very good friend."[16]

The association of Hubbard, Crowley, and Parsons (who headed his own black magic group modeled after Crowley's occult group in England) has given rise to a number of fascinating accounts regarding various "ceremonies" that took place at the Pasadena mansion. Science fiction writer L. Sprague de Camp, who knew both Hubbard and Parsons, remembers how neighbors "began protesting when the rituals called for a naked pregnant woman to jump nine times through fire in the yard."[17]

Paul Rydeen, in his book *Jack Parsons and the Fall of Babylon*, relates this same story. Moreover, in a lengthy excerpt from Rydeen's volume that was printed in the underground magazine *The Excluded Middle*, it was asserted that both Hubbard and Parsons practiced Crowleyan sex magick.[18] Such accusations have appeared before in several unauthorized Hubbard biographies, including *Bare-Faced Messiah: The True Story of L. Ron Hubbard* (1987), *A Piece of Blue Sky* (1990), and *L. Ron Hubbard: Messiah or Madman?* (1987), co-authored by Hubbard's own son, L. Ron Hubbard, Jr.

More recently, a 1995 edition of the British occult book series *Rapid Eye* referred to Hubbard as one of the most famous of all "Thelemic" magicians.[19] The word *Thelema* (Greek, meaning "Will") refers to "the body of philosophy and magickal practices codified by the late Aleister Crowley."[20] The importance of magick in *Thelema* was not lost on Parsons or Hubbard, who reportedly participated in one of the most famous "magickal operations" of the twentieth century: the "Babalon Working."[21]

This advanced sex magick ritual was meant to produce a "moonchild" in fulfillment of a prophecy that Crowley had made in his *Book of the Law*. According to Crowley, his magickal heir would be the much dreaded Antichrist, a "living being in form resembling man, and possessing those qualities of man which distinguish him from beasts, namely intellect and power of speech, but neither begotten in the manner of human generation, nor inhabited by a human soul."[22]

Parsons evidently wanted to be the Antichrist's father and decided that the mother would have to be an "elemental spirit" corresponding to the "Whore of Babylon" (Rev. 17:4–5). Through the use of magick during sexual intercourse with a willing female, Parsons hoped to deny a human spirit access to the unborn child, thereby leaving room for the invoked spirit of "Babalon"—which roughly corresponded to the "mother of the universe"—to possess the fetus.[23]

To find a willing female vessel, Hubbard and Parsons allegedly participated in eleven days of magickal ritual (January 4, 1946 to January 14, 1946). They had no idea whether the rituals had worked until a few days later when Marjorie Cameron, a woman whom neither man had met, mysteriously showed up at the mansion. Parsons later recorded in his journal that she was quite eager to conceive the demon-seed child in her womb. Consequently, from March 2–4 at least three "moonchild" sex magick rituals took place. Hubbard reportedly assisted Parsons and Cameron in all of them.[24]

In a March 6 letter to Crowley, Parsons explained that the instructions for these rituals were channeled from the spirit world "direct through Ron—the seer."[25] Surviving copies of Parson's *Book of Babalon*, which chronicles his alleged magickal exploits with Hubbard, records an interesting set of ceremonial commands that supposedly came forth from Hubbard while he was channeling:

> Display thyself to Our lady; dedicate thy organs to Her, dedicate thy heart to Her, dedicate thy mind to Her, dedicate thy soul to Her, for She shall absorb thee, and thou shalt become living flame before She incar-

nates. . . . Consult no book but thine own mind. *Thou art a god. Behave at this altar as one god before another.* . . . Thou art the guardian and thou art the guide. . . . Envision thyself as a cloaked radiance desirable to the Goddess, beloved. Envision her approaching thee. Embrace her, cover her with kisses. Think upon the lewd lascivious things thou couldst do. All is good to Babalon. ALL. . . . Thou as a man and as a god hast strewn about the earth and in the heavens many loves, these recall, concentrate, consecrate each woman thou hast raped. Remember her, think upon her, move her into BABALON, bring her into BABALON, each, one by one until the flame of lust is high. Preserve the material basis. . . . The lust is hers, the passion yours. Consider thou the Beast raping [italics added].[26]

In the end, no "moonchild" was ever conceived. Parsons had a falling out with Hubbard over a failed business venture, and Hubbard went back to what he loved the most—writing.[27] His first full-length story to be published—"The End Is Not Yet"—appeared in the pages of *Astounding Science Fiction* magazine in August 1947. It was about a nuclear physicist overthrowing a dictatorial system with the creation of a new philosophy. Three years later Hubbard had another article printed in *Astounding Science Fiction*. That piece, although nonfiction, would become a book—*Dianetics: The Modern Science of Mental Health*.

Scientology Basics

Dianetics hit the mid-1950 best sellers list almost immediately. A year later, however, its sales had dried up, the research foundations he established for his "poor man's psychoanalysis" had fallen into financial ruin, and his writing future looked bleak. But the ever-creative L. Ron Hubbard would bounce back by 1954 with his most brilliant idea yet: a new religion— Scientology (i.e., *Dianetics* with a spiritual twist).

The religion of Scientology can purportedly help people handle "any and all" problems.[28] It is founded upon the psychotherapeutic techniques outlined in *Dianetics*. In fact, simply reading this volume is often a person's first step toward becoming a Scientologist. The book is so important to the church that members actually mark time by its publication date. To illustrate, Scientologists consider the year that saw President Bill Clinton reelected to office as being A.D. 46 (After *Dianetics*).[29]

Hubbard's theories rest on a presupposition that the mind is composed of two parts: 1) the "analytical mind," that conscious part of us by which we perceive, reason, think, and remember; and 2) the "reactive mind," a part of us that might best be understood as a sort of subconscious.[30] The reactive mind "works on a totally stimulus-response basis."[31] It is not controlled by the analytical mind, nor is it even perceived by the analytical mind. Nevertheless, it is said to exert tremendous influence over us.

Dianetics explains these concepts and further describes "engrams," which are "mental recordings" of past experiences of physical pain, unconsciousness, and any real or imagined "threat to survival."[32] These, although unknown to our analytical mind, reside in our reactive mind and cause unhappiness, sickness, behavioral aberrations, a negative outlook on life, violent responses to various situations, and in many cases, illness. In short, they are the single source "of all human failings."[33]

According to *Dianetics*, there exist an infinite number of engrams that can come from an equally vast number of negative experiences that have been recorded in the reactive mind. We can even get engrams—which Hubbard parallels with what he describes as moments of "unconsciousness"[34]—while still in our mother's womb. This location, in fact, seems to be one of the most dangerous of all engram-producing places:

> Mama sneezes, baby gets knocked "unconscious." Mama runs lightly and blithely into a table and baby gets its head stoved [sic] in. Mama has constipation and baby . . . gets squashed. Papa becomes passionate and baby has the sensation of being put into a running washing machine. Mama gets hysterical, baby gets an engram. . . . Junior bounces on Mama's lap, baby gets an engram. And so it goes. People have scores of prenatal engrams. . . . They can have more than two hundred. And each one is aberrative [a cause of irrationality and/or deranged behavior]. Each contains pain and "unconsciousness." Engrams received as a zygote are potentially the most aberrative. . . . Those received as an embryo are intensely aberrative. Those received as a foetus are enough to send people to institutions all by themselves.[35]

Hubbard says that some of the most destructive prenatal engrams are received by babies whose mothers attempt to abort them with douches and knitting needles.[36] In *Dianetics*, he plainly states that attempted abortions are "very common," and their results are terrible:

[I]t is a scientific fact that abortion attempts are the most important factor in aberration. . . . A large proportion of allegedly feeble-minded children are actually attempted abortion cases, whose engrams place them in fear of paralysis or regressive palsy and which command them not to grow but to be where they are forever. . . . [M]any billions [of dollars] America spends yearly on institutions for the insane and jails for the criminals are spent primarily because of attempted abortions done by some sex-blocked mother. . . . The case of the child . . . upon whom abortion has been attempted, is not hopeless. If he is treated with decency after he is born and if he is not restimulated by witnessing quarrels, he will wax and grow fat until he is eight and can be cleared, at which time he will probably be much startled to learn the truth. . . . All these things are scientific facts, tested and rechecked and tested again.[37]

Scientology further teaches that "Man exists in a partially hypnotized state" and that church processes are "methods of 'unhypnotizing' men to their own freer choice and better life."[38] Engrams are similar to post-hypnotic suggestions.[39] Anything reflective of an engram (e.g., word, picture, object) will "key-in" that engram and cause the person to respond negatively to whatever is stimulating the hidden memory.[40]

For example, words spoken to a pregnant woman after she falls—e.g., "Did you hurt yourself, Margaret? Let me help you get up"—might be recorded in an unborn baby as a "pain" or "fear" engram. Consequently, when the name "Margaret" is heard by that child, he or she may become terrified or feel pain. As an adult, that person might also experience fear of looking to others for help. Hubbard's solution to such prenatal engrams is simple: "If she [a pregnant woman] falls, she should be helped—but *silently*."[41] At the same time, Hubbard warns that people should not maintain silence by "a volley of 'Sh's,' for those make stammerers."[42] Furthermore, such careful word monitoring should be maintained around children and adults as well:

Maintain silence in the presence of injury. . . . Say nothing and make no sound around . . . [an] injured person. To speak, no matter what is said, is to threaten his sanity. Say nothing while a person is being operated upon. Say nothing when there is a street accident. Don't talk! Say nothing around a sick child or an injured child. Smile, appear calm, but say nothing. . . . [A]ctions are all that can be done around the sick and injured unless one has an active desire to drive them into neurosis or insanity or, at best, to give them a future illness. And above all, say nothing around a woman who has been struck or jarred in any way. Help her. If she speaks, don't answer. Just help her. You have no idea of whether she is pregnant or not.[43]

Engrams can also be caused by other kinds of experiences. Consider these examples from *Scientology: A World Religion Emerges in the Space Age*:[44]

Mr. A has a tonsillectomy under anesthetic. During the operation, the surgeon, who wears glasses, comments angrily to a clumsy nurse, "You don't know what you are doing." Mr. A recovers. A few months later, Mr. A, a bit tired during a hard day at the office, has an argument with his employer (who happens to also wear glasses), and who says "You don't know what you are doing." Mr. A suddenly feels dizzy, stupid, and gets a pain in his throat. There is installed a kind of conditioned somatic response.

How does someone get rid of their engrams? That can only be done through Scientology.[45] A person must go to a Scientology office/church for face-to-face "auditing" sessions with a church counselor, whose role is to help the convert discover where in his or her psychological makeup there might be some hidden engramic trauma.[46] An "invaluable and indispensable tool" used in these sessions is the *electrometer* ("E-meter"),[47] a crude lie detector that Scientology bills as "the only instrument known to man that can accurately measure thought."[48]

An E-meter purportedly reads a person's reactive mind via two tin cans attached to wires that are hooked up to the main machine. The person holds these cans while they are asked various questions and given numerous directions or commands. The procedure gets them to reveal intimate details about their life. An auditor "reads" the person's reactions on the E-meter and in so doing helps the person learn about him- or herself.[49]

It is widely recognized, however, that the battery-operated contraption is simply an electrogalvanometer that measures changes in the electrical resistance of one's skin based on how moist it is. When the skin moisture of the person holding the cans fluctuates, so does the E-meter. Nevertheless, Scientologists insist that they can, through E-meter auditing, help persons bring engrams into their analytical mind realm, where the engrams can be consciously recognized and released.[50]

Going Clear

Scientologists claim that engram eradication, also known as going "Clear" of one's reactive mind, enables someone to "perceive, recall, imagine, create and compute at a level high above norm."[51] It allegedly improves one's "social attitudes . . . fertility . . . artistic creativity . . . [and] reaction time."[52] "Clear" is the first significant level of achievement a Scientologist reaches.[53] The process, however, is far from pleasant. Hubbard warned that erasure of an engram is accompanied by yawns, tears, sweat, odor, panting, urine, vomiting, and excreta.[54] But after these irritations cease, "Clears" can expect increased intelligence,[55] better appearance,[56] and immunity from 70 percent of all known diseases.[57] A "Clear" can also "control all of his body fluids,"[58] "confront anything and everything in the past, present and future . . . has no vicious reactive mind and operates at total mental capacity . . . can create energy at will . . . [and] can have or not have at will anything in the universe."[59]

In Hubbard's 1954 book *The Creation of Human Ability*, numerous examples are given of the kind of unusual, repetitive questions and commands used while auditing a preclear. The following text is taken from the directions for two auditing runs in the "Intensive Procedure: Route II":

R2-26: In this Intensive Procedure only two steps are employed. . . . The first consists of these commands, "*Be completely certain that the wall [in this room] is [really] there*". And when the preclear has become . . . completely certain that the wall is there, touching it, pushing against it, and so forth, the auditor then says, "*Sit down, take this (your) watch*", "*Now predict that the wall will be there ten seconds from now*", "*Have you done so?*" "*All right wait ten seconds by your watch*". And when this is done, [ask] "*Is the wall still there?*" And when the preclear has answered, [say] "*Now make absolutely certain the wall is there*" and the preclear does so by touching it, pushing at it, kicking it. [Then say] "*Now make very sure that the wall is there*". And when the preclear very vigorously has done so, [say] "*Now predict that it will be there in ten seconds*". And when the preclear has done so, the remainder of the commands are given and this is repeated over and over. . . . [Then say] "*Start laughing*" . . . no matter what the preclear says thereafter, or what arguments he advances, or how many things he asks about, or how many reasons he wants or gives, the auditor merely says (adding words that urge the preclear), "*Start laughing*". And when the preclear at length does so, no matter how half heartedly, [say] "*Keep* *on laughing*". The two commands which are used . . . without giving the preclear any reason whatsoever are, "*Start laughing*" and "*Keep on laughing*". This process is then done until the preclear can actually enjoy a laugh without any reason whatsoever.[60]

Clear is really just the beginning point of mental/spiritual growth in Scientology.[61] After reaching Clear, church members are encouraged to proceed deeper into their faith because although cleared, they still face grave spiritual dangers. A vast array of "courses" are offered for Clears, some of the most crucial being the OT classes ("Operating Thetan," an advanced Clear). Skipping courses is usually not allowed because "understanding of and ability to apply OT materials are dependent upon having fully attained the earlier states of awareness and abilities."[62]

Scientology spokesperson Leisa Goodman rightly comments that reserving a portion of religious texts "for those who have attained specific levels of spiritual advancement has well-established precedents in other religions."[63] It should be noted, however, that Scientologists who desire spiritual growth must pay for it. As Hubbard taught, "MAKE MONEY, MAKE MORE MONEY, MAKE OTHERS PRODUCE SO AS TO MAKE MONEY."[64]

For many, the path toward Scientology's brand of enlightenment begins with a free personality test that takes approximately one hour. Next comes various "auditing" sessions, which are modestly priced. After these initial courses, fees increase exponentially, all in an effort to bring a person to Clear. But reaching Clear only puts members in a position of having to pay even larger fees if they want to spiritually advance and learn the mysteries of their religion on "The Bridge To Total Freedom."[65]

A 1990 *Los Angeles Times* investigative series on Scientology estimated that it costs anywhere from $200,000 to $400,000 to go from the initial free test to the OT 8 level, a course called "Truth Revealed." As of 1990, only 900 members had reached this level of advancement.[66] Levels OT 9–OT 15 have since been added to the ever-growing list of auditing courses.[67] These advanced courses allegedly result in greater spiritual insight, increased emotional control, higher intellectual capabilities, sharpened memory, and better health. Church officials maintain that OTs can actually project themselves out of their body "to view the body or control the body from a distance."[68] Consequently, they do not "need a body to communicate or work."[69] It is also claimed that OTs can read minds and "control matter, energy, space and time."[70]

Scientology's graduated levels of spiritual knowledge has been the source of countless complaints from former members and the general public. Many people have argued that had they known what was in the more advanced levels, they would never have begun their expensive journey toward spiritual fulfillment a lá Scientology. Fortunately, a general picture of Scientology's worldview and its doctrines can now be constructed from materials released to the public. Some observers remark that its teachings read more like a science fiction thriller than anything else, as the following synopsis of Hubbard's cosmology reveals.[71]

The World According to Hubbard

Trillions of years ago, long before anything as we know it existed, there were countless immortal beings known as "thetans," who found themselves bored with eternal life. In an effort to rid themselves of the doldrums, they decided to collectively create the universe and everything in it. Their hope was to have a realm in which to play the "Game of Life" and pass the time.[72] But the thetans soon faced a problem on which they had not planned. As *spiritual* beings, they could not function within their *physical* creation. The thetans solved this dilemma by building bodies for themselves, the human form being only one of many different appearances.

Unfortunately, the thetans forgot their *true* identities and began believing they were just physical beings. In forgetting who they were, these thetans, now trapped in physical bodies through ignorance, became vulnerable to painful experiences—"engrams." Even when the thetan's host body died, their engrams remained with them, only to cause more problems after the thetan reincarnated into yet another body. Each human lifespan produced more engrams, which in turn created even more engrams, and so on, and so on throughout innumerable lifetimes on earth.

All modern-day humans are merely thetans who have reincarnated into the latest generation of physical bodies.[73] We are all still playing "the game" we started so long ago—we just do not know it. Everyone, of course, is rife with engrams, which are the real cause of society's woes. Scientology's primary goal is to purge each person/thetan of his or her engrams. The ultimate aim of Scientology is to "clear" the entire planet, thereby eradicating the global effects of our reactive minds: "war, pollution, insanity, drugs, and crime."[74] In order to achieve this goal, every individual on the earth would, of course, have to embrace Scientology. Consequently, the church has implemented a number of social programs/front organizations that seem to be part of a massive effort at spreading the gospel of Scientology. These include: Narconon, Criminon, Applied Scholastics, Citizens Commission on Human Rights, American Citizens for Honesty in Government, and The Way to Happiness Foundation.[75]

More about Engrams

According to Hubbard, many of our engrams date back to long before our present lifetime. Some were recorded trillions of years ago through planetary wars with other beings. Others were deliberately inflicted on us by evil, power-hungry thetans. These latter engrams—known as "implants"—are some of the most destructive of all. "Implants," Hubbard once remarked, "result in all varieties of illness, apathy, degradation, neurosis and insanity and are the principal cause of these in man."[76]

Some of the worst implants are allegedly recorded right after we die, just before being reincarnated into another body. Hubbard revealed this discovery during a lecture given on July 23, 1963. It seems he learned about these insidious "Between Lives Implants" while traveling through the universe in spirit form.[77] Hubbard said that after a human body ceases to function, we thetans go to a "landing station" on Venus, where evil thetans implant us with lies about our past lives and our future. One of the most heinous implants involves our mode of reincarnation. We are made to think that our return to earth happens when we are lovingly placed inside a newborn baby's body. But Hubbard revealed the *true* story:

> Of all the nasty, mean and vicious implants that have ever been invented, this one is it. And it has been going on for thousands of years. It's the most complete memory wipeout system and the biggest bunch of lies that anybody ever had anything to do with. . . . [T]hey show you a picture of being sent directly down to Earth and channeled straight into the

body of a newborn baby. . . . [W]hat actually happens to you [is] you're simply capsuled and dumped in the gulf of lower California. Splash! To [profanity deleted] with ya. And you're on your own, man. And if you can get out of that and through that and wander around through the cities and find some girl who looks like she's going to get married or have a baby or something like that, you're all set. And if you can find a maternity ward to a hospital or something, you're okay. And you just eventually just pick up a baby. You're strictly on your own, man. In a state of total amnesia. . . . Well, in this sequence you're [also] given a compulsion that the next time you die you must appear on the landing stage. And that's it. That's the whole ruddy, lousy, cotton-picking lot. . . . [T]his is the most vicious engram I have ever seen set up.[78]

Venus is not the only "landing station" site. According to Hubbard, there are some on Mars, and even some on earth![79] Hubbard discovered that these stations have been used to impart all kinds of different implants, including the following:[80]

the Jack-in-the-box: The thetan area is invaded by MEST [Matter, Energy, Space, Time] beings. . . . The MEST beings use theta traps. One of these is to give to thetans pretty little boxes. These boxes contain a stack of pictures. . . . [T]hese pictures are very acceptable. The thetan looks over the pictures. He finds they are quite similar one to another. They show, each one, a picture of a box of pictures. When he [the thetan] replaces the lid, the box explodes violently. He instinctively tries to dampen the explosion. He gets his aura of beingness full of pictures which are extremely confusing, being pictures of boxes of pictures. . . . You will find a preclear with this in restimulation to be very curious about cereal boxes which have pictures of boxes of cereal which have pictures of boxes of cereal.

As if things were not bad enough, earthbound thetans have yet another worry: "body-thetans." These bothersome creatures are allegedly attached to our fleshly bodies. They are, of course, invisible. They are also incredibly powerful, and their origins date back to the "catastrophe which laid waste to this sector of the galaxy."[81] Church members allege that ridding oneself of body-thetans is yet another benefit of Scientology. The body-thetan saga, which is taught in the church's OT 3 course and costs advanced church members approximately $6,000, is as follows.

Invasion of the Body-Thetans

Seventy-five million years ago a tyrannical ruler named Xenu (pronounced Zee-new) decided it was time to do something about the overpopulation that was negatively affecting his Galactic Confederation of seventy-six planets. The evil despot knew his solution would have to be a drastic one since the problem he faced was enormous—i.e., approximately 250 billion people per planet. He finally devised a plan that suited his diabolical nature: mass executions. He hired renegades and ordered them to sweep through the Confederation and round up thetan-inhabited beings of all shapes and sizes. Those unfortunate enough to be captured were subsequently frozen by injections of an alcohol/glycol mix and, in spaceships resembling DC-8s, were transported to the designated execution planet—earth, then known as Teegeeach.

Once Xenu's victims were deposited near ten volcanoes located around the world, he had powerful H-bombs dropped on them, which obliterated their bodies. But since thetans are immortal and cannot be destroyed,[82] the blasts merely freed them from their physical encasings. Xenu knew this would happen. He also knew that he could not have disembodied thetans floating around the galaxy. So he had instructed his officers to quickly recapture all of the thetans with "electronic ribbons." The thetans were then pulled back to earth and "packaged" (i.e., stuck together) in tiny, invisible clusters. This procedure was done in two locations: Hawaii and Las Palmas in the Canary Islands.

Their ordeal, however, was not yet over. For thirty-six days the thetans were subjected to a sequence of implants via movies they were forced to watch. The films contained images of God, religion, Satan, psychiatrists, sex, spinning dancers, car accidents, Christ's crucifixion, and scenes from modern-day England, among other things. All of these implants were designed to obscure their memories about who they were, where they came from, and most importantly, what Xenu had done to them.

Afterward, the thetan clusters were released and ended up getting frozen in ice. Aeons later, when the ice melted, the clusters flew out across the planet and began attaching themselves by the thousands to the bodies of unsuspecting humans. Thus, they are called "body-thetans." During the last several million years, these confused thetan clusters have caused humanity endless troubles. All of us, according to

Hubbard, are covered with them. They overwhelm the main thetan who resides within our bodies, and this in turn causes us confusion and internal conflict.

Hubbard discovered all of this back in 1967 and devised a way to get rid of them: the OT 3 course. In OT 3, Scientologists are taught to scan persons' bodies for "pressure points," indicating the presence of thetan clusters. Using techniques prescribed by Hubbard, church members make telepathic contact with their body-thetans and remind them of Xenu's treachery as well as what they went through so long ago. With that, the body-thetans detach themselves, and the Scientologist is freed of their influence.[83]

ACCORDING TO THE BIBLE

However, documentation exists that definitively shows Scientology to be incompatible with Christianity. Scientologists claim that their church "respects all religions" and that their faith does not "conflict with other religions or religious practices."[84] Scientology literature goes so far as to say, "[T]here is no attempt to change a person's beliefs or to persuade him away from any religion to which he already belongs."[85] To those unfamiliar with Scientology, this may indeed seem to be the case, especially because straightforward statements about key theological doctrines are difficult to track down in the labyrinth of materials that Hubbard has produced. However, documentation exists that definitively shows that Scientology is *not* compatible with Christianity. This is the general consensus of evangelical religion researchers who specialize in the field of cults.

In his landmark book *The Kingdom of the Cults* well-known cult expert Dr. Walter Martin explained that his chapter on Scientology showed "the major points at which statements in Scientology materials contradict biblical teaching."[86] In *Evangelizing the Cults*, Kurt Van Gorden writes: "No one who is faithful to God's Word can say that there are no conflicts between Scientology and the Bible."[87] Christian authors John Ankerberg and John Weldon observe: "Scientology teachings are inconsistent with the beliefs of orthodox Christian faith."[88] These assessments represent only a small sample of the many pronouncements against Scientology that have been made by evangelical cult experts and Christian ministers. A brief comparison of Scripture with Scientology statements easily supports their warnings.

THE BIBLE

Scientology	Scripture
"[W]e in Scientology believe that when Man sees the truth about himself and the Universe, the scales of illusion will drop from his eyes and he will see that Truth which previously he could not see or understand. This truth, in the form of cosmological revelation, is contained in the early writings of the Founder of Scientology, L. Ron Hubbard."[89]	"Jesus answered, 'I am the way, and the truth, and the life'" (John 14:6). "Sanctify them by the truth; your word is truth" (John 17:17).
"Mr. Hubbard's writings and lectures on the human spirit comprise the Scripture of the Scientology religion.... As the sole source of the Scriptures, he has no successor."[90]	"All Scripture is inspired by God [i.e., breathed-out by God] and profitable for teaching, for reproof, for correction, for training in righteousness" (2 Tim. 3:16).
	"This is what we speak, not in words taught by human wisdom but taught by the Spirit, interpreting spiritual things in spiritual words" (1 Cor. 2:13).

GOD

Scientology	Scripture
"In Scientology we believe that God exists. As to the form in which He exists, we do not yet have dogma."[91] "Although the existence of the Supreme Being is affirmed in Scientology, His precise nature is not delineated."[92]	"In the beginning was the Word, and the Word was with God, and the Word was God.... And the Word became flesh, and dwelt among us, and we beheld His glory, glory as of the only begotten from the Father.... No one has ever seen God, but God the One and Only [Jesus], who is at the Father's side, has made him known" (John 1:1, 14, 18).
"[E]ach person must seek and know the Divine Nature in and for himself."[93] "We believe that by spiritual revelation, the true nature of God will be revealed to each subjectively."[94]	"For since the creation of the world His invisible attributes, His eternal power and divine nature have been clearly seen, being understood through what has been made, so that they are without excuse" (Rom. 1:18–20).
"There are gods above all other gods.... [T]here is no argument here against the	"Before me there was no God formed, neither shall there be after Me" (Isa. 43:10).

GOD *(cont'd.)*

Scientology	*Scripture*
existence of a Supreme Being. . . . It is amongst the gods, there are many false gods elected to power and position. . . . There are gods above other gods, and gods beyond the gods of the universes."[95]	"[Y]ou are My witnesses. Is there any God besides Me. . . . I know of none" (Isa. 44:8).
"So he (the thetan) has as far as we can see in the manufacture of energy, about the same capabilities as those which have been assigned to the Supreme Being in this universe."[96]	"For this reason Thou art great, O Lord God; for there is none like Thee" (2 Sam. 7:22). "Remember this, and be assured. . . . I am God, and there is no other; I am God and there is no one like Me" (Isa. 46:8–9).

JESUS CHRIST

Scientology	*Scripture*
"[T]he Hebrew definition of Messiah is One Who Brings Wisdom. . . . 'Messiah' is from 'messenger.'"[97]	MESSIAH: "[The] Hebrew word masiah is derived from masah, 'to anoint, smear with oil.' . . . The primary sense of the title is 'king,' as the anointed man of God. . . . Jesus was confirmed as the Christ, the Messiah of God [Acts 2:36; Rom. 1:4; Phil. 2:9–11]." [98]
"Neither Lord Buddha or Jesus Christ were OTs according to the evidence. They were just a shade above clear."[99]	"For in Him all the fullness of Deity dwells in bodily form" (Col. 2:9). "Thomas answered and said to Him [Jesus], 'My Lord and my God!'" (John 20:28).
"Somebody somewhere on this planet, back about 600 B.C. found some pieces of R6 [another name for the 36-day implant that created body-thetan clusters], and I don't know how they found it; either by watching madman or something. But since that time they have used it and it became what is known as Christianity; the man on the cross—there was no Christ!"[100] "[T]he Christian church used (and uses) implanting. . . . They . . . invented Christ, who comes from the crucifixion in R6 75 million years ago, and implanted their way to power."[101]	"We did not follow cleverly invented stories when we told you about the power and coming of our Lord Jesus Christ, but we were eyewitnesses of his majesty. . . . And we have the word of the prophets made more certain, and you will do well to pay attention to it" (2 Peter 1:16–19). "That which was from the beginning, which we have heard, which we have seen with our eyes, what we have looked at and our hands have touched—this we proclaim concerning the Word of Life [Jesus]" (1 John 1:1–2).

JESUS CHRIST *(cont'd.)*

Scientology

"You will find the cross as a symbol all over the universe, and the Christ legend as an implant in preclears millions of years ago."[102] "The symbol of the crucified Christ is very apt indeed. It's the symbol of a thetan betrayed."[103]

Scripture

"God was pleased to have all his fullness dwell in him [Jesus], and through him to reconcile to himself all things, whether things on earth or things in heaven, by making peace through his blood, shed on the cross" (Col. 1:19-20).

"He forgave us all our sins, having canceled the written code, with its regulations, that was against us and that stood opposed to us; he took it away, having nailed it to the cross. And having disarmed the powers and authorities, he made a public spectacle of them, triumphing over them by the cross" (Col. 2:13-15).

MAN / SIN

Scientology

"[M]an is basically good—a fact which flies in the teeth of old religious beliefs that man is basically evil. . . . Man is basically good but he could not attain expression of this until now."[104]

"It is a basic tenet of Scientology that man is basically good."[105] "Scientology is . . . predicated upon the fundamental belief that man is basically good."[106]

"Absolute good and absolute evil do not exist in the MEST [matter, energy space, time] universe." [107]

Scripture

"The heart is more deceitful than all else and is desperately sick" (Jer. 17:9).

"[T]he hearts of the sons of men are full of evil, and insanity is in their hearts throughout their lives" (Eccl. 9:3)

"[O]ut of the heart come evil thoughts, murders, adulteries, fornications, thefts, false witness, slanders" (Matt. 15:19–20).

"[N]othing good dwells in me" (Rom. 7:14-25).

"There is none righteous, not even one. . . . [A]ll have sinned and fall short of the glory of God" (Rom. 3:10, 23).

"But solid [spiritual] food is for the mature, who by constant use have trained themselves to distinguish good from evil" (Heb. 5:14).

"Depart from evil, and do good" (Ps. 34:14).

SALVATION

Scientology	*Scripture*
"Nobody but the individual could die for his own sins—to arrange things otherwise was to keep man in chains."[108]	*"He himself bore our sins in his body on the tree, so that we might die to sins and live for righteousness; by his wounds you have been healed" (1 Peter 2:24).*
"It is despicable and utterly beneath contempt to tell a man he must repent, that he is evil."[109]	*"Repent, then, and turn to God, so that your sins may be wiped out" (Acts 3:19).* *"In the past, God overlooked such ignorance, but now he commands all people everywhere to repent" (Acts 18:30).*
"There are probably many types of redemption."[110] "[T]here are many different paths to God for different people."[111]	*"Salvation is found in no one else [but Jesus], for there is no other name under heaven given to men by which we must be saved" (Acts 4:10-12).*
"[Scientology] brings man to total freedom and truth."[112]	*"It is for freedom that Christ has set us free. Stand firm, then, and do not let yourselves be burdened again by a yoke of slavery" (Gal. 5:1).*
"[T]he Church of Scientology represents spiritual freedom for millions of people the world over."[113]	*"You shall know the truth. and the truth shall set you free" (John 8:32).* *"[T]hrough Christ Jesus the law of the Spirit of life set me free from the law of sin and death" (Rom. 8:2).*
"Scientology has accomplished the goal of religion expressed in all Man's written history, the freeing of the soul by wisdom."[114]	*"The fear of the Lord is the beginning of wisdom" (Prov. 1:7).* *"Christ [is] the power of God and the wisdom of God" (1 Cor. 1:24).*

CHRISTIANITY

Scientology	*Scripture*
"The whole Christian movement is based on the victim.... A Scientologist is not a victim.... We can win by converting victims. Christianity succeeded in making people into victims. We can succeed by making victims into people."[115]	*"Who shall separate us from the love of Christ? Shall trouble or hardship or persecution or famine or nakedness or danger or sword? ... No, in all these things we are more than conquerors through him who loved us" (Rom. 8:35-37). "For God has not given us a spirit of timidity, but a spirit of power, love and of self-discipline" (2 Tim 1:7).*

CHRISTIANITY *(cont'd.)*	
Scientology	*Scripture*
"[Scientology] is a far more intellectual religion than that known to the West as late as 1950."[116]	*"Love the Lord your God with all of your heart and with all your soul and with all your mind" (Matt. 22:37).*
	"Do not conform any longer to the pattern of the world, but be transformed by the renewing of your mind" (Rom. 12:2).
	"Set your mind on things above, not on earthly things" (Col. 3:2).
	"[W]hatever is true . . . noble . . . right . . . pure . . . lovely . . . admirable . . . excellent . . . or praiseworthy—think on these things" (Phil. 4:8).

Reincarnation

Another key concept in Scientology is reincarnation. To a Scientologist, personal salvation is freedom from the cycle of birth and death.[117] Scientology maintains that most major religions, including Christianity, have taught this:

Like the Buddhist, Taoist, the Hindu, and the early Christian, Scientology believes that the immortal being has assumed many bodies in his evolution in the physical universe toward an ultimate realization and freedom from material bondage.[118]

The Egyptians, Hindus . . . Christians, Romans, Jews and Gnostics all believed in reincarnation and the rebirth cycle. It was a fundamental belief in the Roman Catholic Church until 553 A.D. when a company of four monks held the Synod of Constantinople, (without the Pope present) and decided the belief could not exist. They condemned the teachings of reincarnation as heresy and it was at this time that references to it were expunged from the Bible.[119]

Such statements are simply untrue, not only theologically, but also historically. Reincarnation is completely antithetical to Christianity and always has been. None of the early church fathers embraced reincarnation. Many of them, in fact, spoke out against it, including Justin Martyr (c. 100–165), Irenaeus (c. 120–202), Tertullian (c. 160–215), Clement of Alexandria (c. 155–220), Jerome (c. 345–419), and Augustine (345–430).[120]

Hubbard's comment regarding the Synod of Constantinople reveals an even greater ignorance of basic church history. There were actually four councils held at Constantinople, in the years 381, 553, 680, and c. 879. *None* of them dealt with reincarnation. Furthermore, the Second Council to which Hubbard refers was actually attended by 165 bishops, not four monks. The issues they discussed dealt primarily with the nature of Christ.[121] It is true that a list of condemnations were issued at about the same time. These, however, "were issued against (among other things) the notion of the preexistence of souls . . . but there was no mention made of reincarnation."[122]

Biblically, Hebrews 9:27 clearly states that "it is appointed for men to die once, and after this comes judgment." Those who have received Christ as their personal Savior will immediately be in the presence of God (Phil. 1:21–23; 2 Cor. 5:8). Individuals who have not come to a saving knowledge of Christ during this lifetime will first go to an intermediate state of punishment where they will await a final judgment (Job 21:30–34; Isa. 14:9–11; 2 Peter 2:9). At the final judgment they will be told to depart from the Lord's presence (Matt. 7:23) into what Scripture terms "the lake of fire" (Rev. 20:10–14). In short, "now is the day of salvation" (2 Cor. 6:2).

WHAT'S THE ATTRACTION?

One of the most powerful attractions to Scientology lies in the influential endorsements of its many Hollywood celebrity members, including jazz pianist Chick Corea; singer Al Jarreau; actress Karen Black; politician/entertainer Sonny Bono; Priscilla Presley; her daughter, Lisa Marie Presley; and Nancy Cartwright (the voice of Bart Simpson). Perhaps the most notable Scientologists are superstars Tom Cruise, Kirstie Alley, John Travolta, and his wife Kelly Preston. Travolta says Scientology "contains the secrets of the Universe."[123] According to Alley: "If you can erase your engrams, then you can get better."[124] Preston believes Scientology is "very much a spiritual science. It creates ways to handle everything, whether it's in your love life or in your work."[125]

Such comments have done much to spread the gospel of Scientology. Celebrities hold great influence over society, especially American society, which has demonstrated a consistent obsession with stars of the silver screen. Moreover, celebrities carry a lot of clout that can be used to silence critics. For example, a June 19, 1995 *Denver Post* article reported that when Lisa Marie Presley found out MTV was preparing a special entitled *New Religions: The Cult Question* and that it included a segment on Scientology, she "made it known to MTV brass that if the report bashes her church of choice, her hubby Michael Jackson's music may not be available to the network any longer."[126]

To pamper these valuable public relations assets, Scientology built a luxurious "Celebrity Centre" at the old Chateau Elysee, a seven-story mansion overlooking Hollywood. At this location, stars can rest, relax, worship, and of course audit away engrams. From the Celebrity Centre the church also runs a special office that is not only in charge of offering career guidance for the stars but ensuring their "correct utilization" for Scientology.[127]

It was not until January 1997, however, that Scientology aggressively used its Hollywood clout for the first time. In an effort to counteract alleged discrimination against Scientologists in Germany, thirty-four American celebrities published an "open letter" to Chancellor Helmut Kohl.[128] It accused Germany of persecuting Scientologists the way Hitler persecuted the Jews. Signers of the petition included such celebrity heavyweights as actor Dustin Hoffman, actress Goldie Hawn, film director Oliver Stone, talk-show host Larry King, Los Angeles entertainment attorney Bertram Fields, and novelist Mario Puzo, author of *The Godfather*.[129] Noteworthy was the fact that *none* of the signers were Scientologists. Celebrity Scientologists had apparently used their connections to obtain protesters. For example, film director Constantin Costa-Gavras signed it at the request of his friend, actor Dustin Hoffman. Hoffman is close friends with Scientologist Tom Cruise, with whom he co-starred in *Rainman*. (Gavras eventually withdrew his support for the letter, after learning more about Scientology.)

Kohl dismissed the letter as "garbage," charging that the people who signed it "know nothing about Germany and don't want to know. Otherwise they wouldn't have concocted such a thing." Michel Friedman of the Central Council of Jews in Germany was quoted by the *Berliner Zeitung* newspaper as saying: "Comparing the Third Reich's Final Solution ideology with the democratic realities of Germany today is absurd, historically wrong, politically irresponsible." Germany's Family Affairs Minister Claudia Nolte angrily declared, "The U.S. celebrities have insulted victims of the Nazis."[130] The American government agreed: "It is simply outrageous to compare the current German leadership to the Nazi era leadership. We have advised the Scientology community not to run those ads, because the German government is a democratic government, and it governs a free people."[131]

For some people, another attractive aspect of Scientology is its mystery. Scientology thrives on mystery through its policy of making advanced church truths available only to those willing to plunge deeper into the organization (and deeper into their checkbooks). The emotional principle at work here is the same one that binds together adults who join fraternal organizations and children who form "secret clubs," complete with hidden knowledge, private handshakes, cryptic signs, and code-words. Fiction author Hubbard knew the merits of mystery, writing: "If we tell him there is something to know and don't tell him what it is, we will zip people into [Scientology]. . . . And one can keep doing this to a person—shuttle them along using mystery."[132]

RECOMMENDED READING

Ankerberg, John and John Weldon. "Scientology," in *Encyclopedia of New Age Beliefs* (Eugene, OR: Harvest House, 1996).

Behar, Richard. "*Scientology: The Cult of Greed,*" Time, May 6, 1997, 50–57.

Branch, Craig. "Hubbard's Magic," *The Watchman Expositor,* vol. 13, no. 5 (1996).

_____. "Hubbard's Religion," *The Watchman Expositor,* vol. 13, no. 2 (1996).

_____. "L. Ron Hubbard: The Man & His Myth," *The Watchman Expositor,* vol. 13, no. 5 (1996).

Cooper, Paulette. *The Scandal of Scientology* (New York: Tower Publications, 1971).

Corydon, Bent and L. Ron Hubbard, Jr. *L. Ron Hubbard: Messiah or Madman?* (New York: Lyle Stuart, 1987).

Durand, Greg Loren. "The Dangers of Dianetics: Sceintology's Roadmap to Mental Bondage," Internet edition available at http://204.97.103.50/members/14bs/dianetic.htm.

Miller, Russell. *Bare-Faced Messiah: The True Story of L. Ron Hubbard* (London: Michael Joseph, 1987).

Owen, Chris. "Bodies in Pawn: Clams, Marcabs & Galactic Invader Forces," Internet edition available at http://wpxx02.toxl.unl-wuerzburg.de /~cowen/essays/marcabs.html.

Sappell, Joel and Robert W. Welkos. "Scientology Series" (six-part), *Los Angeles Times*, June 24–29, 1990. Internet edition available at http://homepage.clstron.nt /~davel/la90.html.

Scientology: Cult of Greed & Power, Internet Site, http://www.entheta.net /Index.shtml.

Scientology: Religion or Not, Internet Site, http://wpxx02.toxl.unl-wuerzburg.de /~krasel/CoS/Index.html.

Who Is Who In Scientology, Internet Site, http://wpxx02.toxl.unl-wuerzburg.de /~krasel/CoS/wholswho.html.

Van Gorden, Kurt. "Scientology," in *Evangelizing the Cults*, ed. Ronald Enroth (Ann Arbor, MI: Vine Books, 1990).

CHRISTIAN IDENTITY: WHITE MAKES RIGHT

There are no words in the English language, or any other, to adequately describe a Jew. You can not, hard as you may try, insult a Jew because the very vilest and foulest things, you can think of to say about him, are nothing but pure and unadulterated flattery in comparison to what he really is.

**THOMAS E. O'BRIEN,
NEW CHRISTIAN (IDENTITY) CRUSADE CHURCH**[1]

Children are little people, little human beings, and that means white people. . . . There's little dogs and cats and apes and baboons and skunks and there's also little niggers. But they ain't children. They're just little niggers.

CHARLES CONLEY, CHRISTIAN IDENTITY MINISTER[2]

Johnny Lee Clary was five years old when he saw a black person for the first time. It happened while he and his father were sitting outside a grocery store in Del City, Oklahoma. "Look, Daddy," he said pointing across the street. "A chocolate covered man!" Johnny's father responded, planting seeds of hate in his boy's heart: "Son, that's a nigger. Say 'nigger,' son. Say 'n-i-g-g-e-r.'"

Johnny eventually learned that black people were not the only ones worthy of the white man's contempt. Persons of Jewish descent deserved to be despised as well. Johnny Lee's daddy would dance around the kitchen singing, "Ak a back a soda cracka, ak a back a boo; if your mother chews tobacco, she's a dirty Jew." Johnny subsequently grew up thinking all Jews were dirty. It was a lesson that would prove difficult to unlearn.

As the years passed, Johnny's home life rapidly deteriorated. His alcoholic mother regularly committed adultery, only to be beaten up by Mr. Clary who had also become a drunkard. Finally, when Johnny was eleven, he watched his father commit suicide. It was an event he would never forget.

Johnny was subsequently shuffled around from relative to relative, being physically abused in every home to which he was sent. All he had left were memories of the days when he and his father were able to enjoy each other's company in peace. But those days were gone forever. By the time he reached fifteen, Johnny was on the verge of suicide. If he could not be with his father in life, he would join him in death.

One day, however, he was watching television and saw a young David Duke discussing the merits of the Ku Klux Klan. Johnny immediately remembered his father mentioning this organization and tuned in to listen. Much of what Duke said echoed the words of Johnny's father. It was so comforting that he sent for some KKK literature.

The Klan ended up being Johnny's family for seventeen years. He quickly rose through its ranks and ended up being the Imperial Wizard of his own Klan. He rubbed shoulders with some of America's most notorious racists/anti-Semites: Richard Butler, founder of the neo-Nazi Aryan Nations; Tom Metzger, founder of White Aryan Resistance (WAR); and David Duke, Louisiana's most famous racist politician.

Amazingly, Johnny believed that he was following Christianity, which according to his KKK brethren was for white people, God's chosen race. Johnny, of course, was *not* practicing Christianity. He had embraced the teachings of the Christian Identity Movement, an amalgamation of religiously inclined racists from the ranks of the KKK, the neo-Nazi community, and various white supremacist groups. It is one of the few spiritual belief systems that thrives on hate.

Johnny's involvement with Christian Identity started coming to an end after he inadvertently ran across this Bible verse: "There is neither Jew nor Greek, there is neither slave nor free man, there is neither male nor female; for you are all one in Christ Jesus" (Gal. 3:28). He also ran across a number of verses on love, such as 1 John 4:16. Johnny gradually came to realize that he had never really been a Christian. Finally, in 1991, he knelt down before God and cried out to Him for a new life with the following prayer:

> Lord Jesus, I've been so wrong—just like the prodigal son whose father forgave him. Lord, I thought I knew You all these years, but I realize I

didn't know You at all. I want to come to You now. Father, I want You to take this hate from me. Come into my heart Lord Jesus, and cleanse me.

Today Johnny Lee Clary tours the world speaking at churches about the love of Christ and the evils of racism, hate, and violence.[3]

HOW IT ALL BEGAN

Christian Identity (also referred to as simply Identity) is a loosely-knit network of churches and independent leaders that began forming in the 1940s when white racists defected from mainstream Christian denominations to organize their own churches. They built their faith by blending racial prejudice with miscellaneous Christian beliefs that were appealing to them (most notably, those dealing with the end-times).

Identity is not a religious sect, nor is it an authoritarian cult or a mainstream denomination. It does not even have a definitive set of beliefs that a person must embrace in order to be accepted as a follower. It is a unique social/political/spiritual movement based on hate. The foundational concept upon which Identity is built involves what is known as "The Ten Lost Tribes of Israel." This myth has a long history that stretches back to approximately 930 B.C. and the death of Israel's King Solomon (compare 2 Sam. 7; 1 Kings 10).

Almost immediately after Solomon died, the twelve tribes comprising the Hebrew nation of Israel fell into civil war and split into two separate kingdoms.[4] Ten tribes set up a northern kingdom known as the House of Israel. The remaining tribes formed a southern kingdom called the House of Judah. Both kingdoms were plagued by wars, invasions, and internal strife. Finally, in 722/21 B.C., the northern tribes were conquered by the Assyrians and taken into captivity. The southern tribes fell to the Babylonians in approximately 586 B.C. and were sent into exile.

The House of Judah remained in captivity as a distinct entity for seventy years. They returned to their homeland as a nation in 539 B.C., after Babylon fell to Cyrus, King of Persia, who decreed that the Israelites could return to Jerusalem (see 2 Chron. 36:21-23; Jer. 25:9–11).[5] The descendants of these Hebrews comprise most of the population of modern-day Israel. Much less, however, is known about those in the northern kingdom. It is assumed that many were assimilated either into the Assyrian nation or into the populace of surrounding countries. A majority of them may have even been absorbed into the tribe of Judah. All we know for certain is that they were deported to Assyria and settled in Halah, Habor, and the cities of the Medes (2 Kings 17:6).

Questions about the northern kingdom's fate have produced several legends surrounding the "lost" ten tribes.[6] One such myth asserts that their descendants are the Caucasians scattered throughout the earth. This concept first gained wide acceptance in Victorian England (1837-1901) when Protestants embraced the notion that they were biologically linked to Israel. Known as Anglo-Israelism, this idea provides a doctrinal basis for Identity, which teaches that "[t]he Germanic kindred (white) peoples are the true descendants of Abraham, Isaac, and Jacob/Israel."[7]

Doctrines of Hate

By the 1920s, Anglo-Israelism had become extremely popular in America. It was especially attractive to members of the Ku Klux Klan, who saw it as religious justification for their white supremacist views. Christian Identity, however, took at least thirty years (1940s–1970s) to arrive at its present theological state. Although Identity believers may often disagree on several peripheral issues—e.g., whether or not Hitler should be idolized, what should be done with non-whites (exportation vs. extermination), the merits of violent action as opposed to the benefits of non-violent political activism, etc.—most adhere to at least five basic premises:

- White people (Aryans) are the Israelites of the Old Testament.
- The Jews are literal descendants of Satan.
- Adam and Eve were not, as mainstream Christianity teaches, the first people. They were the first *white* people.
- All non-whites (blacks, Asians, Middle Easterners, etc.) are descendants of pre-Adamic races and make up an entirely different species than Caucasians.
- Armageddon, which will be a race war between whites and non-whites, is fast approaching.

One of Identity's main tenets is the Serpent Seed theory, which proposes that Jews are the physical descendants of a sexual union between "Mother Eve" and "the serpent" (Gen. 3).[8] This serpent is variously identified as either Satan or a demonic representative of Satan. As such, Jews are literally "Children of the Devil."[9] Most Identity believers see the serpent as a manifestation of Satan himself:

> Satan (the Arch-Angel) sought to make his intrusion into the being of adam kind by cohabitating with Eve and incarnating himself into a physical Seed Line, hence the seed of the serpent (Gen. 3:15).[10]

In this "two seed" theory, Eve's first two sons, Cain and Abel, were only half-brothers, having "the same mother, but different fathers."[11] Cain was conceived by Eve and Satan, while Abel was conceived by Eve and Adam.[12] In Identity theology, Eve's copulation with "the serpent" (Satan) was "original sin."[13] Aryan Nations founder Richard Butler writes, "[T]here are literal children of Satan in the world today . . . the descendants of Cain, who was the result of Eve's original sin."[14] Hence, the following Christian Identity belief:

> The jew has not been born who does not have an utterly EVIL nature that is easily detectable in his eye. Nevertheless, identifying these serpents conclusively will no doubt be a difficult task.[15]

Those familiar with the biblical account of Genesis will recall that Cain killed Abel. In the continuing Identity version of biblical history, Cain left the Garden of Eden after murdering his brother and fathered the Jewish race. The *Doctrinal Statement of Beliefs* published by Kingdom Identity Ministries of Harrison, Arkansas, reads: "We believe in an existing being known as the Devil or Satan and called the Serpent (Gen. 3:1; Rev. 12:9), who has a literal 'seed' or posterity on earth (Gen. 3:15) commonly called Jews today."[16] This belief is also contained in the Aryan Nations statement of beliefs:

> WE BELIEVE that there are literal children of Satan in the world today. These children are the descendants of Cain, who was a result of Eve's original sin, her physical seduction by Satan. We know that because of this sin, there is a battle and a natural enmity between the children of Satan and the Children of The Most High God. WE BELIEVE there is a battle being fought this day between the children of darkness (today known as Jews) and the children of light (God), the Aryan race, the true Israel of the Bible.[17]

With whom did Cain produce his demon progeny? He allegedly inter-married with pre-Adamic races,[18] usually identified as either "mud people" or "beasts of the field."[19] Identity leader Bertrand Comparet comments: "[T]he Bible makes it unmistakably clear that we are not all descended from Adam and Eve, for there were other races on earth, already old, already numerous, when Adam was created."[20] Comparet also writes: "God had millions of the pre-Adamic Asiatic and African peoples around."[21] Predictably, Identity preachers teach that these pre-Adamic, non-white races were insufficient for God's plans. The Lord needed a "special" race, so he created Adam, who was *not* the first man but rather a second type of man—the first of a "superior species."[22] He was the first white man, "the father of the White Race."[23]

According to Identity theology, the battle between Satan and God began immediately after the creation of Adam and Eve. The Devil's first attack was his seduction of Eve. His second assault upon God's white children was the murder of Abel. The Adversary struck a third time when Cain began tainting the blood lines of pre-Adamic races, resulting in the creation of Jews. The fourth diabolical act occurred when the Jewish/Satanic race crucified Christ.

Recently, Satan has allegedly again begun to harass God's "special" white race. His latest plot is to control the whole world through a fiendish series of moves that are inextricably tied to the Jews. Influential Christian Influential Christian Identity pastor Pete Peters has gone so far as to suggest that the Jews (also referred to as Esau-Edom)[24] could have been responsible for the 1995 Oklahoma City bombing:

> Concerning the Oklahoma bombing . . . [W]hat ethnic group would kill innocent women and children? One group that comes to mind is Esau-Edom. Most have never heard of Edom because the word comes from the Bible. . . . Edom has the cursed Canaanite blood in them . . . and are the descendants of Esau.[25]

Although Identity followers regularly attribute all manner of crimes to their Jewish enemies, the primary means by which Jews are supposedly achieving their goal of satanic world domination is much less violent, though far more effective and offensive: Jews are allegedly behind the modern acceptance of interracial marriage and integration.

The Ultimate Sin

According to James Combs, Jews are behind every troublemaking movement geared to "further decay Christian-White society." One such movement has been the "racial-integration operation." Combs says there is "simply NO question about Jews being guilty."[26] He also writes: "[T]he ultimate aim [of Jews] is that Christian-Whites will be physically bred with the colored. Then, conclusively, we would be obliterated as a people and as the only barrier to Jewry's ambitions as *the* world power."[27]

Like Combs, all white supremacists feel that the preservation of their race is being threatened by Jews seeking to corrupt God's holy line of righteous, white children with Satan's seed, as well as with the seed of pre-Adamic "beasts":

> Jews seek to wipe us out as a race ... HOW? By mongrelizing us via miscegenation [interbreeding] with colored races of the world, especially the Congoloid blacks ... "beasts of the earth" of Genesis 1:25.[28]

> Jews are the ones promoting multi-racial immigration and multi-culturalism. ... It has been the Jews' role as Esau-Edom to destroy God's order of things by getting the white race to ignore the natural barriers of distinction between races. The Jew thus runs to the aid and cause of the Negro and colored races to elevate them while lowering the status of the white man. ... Jews, who are mongrels, desire the entire world to be mongrelized, especially the white race.[29]

Besides social and cultural reasons, Identity adherents see several spiritual motives for avoiding integration with other races. First, white Christians must shun the obvious satanic blood line through Cain. Second, interracial marriage is considered "one of the greatest of all sins," even when it comes to non-Jewish, pre-Adamic races.[30] Third, the white race—which is supposedly the modern descendants of ancient Israel—are God's chosen people and as such are "to be above all people and are not to mix with them."[31] Fourth, pre-Adamic races are greatly inferior to Adamic Aryans. Combs, for example, says the "colored are manifestly such culturally-inferior peoples that a unified White people could, if desired, control them."[32]

Even more moderate supremacists such as Jack Mohr and Pete Peters hold that races should not intermarry. According to Mohr, Adam was "a very special human being" and propagated a race of an entirely different order than pre-Adamic people.[33] Peters feels the same way: "[I]nterracial marriage destroys. It violates God's natural genetic law of like begetting like."[34] Mohr and Peters are properly termed moderates because they deny the Serpent Seed doctrine, maintaining instead the classic Anglo-Israel position that Jews are descended from Khazars, Asiatic tribespeople who lived near the Black Sea in the sixth century.[35] Nevertheless, race-mixing is forbidden by both of these Identity leaders. Peters, for instance, declares: "I teach them [his children] also that if they ever did such a thing—never to come around my house with their mate or their half-breed children because they've been traitors to their own sires."[36]

Former KKK Grand Dragon Louis Beam, one of Identity's most flamboyant leaders, agrees: "Racial treason is the greatest crime a member of our race can commit, for from its end results there is no recovery."[37] According to David Tate of the Aryan Nations, "God loves a sinner but hates a race traitor!"[38] White supremacist Roy B. Mansker warns that "judgment will weigh heavy on the race traitors, who are allowing the alien jew to stay in power."[39] According to Richard Butler, "[O]ur greatest enemies are the race traitors in our ranks."[40]

A final reason for not mixing races is found in a 1991 issue of *Christian Patriot Crusader*, a newsletter published by Jack Mohr. Apparently, white supremacists believe that non-white males—especially blacks—are in some way "conquering" the white race every time they "defile" a white woman, who is deemed nothing less than exclusively white man's territory:

An endless succession of Jew produced plays, films and television shows depict Black males making love to White women. . . . This change in national thinking, has made White women open game for Black males. . . . The Negro invasion of the White man's sanctuary is planned as an assault on the seat of his power and the citadel of his greatness—which has been his gene pool. When a Black man overpowers a white woman, he believes that he is exerting a form of superiority over the White race. . . . This is something every White man should remember, when he sees a colored man with a White woman. . . . The Blacks have not yet reached the place where they hang white scalps on their belts, but many are close to it, because Whites have allowed it to happen. Yet the vast majority of White people have become so befuddled by Jewish propaganda, that they believe this breaking down of barriers can go on without it ending in the destruction of their own race. . . . I am firmly convinced, from a study of history and scripture, that if the White man in America settles down to live side by side with the Black, on any terms, it is only a matter of time and not a long time—till he will cease to exist as a White man.[41]

Louis Beam, who is known for his charismatic speaking and writing, tends to express his aversion to "race-mixing" with high levels of emotional language:

At the mailbox I gaze with utter horror upon two young white girls with their black boy friends. Can I not be spared this? Must I be forced to watch this horrible slow-motion, torture/obliteration of my own people? . . . Father [God], can not this biter [sic] cup be passed to another generation? Have mercy and spare me this![42]

Although hatred toward any race is offensive, America is a free country, and its citizens have a constitutional right to hold whatever beliefs they choose. Unfortunately, most white supremacists are not willing to allow others this freedom. The ultimate goal of many white supremacists is nothing less than a complete takeover of America. This final plank in the foundation of Identity is built on their concepts of the "end-times."

Visions of Armageddon

Identity believers assert that America is the Promised Land (i.e., "the New Jerusalem") where all Israelites/whites, in fulfillment of biblical prophecy, will be gathered together just prior to Armageddon.[43] Once this is accomplished, God's "Heavenly Reich on earth" will be born.[44] The earth will then be cleansed of all antichrist/Jewish/multiracial forces by means of extermination.[45] As Identity pastor Thom Robb writes: "Our nation needs to turn back to God's laws and outlaw race-mixing, with the death penalty being the judgment of doing so."[46] Robb voiced an equally chilling message at a 1986 Aryan Nations meeting:

There is a war in America today and there are two camps. One camp is in Washington, D.C., the federal government controlled by the anti-Christ Jews. . . . [T]heir goal is the destruction of our race, our faith and our people. And our goal is the destruction of them. There is no middle ground. We're not going to take any survivors, any prisoners. It's us or them."[47]

It must be remembered that white supremacists are not seeking to establish an Aryan republic out of mere free-floating prejudice. They actually believe it is their God-ordained destiny to create a white utopia, as Richard Butler clearly proclaims in his tract *Who, What, Why, When, Where: Aryan Nations*:

> WE BELIEVE that there is a day of reckoning. The usurper will be thrown out by the terrible might of Yahweh's people [God's white race] as they return to their roots and their special destiny. We know there is soon to be a day of judgment and a day when Christ's Kingdom (Government) will be established on earth as it is in heaven. . . . [T]he saints of the Most High shall take the kingdom and possess the kingdom forever, even for ever and ever. And the kingdom and dominion and greatness of the kingdom under the whole heaven shall be given to the people of the saints of the Most High, whose kingdom is an everlasting kingdom, and all dominions shall serve and obey Him (Daniel 2:44; 7:18; 7:27).[48]

"We're a dispossessed race now," Butler says. "If the white race is to fulfill its divine, destined purpose under scripture as God's word, it must have its own territorial imperative—a homeland of, by and for its own kind."[49] Butler has also stated, "Our mission is to conquer the earth and have dominion over it."[50] In an open letter that appeared in the Aryan Nations publication *Calling Our Nation*, "Dale" Chesson imparted a word of encouragement to fellow Aryans that perfectly illustrates the lengths to which Identity believers are willing to go in order to recapture America:

> The battles are many, large and small, but for us only victory is acceptable, and victory will be ours!! . . . We must remember that when one of OURS gives his life for that which we are fighting, he is not a terrorist, nor a criminal, but a warrior of the highest rank, an aryan warrior!![51]

A short-term goal of Identity adherents is "to see the creation of a national state for the White man, an Aryan Republic within the borders of the present occupied country [America]."[52] The chosen place of this mini-republic is the Pacific Northwest, where many white supremacist organizations (e.g., the Aryan Nations) are already situated. It is from this locale that racists plan to fight the last great battle on "the Day of the Lord." Richard Butler promises, "As His divine race, we have been commissioned to fulfill His divine purpose and plans—the restitution of all things."[53]

The hopes and dreams of all Identity believers were articulated as far back as 1980 in a small article entitled "Why Oppose the Jews." The summary statement leaves no doubt as to what white supremacists want: "Think of an America in the possession of the world's premier race—the White, Aryan peoples."[54]

ACCORDING TO THE BIBLE

Although most Identity believers claim to worship, serve, and follow Christ, their violent lifestyle and hate-filled rhetoric reveal that they are far removed from Christianity. The apostle John wrote: "[L]et us love one another, for love is from God; and everyone who loves is born of God and knows God" (1 John 4:7). John goes on to say that whoever "does not love does not know God" (v. 8) and that if someone says he loves God but hates his brother, "he is a liar" (v. 20).

The Identity notion of pre-Adamic races is also refuted by Scripture. Genesis 3:20 states that Eve became "the mother of *all* the living." Consequently, all human beings are ultimately related. We are all brothers and sisters according to the flesh. Paul the apostle commented on this when he spoke to the multitudes gathered at Mars Hill:

> *The God who made the world and all things in it, since He is Lord of heaven and earth, does not dwell in temples made with hands. . . . He made from one, every nation of mankind to live on all the face of the earth.*
>
> ACTS 17:24-26

Finally, Identity believers advocate prejudice, which God condemns. Romans 10:12, for instance, reads: "For there is no distinction between Jew or Greek; for the same Lord is Lord of all." Paul the apostle additionally taught, "There is neither Jew nor Greek, there is neither slave nor free, there is neither male nor female; for you are all one in Christ Jesus" (Gal. 3:28). It must also be observed that Identity followers believe that Jesus was not a Jew but was a Caucasian. Consequently, they worship "another Jesus" and fall under Paul's 2 Corinthians 11:4 condemnation of false teachings concerning the person of Jesus Christ.

WHAT'S THE ATTRACTION?

Many individuals within the Christian Identity Movement are there through no fault of their own. They were born into racist families and were subsequently raised to believe that all men are *not* created equal. By the time they reached adulthood, a racist worldview was firmly rooted in their hearts and minds. These persons live their life of hatred more out of ignorance than anything else. Unfortunately, this ignorance is reinforced by the limited circle of people with whom they associate—i.e., other racists.

The white supremacist movement into which Christian Identity fits also gives many of its followers a sense of purpose and belonging. There are Klan meetings to attend, neo-Nazi cross-burnings to watch, and white supremacist rallies in which to march. Each event draws the participants closer together in a common cause: to destroy the enemy Jews and all people of color. This is especially attractive to young white males from broken homes, who have a significant amount of displaced anger and a powerful need to be guided by older males. Christian Identity, the KKK, or some other white supremacist organization becomes the father/family they desperately miss.

Tragically, an increasing number of conservatives are being drawn into Identity because of its adherence to a few ethical/moral principles that do not relate to race. These principles, which have been borrowed from mainstream Christianity, include a pro-life stand, support for school prayer, and a rejection of ungodly conduct such as fornication, drunkenness, and swearing. Note the following comments from a fifteen-year-old KKK Youth Corps member. She sounds much like a conservative Christian until midway through her speech:

> [Madalyn Murray O'Hair] banned public prayers from schools. . . . I tell you, I'm a devout Christian, I go to church and I love the Lord and I'm proud of it. You know I'd love to lead prayer in school, but I can't because of her. The only way we can stop her and all these communist niggers out there is to join the Ku Klux Klan. . . . KKK stands for three main things. . . . Number One is God. . . . Two is for Race, which is for the *white*

race—and we all know, the *right* race! . . . Number three is Country, to help make America what it once was.[55]

John Perkins, an African-American Christian leader of the 1960s civil rights movement, was nearly beaten to death by Mississippi highway patrolmen. One might think that he, of all persons, would hate. But John sees a better way: "Evil is a strong force, and hate one of evil's best weapons. But love is, and always has been, stronger than hate. Good is stronger than evil. Light is more powerful than darkness. In the end, love will prevail."[56] In this day when Identity believers are preaching a gospel of hate, it is the responsibility of every true Christian to show the world that the good news of Jesus Christ is centered on love.

RECOMMENDED READING

Abanes, Richard. *American Militias: Rebellion, Racism, and Religion* (Downers Grove, IL: InterVarsity Press, 1996).

Barkun, Michael. *Religion and the Racist Right* (Chapel Hill, NC: University of North Carolina, 1994).

Edwards, Jefferson D. *Purging Racism from the Church* (Grand Rapids, MI: Zondervan, 1996).

Ezekiel, Raphael S. *The Racist Mind* (New York: Viking, 1995).

Perkins, John and Thomas A. Tarrants, III. *He's My Brother* (Grand Rapids, MI: Chosen Books, 1994).

Ridgeway, James. *Blood in the Face* (New York: Thunder's Mouth Press, 1990).

Yancey, George A. *Beyond Black and White* (Grand Rapids, MI: Baker, 1996).

NATION OF ISLAM:
ALLAH'S BLACK SUPREMACISTS

Ain't no use you get mad with me, white people. You are the devil. . . . You are nothing but a devil in the plainest language. The arch-deceivers of the people of the planet earth. The number one hater, murderer, killer, liar, drunkard, home-monger, hog-eater. Yeah, you're number one.

LOUIS FARRAKHAN,
NATION OF ISLAM[1]

In 1969, at the age of sixteen, Alphonso Bernard began his six-year relationship with the Nation of Islam (NOI). He was drawn to the organization not only by its army-like discipline, but also by its call for black men to be leaders filled with dignity, strength of character, integrity, and pride. The message greatly appealed to Bernard, who had grown up in a fatherless home in Brooklyn. Bernard also remembers being attracted to the NOI by the powerful teachings of Elijah Muhammad, an early NOI leader:

[Muhammad] really attempted to address the economic plight of the black man in America, which the Christian church, for me, had failed to do. . . . He began to bring dignity to the black man, and black men began to rehabilitate and reform.

Eventually, however, Bernard grew tired of the incessant hate-filled rhetoric for which NOI members (also known as Black Muslims) have become infamous. For example, during a 1972 interview Muhammad labeled all white people as "devils."[2] In his book *The Supreme Wisdom* Muhammad wrote: "Christianity is a religion organized and backed by the devils for the purpose of making slaves of black mankind."[3]

Bernard simply could not accept such blanket accusations. As a result, he began a spiritual quest that took him through numerous religions, including Hinduism and Buddhism. He finally landed in a Christian church service on January 11, 1975. Speaking that night was Nicky Cruz, the well-known gang member turned Christian minister whose miraculous story is told in *The Cross and the Switchblade*. It was during Nicky's sermon that Bernard suddenly began seeing God "from God's eyes."

In the weeks and months that followed, Bernard faithfully went to services at a nearby Church of God in Christ (COGIC), the nation's largest black Pentecostal denomination. He also bought and read as many different Bible versions and commentaries as he could find. He not only accepted Christ as his Savior but ended up joining the church and becoming a licensed/ordained COGIC minister: "I saw the power of God expressed in their worship. The people were exuberant, quoting Scriptures, and I was so impressed."

Alphonso Bernard has since established his own New York City church with a membership of more than 5,000 people. From his pulpit he preaches discipline, self-reliance, financial independence, and the need for strong male leadership—the same points the NOI stresses to gain converts from the black community. There is, however, a vast difference between his teachings and those of the NOI: Bernard's counsel comes from Scripture and is built upon the love and power of Jesus Christ.

How does Bernard feel about the NOI today? "I know exactly where they are going if they continue this way," he says. "There is only one end to hatred. Hatred has a self-consumptive destiny; once it consumes the enemy, it turns on itself." It is Bernard's prayer that before tragedy strikes, countless NOI members will find lasting peace, joy, and comfort in the Lord.[4]

HOW IT ALL BEGAN

The origins of the Nation of Islam are somewhat mysterious due to the shadowy background and life of its founder, Wallace D. Fard (1891–?). Several contradictory accounts detail events that may or may not accurately retell his life.[5] One story paints him as the son of wealthy Middle Eastern parents who were from the same tribe to which the Islamic prophet Muhammad had belonged. Another saga asserts that he was a

Palestinian Arab who traveled to America after being involved with "racial agitations" in India, South Africa, and London. A third variation tells of how he came to the United States from Jamaica as the son of a Syrian Muslim.[6]

Although each of these accounts provide a different genealogical history, all agree that W. D. Fard, ironically, was white. He first showed up in Detroit as a door-to-door salesman on July 4, 1930 with a self-professed mission to give blacks knowledge of their lost culture, which he claimed could be traced to the Saudi Arabian city of Mecca, and before that to the very foundations of the world. He also claimed to have information about the true and natural religion of all blacks: Islam. The only hope for black people, he taught, was their return to this ancient belief system:

> African Americans were of the lost, but finally found Nation of Islam, the tribe of Shabazz that had been stolen by the "Caucasian cave man" or the "blond blue-eyed devil" and brought as slaves to "the wilderness of North America." He [Fard] had been assigned the task of reintroducing them to their original way of life. They must now return to the fold of Islam and relearn Arabic, their mother tongue. . . . Upon completing this process of reculturalization, God would redeem them by returning them to Mecca. . . . There, they would experience no more suffering but would reunite with their kind and reassume their life as royalty.[7]

Not much more would be known about Fard if it were not for the many law enforcement records that reveal his true identity: Willie D. Ford or Wallace D. Ford. To the FBI, he was better known as #56062, an ex-con who spent three years in San Quentin Prison (1926–1929) for selling narcotics. To the Michigan State Police, Ford/Fard was #98076. The California Bureau of Identification and Investigation called him #1797294. To Los Angeles Police, he was #16448F.[8]

Fard's first brush with the law occurred in 1918, the year he moved to Los Angeles and opened a cafe called Walley's Restaurant. On November 17 he allegedly pulled a gun on R. W. Gilabrand, a customer who had refused to pay a $2 deposit on some steaks before they were put on the grill. When Gilabrand fled, Fard followed him out into the street and proceeded to beat his head into the cement sidewalk.[9] Eight years later Fard started having numerous run-ins with police:

> In January 1926, Fard was arrested for selling a pint of bootlegged liquor. . . . While waiting to appear in court, he was again arrested, this time for selling narcotics. In June of that year, he was sent to San Quentin. . . . He was also fined $401 for selling illegal whiskey. When Fard left prison in 1929, he . . . headed for Chicago and eventually Detroit, where he sold silks door to door and polished his patter that he was a Negro, a biblical authority, and a mathematician.[10]

In Detroit, Fard spun fantastic yarns about Mecca and the glories of the Black Nation, which in America had come under the tyrannical rule of the white man. He often punctuated his stories by displaying fine silks that invariably wound up being sold to listeners who wanted to dress like their black brothers and sisters in Mecca:

> He came first to our houses selling raincoats, and then afterwards, silks. In this way he could get into the people's houses, for every woman was eager to see the nice things the peddlers had for sale. He told us that the silks he carried were the same kind that our people used in their home country, and that he was from there. So we asked him to tell us about our own country.[11]

Fard, eventually known to NOI adherents as Farad Muhammad, also peddled a health diet that he said was the way blacks ate in the Middle East. Denke Majied, an early follower, remembers how Fard reacted whenever he was invited to dinner:

> [H]e would eat whatever we had on the table, but after the meal he began to talk, "Now don't eat this food. It is poison for you. The people in your own country do not eat it. Since they eat the right kind of food they have the best health all the time. If you would live just like the people in your home country, you would never be sick any more." So, we all wanted him to tell us more about ourselves and about our home country and about how we could be free from rheumatism, aches, and pains.[12]

Without hesitation, Detroit blacks accepted Fard's peculiar (and completely erroneous) brand of Islam, which he built from a bizarre smorgasbord of anti-white rhetoric, science fiction, Afro-centric mythology, and anti-Christian propaganda.

Fard's Fantasies

Fard maintained that all of history, as it is generally taught, is wrong. It is nothing but fiction invented by whites in an effort to keep blacks in spiritual/psychological bondage. Earth's true history centers around blacks and is as follows:

> Fard's "Original Man," a black man of Eden, had known only peace and righteousness until Yacub, "the Mighty Scientist of that time," created the devil. Born twenty miles outside of Mecca in the year 8400 B.C., Yacub . . . was a rebel who yearned to overthrow the established order. He began preaching at the age of sixteen. As his teachings spread and caught on, he created confusion and havoc and was thrown in jail. The king finally promised to release Yacub if he and his followers went into exile. Yacub agreed, and led 59,999 of his disciples to the island of Pelan in the Aegean Sea, to the west of Turkey. There, after six hundred years of trying to "graft" a new race from the "germs" of blacks, Yacub created a manlike creature— whites—that was really the "devil" in disguise. Yacub was determined that his synthetic progeny would outnumber blacks. So, in a crude, cruel adventure in birth control, he ruled that ministers could officiate only at weddings of whites and that nurses had to kill all "black babies at birth by sticking a pin into the . . . baby's head or feed . . . [them] to some wild beast."[13]

Yacub's mischief allegedly produced today's world wherein the minority black population is oppressed by the majority devil race of whites. How will blacks ever obtain deliverance? Fard prophesied that one day cataclysmic global destruction will cleanse the planet of all white devils.[14] This in turn will create a heaven on earth:

> Paradisiacal joy would flourish with the ex-masters gone forever and with blacks finally ruling the world into which they had been born to be kings, relying on their "heart[s] of gold, love and mercy," qualities that whites— nasty "two-headed rattlesnakes"—[are] forever incapable of knowing.[15]

Fard went even further, instructing blacks to "prepare for the battle of

Armageddon, which he interpreted to mean the final confrontation between blacks and whites."[16] His goal was to spiritually and psychologically cleanse the black population of America in preparation for that day when they would finally overthrow whites. In his 1996 book *In the Name of Elijah Muhammad*, Mattias Gardell, associate professor in the Department of Theology at Uppsala University, Sweden, gives perhaps the most concise and complete synopsis of Fard's history of the world from beginning to end:

> The Nation of Islam teaches that God is a black man and not an invisible spirit. The African American is not the inferior, so-called Negro but the original man, god of the universe. The primeval black civilization was a divine culture from which originated all science, wisdom, and institutions for human progress. . . . The white man differs from the original species in that he is not a creation of God. His is a man-made race, grafted by the dissatisfied black scientist Mr. Yacub approximately 6,000 years ago. Bent on producing a race evil and powerful enough to transform the original harmony into its opposite, Mr. Yacub set out systematically to drain a number of the original people of divine essence. In intervals, the brown, red, and yellow races appeared before his goal was reached: to create a race absolutely bereft of divinity. This was a race whose members were evil by nature, incapable of acting or thinking decently, or submitting to the law of Islam: the blond, blue-eyed white devils. In his omniscience, God gave the Devil 6,000 years to rule the earth. White world supremacy is equated with the evil era of the Devil and explains the experiences of the darker people in late world history: colonialism, slavery, racist oppression, and poverty. The [Black Muslim] gospel is that the era of the Devil now has expired [as of 1914]. . . . When the mentally "dead" blacks have united in Knowledge of Self and God, white supremacy will fall. God will himself exterminate the devils from the face of the earth in a global apocalyptic fire. Thereafter—in the hereafter—the world will be transformed into the black paradise it is predestined to become, where freedom, justice, and equality (that is, Islam) will be the conditions for eternal times to come.[17]

NOI followers still promote these views, which is not surprising since they also believe that Fard is the most powerful god within their pantheon of cosmic deities. Fard—the *current* "Supreme Ruler of the Universe"—is even greater than the original "self-created" Supreme Being (the "First

One") who "brought the Universe into existence seventy-six trillion years ago."[18] On one occasion a Fard devotee said to his master: "I know who you are. You are God." Fard replied: "Yes, I am the One."[19]

Within a few years of his appearance, Fard had attracted about 8,000 followers. He might have continued gaining converts if not for a horrible murder committed in the name of his teachings. The crime stemmed from Fard's call for NOI members to be as violent toward whites as whites had been toward them. One of Fard's "lessons" included an admonition to "bring in [murder] four (4) devils, and by having and presenting four (4) at one time, his reward was a button to wear on the lapel of his coat; also free transportation to the Holy City of Mecca to see their brother Muhammad."[20]

In November 1932 one of Fard's followers—Robert Karriem—killed John Smith by stabbing him in the heart. Police discovered that Karriem had also planned to murder two women welfare workers because they were "no good Christian[s]."[21] When Fard was taken into custody, he disavowed the murder, admitting to authorities that all of his teachings were "strictly a racket" and that he was simply "getting all the money out of it that he could."[22] In May 1933 police expelled him from Detroit.

Fard later surfaced in Chicago as a traveling salesman for a mail-order tailor. He slowly worked his way out west, "arriving in Los Angeles in 1934 'driving a new car and garbed in flowing white robes.'"[23] No one really knows what happened to Fard after that. The last person to hear from him was his most devoted disciple, Elijah Muhammad. He received a postcard from Fard that had been mailed from somewhere in Mexico.[24] Muhammad, however, remained faithful. In fact, he took over the NOI, positioning himself as "The Messenger" of Allah/Fard.

Elijah Muhammad

After Fard's disappearance, NOI leadership fell to Elijah Muhammad (1897–1975)—a.k.a. Elijah Poole—a Fard devotee from Georgia who had moved to Detroit with his wife and family in 1923. Muhammad continued to propagate his mentor's claims, stating that the entire world would one day recognize Fard as God.[25] In *Message to the Black Man in America* he stated: "We believe that Allah (God) appeared in the Person of Master W. Fard Muhammad, July, 1930—the long awaited 'Messiah' of the Christians and the 'Mahdi' [savior] of the Muslims."[26]

Although Muhammad uncompromisingly taught all he had learned from Fard, he added his own twists to the beliefs. For example, he parroted the teaching that one day all whites would be destroyed but went on to preach that the method of this destruction would be a huge spaceship, which he claimed was described in Ezekiel 10:6–10:

> Ezekiel's wheel would "sparkle" and rain fiery coals upon evil; Muhammad's wheel—the "Mother of Planes"—would measure "one-half mile by a half mile" and be "a small human planet made for the purpose of destroying the present world of the enemies of Allah." This Mother Plane could stay in space for up to a year and carry fifteen hundred bombers equipped with "steel drills . . . [that could] take bombs into the earth at a depth of one mile. . . . The bombers were so "swift that they can make their flight and return to the Wheel . . . almost like a flash of lightning."[27]

Throughout his term as the NOI's leader, Muhammad continually elevated himself in the eyes of his followers until he claimed to be "not only the incarnation of *all* the prophets, but of an entire cast of other Old Testament characters" such as King David, Noah, and Lot.[28] Moreover, he claimed that he had to do exactly what they had done, saying: "When you read about how David took another man's wife, I'm that David. You read about Noah, who got drunk—that's me. You read about Lot, who went and laid up with his own daughters. I had to fulfill all those things."[29]

Muhammad demonstrated how seriously he believed these words by impregnating one private secretary after another until six of them had produced thirteen children.[30] When news concerning these infidelities broke in the early 1960s, it not only caused strife between Muhammad and his wife, Clara, but damaged the reputation of the NOI leader in the eyes of many of his followers. He had preached constantly against black men treating their wives poorly and on the importance of faithfulness in marriage, stating: "Even animals and beasts, the fowls of the air, have more love and respect for their females than have the so-called Negroes of America."[31]

The revelation of Muhammad's indiscretions began a bitter war of words between two of the NOI's most influential spokespersons: Malcolm X and Louis X (a.k.a. Louis Farrakhan). In the end, Louis would rise to succeed Muhammad, and Malcolm would fall dead in a barrage of gunfire.

Malcolm & Louis: Friends to Enemies

Malcolm Little (1925–1965), who would rise to prominence as Malcolm X, remains perhaps the most celebrated of all NOI leaders. Although murdered in 1965, he continues to be idolized by countless people— men, women, teens, and children—who wear baseball caps, sweatshirts, and T-shirts emblazoned with a large white X.[32] To Malcolm, this letter signified his disdain for White America. It symbolized the "unknown" and served as a substitute for what Malcolm referred to as his slave name.[33]

Malcolm was in his early twenties when he joined the NOI in 1949. Before that he was little more than "a hustler, a scam artist, a player of games" on the mean streets of Boston.[34] Eventually he ended up serving six and a half years of a ten-year prison sentence for robbery.[35] It was after his release from jail in 1952 that Malcolm attended his first NOI meeting in Detroit. In September of that year he went to Chicago to hear Muhammad speak and knew for certain that the NOI was his new home.

Muhammad sent Malcolm back to Detroit with orders to begin recruiting new members. Eventually he was sent to Boston, where he held nightly meetings and began raising up an army of NOI followers that ranged in age from their mid-teens to early twenties.[36] From Boston, Malcolm went to Harlem, where he greatly multiplied the membership of NOI's Temple No. 7. It was from this site that Malcolm also began generating national attention for the NOI. All the while he worked hand in hand with Louis X (1934–), yet another charismatic leader of the Nation.

Unlike Malcolm, Louis X/Farrakhan—born as Louis Eugene Walcott (often called "Gene")—studied hard and excelled in music. As a child, he even sang in the church choir and played the violin in Sunday concerts. Elma Lewis, whose mother was Farrakhan's godmother, remembers how the women at the Episcopalian church loved Gene: "He behaved. He was obedient. He was mannerly. He was faithful and kind. He was everything you would want a child to be."[37] But unknown to his family and friends, young Gene Walcott often cried himself to sleep at night as he eavesdropped on his mother and her friends talking about the plight of blacks. During a 1995 speech, Farrakhan explained that what disturbed him the most was the inconsistency between what Christians said and what Christians did:

I would wonder why, if God had sent a deliverer to an oppressed people in the past, why that same God wouldn't send *us* a deliverer? I never
heard my pastor speak on the question of the liberation of my people. I
couldn't understand why we would have to be buried in a separate
cemetery if we were all going to the same heaven. I couldn't understand
why it was an honor to go downtown to sing with a white choir in a
white church. As a youngster, I loved Jesus and I loved scripture, but I
just wanted answers.[38]

Throughout his childhood and teens, Gene drifted further away from
his Christian roots in hopes of finding someone who would deliver the
black community from its suffering. A complete denial of Christianity
occurred when he traveled to the South:

I went to college in the South and felt the victimization of black people
and knew that something was wrong with Christianity, the way that it
was practiced, because I couldn't go to a white church, except to sit in the
balcony. . . . [T]hat was not the teachings of Jesus.[39]

Meanwhile, he also continued to sharpen his many talents—most
notably, his musical abilities. He became an accomplished calypso singer
known as "The Charmer" who performed in a variety of clubs and theaters
throughout the country. It was during an eight-week tour with a show
called "Calypso Follies" that the young Louis Walcott was introduced to
the NOI. The year was 1955. The place was Chicago. The contact was an
old friend named Rodney Smith, whom Gene just happened to meet on the
street. Smith, a recent convert to the NOI, invited Walcott to attend the
group's upcoming annual convention, where Elijah Muhammad would be
preaching.

Gene went to the meeting and joined the NOI immediately. He did not
feel completely at ease with his decision, however, until a few months later,
when he heard Malcolm X speak.[40] Walcott subsequently adopted the
name Louis X and, together with Malcolm, did much to spread the NOI's
gospel. They worked side by side and quickly rose to prominent positions
in the organization. Elijah appointed Malcolm as his national representative, while Louis was put in charge of Boston's NOI Temple No. 11, which
he gradually turned into one of the most prosperous NOI sites. Both were
fiercely loyal to the NOI until Malcolm found out about Muhammad's

promiscuous lifestyle. In *Prophet of Rage* journalist Arthur Magida explains how the situation affected Malcolm:

> Malcolm began backpedaling from speaking about morality, replacing it with politics, current events, and social doctrine and trying to engineer an exit for himself from the Nation, or at least from Elijah Muhammad. He could not represent Elijah after losing faith that the Nation stood for moral reformation.[41]

Malcolm continued in rebellion by blatantly disregarding orders from Muhammad regarding the cessation of all public statements by NOI members. An even more significant act of defiance, which placed Malcolm firmly in the traitors' camp, was his full disclosure to the press of Muhammad's many liaisons and their resulting out-of-wedlock children.[42] Louis X/Farrakhan later explained why he himself had no problem accepting Muhammad's romantic escapades with numerous secretaries:

> Elijah Muhammad didn't have secretaries—he had wives. . . . If Elijah Muhammad had wives, what's the problem? . . . [S]ome of them in Africa don't just have one or two or three or four. They have many. Some of the Islamic kings have many wives and concubines. . . . If Elijah Muhammad believed himself to be the messenger of Allah and acted on that belief, who can judge him? Certainly not you. Certainly not Malcolm.[43]

Malcolm, however, felt differently and proceeded to say so publicly. Finally, in January 1964, he was removed by Muhammad as the Harlem Temple's minister and as the NOI's national representative. Malcolm resigned from the NOI in March after hearing of "several plots within the Nation to kill him."[44] He subsequently formed his own organization—Muslim Mosque, Inc.—which directly challenged the NOI's long-held position as America's spiritual/social haven for blacks.

Malcolm also preached that ultimate peace between blacks and whites could only be achieved by working with, and recognizing the positive efforts of, many organizations that included other religions and other races. His enlightenment seemed to spring from two extensive trips in 1964 that took him to Africa and Mecca, where he learned that the "Islam" practice by the NOI had little to do with orthodox Islam.

After embracing "the brotherhood of man" that he had experienced by seeing the many hues of skin color in the Muslim pilgrims from around the world, he condemned Elijah Muhammad as a "faker" who had hawked his "distorted religious concoction" and "racist philosophy" as authentic Islam, intending "only to fool and misuse gullible people." . . . Malcolm defended "every man's right to believe whatever his intelligence leads him to believe is intellectually sound" and pledged to "never rest until I have undone the harm I did to so many well-meaning Negroes who, through my own evangelistic zeal, now believe in [Elijah Muhammad] even more fanatically and blindly than I did."[45]

Malcolm's change of heart, especially toward Elijah Muhammad, had devastating effects on the NOI, which lost half of its membership (anywhere from 50,000 to 500,000). Louis X's Boston congregation alone lost more than 60 percent of its members, leaving it with a congregation of fewer than 100. Louis responded by writing a scathing three-part series for the NOI periodical *Muhammad Speaks*:

Louis attacked Malcolm's "cupidity," "lying," "jealousy," "treachery," and "defection." Malcolm was to Elijah what Judas was to Jesus or what Moseilma, a false prophet in Islamic lore, was to Muhammad. A cheat and a scoundrel, Malcolm "had benefited and profited most from [Elijah's] generosity" and had "played the hypocrite on both sides," against the white man of America and against Muhammad, too. Consorting with heathens, Malcolm had "made the foolish and ignorant mistake . . . [of saying] his best friends were among such non-believing people as Hindus . . . Jews, Christians, Catholics, and even 'Uncle Toms.' He really made a fool of himself. . . . No Muslim is a Muslim who accepts such people as his brothers."[46]

Louis X/Farrakhan then made a statement that has prompted endless speculation about his possible involvement in the assassination of Malcolm X: "Only those who wish to be led to hell, or to their doom, will follow Malcolm. The die is set, and Malcolm shall not escape. . . . Such a man as Malcolm is worthy of death, and would have met death if it had not been for Muhammad's confidence in Allah for victory over his enemies."[47]

Faithful NOI members quickly reacted to Louis's words. On February 14, 1965, Malcolm and his family narrowly escaped death when Molotov cocktails were thrown through the family's living room window. The next day, at a meeting of his newly formed Organization of Afro-American Unity (OAAU), Malcolm lashed out: "I've reached the end of my rope. . . . My house was bombed by the [Black] *Muslims* . . . [a] criminal organization [led by] a senile old man interested in nothing but money and sex."[48]

One week later, on February 21, Malcolm stood at the podium of another OAAU meeting being held at the Audobon Ballroom in Harlem. Seconds after beginning his speech, a scuffle broke out in the audience. As he asked for calm to prevail, three NOI members rushed the stage with guns blazing. The first shotgun blast hit Malcolm directly in the chest. Two of the assassins then stood over Malcolm and proceeded to empty their handguns—a Luger and a .45 caliber revolver—into his dying body.[49]

The NOI power struggles, splinterings, and defections that ensued were marked by heated rhetoric and, in the early 1970s, horrific violence marked by brutal murders and/or suicides. This decade of turbulence finally climaxed in 1975 when Elijah Muhammad died of heart congestion, and leadership of the NOI was passed to Wallace Muhammad, Elijah's son. Wallace eventually repudiated many of his father's teachings including color-consciousness, racism, and the deification of Fard.

By 1984 Wallace's group had lost much of its influence in the black community and was subsequently disbanded. Years earlier, however, a splinter group retaining the name "Nation of Islam" had broken away from Wallace in order to stay true to the teachings of both Fard and Elijah. This break-away sect thrived and to this day has continued to grow in power under the leadership of none other than Louis Farrakhan.

Farrakhan's NOI

Farrakhan did not gain prominence outside the black community until 1984 when he endorsed and publicly appeared with presidential hopeful Jesse Jackson. The move enabled Farrakhan to finally garner widespread attention for himself and the NOI faction that he had been leading since 1978/79. He and his 70,000–100,000 member NOI[50] have since become a powerful force within the black community, rivaling the dynamism of Martin Luther King's civil rights movement.

The October 16, 1995, NOI-sponsored Million Man March, which drew anywhere from 600,000 to 1,000,000 African-American men to Washington

D.C., showed that the NOI's influence is indeed great. Farrakhan's beliefs, however, differ greatly from those espoused during the 1960s civil rights movement. Dr. King preached a prejudice-free ideology marked by tolerance, inclusiveness, peace, and Christian love. Farrakhan, on the other hand, spreads a philosophy built on little more than religious intolerance, racist conspiracy theories, and anti-Semitism.

Sometimes Farrakhan's statements even take on a decidedly anti-American tone. During a February trip to Iran, for instance, Farrakhan "pledged to help Islamic mullah overthrow the United States, which he called the 'Great Satan.'"[51] In yet another speech, Farrakhan praised Libyan leader Muammar Gaddafi as a "Freedom Fighter" and asserted that "Terrorism is like beauty; it is in the eye of the beholder."[52] He has further declared that "God will destroy America by the hands of Muslims."[53]

Farrakhan is perhaps best known for his conspiracy theories, all of which portray blacks as victims. For example, he maintains that Elijah Muhammad did not die but only appeared to die in order to escape a U.S. government conspiracy to kill him. The most interesting aspect of this plot is how Farrakhan learned of it. It came to him via a "black man who heard about it from a white prostitute who had heard about it from a white doctor who had hired her for an 'orgy' in Phoenix, Arizona."[54] But Allah was too smart for the Feds and rescued his servant Elijah Muhammad by having black angels bodily transport him to heaven.[55] "We believe that Elijah Muhammad is not dead physically," explains Farrakhan. "[H]e is alive. . . . [D]uring that time in the hospital he went through what they call death. . . . [H]e was made to appear as though dead. [But] I believe that he escaped."[56] Elijah Muhammad is "a man who today sits on the right hand side of God the Almighty, soon to return and deal with the living and the dead."[57]

The most infamous conspiracy theories propagated by Farrakhan and his NOI involve people of Jewish descent. Like adherents to Christian Identity (see Chapter 5), NOI followers portray Jews as the world's worst troublemakers. The NOI has charged the Jews collectively as a race with injecting black babies with the AIDS virus, bringing the U.S. into World War I, financing "all sides" of World War II, engineering the federal deficit, and causing the hole in the ozone layer.[58] In 1992 Farrakhan wrote: "We know that the Jews are the most organized, rich, and powerful people, not only in America but in the world. They're plotting against us even as we speak."[59] Farrakhan's views are clearly outlined in the NOI's book *The*

Secret Relationship Between Blacks and Jews, which alleges that Jews master-minded America's slave trade.

Several NOI spokespersons have shown disdain for Jews. Two days before the Million Man March, NOI's national youth minister stated: "All you Jews can go straight to [profanity deleted].... I say to Jewish America, 'Get ready. Knuckle down. Put your boots on, because we're ready and the war is going down.'"[60] That same evening NOI's national spokesman Khallid Abdul Muhammad called the Jew a "parasite who comes into our community and takes out trailer and tractor loads of money on a daily basis."[61] It was also Khallid who in November 1993 unleashed some of the most potent anti-Semitic rhetoric to be heard publicly in recent years:

> [Jews exploit blacks] on a daily and consistent basis. They sell us pork and they don't even eat it themselves.... A wall of liquor keeping our people drunk and out of their mind, and filled with the swill of the swine, affecting their minds.... [Jews are] stealing rubies and gold and silver all over the earth. That's why we can't even wear a ring or a bracelet or a necklace without calling it "Jew-elry." We say it real quick and call it "jewelry," but it's not jewelry. It's "Jew-elry," 'cause you're the rogue who's stealing.... The Jews have told us, "Ve have suffered like you. Ve, ve, ve, ve marched with Dr. Martin Luther King, Jr. Ve, ve, ve were in Selma, Alabama. Ve, ve were in Montgomery, Alabama. Ve, ve were on the front line of the civil rights marches. Ve have always supported you." But ... what [the Jews] have actually done, brothers and sisters, is used us as cannon fodder.... Everybody always talk[s] about Hitler extermi-nating six million Jews ... But don't anybody ever ask what did they do to Hitler? ... They went in there, in Germany, the way they do every-where they go, and they supplanted, they usurped, they turned around, and a German, in his own country, would almost have to go to a Jew to get money. They undermined the very fabric of the society.... You [Jews] are a European strain of people who crawled around on all fours ... eatin' juniper roots and eatin' each other.[62]

Khallid's three-hour tirade also attacked whites, going so far as to call for nothing less than their deaths:

> If we want to be merciful at all, when we gain enough power from God Almighty to take our freedom and independence from him [the white man], we give him twenty-four hours to get out of town by sundown....

If he won't . . . we kill everything white that ain't right in South Africa. We kill the women, we kill the children. We kill the babies. We kill the blind, we kill the crippled, we kill 'em all. We kill the faggot, we kill the lesbian, we'll kill them all. . . . [W]hy kill the babies? . . . Because they gonna grow up one day to oppress our babies. . . . Why kill the women? . . . [B]ecause . . . [they are] the army's manufacturing center. . . . Kill the elders, too . . . if they're in a wheelchair, push 'em off a cliff in Capetown . . . or Johannesburg . . . or Port Sheppiston or Darbin [sic]. How the [profanity deleted] you think they got old? They got old oppressing black people. . . . And when you get through killing 'em all, go to the [profanity deleted] graveyard and dig up the grave and kill 'em all, [profanity deleted], again. 'Cause they didn't die hard enough. And if you've killed 'em all and you don't have the strength to dig 'em up, then take your gun and shoot in the [profanity deleted] grave. Kill 'em again. Kill 'em again, 'cause they didn't die hard enough.[63]

Like Muhammad, Farrakhan and his NOI also declare that doomsday for whites is fast approaching. According to Farrakhan, America, and ultimately the whole earth, will be obliterated by a big UFO that was built in Japan aeons ago by Allah's scientists, who originally used it to make the planet's mountains:

[God's] intention is the total destruction of America. . . . God will do it Himself. . . . [T]he last fight . . . will be in East Germany, and there she (America) will be destroyed. . . . When the power of the Soviet Union was broken, many of you that were in the armed forces in Europe were called back to America. You don't have jobs but soon they are going to ask you to go back to Europe. The Messenger [Elijah Muhammad] said that you would go away in the thousands and you will return in the tens. And when you return there will be no such thing as an American government. . . . He said that all of America's possessions will be taken one by one, and all of her fortifications will be destroyed. . . . He said that England is going to trick America into war. He said white America will be destroyed mercilessly, that not even her own (white) brother or sister will show mercy on her. . . . The final thing is the destruction. The Honorable Elijah Muhammad told us of a giant Motherplane that is made like the universe, spheres within spheres. White people call them unidentified flying objects (UFOs). Ezekial [sic], in the Old Testament, saw a wheel that looked like a cloud by day but a pillar of fire by night. . . . [T]hat wheel was built on the island of Nippon, which is now called Japan, by some of the original scientists. It took 15 billion dollars in gold at that time to build it. It is made of the toughest steel. America does not yet know the composition of the steel used to make an instrument like it. It is a circular plane, and the Bible says that it never makes turns. Because of its circular nature it can stop and travel in all directions at speeds of thousands of miles per hour. He said there are 1,500 small wheels in this mother wheel which is a half mile by a half mile. This Mother Wheel is like a small human built planet. Each one of these small planes carry three bombs. . . . [T]hese planes were used to set up mountains on the earth. . . . That's how the earth is balanced, with mountain ranges. The Honorable Elijah Muhammad said that we have a type of bomb that, when it strikes the earth a drill on it is timed to go into the earth and explode at the height that you wish the mountain to be. If you wish to take the mountain up a mile, you time the drill to go a mile in and then explode. The bombs these planes have are timed to go one mile down and bring up a mountain one mile high, but it will destroy everything within a 50 square mile radius. The white man writes in his above top secret memos on the UFOs. He sees them around his military installation like they are spying. The Honorable Elijah Muhammad said that Mother Plane is so powerful that with sound reverberating in the atmosphere, just with a sound, she can crumble buildings. And the final act of destruction will be that Allah will make a wall out of the atmosphere over and around North America. You will see it, but you won't be able to penetrate it. He said Allah (God) will cut a shortage in gravity and a fire will start from 13-layers up and burn down, burning the atmosphere. When it gets to the earth, it will burn everything. It will burn for 310 years and take 690 years to cool off.[64]

Farrakhan maintains that the Motherplane is "a dreadful looking thing" and that the truth of its existence is actually known to some white people who, in a conspiratorial effort to fool people into believing such a ship is unreal, are now making movies "to make these planes look like fiction."[65] The 1996 movie *Independence Day* is but one of these films that Farrakhan sees as a plot to blind the populace to the reality of their impending destruction by the Motherplane. The film's hidden meaning was explained in the July 1996 issue of the NOI's official newspaper, *The Final Call*:

The movie's acronym, ID4, "is a bio-genetic reference to a genetic inhibitor which ceases certain procedures in evolution and life, according to researchers at M. I. T.," the alma mater of the "Jewish genius" played by Jeff Goldblum. Its menacing "mother ship" is a ripoff of the NOI's very own "Mother Plane." . . . [According to Farrkahan] former President Ronald Reagan and former Soviet Union President Mikhail Gorbachev spent five hours in confidential talks during the 1985 Geneva Conference, discussing what military strategies to take in the event of alien attack against earth. But such military countermeasures are futile [says Farrakhan]: "All of the methods used by the government to harm the real 'Mother Plane' have failed, just as their efforts to crush the Nation of Islam have failed." . . . The film's "happy ending"—another Hollywood Jewish coverup—also falsifies the apocalyptic future in which the extraterrestrial will win as part of Allah's judgment against the white man.[66]

Farrakhan does not accept Muhammad's tales about a "Motherplane" on mere faith. He claims to have been beamed up to Allah's spaceship on September 17, 1985. The vision occurred while he was sitting atop a Mexican Pyramid:

When he got to the top of the mountain, a UFO appeared. Farrakhan immediately realized the importance of the moment. In the cosmology of the Nation, God supervises humanity from a great manmade planet circling Tellus. This planet . . . is known in the NOI as "the Mother Ship" or "the Mother Wheel." . . . In this heavenly abode is a magnificent city, prepared as a residence for the new civilization that is to replace the present world order after the battle of Armageddon. On the Mother Wheel too, are small spacecraft carriers, called "baby planes," piloted by helpers of God. Frequently, the smaller crafts visit earth on various expeditions ordered by God, such as when Elijah Muhammad was rescued from hired assassins in 1975. . . . [A] voice called Farrakhan to come closer. . . . He obeyed, and as he walked closer, a beam of light, resembling the sunlight piercing through a window, came out of the wheel. Farrakhan was told to relax and was brought up into the plane on this beam of light. He was placed next to the pilot. Farrakhan could feel his presence but could not see him. The spacecraft took off with Farrakhan, who knew that the pilot was sent by God and was to take him to the Mother Wheel. Approaching the manmade planet, the pilot turned the spaceship around and with great speed backed into a tunnel in the main wheel. . . . After docking, the door opened and Farrakhan was escorted by the pilot to a door and admitted into a room, which was totally empty except for a speaker in the ceiling. From that speaker Farrakhan heard the well-known voice of the Honorable Elijah Muhammad, which confirmed his being alive. Farrakhan was authorized to lead his God-fearing people through the latter days. . . . As the Messiah was speaking, a scroll full of divine cursive writing was rolled down inside Farrakhan's head. Farrakhan for a moment saw a reflection of this scroll, containing the full message from God to humanity, before it was gone, placed in the back of his brain. Then Elijah Muhammad said, "I will not allow you to see me now. You have one more thing to do, then you can come and be with me, and I will show myself to you face to face." The Messiah did not say exactly what this last thing Farrakhan had to do was, but left it to Farrakhan to find out. Farrakhan believes the relevant information has been put into him already and will appear when the time has come. Elijah Muhammad then started telling Farrakhan about a war that President Reagan was planning and ordered him to hold a press conference to expose Reagan's evil schemes and tell him and the rest of the world from where he got his information. . . . Elijah Muhammad then dismissed Farrakhan . . . [who] was escorted back to the little wheel by the same pilot, whom he still could not see but only could feel his presence. The spacecraft shot out of the tunnel and then stopped abruptly. The pilot then took the plane up to a terrific height and maneuvered the vehicle to allow Farrakhan to look down on the wheel. Farrakhan saw a city, a magnificent city, the New Jerusalem, in the sky. Instead of going back to Mexico, the craft carried Farrakhan with tremendous speed to Washington, D.C., and dropped him off outside the city. He walked into the capital and delivered his announcement, the final warning to the United States government.[67]

Farrakhan's vision was confirmed to him after leaving Arizona for a speaking engagement in New York. He claimed that he was followed by "a fleet of divine space carriers." According to Farrakhan, "the news reported that fifteen squadrons of four little wheels, going at the speed of 150 miles per hour, were seen moving from the Southwest to the Northeast." Farrakhan claims that everywhere he went the wheel followed to remind him of his mission and to assure him that he is backed by God: "The Messiah is alive. He is in the world. The power of God is present in America with me."[68] Farrakhan seems to be, as one writer has put it, "on the black path of deification."[69] At a 1989 dinner, in fact, the NOI leader admitted: "I am the man everybody is looking for. I am a Messiah. Elijah

Muhammad was raised by Master Farad Muhammad to become the Messiah and he raised me to become the little Messiah."[70]

ACCORDING TO THE BIBLE

As far back as Fard, the NOI has espoused unbiblical and socially offensive views, which Farrakhan and his followers continue to vehemently preach. Fard's divinity and Muhammad's messianic status are only two of the many doctrinal planks upon which the NOI's religious system is based. Its theological landscape is an eclectic mixture of Fard's home-grown version of Islam, pseudo-Christian views involving the end-times, old Jewish parables, rituals gleaned from the black church, and finally, pure science fiction.

GOD & GODS

NOI	Scripture
"[Fard] is God Himself. He is the One that we have been looking for the last 2,000 years to come. He is the One, and His Word bears witness to the fact that He is the One."[71]	"[T]here is one God, and one mediator between God and man, the man Christ Jesus" (1 Tim. 2:5).
"Allah teaches me that He is a man—not something that is other than man."[72] "If I [Elijah Muhammad] would say that God is not a man, I would be a liar before Him and stand condemned."[73]	"God is not a man" (Num. 23:19; cf. 1 Sam 15:29, Hos. 11:9).
"Some enemies of the True God, the Visible God, have deceived you and are making you think that there is no such thing as a visible god. I want to say to you, my friends, if you don't have one that is visible—see Allah the visible way!"[74]	"No one has ever seen God" (John 1:18). "He [Jesus] is the image of the invisible God" (Col. 1:15). "Now to the King eternal, immortal, invisible, the only God" (1 Tim. 1:17; cf. 1 Tim. 6:16).
"[A] council of twenty-four imams—gods or black scientists—was established [to help the Supreme God]. It is composed of twelve greater imams, the first God and the next eleven ones, and twelve lesser imams,	"Before Me there was no God formed, And there will be none after Me" (Isa. 43:10).

GOD & GODS

NOI	Scripture
referred to in Revelation as the 'four and twenty elders.' . . . Their number will always remain intact, but their seats will be filled by a succession of Gods, as no God lives forever. . . . For each cycle [of earth time], a Supreme God from the divine council is in charge, taking his turn in contributing to the evolutionary process that shaped the present world. After completion of a cycle [every 25,000 years], 'another God would be given a chance to show forth his Wisdom to the people.'"[75]	*"[Y]ou are My witnesses. Is there any God besides Me. . . . I know of none" (Isa. 44:8).*

JESUS

NOI	Scripture
"[Jesus] was only a prophet and not the equal of Moses and Muhammad."[76]	*"For in Him all the fullness of Deity dwells in bodily form" (Col. 2:9)*
	"Thomas answered and said to Him [Jesus], 'My Lord and my God!'" (John 20:28).
"[Jesus'] religion was Islam."[77]	*"Joseph and Mary took him [Jesus] to Jerusalem to present him to the Lord (as it is written in the [Jewish] law of the Lord . . .), and to offer a sacrifice in keeping with what is said in the [Jewish] Law of the Lord" (Luke 2:21–24).*
	"The Samaritan woman said to him [Jesus], 'You are a Jew and I am a Samaritan woman'" (John 4:9).
"Jesus can't save, only Christ can save. Jesus couldn't save as Jesus. He had to be exalted to the right hand of the Father . . . then that Jesus, the Christ, became the Savior and Lord of all."[78]	*"He himself bore our sins in his body on the tree, so that we might die to sins and live for righteousness; by his wounds you have been healed" (1 Peter 2:24).*
	"Salvation is found in no one else [but Jesus], for there is no other name under heaven given to men by which we must be saved" (Acts 4:10-12).

JESUS' RESURRECTION

NOI	Scripture
"[Christians worship] a dead Jesus and his dead disciples."[79]	"Jesus answered them, 'Destroy this temple and I will raise it again in three days'. . . . But the temple he had spoken of was his body. After he was raised from the dead, His disciples recalled what he had said. Then they believed the Scriptures and the words that Jesus had spoken" (John 2:19–22; cf. Acts 10:39–41).
"[Jesus'] body is still . . . in Palestine and will remain there."[80]	"[H]e was taken up before their very eyes, and a cloud hid him from their sight. . . . [S]uddenly two men dressed in white stood beside them . . . [saying] 'This Jesus, who has been taken up from you into heaven, will come in just the same way as you have watched Him go into heaven'" (Acts 1:9–11).

SALVATION / ATONEMENT

NOI	Scripture
"You have to repent for being the fool, the clown, the buffoon, the pimp, the punk, the hustler. You have to atone."[81]	"Christ was sacrificed once to take away the sins of many people; and he will appear a second time, not to bear sin, but to bring salvation to those who are waiting for him" (Heb. 9:28).
	"[W]e have been made holy through the sacrifice of the body of Jesus Christ once and for all. . . . [L]et us draw near to God with a sincere heart in full assurance of faith, having our hearts sprinkled to cleanse us from a guilty conscience" (Heb. 10:10, 22).
"[W]e must give up our slave names . . . give up all evil doings and practices and do only righteousness or we shall be destroyed from the face of the earth."[82]	"He himself bore our sins in his body on the tree, so that we might die to sins and live for righteousness; by his wounds you have been healed" (1 Peter 2:24).
"Jesus represents a body of knowledge to which he asks his disciples to discipline their lives. In our willingness to discipline every aspect of our lives to the word and example of the Jesus, to that degree we have salvation."[83]	"For it is by grace you have been saved, through faith—and this not of yourselves, it is the gift of God—not by works so that no one can boast" (Eph. 2:10; cf. John 3:16, Rom. 10:9).

BLACKS

NOI	*Scripture*
"Black Man, the Original Man is the God."[84] "[T]he Black Man by nature is divine."[85] "Man is God and God is man."[86]	*"Thus says the Lord. . . . [Y]ou are my witnesses. Is there any God besides Me? Or is there any other Rock? I know of none" (Isa. 44:6, 8).*
"The Original Man . . . is none other than the Black Man. He is the first and the last, and the Maker and owner of the universe."[87]	*"Thus says the Lord . . . and his Redeemer, the Lord of hosts; I am the first and I am the last, and there is no god besides Me" (Isa. 44:6).*
"[Blacks are] sacred vessels of the Temple of God."[88]	*"[T]o those sanctified in Christ Jesus. . . . Don't you know that you yourselves are God's temple and that God's Spirit lives in you?" (1 Cor. 1:1; 3:16).*
	"If anyone acknowledges that Jesus is the Son of God, God lives in him and he in God" (1 John 4:14–15).

ELIJAH MUHAMMAD

NOI	*Scripture*
"I know you think Elijah is dead. . . . I'm here to tell you that he is as alive as you sitting right down there in that seat. . . . He and God are together and his return is imminent. . . . [He] has been exalted to the right hand of God to control the forces of nature."[89] "[Elijah Muhammad is] a man who today sits on the right hand side of God the Almighty, soon to return and deal with the living and the dead."[90]	*"[S]et your hearts on things above, where Christ is seated at the right hand of God" (Col. 3:1; cf Heb. 12:2).*
	"[You are saved] by the resurrection of Jesus Christ, who has gone into heaven and is at God's right hand—with angels, authorities, and powers in submission to him" (1 Peter 3:21–22).
	"You know what has happened throughout Judea . . . how God anointed Jesus of Nazareth with the Holy Spirit and power. . . . We are witnesses of everything he did. . . . He ordered us to preach to the people, and solemnly to testify that this is the One who has been appointed by God as Judge of the living and the dead" (Acts 10:37–42).
"I warn you that when you turn me down and refuse this truth, you are turning down the Lord, the Savior, the Messiah and the	*"[I]f anyone says to you, 'Look, here is the Christ!' or, 'Look, there he is!' do not believe it. For false Christs and false prophets will*

ELIJAH MUHAMMAD *(cont'd.)*

NOI	Scripture
Deliverer that you seek. This Deliverer is the Honorable Elijah Muhammad."[91]	*appear and perform signs and miracles to deceive the elect" (Mark 13:22).*
"[Jesus] didn't save the world. It's still a misery out there. But he pointed towards the coming of a Saviour [i.e., Elijah Muhammad] who was to raise the dead [i.e., enlighten black people to the truth about themselves and God]."[92]	*"[Grace] has now been revealed through the appearing of our Savior, Christ Jesus" (2 Tim. 1:10).* *"He saved us through the washing of rebirth and renewal by the Holy Spirit, whom he poured out on us generously through Jesus Christ our Savior" (Titus 3:5–6; cf. 2 Peter 3:18; 2:20; 1 John 4:14–15).*

Black vs. White?

More disturbing than the NOI's bizarre conspiracy theories and fantastic tales about UFOs are the many vitriolic statements for which the group has become infamous. Historically, the organization has gone out of its way to issue blanket condemnations of all white people and Christianity, which has consistently been characterized as "the white man's religion." Consider the following words of Malcolm X:

> As "Negro Christians" we idolized our Christian Slavemaster, and lived for the day when his plurality of white gods would allow us to mingle and mix up with them. . . . We were supposed to be a part of the "Christian Church," yet we lived in a bitter world of dejection . . . being rejected by the white "Christian Church." In large numbers we became victims of drunkenness, drug addiction, reefer smoking . . . in a false and futile attempt to "escape" the reality and horror of the shameful condition that the Slavemaster's Christian religion had placed us in. . . . Fear ruled us, but not fear of God. We had fear of the Slavemaster. . . . We called ourselves "Negro Christians," yet we remained an ignorant, foolish people, despised and REJECTED by the white Christians. We were fools![93]

NOI members habitually brand all whites or all Christians as devils or anti-black. At the same time, the NOI makes supremacist statements that place all black people on a racial pedestal simply because they are black.

Such comments only serve to further divide America along racial lines. Consider the following remarks:

> [B]y nature they [white people] were created liars and murderers, they are the enemies of truth and righteousness, and the enemies of those who seek the truth.[94]

> The human beast—the serpent, the dragon, the devil, and Satan—all mean one and the same; the people or race known as the white or Caucasian race.[95]

> White people are born devils by nature. They don't become so by their deeds.[96]

> Thoughtful white people know they are inferior to black people. . . . When you want strong coffee, you ask for black coffee. If you want it light, you want it weak, integrate it with white milk. Just like these Negroes who weaken themselves and their race by this integrating and intermixing with whites.[97]

> Christians preach love but practice hate and tyranny, and use God to cover up their corrupt and dirty practices.[98]

Such divisive language has caused much of the opposition to the NOI to come from blacks, many of whom are well-respected and influential. In 1985 Congressman Charles Rangel of New York's 16th district (Harlem) stated that "the hatred spewed by Farrakhan is scurrilous and intolerable."[99] In 1995 General Colin Powell voiced similar sentiments in an especially pointed way. He not only refused to attend the "Million Man March" but went so far as to compare Farrakhan with police officer Mark Furhman, the infamous white racist of the O. J. Simpson trial.[99]

Obviously, the NOI does not represent the views of all black people. The NOI does not even represent Islam. Orthodox Muslims do not believe God is a man. Nor do they believe the NOI's version of how white people were created. Moreover, Islam teaches racial harmony, as opposed to racial separatism. According to Ibrahim Hooper of the Council on American-Islamic Relations, the NOI is definitely "outside mainstream Muslim beliefs because of Farrakhan's racist views."[100] It has "always been regarded by serious Muslim organizations as a fringe group of heretics."[101]

WHAT'S THE ATTRACTION?

A 1996 *Newsweek* poll found that although 41 percent of blacks view Farrakhan unfavorably, another 41 percent approve of him.[102] A 1996 survey by *Time*/CNN revealed that 59 percent of blacks believe Farrakhan speaks the truth and is a good role model for black youth; 50 percent of blacks feel he has been a positive force on the black community.[103] Why? It may be because since the days of Elijah Muhammad, the NOI has given blacks a "sense of dignity, a conviction that they are more than the equals of whites" and that they are destined to rule the earth.[104] This is especially important in the 1990s, an era wherein black males comprise only 7 percent of America's population but constitute 48 percent of the prison population.[105]

Much of the NOI's success can be attributed to its focus on meeting the emotional/psychological needs of black men, many of whom feel angry, frustrated, and lost in a society that continues to harbor anti-black prejudice. To many individuals in the black community, Farrakhan is "the standard by which courageous black manhood is measured."[106] He himself has said as much by maintaining that he represents the "last chance" black people have to attain freedom, justice, and equality.[107]

It cannot be denied that Farrakhan and his NOI bring some admirable instructions to black males. The pledge recited at the Million Man March, for instance, provided high ideals for those in attendance: "I . . . will strive to improve myself spiritually, morally, mentally, socially, politically, and economically."[108] For Ben White, one of the many black men who marched in Washington, the event gave him a fresh resolve: "[T]o watch my mouth, treat my brothers and sisters with respect, get my life together, and carry the message back to the community."[109]

But when all is said and done, the belief system taught by the NOI is nothing but white supremacy in reverse. Black Muslims—like the white racists they so despise—propagate racial division, racial superiority, and a patently false view of history. NOI members, in their zeal to fight the evil of bigotry, have themselves become racists. In 1965 cult expert Dr. Walter Martin gave a wise piece of advice concerning Christian interaction with Black Muslims, which still holds true today:

The Christian attitude in the midst of all this, must be one of patience, love and firm resolve. We must turn the other cheek to their abuses and strive to guarantee for them and for all Americans, regardless of race, their just rights under the laws of our land. In this way, we shall indeed demonstrate to them the love and teachings of Jesus Christ.[110]

RECOMMENDED READING

Brackman, Harold. *Ministry of Lies: The Truth Behind the Nation of Islam's "The Secret Relationship Between Blacks and Jews"* (New York: Four Walls, Eight Windows, 1994).

Cross, Haman and Donna E. Scott. *What's Up with Malcolm?* (Chicago: Moody Press, 1993).

Gardell, Mattias. *In the Name of Elijah Muhammad: Louis Farrakhan and the Nation of Islam* (Durham, NC: Duke University Press, 1996).

Glegg III, Claude Andrew. *An Original Man: The Life and Times of Elijah Muhammad* (New York: St. Martin's Press, 1997).

Lincoln, C. Eric. *The Black Muslims in America* (Grand Rapids, MI: William B. Eerdmans, 1961; 1994 edition).

Magida, Arthur J. *Prophet of Rage* (New York: Basic Books, 1996).

MOON'S
MOONIES

The whole world is in my hand, and I will conquer and subjugate the world. . . . The time will come, without my seeking it, that my words will almost serve as law. If I ask a certain thing, it will be done. If I don't want something, it will not be done.

**REV. SUN MYUNG MOON,
FOUNDER, UNIFICATION CHURCH[1]**

After completing high school in 1986, Ingo Michehl decided to leave his native Germany and travel to the United States for a three-week stay, during which time he would evaluate several universities. He would first visit a family in Auburn, California, with whom he had stayed on a previous trip to the U.S., then go on to San Francisco, and finally catch a flight to Florida. From there, he would return home.

Ingo's trip went as planned until he arrived in San Francisco, where he was approached by two Japanese university students, Hitomi Kanepa and her male companion, Yoshihisa Nozawa. They seemed to immediately recognize Ingo as a foreign visitor and invited him to their "international student club." Because Ingo had already begun thinking of himself as an international student, he gratefully accepted their invitation. He had no idea that their "club" was actually a local chapter of the Collegiate Association for the Research of Principles (CARP), a controversial evangelistic arm of Reverend Sun Myung Moon's Unification Church.

At the club Ingo was encouraged to join CARP in order to meet more international students with whom he could exchange exciting new ideas and philosophies via "workshops." The high energy of his new friends and their enthusiasm for the workshops quickly convinced Ingo that their seven-day instructional course presented an opportunity he could not pass up, even though it meant altering his travel plans. He still did not know that the group was part of Moon's religious organization, nor was he told that the workshops were designed to recruit full-time members for CARP. Ingo can still remember how the workshop he attended at a CARP camp retreat affected him:

> I was overwhelmed with the love I was shown by members. Everyone was serving each other, surprising each other with little "love bombs" (tokens of one's affections such as secret notes of affirmation, etc.). I was led to believe it was the ideal world family of true love.

At this time Ingo was emotionally and psychological drained on several levels, which made this experience with CARP especially positive. He was far from home, uncertain about his future, and very lonely. Furthermore, he had recently broken up with a long-time girlfriend back in Germany, which left his heart "shattered and vulnerable, starving for love." Consequently, Ingo did not return home but instead became a member of CARP and began serving the needs of the Unification Church.

Ingo's life suddenly turned into a torturous grind. He was called upon to work eighteen to twenty hours a day to "further the cause of establishing a totalitarian theocracy under the leadership of the self-declared messiah Sun Myung Moon." This would not have surprised Ingo had he known about the directive Moon presented in a 1973 speech: "If we have money we can make reality. You must not sleep much, rest much, eat much. You must work day and night to make this great task a reality—a success."[2]

Even after his three-week visa expired, Ingo stayed in the U.S. to work for CARP as an illegal alien. He was instructed to join the Mobile Fundraising Team (MFT), which traveled cross-country and sold various products (e.g., laser etchings) on American streets—without a permit. According to Ingo, there was nothing more important than working and raising money for Moon's cause:

> I was not the only illegal alien CARP entertained. . . . Most of the team members were foreigners (predominantly Japanese and European travelers who had been recruited during their vacation much like me). All 11 of us slept in a Ford van, traveling at night and fundraising during the day. We heard of a few other teams who had serious accidents, with even some people getting killed because "the driver had been invaded by

Satan." What that meant was that the driver had fallen asleep behind the wheel. I met several members with severe health problems due to such accidents. And the medical care for them—as later for me when I developed back problems due to carrying my 25 pound backpack day in and day out—was insufficient, if provided at all. . . . Other illegal activities we were led to engage in through our leaders were such things as sleeping with 5 or 10 people in a 1 person bedroom (without paying the extra amount), sneaking into state parks to sleep there, use the showers and leave before they would open so we would not have to pay. All this was justified because according to Rev. Moon's teaching, the end justifies the means—and we were working and living to help America and the World. Moon himself once stated upon being asked about "white lies" by a member: "If you tell a lie to make a person better, then that is not a sin. . . . Even God tells lies very often."[3] This may account for the practice of "heavenly deception," which we were taught [to use] in order to accomplish the group's goals. So when I later went to recruit new converts, I likewise hid the true identity of the group—"for the better of the newcomer" who would otherwise not join. The end justifies the means.

Ingo's family in Germany was grief-stricken. They tried desperately to contact their son and convince him to come home, but most of the attempts by Ingo's father to reach him were blocked by CARP leaders, who proceeded to tell Ingo that Satan was attempting to destroy his spiritual life through his parents. Ingo was also taught that if he ever left the Unification Church, he would instantly be at the mercy of the Devil.

We were taught that upon leaving the church, Satan would invade us completely, destroy our family, cause us to become insane, or die through some horrible accident. We would continuously hear testimonies about members who would not "unite" with their leaders [fully commit]. One story told to us was about a disobedient member's child who had been born without ears. Another disobedient member had developed cancer—Satan's punishment.

After three years as a "Moonie," Ingo was having serious doubts about his involvement with the church. Fear of losing his salvation, however, kept him working day and night. He finally graduated from Mobile Fundraising Team in 1989 and was sent to Chicago to serve as a street fundraiser and an evangelist at the University of Illinois, Chicago (UIC). By 1993

Ingo had become the area's top fund-raiser. At the same time, however, he had been having numerous confrontations with one of his leaders, Mr. Yoshizumi. The tense relationship came to a climax on Easter weekend when Yoshizumi physically struck Ingo several times for not having sold a prescribed quota of flowers.

But Ingo still could not bring himself to leave. Then, within a few weeks, Ingo met a Christian engineering student on the UIC campus who was able to demonstrate that Moon's teachings contradicted the Bible in many places. Ingo knew that the Bible was God's revelation to man and also understood that a new revelation from God cannot contradict revelations He previously imparted. Consequently, Ingo decided that Moon and his organization *must* be wrong.

Ingo left the church on Mother's Day 1993 but still faced many difficulties. For example, he had suffered a partially collapsed lung due to his confrontation with Yoshizumi. When he returned to Germany, he faced criminal charges for having evaded that country's mandatory draft. Fortunately, Ingo's lung re-inflated on its own, and the German government dropped Ingo's draft requirement in lieu of a fine. Today Ingo is a Christian and lives in Germany with his family.[4]

HOW IT ALL BEGAN

Since the mid-1970s, the Unification Church (UC)—officially, the Holy Spirit Association for the Unification of World Christianity (HSA-UWC)—has been the subject of countless cult-related books, magazine articles, and newspaper stories. Critics of the multi-million dollar organization maintain that its founder/leader, Reverend Sun Myung Moon, enjoys totalitarian control over his followers and is committed to doing whatever it takes to achieve his ultimate goal: the unification of all religions into one global religious-political system[5] over which he will reign as humanity's messiah.

Former members accuse Moon's disciples (commonly known as Moonies) of making converts and raising financial support through the use of mind-control techniques, deceptive recruiting tactics, and financial improprieties.[6] UC members, most of whom vehemently reject the designation "Moonies," allegedly will stop at nothing to further the plans of their spiritual "True Father." As a result, the UC is seen by many people as the quintessential religious "cult."[7] Moon, of course, is viewed as the epitome of a cult leader—shrewd, authoritarian, charismatic, deceptive, and obsessed with his self-proclaimed identity as a divinely-appointed messenger of God.

Moon's role as a religious leader dates back nearly as far as his birth in Pyungan Buk-do, Korea, on January 6, 1920. According to one UC publication, the event was as significant as Jesus' birth in Bethlehem.[8] UC members claim that their leader, even as a young boy, was spiritually advanced and insightful well beyond his years.[9] Moon himself has said as much, stating that from childhood he was clairvoyant and could see through people's spirits.[10]

Not until the age of sixteen, however, did Moon learn that he was God's chosen messiah, a second Christ, destined to usher in the kingdom of heaven. This revelation came to Moon while he was in prayer during a 1936 Easter morning sunrise service: "Jesus appeared to him and told him that he was chosen to complete the mission Jesus had begun 2,000 years ago."[11] (Moon would later meet and converse with Moses and Buddha.)[12] He subsequently embarked on an "intense search for the universal truth" during which he sought to answer a number of perennial questions: What is man? Who is God? Who is Satan? Why does God allow evil to exist? What is salvation? Who was Jesus Christ? Did Jesus complete His mission? When will the world end?[13]

Moon claims that his quest was marked by constant spiritual, physical, and mental suffering. Nevertheless, he pressed on until one day he received truths from God that "had never before been known to man."[14] This supposed impartation of knowledge from above supposedly solidified Moon's role as the world's savior and gave him complete victory over the forces of darkness in the spiritual dimension. It was a monumental event, to say the least, as the following excerpt from the UC pamphlet *Sun Myung Moon* explains:

> After nine years of search and struggle, the truth of God was sealed into his [Moon's] hands. At that moment he became the absolute victor of heaven and earth. The whole spirit world bowed down to him on that day of victory, for not only had he freed himself completely from the accusation of Satan, but he was now able to accuse Satan before God. Satan totally surrendered to him on that day, for he had elevated himself to the position of God's true Son. The weapon to subjugate Satan then

became available to all mankind. . . . The spirit world has already recognized him as the victor of the universe and lord of creation. The physical world has now only to reflect what he accomplished. . . . The spiritual victory in which he was sealed as the Son of God and victor over Satan is only the beginning of his story.[15]

But gaining spiritual revelations and fully recognizing himself as a second "Son of God"—i.e., a second Messiah—was only the first stage of Moon's mission. The second stage of his assignment began in 1946, shortly after World War II, when God directed him to preach his revelations to the people of Pyung-yang, the capital of what had by then already become Communist North Korea. It was from this site that Moon felt he would begin establishing the kingdom of heaven on earth.

He soon acquired a small following, as well as the attention of Communist authorities, who proceeded to arrest Moon and throw him into prison. The official UC version of the story paints Moon as God's suffering servant who, after being tortured *to death*, was "tossed out into a cold winter night."[16] The dramatic saga continues with Moon's corpse being found by grieving devotees who immediately began funeral preparations but ceased their activities three days later he when came back to life!

Moon again began to preach his message—known as the Divine Principle—only to be re-arrested and sent to a Communist labor camp at Hung-nam in North Korea. Once more the UC's official account of Moon's experience seems somewhat exaggerated. He is portrayed as nothing less than a divine holy man who is filled with unparalleled love, self-sacrifice, strength, honor, courage, and wisdom—everything one might expect from a messiah:

> From the very first day that he entered Hung-nam, he set aside one-half of each meal and divided it among his fellow prisoners. The total portions alone were not adequate to feed even a small child, yet for three months Sun Myung Moon lived on half of the meal that was served. Though many of his devout followers walked more than a hundred miles to bring him food and clothes, he never kept any of their gifts for himself, but always distributed them among his fellow prisoners. . . . He was indeed innocent, a man "smitten and afflicted" [cf. Isa. 53:4] for the transgressions of humanity. Throughout his imprisonment, no one saw Sun Myung Moon sleep. After a long, arduous day, the tired prisoners would fall down to sleep

immediately upon finishing their scanty meal. As each one dropped off to sleep, he could see the dim figure of Sun Myung Moon sitting in the prayer position.... When the prison guards aroused the prisoners from their sleep early in the morning, Sun Myung Moon was already in the same prayer position they had seen him in the evening before.... Though the work quotas set by the prison authorities were impossible for the tired and hungry prisoners to attain, Sun Myung Moon shocked even the Communist authorities by surpassing the daily work quota.... Though he never revealed a single word concerning the Divine Principle or his mission, every prisoner soon recognized him as a man of God.... Some had dreams or visions in which God showed them that prisoner #596 [Moon] was His Son. Several prisoners saw him on a great and glorious throne of God with his face shining like a sun, looking down on the entire world. Thus, in the midst of his hardships, God sent him followers.[17]

After United Nations forces liberated the Hung-nam work camp in 1950, Moon spent the remainder of the Korean War and the post-war years preaching and gathering disciples throughout Korea. It was during this period that he authored the first draft of *Divine Principle*, which organized his many revelations into a coherent belief system. Finally, in 1954, Moon founded the UC and began building what would eventually grow into a global empire:

Moon made the acquaintance of the authoritarian leader of South Korea, General Park Chung Hee.... Moon's fervid anti-Communism and support for the government's policies resulted in a good working relationship with Park. Moon's business activities also began to grow, and he became board chairman of South Korean concerns as diverse as a pharmaceutical company specializing in Ginseng tea and a corporation that manufactured shotguns.[18]

By 1958 Moon had expanded his organization enough to send a missionary to Japan. One year later the UC sent missionaries to America under the leadership of Young Oon Kim, an English-speaking former university professor. But the UC met with little success in the U.S. until 1972, when Moon emigrated to America with his second wife, Hak Ja Han (they married in 1960). Moon alleges that during a 1972 New Year's Day revelation God instructed him to move to America.

Almost immediately the group began to grow through zealous evangelistic efforts and massive outreach programs that included a series of "Day of Hope" rallies in major American cities. By 1976 the UC in the U.S. had attracted several thousand followers and had even established a Unification Theological Seminary in Barrytown, New York. Unfortunately for Moon, the UC also drew intense scrutiny from counter-cult organizations and concerned parents of young converts. Its inner workings, fundraising tactics, and political meddling soon brought widespread criticism and investigations:

> Moon's anti-Communism was adopted as part of the sect's reinterpretation of Christian doctrine. Moon himself entered directly into the political arena. During the Watergate investigations, he organized a media campaign to support the beleaguered President, investing $72,000 in the effort. His position, as announced in his newspaper advertisements, was that "at this moment in history, God had chosen Richard Nixon to be President of the United States." As the Watergate crisis was mounting, Moon brought 1,500 followers to demonstrate in Lafayette Square across from the White House. . . . Moon was invited to meet with the President the next day. It was later revealed that the church had committed other resources to political activities, creating a quasiautonomous group called the Freedom Leadership Foundation to promote public relations and conservative political causes. Such political activities, however, compromised the movement's protection under the First Amendment. Moon's overseas political ties also caused concern. It was suggested that his church had links to the Korean government through certain members, such as Moon's translator, Colonel Pak, a fourteen-year veteran of the Korean army who served as a Korean military attaché in Washington during his early days in the church. In response to rumors of a relationship between the church and the Korean CIA, a congressional investigation was undertaken by Donald Fraser, chairman of the House Sub-Committee on International Organizations. . . . The sect's finances garnered considerable public attention. . . . Mobile fund raising teams traveled throughout the country and raised money in public places from the sale of small specialty items such as flowers or ginseng tea. It was reported that each of hundreds of members brought in from one to five hundred dollars on an average day, usually not revealing their affiliation. The church also made sizable real estate acquisitions that were heavily mortgaged and served as long-term investments. Properties such as Moon's own residence on the Hudson River, a twenty-five acre estate

purchased for $556,000, and the New Yorker Hotel in mid-Manhattan, bought for $5.6 million and used to house followers, were widely perceived as lavish acquisitions made with funds earned by impressed labor.[19]

Eventually a report by the House Sub-Committee on International Organizations stated that it had "found evidence that Reverend Moon's international organization had systematically violated the United States tax, immigration, banking, currency, and foreign-agent registration laws, as well as state and local laws on charity fraud."[20] This led to Moon's 1981 indictment for filing false tax refunds. He had failed to report more than $150,000 of his income in a three-year period. Moon had also deposited $1.6 million in New York bank accounts and failed to report interest on it.[21]

In 1982 Moon was convicted of tax evasion and was sentenced to eighteen months in prison. Surprisingly, his imprisonment only strengthened the UC's position on the American religious scene. Many sociologists, religious leaders, and "religious rights" crusaders painted Moon as less of a criminal and more of a sincere religious leader suffering unjust persecution at the hands of the U.S. government.[22] After thirteen months in jail (July 20, 1984–August 20, 1985), Moon was released to pursue his dream of a utopian society bound together by his Divine Principle.

GOING MAINSTREAM

Thanks to a new public relations campaign built on conservative politics and "family values," the UC has made significant steps toward merging with America's mainstream religious community. During the 1990s the UC sponsored several conferences throughout the world under the banner of Moon's Family Federation for World Peace and his Women's Federation for World Peace. Conference attendees and speakers included such respected conservatives as Christian Coalition executive director Ralph Reed, Family Research Council president Gary Bauer, Jerry Falwell, Robert Schuller of the Crystal Cathedral, and Concerned Women for America president Beverly LaHaye.[23]

Similar events held by other UC front groups have also been attended by conservative heavyweights. As far back as 1988 the National Association of Evangelicals (NAE) had issued a warning to its members about "Unification Church attempts to infiltrate their ranks by joining with organizations that seem to have conservative goals."[24] Nevertheless, evangelicals have continued to rub elbows with Moon-affiliated groups, due in part to the enormous speaking fees paid by Moon; confidential industry sources reveal that some of the payments have topped $100,000.[25]

Christian sociology professor Ronald Enroth comments: "In a sense they have bought legitimacy. One of the main goals of the Unification Church is to receive legitimacy by association. They constantly play up their association with the respectable mainstream."[26] For example, one of the main speakers at a December 1995 Unification conference entitled "Christian Ecumenism in the Americas" was Jerry Falwell. A 1997 *Cornerstone* magazine article reported: "Unification publications used Falwell's appearance there to lend an aura of legitimacy and acceptance to Moon's world mission. . . . [T]he Unification Church published a photograph of Falwell and Moon in a bear hug."[27]

The Republican Party, too, has been represented at UC-backed events. Republican speakers have included former President George Bush; his wife, Barbara Bush; GOP vice presidential candidate Jack Kemp; and Marilyn Quayle (wife of former vice president Dan Quayle).[28] In fact, Bush traveled to Buenos Aires to address those attending the inauguration of Moon's new Spanish language newspaper, *Tiempos del Mundo*. During his speech he "praised the [conservative-oriented] *Washington Times*, a daily newspaper owned by Moon, for its 'defense of liberty and democracy.'"[29]

Other notable participants at UC-related events include comedian Bill Cosby; Olympic gold medal speed skater Dan Jansen; Coretta Scott King, wife of the late Dr. Martin Luther King; ABC news anchorwoman Barbara Walters; film actor Christopher Reeves; singer Pat Boone; and former British Prime Minister Sir Edward Heath.[30] Some of these celebrities, like some conservatives (e.g., LaHaye, Reed, Bauer), had no idea who was sponsoring the event at which they were appearing. Cosby, for instance, tried to pull out of his engagement after learning of Moon's involvement but was forced to go through with his performance after being threatened with litigation.[31] Not everyone, though, is as concerned about their participation in Moon-related events. For example, George Bush and his wife steadfastly defend their appearances at UC gatherings:

According to Bush spokesman Jim McGrath, "the former President and his wife are aware of the Federation's [Women's Federation for World Peace] origins and complaints by anti-cult groups and relatives of Moon's followers, but do not intend to change their speaking plans. . . . [T]he public outcry against this may be having some effect. McGrath promised that Bush's fee for a recent Moon sponsored event in Washington would be donated to charity. His fees reportedly run $80,000 per speech. . . . However, he [Bush] continues to speak at Moon's conferences, and has made much more than the estimated $80,000 he pledged to give to charity. His and Mrs. Bush's past speaking engagements at functions sponsored by Moon's Women's Federation for World Peace were quite lucrative. Neither Bush's representatives nor Moon's group would reveal how much was paid for their appearances. However, estimates have run as high as one million dollars for his six appearances.[32]

It is undeniable that Moon has been trying to associate himself with famous persons in an effort to capitalize on their positive public image. He has often had his picture taken with high-profile personalities, only to have the photographs appear in UC publications distributed to the public.[33] In a 1974 speech Moon emphasized the importance of also getting written endorsements by well-respected individuals:

As you know they have sent many telegrams and congratulatory messages. In doing this they are lending us the entire weight of their names. . . . This will lift our movement up to the pinnacle. . . . When you go get the proclamations in your various cities and you must meet the Mayors, it is easy because your foundation has been laid. All you have to do is show other proclamations, other letters, and say what other people have done to honor Father.[34]

Although the UC is pushing for legitimacy, it still has critics who are extremely worried that Moon's growing list of connections with big business, respected conservatives/evangelicals, and politicians will give the UC undue influence not only in foreign countries but in the U.S. as well.[35] Moon himself admitted in 1973 that "when it comes to our age, we must have an automatic theocracy [God-centered government] to rule the world. So we cannot separate the political field from the religious. God's loving people [Moonies] have to rule the world—that's logical."[36]

Evangelical counter-cult organizations are especially disturbed by the UC-sponsored engagements because Moon and/or his wife usually play a prominent role in their events. Watchman Fellowship notes that the Moons will typically deliver "the keynote address, in which they will present Unification theology."[37]

The Divine Principle

All of the UC's theology is rooted in Moon's *Divine Principle*, which he claims can solve every "political and economic situation in every field."[38] It is allegedly the "unchanging truth of God"[39] that "inherits and builds upon the core truths which God revealed through the Jewish and Christian scriptures, and encompasses the profound wisdom of the orient."[40] In reality, however, Moon's worldview is a heretical tapestry woven from bits and pieces of Christianity, Taoism, Buddhism, Confucianism, Korean Shamanism, and occultism.[41] Like all pseudo-Christian cults, the UC uses orthodox-sounding terms that conceal concepts that radically depart from the Christian faith. *Divine Principle* significantly perverts nearly every major Christian doctrine, including God's nature, the person and work of Jesus Christ, original sin, the fall of Adam and Eve, salvation, heaven, and hell.

All of the UC's beliefs revolve around the foundational idea that Moon is humanity's messiah, sent to complete the mission that Jesus failed to complete: i.e., the spiritual *and* physical salvation of humanity. As the introduction to *Divine Principle* states: "With the fullness of time, God has sent one person to this Earth to resolve the fundamental problems of human life and the universe. His name is Sun Myung Moon."[42]

How is Moon going to save humanity? To answer this question, one must first understand Moon's view of God. According to Moon, God is "male and female—or masculine and feminine."[43] Such a concept reflects Taoism, the Eastern religious philosophy that teaches that creation is interconnected by a cosmic energy that has two sides: one "masculine" (*yang*) and one "feminine" (*yin*).[44] Moon admits that his theology is rooted in Taoism's yang/yin principle as well as Taoism's concept of a "Great Ultimate," or the "Ultimate Void" out of which arose the yang and yin.[45] However, he puts a Christian spin on Taoism by declaring that the Great Ultimate is actually "a God with personality" (i.e., the personal God of the Bible).[46]

Deeply intertwined with Moon's ideas about God are his views on human nature. Again Taoistic principles are the basis of his beliefs. Moon asserts that human beings, like God, have a positive and negative side. He additionally theorizes that God's will for His creation can only be fully realized through "reciprocal relationships" (i.e., when the opposite sides of one person are united with the opposite sides of another person through marriage). Furthermore, God Himself can only have full expression within creation by entering into a *divine* reciprocal relationship with a man and woman who, through their own reciprocal relationship, have produced children. This "union" of God with a married couple and their children produces what Moon calls the "Four Position Foundation," which he describes as "an unchanging foundation of power . . . . the most basic foundation where God's purpose of creation is perfected."[47]

Moon alleges that God's desire for the formation of Four Position Foundations goes all the way back to Adam and Eve, who were created and placed in the Garden of Eden in order to: 1) have dominion over creation; 2) attain individual perfection and unity with God; 3) unite with each other as husband and wife, thereby reaching perfection within their own "reciprocal relationship" (physical union); and 4) join as husband and wife in a perfectly loving "reciprocal relationship" with God (spiritual union).

As perfected humans in union with each other and God, they were to raise children who would in turn create yet more reciprocal relationships with each other and God. The physical/spiritual multiplication of reciprocal relationships would have eventually led to the establishment of the "Kingdom of Heaven on Earth." Ultimately, after everyone had lived through their appointed time on earth, died, and gone to the spirit world, the kingdom of heaven in *that* realm would have been established.[48] Moon says this was God's original purpose of creation. Adam and Eve were to be the "True Parents"—spiritually and physically—of humanity. Their union with each other (physically) and their union with God (spiritually) would have produced the "True Family," from whom would have come "true society, true nation, and true world."[49]

But instead of fulfilling their mission, Adam and Eve sinned and ruined God's plan to have His creation reflect His dualistic divine nature through reciprocal interaction. How did Adam and Eve frustrate God's plans? According to Moon, the world has turned out badly not because Adam and Eve ate from the Tree of Knowledge, but because Eve had sex with Satan, symbolized by the serpent in Genesis 3. Moon extracts this doctrine from the Bible by using a highly esoteric interpretation of Genesis that defines the Tree of Knowledge as being symbolic of perfected womanhood and the Tree of Life as being symbolic of perfected manhood:

> Just as there was a tree [of life] in the Garden of Eden which symbolized a perfected man . . . . [t]he tree of knowledge represents the ideal woman, perfected Eve. . . . We read that before they fell, Adam and Eve were both naked, and were not ashamed. After the Fall, however, they felt ashamed of their nakedness. Adam and Eve's sexual parts were the source of their shame because they were the instruments of their sinful deed. . . . [H]uman beings fell through an act of illicit sexual intercourse. . . . The tree of the knowledge of good and evil was shown earlier to symbolize Eve. What does the fruit of this tree represent? It signifies the love of Eve. As a tree multiplies by its fruit, Eve should have borne good children through her godly love. Instead, she bore evil children through her satanic love. . . . This is why Eve's love is symbolized by the fruit of the tree of the knowledge of good and evil, and why Eve is symbolized by the tree. What did eating the fruit of the tree of the knowledge of good and evil signify? . . . Eve's eating of the fruit of the tree of the knowledge of good and evil denotes that she consummated a satanic love relationship with the angel [Satan/serpent] which bound her in blood ties to him. . . . God created human beings with two components: the spirit self and the physical self. The human Fall likewise took place in two dimensions: the spiritual and the physical. The fall which took place through the sexual relationship between the angel and Eve was the *spiritual fall,* while the fall which occurred through the sexual relationship between Eve and Adam was the *physical fall.* . . . Perfect Adam and Eve were supposed to have become an eternal husband and wife in God's love. But Eve, who in her immaturity had engaged in the illicit relationship with the Archangel, joined with Adam as husband and wife. Thus, Adam fell when he, too, was still immature. This untimely conjugal relationship in satanic love between Adam and Eve constituted the physical fall.[50]

The importance of Moon's Garden of Eden saga cannot be overstated. This is the doctrine upon which he builds several other key concepts involving such important doctrines as the nature of man, the problem of sexual immorality in society, and most importantly, the role of Jesus Christ in the salvation process.

Jesus Christ: God's Failure

The UC teaches that when Eve had sexual relations with Satan, she somehow inherited elements of his evil nature. These sinful elements were then passed on to Adam when she had sex with him in an effort to unite with the one whom she realized was supposed to be her mate. Adam and Eve in turn passed on Satan's nature to their offspring. From that time forward, every human being has been born with Satan's spiritual nature. According to Moon's teaching, even though we are physically the descendants of Adam and Eve, we are literally the spiritual "lineage" of the Devil.[51]

Here is where the need for a savior enters the UC's theological landscape. According to Moon, the fall of Adam and Eve resulted in the creation of a Four Position Foundation with Satan rather than with God. Like the elements of Satan's nature, this Four Position Foundation was passed on to all humanity. Moon further asserts that in order to obtain deliverance from this satanic union, a messiah/savior—a perfected man (i.e., a second Adam)—needed to come to earth and create what Adam and Eve had failed to create: a Four Position Foundation with God. This savior would essentially provide another chance for everyone to live in union with God as a reflection of the divine nature.

Like Adam, the messiah would have to find a perfected woman (i.e., a second Eve), unite with her through marriage and sex, subsequently unite with God spiritually, then have a family, which would in turn produce what God wanted all the way back in the Garden of Eden: the kingdom of heaven on earth. What about persons who are not directly related to the savior's "true family"? According to Moon, they could be saved by joining themselves to the savior and his wife through faith. Such a alliance would provide *physical* deliverance (due to the savior's union with his wife) and *spiritual* deliverance (due to the union of the savior and his wife with God). By faith, individuals would come into the True Family and claim the savior as their True Father and his wife as their True Mother.[52]

The man known as Jesus was supposed to have secured complete salvation (physical and spiritual) for humanity, but he failed to do so because he was crucified before he could produce a True Family.[53] In Moon's words, "physical salvation was left unaccomplished. . . . The salvation which Jesus provided . . . is limited to the spiritual dimension. It does not resolve the original sin, which is transmitted through our physical bodies and remains active within us."[54]

According to Unification theology, Jesus was not God in the flesh. He was a mere man who, after reaching spiritual maturity, tried to save humanity.[55] But he failed to complete his task and only opened up a way for people to obtain *spiritual* salvation through faith in his message. This way was created when Jesus and the Holy Spirit "worked in oneness to grant spiritual rebirth by spiritually engrafting believers with themselves."[56] They somehow became the *spiritual* True Parents of humanity: "When we believe in Jesus as the Savior through the inspiration of the Holy Spirit [the feminine side of God], we receive the love of the spiritual True Parents, which is generated through the give and take between Jesus, the spiritual True Father, and the Holy Spirit, the spiritual True Mother."[57]

Neither Moon nor any other high-ranking UC official has ever explained exactly *how* the Holy Spirit and Jesus—who was resurrected only as a spiritual being—were able to join together and become spiritual True Parents. The concept is simply accepted as a fact by UC members despite a number of obvious questions: Did these two spiritual beings unite sexually? Why did Jesus make the Holy Spirit the spiritual True Mother? If Jesus was resurrected spiritually, and if spirit beings can have sex with humans (e.g., Satan with Eve), then why did Jesus not just continue to seek out a physical female with whom he could mate? If spiritual *death* occurred when a spirit and a physical woman had sex, then could not spiritual rebirth have occurred through sex between a spirit (i.e., Jesus) and a woman?

All of these questions remain unanswered. Furthermore, Moon arbitrarily claims that Jesus' spiritual resurrection brought into existence a heretofore unknown spiritual realm he has labeled "Paradise." This is the destination "for those spirits who have attained the level of life spirits [a second stage of spiritual growth] by believing in Jesus during their earthly life."[58] This location is *not* the kingdom of heaven. In fact, even Jesus himself could not get into heaven because he had failed in his mission:

Jesus . . . could not enter the Kingdom of Heaven. He instead went to Paradise. In order to enter the Kingdom of Heaven, Jesus would have had to form a family. . . . Jesus was to marry, form a family, serve and live with God in that family, and then enter the Kingdom of Heaven with that family. He could not enter the Kingdom of Heaven by himself alone.[59]

Although Jesus opened up the way to *spiritual* salvation, he did nothing to secure our *physical* salvation, which must be obtained if one is ever going to enter the kingdom of heaven on earth and ultimately the kingdom of heaven in the spirit world. Consequently, another messiah is needed, a True Father who procreates a True Family with a True Mother wife. Moon explains:

> Adam and Eve were supposed to be the True Parents of mankind. . . .
> When they failed, God intended Jesus to be the True Parent of mankind.
> When he was crucified on the cross, God promised another messiah. He
> is coming to consummate the ideal of God-centered True Parents. He will
> generate a new family of God through restoring the family unit under
> God's ideal. . . . Mankind's ultimate fulfillment . . . is to become true sons
> and daughters of God.[60]

Moon is allegedly this messiah, the Lord of the Second Advent through whom the world will be blessed. In the December 1995 issue of *Unification News*, Dr. Tyler O. Hendricks, president of the Unification Church of America, stated: "The Messiah is the incarnation of God . . . . [T]he UC is the church which demands continual sacrifice of its members, centering on the fate of one individual, the Messiah, Reverend Sun Myung Moon."[61] Moon supposedly fulfills the second coming of "Christ."[62] Several publications, such as *Divine Principle*, seem to indicate that Moon is a sort of reincarnation of Jesus himself, who has returned to fulfill his mission:

> We who receive salvation based on Jesus' crucifixion cannot unshackle
> ourselves from the chains of sin, due to the original sin still active deep
> within us. Therefore, to uproot the original sin, which he could not
> remove through the crucifixion, and to complete the work of physical sal-
> vation, Jesus must come again on Earth. Only then will the purpose of
> God's work of salvation be fulfilled both spiritually and physically.[63]

Moon's wife, because she is the True Mother, also holds a prominent place in UC theology. In fact, according to some aspects of Unification theology, the couple have "equal status in the restoration [of earth], and this equality is indicated by the invocation of 'True Parents' rather than 'Rev. Moon' in the prayer life of the members."[64] Moon's final accomplishment will allegedly be the establishment of one "global nation under God," wherein earth's entire population speaks one language (i.e., Korean)[65] and embraces one religion led by Moon, the ultimate messiah:

> [A]ll religions are converging toward one religion. . . . The returning Christ, who comes as the center of Christianity, will attain the purposes which the founders of religions strove to accomplish. Therefore, with respect to his mission, Christ at his return may be regarded as the second coming of the founder of every religion. . . . One person, Christ at the Second Advent, will come as the fulfillment of all these revelations. The Lord whose coming has been revealed to believers in various religions, including the Maitreya Buddha in Buddhism, the True Man in Confucianism, the returning Ch'oe Su-un who founded the religion of Ch' ondogyo, and the coming of Chongdoryong in the *Chonggamnok* [a Korean religious text], will be none other than Christ at the Second Advent.[66]

Only by faith in Moon can anyone gain access to the kingdom of heaven. A 1976 "Declaration of Unification Affirmations" states: "Christ will come as before, as a man in the flesh, and he will establish a family through marriage to his Bride, a woman in the flesh, and they will become the True Parents of all mankind. Through our accepting the True Parents . . . obeying them and following them, our original sin will be eliminated and we will eventually become perfect."[67]

In addition to these benefits, all Moonies become "divine" spirits. As such, they can "accurately feel and perceive every reality in the spirit world."[68] This ability, too, was not available until now because Jesus failed in his mission.[69] Interestingly, persons who express faith in Moon by joining the UC still must earn their salvation by leading a good life and zealously "attending" to God and His earthly representative, Reverend Moon.[70]

It has also been noted that there exist some rather peculiar views in the UC covering a wide range of topics. For example, Moon believes that Koreans are now God's chosen people (i.e., modern-day Israel)[71] and that Korea is "the place most dear to God and most abhorred by Satan."[72] He also has made some rather odd statements concerning sexual organs, which he believes are extremely important to one's spirituality. Consider the following excerpt from the speech he delivered at the 1996 inauguration of his Buenos Aires newspaper:

> All of you presidents and distinguished guests are famous, but there is something that you do not know. You do not know what makes man man, and woman woman. The answer is: the sexual organs. Is there anyone here who dislikes the sexual organs? If you like them, how much do you like them? Until now you may not have thought it virtuous to value the sexual organs, but from now you must value them. . . . If humanity were to go beyond the traditional categories of virtue, religion and any other human norms, but were absolutely in harmony with the sexual organs, earning the welcoming applause of God, what kind of world would it be?[73]

During this same speech, Moon made a number of bizarre comments regarding bodily functions, which to Moon illustrated man's oneness with himself and somehow demonstrated why people, like God, need to have an object partner in order to feel love:

> You use the bathroom each morning. When you defecate, do you wear a gas mask? This is not a laughing matter but a serious one. If you are near someone else defecating, you will quickly move a good distance away. But when you smell your own feces, you do not even notice it. This is because that fecal matter is one with your body. Therefore, you do not feel that it is dirty. When you were young, did you ever taste the dried mucus from your nose? Does it taste sweet or salty? It's salty, right? Since you can answer, you must have tasted it! Why did you not feel that it was dirty? It is because it was part of your body. Reverend Moon has figured out something that no one in the world knew. When you cough up phlegm, you sometimes swallow it, right? . . . Why do you not feel it is dirty? Because the phlegm was one with your body. We all eat three meals a day, breakfast, lunch and dinner. If you go about twelve inches down from your mouth, there is a fertilizer factory. By eating three meals a day, we are providing raw materials for fertilizer factories. After knowing that, can you still take food into your mouth with a fork and spoon? We know that there is a fertilizer factory in our stomach, but we live on without feeling its presence. Why do we not feel it? It is because we are one with it.[74]

Also noteworthy is the way in which Moon consistently refers to himself in the third person, freely using self-exalting terms and descriptions.

He seems fairly confident that no one is his equal, especially in matters of spirituality. Consider the following remarks:

> Reverend Moon is an intelligent man. I am not doing what I am doing because I am inferior to you. . . . You cannot reject Reverend Moon's Divine Principle, which contains content beyond your wildest dreams presented through logical explanations and in well-ordered structure. . . . You have to realize that Reverend Moon overcame death hundreds of times in order to find this path. Reverend Moon is the person who brought God to tears hundreds of times. No one in history has loved God more than Reverend Moon has. That is why even if the world tries to destroy me, the Reverend Moon will never perish. It is because God protects me. If you step into the realm of the truth Reverend Moon teaches, you also will gain God's protection.[75]

> Reverend Moon is the only one who knows all the secrets of God.[76]

> Within this world there is no individual whom God loves more than Reverend Moon. There is no one else who knows God more than Reverend Moon.[77]

Moon's exalted status within the UC belief system is perhaps best illustrated by the contents of *Victory of Love*, a 1992 book published by the Unification Church. This volume contains spirit messages that were "channeled" (see Chapter 1) by various mediums. The source of the communications were allegedly Moon's dead son, Heung Hin Nim, and Jesus Christ. The messages from "Jesus Christ" place Moon and his wife ("True Parents") on a level that is clearly divine. In fact, the channeled "Christ" admits that one day he will actually bow down to the True Parents:

> [Spirit message from "Jesus Christ":] You must proudly wear the name of your True Parents [Mr. and Mrs. Moon]. . . . I will lift the Crown of Glory and place it on our Parents head. I will bow before their throne. I will bow before the eyes of my sheep and they will know. . . . Bring them [i.e., evangelical Christians] to the throne of our True Parents, the mighty throne of heaven. And I will place the Crown of Glory on our True Parents head. I will lead them. I will show them that the Lord of Lords and the King of Kings and the King of Glory is our precious Lord Sun Myung Moon and his beloved bride Hak Ja Han. They reign as

king and queen of the entire universe. And that I, Jesus of Nazareth, known as the Christ, bow in humility before them. . . . I bow before our precious Lords, our True Parents, Sun Myung Moon and Hak Ja Han. These names are the sun and the moon. These names are the light of the world.[78]

ACCORDING TO THE BIBLE

In response to evangelical criticism, Reverend Moon has relentlessly attacked the Christian church, stating that it has been mobilized by "satanic power" to come against the UC.[79] "Christianity has departed considerably from the original will or dispensation of God," declares Moon. "This is the most important reason that God needs man to have an absolutely new and totally fresh outlook. . . . The Divine Principle is that new revelation."[80] He has additionally charged that the Christian clergy are not only like the hypocritical priests and scribes of Jesus' day, but that they are "entirely ignorant of God's providence in the Last Days."[81]

It is not as if Moon thinks his teachings are compatible with the doctrines of Christendom. On the contrary, Moon has acknowledged that his views are heretical from a Christian perspective. In 1996 he stated: "Christians entrap us, crying heresy because our doctrines differ, and they try to destroy us. But in this case, this so-called heretical cult [UC] is on the side of truth."[82] On an earlier occasion, he admitted: "I can understand why Christians call us heretics."[83]

Nevertheless, Moon maintains that he is right and Christians are wrong. As he puts it, "From God's point of view, my revelation is deeply orthodox."[84] He has gone so far as to proclaim, "[Y]ou must trust my teaching, my words 100 percent because they are not my own. They are God's words."[85] The Bible, however, reveals that Moon's "revelations" are far from orthodox, especially with regard to the person and work of Jesus Christ.

To begin with, Unification Theology teaches that Jesus was not born of a virgin. Contrary to passages such as Isaiah 7:14 and Matthew 1:18–25, Moon claims that Jesus was born as a result of illicit sex between Mary and the aged priest Zacharias, the husband of Mary's cousin, Elizabeth:

> Though an elderly man, Zacharias was not impotent, for he had just made his wife Elizabeth pregnant in spite of the fact that she was past the

normal time of childbearing. . . . As soon as the young girl heard that she had been chosen to give birth to the Son of God, she "went with haste and entered the house of Zacharias" (Luke 1:39). By giving herself to the aged priest, Mary would prove that she was truly a hand-maiden of the Lord. Such an act of total surrender, far from being considered immoral in the ancient world, revealed the highest degree of spiritual dedication. By uniting with the priest, Mary "found favor with God."[86]

Scripture nowhere hints at such a blasphemous concept. In fact, if Mary would have committed fornication/adultery with Zacharias, both of them would have been subject to stoning, according to the Law of Moses (Lev. 20:10).

The UC also asserts that Jesus "did not come to die on the cross."[87] His death "was not the Will of God."[88] According to Unification Church member Young Oon Kim, UC theology "diametrically contradicts the Fundamentalist view that Jesus' sole mission was to atone for the sins of mankind by dying on the cross."[89] Consequently, Unificationists "do not glory [boast] in the cross and rather insist that for Jesus the cross only aroused feelings of extreme bitterness and sorrow. It was not something to be proud of but something terribly shameful."[90]

Paul the apostle viewed Jesus' crucifixion quite differently, saying: "[M]ay it never be that I should boast, except in the cross of our Lord Jesus Christ" (Gal. 6:14). It was indeed God's will for Jesus to die on the cross (Col. 1:19-20). His death not only paid the penalty for our sins (1 Peter 2:24) but once and for all canceled out our debt to the law, nailing it to the cross. "When He had disarmed the powers and authorities, He made a public display of them, having triumphed over them by the cross" (Col. 2:15).

Moreover, our Lord explicitly said that His purpose for coming was to first preach the Gospel of God's kingdom (Mark 1:38; Luke 4:43) and then to die (John 12:27) so that He could draw all men to Himself (John 3:14; 12:32), take away the sins of humanity (1 John 3:5), and destroy the works of the Devil (1 John 3:8). Jesus repeatedly told His disciples what would occur (Matt. 16:20–21; 26:2; Luke 18:31–33). In fact, Jesus' crucifixion had been part of God's sovereign plan since before creation (Eph. 3:11; 1 Peter 1:20). According to 1 Corinthians 1:18, the cross is foolishness only to those who are spiritually perishing.

Moon also denies Christ's physical resurrection. According to *Divine*

Principle, Jesus is no longer a man. He is a divine spirit.[91] Leading UC theologian Young Oon Kim clearly states: "Jesus' resurrection was spiritual and not physical."[92] But again, the UC position directly contradicts the Bible. Jesus prophesied in John 2:19, 21 that after His death He would resurrect His own "body." Also, 1 Timothy 2:5 reveals that the "man" Christ Jesus is now the heavenly mediator between God and men.

There are, of course, numerous other heretical doctrines promoted by the UC; too many, in fact, to rebut in a chapter of this size. However, a final observation must be made on Moon's claim that he is the Messiah. In *The Kingdom of the Cults*, the late cult expert Dr. Walter Martin noted: "The warning of the Lord Jesus against false Christs and false prophets [Matt. 24:5, 11] is most apropos where Moon is concerned, for he can make no genuine claim to messianic office being Korean, for as Christ said, 'salvation is from the Jews' (John 4:22)."[93]

WHAT'S THE ATTRACTION?

Spiritual truth seekers join the UC for a number of reasons. Many Korean Moonies, for example, undoubtedly receive an exalted sense of self through the group's teaching that Koreans are God's chosen people for this era. Moreover, Moon's theology does not do away with Korean traditions or spiritual teachings (shamanism, spiritism, etc.) but rather incorporates both into a home-grown religious system. Koreans can adopt UC theology and feel "Christian," yet not be forced to reject their spiritual heritage.

Additionally, it is important to understand that throughout the centuries Koreans have suffered horrible persecution from neighboring countries. Moon's ideology puts this suffering in a spiritual light, explaining it as God's way of preparing them to be God's elect messengers for the last days. Moon writes: "[T]he Korean people had also to suffer under a nation of Satan's side for a period which fulfills the number forty [a significant prophetic number to Moon]. . . . This was the forty-year period during which Korea suffered untold hardships as a colony of Japan."[94]

In a 1977 interview Moon explained: "Today Korea has much in common with God's heart. From their own experience of suffering and tragedy, Koreans can readily understand God's sorrow and broken heart. They can readily respond to the call of God."[95] By taking this approach to Korea's painful past, Moon provides great comfort to individuals who have suffered, as well as to persons who have had loved ones suffer throughout the generations.

Non-Korean UC members can be attracted to the group for other reasons. In the case of Ingo Michehl, "love bombing" was very instrumental in his becoming a UC member. He was overcome with how much "love" he was receiving from total strangers. Young people are especially vulnerable to this aspect of the UC. Frequently a UC recruiter purposefully approaches a member of the opposite sex in a deliberate attempt to heighten the "love-bombing" experience by adding to it "an unspoken but recognized element of sexuality to the interaction."[96] A lonely young person might easily interpret the favorable feelings accompanying such an experience as being indicative of the group's spirituality or true "love." One former member recalls the following:

> It worked better from female to male than the other way around. Some of them [women] would walk up and put their arm through some guy's arm or grab his hand or something like that. Kind of cute—nothing lurid about [it]—kind of like junior high teasing.[97]

The UC also provides a vehicle through which people can feel as if they are actively creating a better world—the kingdom of heaven on earth. Consider the following words from a twenty-four-year-old former Moonie: "I felt part of a wonderful movement, filled with beautiful people, a beautiful leader, a view that will change the world. We were going to do it—we can do it. You can't match that . . . those few minutes is an experience that few people ever experience in their entire lives."[98] Not surprisingly, an early UC recruitment poster reads: "If you want to change this world and are longing to find the way . . . you are the person who should hear the Divine Principle Seminar!"[99]

Finally, the UC appeals to many people because it conveys a strong sense of "family," something that has been all but lost in recent years. As one UC publication states: "More than ever we are a Family, serving each other as daughters and sons, brothers and sisters, mothers and fathers, under Our True Parents."[100] Sociologist Ronald Enroth observes the following:

> The new cults offer young people a context where they are accepted, cared for, loved, fed, housed, and made to feel important. . . . These 'spir-

itual' families replace the members' natural families. Biological parents are often castigated, ignored or viewed as tools of Satan. Thus while exploiting the human desire to be part of a familial group, the cults undermine the God-ordained social institution of the family by substituting their own spiritualized versions.[101]

Sadly, the UC and similar "families" will never be able to provide what so many individuals are seeking: the peace and joy that comes from joining God's family of born-again believers, who by faith in Jesus Christ are set free to serve their Father in heaven (Rom. 8:15–16).

RECOMMENDED READING

Beverly, James A. "The Unification Church," in Ronald Enroth, ed., *Evangelizing the Cults* (Ann Arbor, MI: Servant Publications, 1990).

Kemperman, Steve. *Lord of the Second Advent* (Ventura, CA: Regal Books, 1981).

Martin, Walter. "Unification Church," in *The Kingdom of the Cults* (Minneapolis: Bethany House, 1965; 1997 edition).

Underwood, Barbara and Betty Underwood. *Hostage to Heaven* (New York: Clarkson N. Potter, Inc., 1979).

Waldrep Bob. "Unification Church Influence in America," *Watchman Expositor*, vol. 13, no. 5 (1996).

ALL IN
"THE FAMILY"

WE HAVE A SEXY GOD AND A SEXY RELIGION WITH A VERY SEXY
LEADER WITH AN EXTREMELY SEXY YOUNG FOLLOWING!

"MOSES" DAVID BERG,
FOUNDER OF CHILDREN OF GOD/THE FAMILY [1]

A mericans will forever remember the 1960s as a turbulent decade of change marred by vivid images of a controversial war in Vietnam, rioting in the streets, illicit drug use among youths, and a generation of teens and young adults ("hippies") who preached a radical anti-establishment message built on the provocative motto, "Make Love, Not War." That era also gave birth to the "Jesus Movement," which prompted thousands of young people throughout America and Europe to give their lives to Christ. It was this religious movement that Sylvia and Arnaldo Padilla thought they had found in 1972 when they visited a London-based commune started by the Children of God (COG), a group known today as The Family.

To the Padillas, members of the COG—who considered themselves revolutionaries or radicals for Jesus—possessed a vibrant faith that seemed to have no boundaries. They boldly proclaimed their beliefs, constantly appealed to the Bible, and tirelessly ministered to the poor, homeless, destitute, and anyone else society had discarded. The group showed a kind of faith that had long been absent from England's spiritually dead denominations. Moreover, the COG's outreaches were "saving" people by the dozens. Sylvia and Arnaldo, both of whom were only thirty years old, quickly agreed that true New Testament Christianity was only to be found in the COG. They subsequently joined the group and, with the help of its members, brought revival to the community in which they were living. Sylvia remembers, "People who had been sitting on the [spiritual] fence for ages made decisions for Christ."

Soon, however, the focus of their life in the COG dramatically changed. They were relocated to a Costa Rican commune and gradually introduced to sexually-oriented literature written by the group's prophet-leader, David Berg. The writings were filled with pornographic teachings that members *had* to follow in order to prove their commitment to God. Arnaldo, who had been promoted into the group's hierarchy, seemed unfazed; Sylvia convinced herself that the teachings were only spiritual. For example, she assumed that when Berg said each woman in the group was to function as a wife for *every* man, he meant that all of the members were spiritually united in Christ.

Eventually, though, group leaders made it clear to her that Berg's directives were to be taken literally. They proceeded to ask her why she had not been willing to participate in sexual "sharing" with other men in the commune. Sylvia was shocked. Even more traumatic was Arnaldo's news: while traveling abroad, he had been having sex with numerous women in the COG communes located throughout the world.

Sylvia had been living in Costa Rica for nearly four years and believed with all of her heart that Berg was God's end-time prophet. Nonetheless, she asked herself, "Could I have been wrong?" Sylvia ultimately decided that Berg *must* be right and that she would have to change. In retrospect, she remembers being psychologically ready to go in that direction anyway, due to the overly intimate and sexually oppressive environment of the COG commune:

> I and my husband would go off to our bedroom in the same house with young men who had either never had a sexual relationship, or who at one time did have a relationship, but no longer had someone to be with. I used to feel almost guilty. I felt sorry for them. I couldn't help it. It was so blatant that my husband and I were going off together. We were a fairly young couple, and they had nobody. I used to think, "Poor guys, it must be very hard for them." But it never occurred to me to do anything about it until my husband, who'd been away somewhere, phoned me and told me about the fun and games that he'd been having. I was so shocked. And then I had so much pressure on me to obey that I thought, "Well, who's the most needy of all these guys around here." I was taught that it was a total sacrificial thing. Many, many of us women reacted in that way. And

we ended up being abused, actually. If a man requested it of you, and you refused, you were considered very selfish, self-centered, disobedient, and just partial to your own husband. It was absolutely a man's world. Any man who wanted it, he'd just have to ask for it. There were a lot of pregnancies and sexually transmitted diseases because the group frowned upon using birth control of *any* kind. It was terrible.

Within a few years Sylvia was also engaging in "Flirty Fishing," Berg's approach to evangelism that called for his female followers to have sex with prospective converts to show them "Jesus' love." What about the many biblical passages condemning adultery and fornication? Sylvia recalls being taught that these verses were only to be taken spiritually. Berg said, "When the Bible talks about adultery, it really means spiritual adultery—idolatry."

By 1988 Sylvia had served as a sexual partner for perhaps as many as fifty to sixty different men. But it gradually became too much for her to handle, and she prayed that God would not allow any more men to ask her to "share." Miraculously, the men immediately ceased approaching her. Arnaldo, however, continued to indulge in unbridled sexual promiscuity.

In 1991 the Padillas moved back to England and were no longer closely monitored by the group's leadership. Sylvia found her separation from the commune to be life-changing. She walked her youngest child to school daily, and her stroll home provided twenty minutes of something that she had not enjoyed for eighteen years: solitude. She used it to pray and critically think about her time in the COG. One day Sylvia finally realized, "This is *not* the Christian life."

Sylvia proceeded to ask the Lord to *please* send her a Christian friend who could guide her. Within days a former COG member who had recently moved to England from India called the Padilla home. He visited and shared with Arnaldo and Sylvia about how God had led him out of the COG. He then invited them to a church he was attending. One month later the Padillas found themselves walking through its doors. The service had already started, and worship songs filled the sanctuary. According to Sylvia, her soul was immediately flooded by God's love. She nearly collapsed:

> I went into the lobby and felt this extraordinary sensation come all over me. Everybody was singing. It was very crowded and everyone was prais-

ing the Lord in song and I immediately wanted to cry. I could hardly get to my seat. When I got to my seat, I plunked down because I couldn't stand. And I sobbed my heart out for 2 1/2 hours. It was just because the Holy Spirit was there. Occasionally, I would stop crying, look up at the ceiling, and think: "Oh God, this is just like being in heaven." Then I'd look at the words of the songs: "ALL HEAVEN DECLARES THE BEAUTY OF THE RISEN LORD. WHO CAN COMPARE WITH THE BEAUTY OF THE LORD." I'd read these words and just burst into tears again. It was the real thing. And then, "REJOICE, REJOICE, CHRIST IS IN YOU, THE HOPE OF GLORY IN YOUR HEART." I hadn't heard anything like that for over eighteen years. I just boo-hooed my whole way through.

Sylvia returned to the church every week and made new friends with whom she could pray. She also received biblical counseling and within a month renounced the COG, telling Arnaldo: "We should leave [the COG]. It's not right. It's very, very wrong." He agreed and notified the group that he and his wife were leaving "The Family."

Unfortunately, Arnaldo left Sylvia three years later to return to the group. Sylvia, however, has remained faithful to God. She also is optimistic about the future, especially now that her six children—aged fourteen to twenty-eight—are out of the group and living with her. "God has been so merciful," she says. "He gave me the most encouraging word one day while I was in prayer. He said, 'I'm not going to use you *in spite* of those eighteen years. I'm going to use you *because* of them.'" Sylvia has since become such an influential and well-known critic of the COG that British TV produced a 1996 documentary about her life. She continues to help victims of The Family find freedom in Christ.[2]

HOW IT ALL BEGAN

As of 1997, "The Family"/COG had an estimated membership of 10,000-12,000 full-time members (including 3,000-4,000 children/teens) and perhaps 5,000 "TSers" (Tithe Supporters) who, though not living in any of its communes, financially support the group. "The Family" is arguably one of the most spiritually, emotionally, and psychologically destructive religious belief systems in existence. At the very least it is "one of the most controversial religious groups of recent decades."[3]

"The Family" promotes a wildly heretical and sexually perverted set of doctrines including: 1) the Holy Spirit is a scantily clad woman (God the Father's wife); 2) Jesus was conceived through sexual intercourse between the angel Gabriel and Mary;[4] 3) Jesus fornicated so frequently with His female disciples that He may have contracted venereal diseases;[5] 4) Jesus participates in heavenly sex orgies;[6] and 5) members of "The Family" may in many cases fornicate and commit adultery as long as they "do it in love."

These and other beliefs can be traced directly to the group's founder, David Brandt Berg (1919–1994), who continues to be revered by members of The Family as "Moses" Berg, a man with "a deep abiding faith in Jesus, and love for God and his fellow man." His followers claim he was "uncompromising in his devotion to God and his denunciation of evil, yet he was an intensely warm, loving man."[7] But many others—Christian journalists, secular investigative reporters, religion researchers, former COG members, and evangelical cult-watchers—have categorized Berg differently. He has been labeled a "satanic" prophet, a sexually deviant "wolf among the flock," and a cult leader who was "undoubtedly evil."[8]

A Man Called David

David Berg was born in California to Hjalmer and Virginia Berg, two traveling evangelists. He grew up as "a very lonesome little boy" who by his own admission "had hardly any friends."[9] He also had very little contact with his mother because she was so busy preaching on the evangelistic circuit.[10] Only when Berg reached adulthood was he able to travel with his parents. After his father died, he continued touring with his mother, functioning as "her chauffeur, secretary and singer."[11]

In 1944 Berg married Jane Miller, with whom he would eventually have four children: Linda, Paul, Jonathan, and Faith. Then, in 1949, he was asked to pastor a Christian and Missionary Alliance church in Valley Farms, Arizona. But within two years Berg resigned as pastor and spent the early 1950s wandering around the country trying to find a place to belong.[12]

He finally found a ministerial niche with Fred Jordan, who had started his own television ministry as well as missionary "Soul Clinics" in Los Angeles, California, and Mingus, Texas. For approximately fifteen years (1952-1967) Berg publicly "served God" by promoting Jordan's gospel broadcasts and training missionaries.[13] His private life, however, was hardly Christian. He "visited prostitutes and indulged in adulterous affairs. He also began sexually molesting his youngest child, Faith, and by the time she was twelve he was having intercourse with her."[14] (Berg's eldest daughter, Linda, has testified that as a child she, too, was sexually molested by her father.)[15]

In 1967 Berg moved to Huntington Beach, California, where he took over the Light Club, a coffeehouse formerly operated by Teen Challenge (the national youth ministry founded by famous Assemblies of God minister David Wilkerson). He preached a radical, anti-church/anti-establishment/anti-government message that reverberated in the streets as a "Gospel of Rebellion." It spoke to the hippies who frequented the Light Club in search of life's meaning, and Berg soon had a sizable following. They called themselves Teens for Christ:

> By July 1968 the Light Club Mission was being totally supervised by Paul, Jonathan, and Faith Berg. They sang; played their guitars; preached Jesus, endtime prophecy, and the Warning Message; and never mentioned the word *church*. The radical youth loved it. Teens for Christ had a message that was reaching the dropouts. They began to run the mission full-time, keeping it open seven days a week. Local businesses were petitioned to donate free sandwiches for the lost and wayward youth, and they gladly obliged. A steady stream of hungry hippies soon patronized the Light Club. . . . The Light Club Mission filled daily with hungry souls—both physically and spiritually—in need of love and direction. It was this condition that made so many in the hippie generation susceptible to the cults. The counterculture afforded them a vehicle by which to drop out, but there was nothing to drop into. Everyone needs a place, and simply being a dropout is good only for a while; the counterculture deceived the youth because it soon took on the nature of a sieve: the youth were dropping through its small but very real holes and finding themselves ever so lost. . . . David Berg had found his element: the Original Hippie had found his lost and beleaguered flock of hippies. The shepherd and his sheep united. . . . David Berg— in a state of rebellion against the "church system," the American government, his family and religious heritage, and most of all, God—had found an audience of rebellious youth. . . . His bitterness against the church, his rejection of the social establishment and the capitalistic system, his contempt for parental authority—all crystallized into a Gospel

of Rebellion. The kids understood him; he spoke their heart; there was no generation.[16]

According to Berg, his followers were just like Jesus and the apostles: "Dropouts, system rejects, but truth seekers and 'true' lovers of God."[17] Berg's gospel not only legitimized their rebellion but gave them the self-respect so many of them were desperately seeking. Consider the following excerpt from a December 1968 sermon:

> What's the matter with these people [speaking of the churches]? Why are they so afraid of us? Let's face it, it's the power of God! They're afraid of God and you represent God! The community is actually afraid of us! Why do they get all uptight when we walk into a church? They're afraid! They're scared! What are they afraid of? . . . It's God, let's face it! You got'm scared, kids! Hallelujah! You got'm scared![18]

As Berg's estranged daughter, Linda, notes in her autobiography: "The formerly lost, hungry, dirty, groping, and confused hippie had suddenly become 'God's representative,' and the world was trembling at his presence!"[19] But Berg's "Revolution for Jesus," which often included mass distribution of literature on public streets and angry protests, soon caused his small flock to have problems with the police. At one point a number of his Teens for Christ were arrested for demonstrating outside local schools.[20]

The whole group ended up fleeing the state in 1969, prophesying as they left that God would punish their "enemies" by destroying California by an earthquake.[21] That year also saw Berg leave his wife to live in adultery with a young convert named Karen Zerby (renamed Maria). He claimed in a "prophecy" that God had ordained the replacement of his wife (representing the "old church") with Maria (representing the "new church").[22] Thus began Berg's use of personal revelations to justify the wanton sexuality for which his group would become infamous.

In 1970, after touring the country in a convoy of trailers, Berg and his band of approximately 200 "revolutionaries for Jesus" established a commune near Thurber, Texas. Once again, their scathing rebukes of "churchianity," the government, and the corrupt "system" won countless converts; so many, in fact, that Berg's disciples were soon traveling to other cities to establish more communes. It was during this period that a newspaper reporter dubbed Berg and his devotees the "Children of God" (COG).

Two years later the COG had a strong foothold in Britain and boasted a membership of nearly 2,500 disciples in 134 communes throughout forty-one countries. It had also established a reputation for being an abusive and decadent sex cult that used deceptive recruiting tactics to lure teens/young adults away from their families. Hundreds of complaints were lodged against them by former members, angry parents of young followers, and law enforcement authorities. This "persecution" (as COG members called it) caused them to go underground for the 1970s-1980s, during which time they assumed a variety of names including The Family of Love and Heaven's Magic. The COG almost completely disappeared from America, taking up residence in numerous foreign countries. But there, too, critics charged them with practicing rampant sexual promiscuity, adultery, pedophilia, child abuse, prostitution, and group sex. Most of these acts have been documented by former members and literature seized in police raids. The COG has even been involved in publishing child pornography and making videos of nude children dancing provocatively.

According to professor Stephen Kent, sociologist at the University of Alberta, Canada, the group's obsession with sex can be directly linked to Berg's own sexual fixations, which stem from events during his childhood that involved erotic experiences followed by physical, mental, emotional, and sexual abuse by various adults:

> [Berg] had early erotic experiences . . . these sexual experiences involved adults either humiliating or shaming Berg. . . . Furthermore, he suffered severe beatings from his father. Each of these traumatic circumstances haunted Berg well into adulthood, but when he reached his fifties he suddenly found himself leading hundreds, then thousands, of hippies whose ideas of sex were very different from the ones with which he had been reared. In the COG social environment, Berg would "work out" his childhood sexual traumas through the deviant policies and practices that he initiated in the name of God.[23]

Despite the many controversies that have surrounded the COG, the 1990s saw Berg and his followers resurface in America as "The Family," complete with a freshly sanitized public image that appears to reflect conservatism, high morals, and mainstream Christianity. The Family's efforts to present itself as a clean-cut Christian organization have been so successful that the group's singing troupe performed for President George Bush during the official opening of the 1992 White House's Christmas season and have continued to appear every year since.[24]

Berg finally died in 1994, leaving a wretched legacy that continues to thrive under Karen Zerby (a.k.a. Maria) and a high-ranking member named Steve Kelly (a.k.a. King Peter). COG members not only continue to propagate Berg's many heretical doctrines, including those that condone sexual promiscuity, but have introduced even more debased practices into the group such as masturbating while praying to Jesus. This practice, which they term the "Loving Jesus Revelation," is explained as a new way to love Jesus and have spiritual sex with Him.[25] In response to critics, one member of The Family has stated: "Why shouldn't you bring prayer into your lovemaking as much as anything else. For the majority of Christians it will be impossible to accept. . . . But it is a personal conviction on the part of the members of the group."[26]

Recently The Family has linked up with other religious groups such as Scientology, the Jehovah's Witnesses, and the Unification Church ("Moonies") to form the International Federation of Religions and Philosophical Minorities. This organization's stated purpose is to defend the religious rights of its members and to share information about individuals supposedly attacking their religious freedoms (e.g., counter-cult ministries, the media, ex-members, etc.).[27]

There are indeed many persons who believe that The Family *should* be attacked, even banned, due to the psychologically destructive and morally bankrupt nature of its belief system. Especially disturbing to opponents of The Family are its teachings and practices that have encouraged children/teens to participate in sexual activities: i.e., pedophilia, child pornography, adult-child sexual contact, child-child sexual relations.

Members of The Family maintain that they are innocent of all such charges. But these denials are contradicted by Berg's own writings (known as Mo Letters), which represent the bulk of The Family's holy scriptures, which are viewed by group members as God's Word. The Family has consistently tried to keep these authoritative texts hidden from non-members. The materials are even letter-coded so that sensitive material will not fall into the hands of enemies. The more restrictive a publication is rated, the more likely it is to contain information that the general public and law enforcement agencies would find objectionable:

- "GP" – "General Public," can be sold on the street to non-members.
- "DFO" – "Disciples and Friends Only," for all members and their sympathetic friends.
- "DO" – "Disciples Only," for all members.
- "LTO" – "Leadership Training Only," for members being trained for high-ranking positions.
- "LO" – "Leaders Only," for high-ranking members only.[28]

In a 1971 "FOR LEADERS ONLY" letter, Berg noted that all "LO" letters were to be seen *only* by the commune's advisor, his wife, and the immediate staff of his "top most trusted leaders who can take the real heavy stuff, including shocking revelations, radical revolutionary information . . . and drastic and fanatical changes, etc.—the real strong [spiritual] meat for very mature brothers and sisters who can take almost anything without being offended."[29] Fortunately, defectors from The Family have been able to deliver these revealing documents to outsiders, including journalists and religion researchers.

In an effort to expose the doctrinal teachings of The Family, I will quote from some of the most closely guarded texts published by Berg. The quotations contained in the following pages are highly offensive. Consequently, some of the words have been slightly altered in an effort to soften their impact. (Note: The Family's literature contains extensive use of capital lettering, boldface type, and underlining. These stylistic choices by Berg have been reproduced exactly as they appear in the original documents.)

Sex, Lies, and Videotape

An informed opinion of The Family cannot be made unless it is clearly understood that uninhibited sexual expression is the foundation upon which the group is built. This facet of the organization sprang from Berg's self-confessed inability to control his own sexual urges. He interpreted this lack of self-control to mean that such urges were natural and godly.

Berg subsequently taught that *everyone* should fully indulge their sexual appetites and punctuated this belief by incessantly talking about sex:

> I don't <u>always</u> talk about sex, just *most* of the time! . . . <u>MAYBE SOME OF YOU</u>
> <u>ARE GETTING BORED WITH SO MUCH TALK ABOUT SEX</u>! It's a neverending
> source of wonder to me. . . . I'm wild about sex & I tell the World about
> it![30] I've tried everything & everybody, but after all these years I still want
> more [sex]! So if you're as sex-crazed as I am personally, I can offer you
> no hope of a cure. . . . <u>SO AFTER ALL THESE YEARS OF CONSTANT SEXUAL</u>
> <u>ACTIVITY & MANY WOMEN LATER</u> I've finally given up & decided there's
> no cure for sex! I keep wanting more every day & I'm constantly yielding
> to my sexual appetite for more women & more sex, & have finally come
> to the conclusion that the only thing I can do about it is to constantly sat-
> isfy that craving with more!—More, more, more!—<u>Hallelujah</u>![31]

Berg was not always so sexually uninhibited. He claims he was "tormented" until almost fifty years old (1968/69) by intense guilt and anxiety
over his sexual past, all the while blaming his parents—especially his
mother, the authority figure in his home—for making him feel dirty and
sinful. Investigations of Berg's life also reveal that he and his wife, Jane,
were plagued by sexual dysfunction.[32] His frustrations were further intensified by numerous ministerial failures for which he was constantly
ridiculed by both his mother and wife.[33] Interestingly, it was the death of
Berg's mother in 1968 that seemed to propel him toward sexual debauch-
ery. In one early Mo Letter, Berg described with great bitterness the psychosexual torture he had endured and encouraged his flock of young
admirers to enjoy what he had been denied for so long:

> **ENJOY YOURSELF AND SEX AND WHAT GOD HAS GIVEN YOU TO ENJOY,**
> **WITHOUT FEAR OR CONDEMNATION!** For "perfect love casts out all
> fear," for **fear** hath **torment**, particularly sexual fears [which] can be
> physical **torture! I know**, because **I myself personally suffered for years**
> **the tortures of the demons of hell with their [profanity deleted] chur-**
> **chy attitudes towards sex** with which they had filled me!—And I don't
> want you to suffer, as I did.[34]

The previous quotation reveals yet another hallmark of Berg's teachings: profane, often X-rated language. Ironically, The Family still regards

Berg as a prime example of Christian love and godly leadership. The following quotations, which represent only a minuscule sampling of his warped teachings, show Berg to be anything but a Christian:

> [Sexual obscenity deleted] is no sin! It was <u>commanded</u> by God. . . . <u>THEY SAY YOU SHOULDN'T USE SUCH NAUGHTY WORDS</u> . . . But you <u>understand</u> it, don't you?[35] Just lookin' at you girls I can hardly keep my hands off you! The Lord gave us that hunger when we see you to want to get ahold of you & love you & kiss you & [sexual obscenity deleted] ya! PTL [Praise the Lord]![36]

During the formative years of The Family, Berg's sexual obsessions quickly led to his sanctioning of various activities that are explicitly prohibited by Scripture.[37] To date, members of The Family are still permitted to indulge in adultery and fornication, two practices that Berg had sanctioned as far back as the early 1970s:

> <u>I'M NOT SELFISH WITH MY WIVES, I GIVE THEM AWAY RIGHT AND LEFT</u> & share them with others who need help & need wives.[38] <u>WE BELIEVE IN SHARING</u> . . . in coming home and sleeping with the same mate nearly every night, but often after we've been out sleeping awhile with somebody else![39] We have a little orgy now & then, we don't publicise [sic] it or do it in front of reporters, although we have had it in front of a few guests! As long as it's all in the Family, why not?[40]

Berg justified sexual sharing by painting it as a mark of pure worship and dedication to God. His rationale was that true spiritual marriage meant a marriage of the whole Family, which worked itself out to mean that everyone should "share" everything, including husbands and wives:

> <u>GOD WILL HAVE NO OTHER GODS BEFORE HIM, NOT EVEN THE SANC-TITY OF MARRIAGE GOD! THE FAMILY MARRIAGE, IS THAT OF PUTTING THE LARGER FAMILY, THE WHOLE FAMILY, FIRST</u>, even above the last remaining vestige of private property, your husband or your wife![41]

Berg even taught that sex ("sharing") between children, as well as sex between children and adults, was acceptable. Incest, too, was encouraged:

**WE WANTED TO ADD A WORD ABOUT THE CHILDREN'S <u>SEX</u> & <u>LOVE LIFE</u>
TOO.** We have not really interfered. . . . Rubin [age 6] & Jonas [age 8 1/2]
both have their little lovers among other little sisters who visit sometimes.[42]

<u>I THINK THE TEENAGE YEARS WERE WHEN I NEEDED SEX THE MOST!</u> Isn't
it ridiculous though, that it's just at the age when you need sex the most
that it's the most forbidden? . . . I hope all of our young kids have plenty
of sex. I hope they won't have all those frustrations . . . from sex depri-
vation. . . . [W]hy did the <u>Lord</u> make you <u>able</u> to have <u>children</u> at the age
of 11, 12 & 13 if you weren't supposed to have <u>sex</u> then?[43]

<u>WHAT ABOUT INCEST?</u>. . . . [W]e'll just have to tell the kids that it's not
prohibited by God, but you'd better watch out. . . . <u>IT IS THE MOST DAN-
GEROUS FORM OF SEX & THE MOST PROHIBITED BY THE SYSTEM</u> [outside
The Family]! . . . The System & the Systemites are so absolutely crazy on
the subject. . . . [T]hat's just the way they are!—Insane! . . . <u>I'M TALKING
ABOUT NATURAL NORMAL GODLY LOVE AS MANIFESTED IN
SEX</u>, as far as I'm concerned for whomever!—There are no relationship
restrictions or age limitations in His Law of <u>Love</u>.[44]

The Family went so far as to produce a 1979 pictorial booklet entitled
My Little Fish, which demonstrated how sexual contact between adults and
children makes for the ideal family environment. Although the photographs appearing in the publication are of poor quality, they clearly show
toddlers engaging in sexual acts with each other. They also show a naked
adult female manually stimulating and orally copulating with a small boy.
The captions accompanying each picture extol the benefits of such activities.

Allegedly such practices are now forbidden. However, many cult
watchers, former members, and concerned citizens around the world
doubt that these activities have completely ceased because Berg's writings
clearly established them as expressions of their central, distinctive doctrine:
The Law of Love. Furthermore, a June 1991 letter printed and distributed
by The Family reveals that documents such as *My Little Fish* were purged
from the group's files only because opponents were using them to prove
their accusations of child abuse:

> To our ungodly enemies and vengeful false accusers, some of our per-
> fectly pure doctrines and views regarding God's Own natural & beau-

tiful sinless creation are very "defiled" & "impure" in their soiled minds! . . . [T]hey're so offended by some of our views . . . & publications & pictures, that they seem bent on using (misusing) them to try to substantiate their very false & malicious accusations against us that we abuse our own dear children! So for this reason, we are now initiating an extensive "purge" of our publications. Thank the Lord, most of our publications will come through this purge with only a few pages missing.[45]

In addition to special publications such as *My Little Fish*, there are the Mo Letters, which number well into the thousands. A majority of these are filled with licentious cartoon illustrations. Some of these depict an elderly, white-bearded Berg. As offensive as these illustrations are, they are not nearly as detestable as the countless pornographic video tapes made by The Family that contain heterosexual acts, lesbian encounters, masturbation, nude dances, orgies, and strip teases, some of which involve pre-pubescent girls as young as three and four years old. Throughout his term as leader of The Family, Berg often sent out directives concerning these tapes:

> CAMERAMAN . . . BE NOT AFRAID OF THEIR FACES. . . . Our kids' faces are their credentials! . . . You should seldom get further away than waist-up. . . . BE SURE NOT TO FOOLISHLY LABEL ANY OF THE TAPES themselves inside with such curiosity-arousing investigation-inspiring & perhaps even illegal titles such as "Love Tape" or "So & so strips" or any other sexy titles.[46]

One of the most controversial aspects of The Family's sex-oriented belief system was its evangelistic practice of "Flirty Fishing" (FFing), which amounted to little more than outright prostitution. Female members were instructed to go out into the community—e.g., to bars, nightclubs, the beach, or the park—and "convert" strangers by showing them Jesus' love through having sexual intercourse with them. Berg affectionately referred to the women who engaged in this activity as "hookers for Jesus."

FFing

FFing began in 1976 when Berg started teaching that by sexually giving themselves to strangers, his female disciples were actually showing Jesus' love:

THAT'S THE WHOLE BASIC DOCTRINE OF FFING, THAT SEX
PROVES LOVE. . . . [T]hese girls are willing to go to bed with these men to
prove they love them. . . . By [sexual obscenity deleted] '[e]m. . . . SEX PROVES
LOVE, TRUE LOVE!—TRUE LOVE IS PROVEN BY SEX! That's one of the major
ways to prove it, either by [sexual obscenity deleted] or dying. . . . That's
the whole idea of FFing, if by sex you can prove there is Love, thereby you
prove there is God, because God is Love. If you can prove to these men
through sex that you love them, therefore you prove that Love exists.[47]

Berg also likened FFing to self-sacrifice, saying that women who gave
themselves in bed to strangers were being "crucified" just like Jesus, who
lovingly gave Himself to the world by dying on the cross.[48] Time and again
this perverted doctrine was graphically illustrated in Mo Letters. Each
drawing would be accompanied by crude and offensive captions.

Even in 1976 when female COG members began catching sexually
transmitted diseases, Berg would not relent. He explained:

IF WE SUFFER DISEASES OR AFFLICTIONS OR INFIRMITIES AS A RESULT [of
women flirty-fishing], WE ARE SUFFERING FOR THEIR SINS [the sins of
non-members with whom the women are having sex], NOT OURS. We
are suffering for their sins as Jesus did for ours in order that we and they
might be saved. Hallelujah! Thank You Jesus![49]

FFing was widely practiced until 1987 when a Family member died of
AIDS. In 1997 The Family's Internet web site offered a statement about
FFing that provided an explanation as to why it was discontinued:

In 1976 . . . [Berg] contended that, in certain circumstances, it would be
acceptable for a Christian to have sexual relations with someone in an
effort to demonstrate a tangible manifestation of God's Love, thereby
helping them to come to a saving knowledge of Jesus Christ. This doctrine became known as "Flirty Fishing," a term that David adapted from
Jesus' admonition to His disciples to "follow Me, and I will make you
fishers of men" (Matthew 4:19). It was practiced by many Family members until 1987, when it was discontinued, largely due to the need to
spend more time in other forms of outreach.[50]

It is noteworthy that The Family nowhere admits that FFing was/is sinful. Instead, the group maintains that it stopped FFing in order to spend

more time evangelizing in other ways. Significantly, this statement goes on to positively present Berg's perverted biblical arguments *justifying* FFing, even though the spiritually and psychologically damaging practice is allegedly now banned:

> Would you do it for Jesus?—Then why not for others? "If a brother or sister be naked and destitute of daily food (including sex?), and one of you say unto them, 'Depart in peace, be ye warmed and filled'; notwithstanding ye give them not those things which are needful to the body (sex?), what doth it profit?"
>
> What better way to show them the Love of God than to do your best to supply their desperately hungry needs for love, fellowship, companionship, mental and spiritual communication, and physical needs such as food, clothing, shelter, warmth, affection, a tender loving kiss, a soft warm embrace, the healing touch of your loving hands, the comforting feeling of your body next to theirs—and yes, even sex if need be!
>
> What greater way could you show anyone your love than to give them your all in the bed of love? How much more can you show them the Love of God than to show them His Love to the uttermost through you? How much more love can you show them than this?
>
> There's no amount of love that could possibly be illegitimate to try to win a soul! There's no sin in love to begin with, and there's no "sin" so great that God would condemn you for it when it's done in love . . . because when it's love it can't be sin.
>
> The only price that's worth it is an immortal undying soul! That's the price we'd even go to bed for! The salvation of an eternal soul!—And that is worth it!
>
> The greatest need of man is love, so the greatest service to man is love! That's why FFing is such a service. It is the greatest, most sacrificial service that anyone can possibly give, outside of actually dying, because it is laying your life on the line. You are laying down your life or your wife for love, love of the Lord. Unselfish love! I'm not just talking about fleshly gratification, but for the love of someone, sacrificial love, even risky love, dangerous love![51]

The Family's presentation of these arguments seem to support accusations by former members who maintain that although FFing has *officially* ceased as a widespread practice, exceptions are routinely made if high government officials or wealthy individuals are interested in experiencing the group's version of "God's love." In a 1997 interview with London's *Sunday Telegraph Magazine*, a current member of The Family explained their views on sex in this way: "If someone is hungry you should feed them and if they are thirsty you should give them something to drink. . . . That is Christian charity. Father David teaches that if someone in our community needs sex, we can give it to them. The sexual urge is like water. You can't compress [sic] it."[52]

All You Need Is Love

The Family's sexual excesses have been, and continue to be, legitimized through Berg's two-fold teaching on salvation. He taught that because of Adam's disobedience in the Garden of Eden, everyone is a sinner who is "absolutely unable to attain to righteousness without the saving power of Jesus Christ."[53] Although this statement is true, Berg went on to couple it with a patently false teaching. He asserted that if salvation is indeed obtained entirely apart from works, then the only real "law" anyone needs to follow is Christ's "law of love," which in turn ended up meaning that "Christians" can do whatever they please as long as it is done in love:

> WE DO NOT HAVE TO KEEP THE TEN COMMANDMENTS! . . . We now only have to keep God's law of love. . . . We are totally, utterly free of the old Mosaic law. . . . [A]ll things are lawful to us in love, praise God! As long as it's done in love it keeps God's only Law of Love![54]

Adherence to this "Law of Love" quickly evolved into a license for sexual promiscuity; sex subsequently became the ultimate expression of "God's love." In fact, The Family began to teach that there existed absolutely no qualitative difference between fornication/adultery and God's love. It has even gone so far as to equate indulgence in sex with how Jesus laid down His life on the cross.

Such teachings directly contradict Paul the apostle, who in Romans 6:1–2 stated: "What shall we say, then? Are we to continue in sin that grace might increase? May it never be! How shall we who died to sin still live in it?" The apostle John penned a similar thought in 1 John 3:4–10:

> *Everyone who sins breaks the law; in fact, sin is lawlessness. But you know that he appeared so that he might take away our sins. And in him is no sin. No one*

who lives in him keeps on sinning. No one who continues to sin has either seen him or known him. Dear children, do not let anyone lead you astray. He who does what is right is righteous, just as he is righteous. He who does what is sinful is of the devil, because the devil has been sinning from the beginning. The reason the Son of God appeared was to destroy the devil's work. No one who is born of God will continue to sin, because God's seed remains in him; he cannot sin because he has been born of God. This is how we know who the children of God are and who the children of the devil are.

Although the meaning of this passage is fairly plain, it ultimately says little to members of The Family because they understand "sins" only in terms of acts that Berg identified as being against the "Law of Love." According to Berg, "sins" fall into only two categories: 1) things that someone may *believe* in their mind to be sinful; and 2) anything Berg has explicitly called sinful. As we have seen, numerous sexual sins ended up being justified in The Family. Consider the following rationalization for committing adultery with prospective converts involving the "Law of Love":

GOD'S ONLY LAW IS LOVE, and if what you're doing is in love and you're not hurting any innocent party, then it is perfectly legal for you ... now hurting guilty parties, that's something we can't avoid. (... SAY A MAN WAS MAKING LOVE WITH ONE OF US AND HIS WIFE HADN'T GIVEN HIM THE LOVE THAT WE CAN GIVE HIM ... she's not innocent, she's guilty ...). . . . So if she isn't giving him love then it's all right if he gets it from somewhere else) And it's her own fault and she's the guilty party.[55]

Again, the only "sins" that have ever been recognized by The Family are those deeds that Berg labeled as such. As he put it: "IF YOU PERSIST IN YOUR DEFIANT & FLAGRANT DISOBEDIENCE TO GOD & HIS WORD & ME . . . you should then be cast out of the Home & the Family."[56] This statement is only one example of the way in which Berg placed himself on par with God. Almost from the very beginning of his so-called ministry, he claimed divine authority over his flock. By convincing them that he was God's mouthpiece, he was able to mold his group into one of the most doctrinally heretical and socially perverse religious groups in contemporary society.

ACCORDING TO THE BIBLE

It is not difficult to find countless passages in Scripture condemning the many sexual sins that at one time or another have been, and continue to be, practiced by The Family: adultery (Ex. 20:14; Deut. 5:18; Prov. 6:24–35; Mal. 3:5; Matt. 15:19; Rom. 13:9–10; 1 Cor. 6:9, 15-16); fornication and sexual immorality (Matt. 5:28; 15:19; Rom. 1:26-27; 13:13; 1 Cor. 6:9; 7:2); lust (Matt. 5:27–28, 32; 1 Thess. 4:5; 1 John 2:16); incest (Lev. 18, 20; Ezek. 22:11; 1 Cor. 5:1–2); religious prostitution/harlotry (Lev. 19:29; 21:9; Deut. 23:17; Isa. 4:12-14); and profane/obscene speech (Phil. 4:8; Col. 3:8; 4:6; Titus 2:8).

Perhaps the most baffling aspect of The Family is how its members can continue to call themselves Christians while engaging in such sinful behavior. Also puzzling is how The Family's sexual escapades could be molded into a religious belief system that includes a pseudo-Christian theology, Christology, soteriology, and eschatology. To understand these issues, our doctrinal survey of The Family must begin with its view of Berg, who touted himself as God's end-time prophet in possession of truth that eclipsed the authority of the Bible.

He continuously encouraged obedience to him, while discouraging reliance on Scripture, saying: "<u>YOU HAVE GOT TO BELIEVE IN THE LORD AND IN ME</u>, that I am a <u>new</u> prophet of a <u>new</u> day of a whole lot of <u>new</u> things that Paul [the apostle] never even thought about!"[57] In one Mo Letter, Berg reproduced what he purported to be a "word" from the Lord: "'He that doesn't receive David [Berg] doesn't receive Me', the Lord said! (Tongues:) 'Blessed are the words & blessed is the tongue that I have given David!'"[58] He went so far as to state that his Mo Letters, although he physically wrote them, were actually being authored by "God by His Spirit."[59]

Furthermore, Berg maintained that the Bible was corrupt and unreliable and that only he was able to impart truth to persons wanting to follow God. He even taught that many parts of the Bible have become irrelevant for today's society. Consequently, God had to impart new truths not contained in Scripture. Berg, of course, claimed that he was the chosen vessel through which these so-called truths were to be given:

> **[S]ome of the parts of the Bible are no longer up to date!** . . . They're the rules God's people used to live by, not the rules they're supposed to live

by today![60] A LOT OF THINGS THAT PAUL SAID WERE RIGHT FOR HIS TIME AND HIS DAY, BUT THEY DON'T NECESSARILY BIND US TODAY.[61]

IT'S A DAMNABLE DOCTRINE OF CHURCH DEVILS TO CONFINE ALL THE TRUTH AND REVELATIONS OF GOD strictly to the Bible. . . . WHAT GOD HAS GIVEN ME is filling in some of the remaining details of Biblical truth.[62] If God has spoken at all and shown me these things at all. . . . it is His Words for today and it supersedes anything else that has ever been given, if it is different.[63]

Berg believed himself to be a direct channel to God no matter what he did. On more than one occasion he boasted that drunkenness actually brought him closer to the Lord. Berg even encouraged his flock to follow his example:

WHEN I GET DRUNK I YIELD TO GOD'S SPIRIT. . . . if you get intoxicated, why, it just makes you even more free in the spirit.[64]

DON'T YOU UNDERSTAND? WINE OPENS THE GATE OF REVELATION! And if you give me a little more wine, I give you a lot more revelation. . . . I have to have wine to open my mouth to give you some more revelation.[65]

Drunkenness, of course, is condemned in the Bible (Rom. 13:13; Gal. 5:21). But Berg knew this and in fact warned his devotees that "churchy" people would object. *Mo Letter 635* reads: "SOME OF THESE PEOPLE HAVE HAD THEIR RESERVATIONS AND THEIR DOUBTS . . . especially those of strong churchy Biblical backgrounds. Therefore some of the things that I have said are going to raise questions in their minds and I'm sure the Devil is going to supply them with lots of Scriptures and say, 'Well now, but, the Bible says so and so.'"[66] In reality, God has condemned Berg and The Family.

Holy Spirit (of Love)

Although Berg occasionally depicted God as being a "part" of all creation,[67] his more common teaching was that there existed three completely separate divine beings known as the Father, Mother (Holy Ghost), and Son. These deities comprised Berg's version of the Trinity,[68] explicitly rejecting the orthodox Christian concept of the Trinity: "I don't even believe in the Trinity. You can't find that word in the Bible. . . . I believe in the Father and I believe in the Son, Jesus, and I believe in the Holy Ghost."[69]

As with most of The Family's doctrines, their concept of God revolves around sex. According to Berg's perverted theology, all three of his celestial deities are sexually active, especially God the Father and "His Mate," the Holy Spirit/Ghost.[70] Berg wrote: "God has such thrills and intoxications of the Spirit in store for you," going on to promise full intimacy with a naked God in a spiritual orgy.[71] Predictably, Berg was particularly interested in making lengthy comments to his followers about the Holy Spirit. As always, his teachings were accompanied by an endless series of lewd illustrations.

> I ALWAYS DID THINK OF GOD AS OUR HEAVENLY FATHER AND HIS SPIRIT OF LOVE AS OUR HEAVENLY MOTHER. . . . His beautiful Holy Spirit, God's Spirit-Queen of Love. . . . the Heavenly Lover and Mother-God, the Queen of Love.[72]

Berg went so far as to allege that during a "spiritual" experience he went to heaven and had sex with the Holy Ghost/Mother.[73]

Scripture, of course, nowhere supports Berg's contention that the Holy Spirit is a promiscuous love goddess.

Occultism

In addition to preaching heretical doctrines, The Family also promotes occultism, which Berg introduced in 1970 when he received a "spirit helper" named Abrahim. This entity was allegedly sent by God to be his guardian angel/spirit guide. Berg claimed that it eventually began taking possession of him:

> PEOPLE DO COME BACK & ARE HELPFUL TO SOMEONE, LIKE ABRAHIM IS TO ME. He is with me all the time, virtually incarnated in me. . . . I never go any place without him. He travels with me. . . . I'm his vehicle now just like his body was before.[74]

According to Berg, there exist countless spirits (gods/goddesses) who are more than willing to guide members of The Family through life. It did not take long for him to begin telling his followers to summon these spirits and yield themselves to being possessed by them. He maintained that "Christians" simply needed to make their minds go blank and give over their bodies.[75] Berg soon blended spirit possession with sex, claiming that it was actually possible to have sex with spiritual entities.[76] He encouraged his female followers to have sex with male spirits, while male members of The Family were encouraged to have sex with female spirits.[77]

Such activity is commonly discussed in occult literature that examines the lore surrounding the existence of incubi (male spirits) and succubi (female spirits). These demonic entities are said to take physical form in order to have sexual intercourse with humans. According to the *Dictionary of Mysticism and the Occult*, the incubus is a "male spirit or demon believed to visit women during the night and subject them to sexual depravity, lust, and terrifying nightmares. . . . The female equivalent of the incubus is the succubus."[78] Involvement with occultism is but one more reason why The Family remains a non-Christian religious group that promises to bring great spiritual, emotional, and psychological harm to persons who participate in its deeds of darkness and depravity.

WHAT'S THE ATTRACTION?

As we have seen, The Family is heretical and objectionable on numerous levels. Nevertheless, it continues to draw many young people. One of its main attractions is obviously the sex that is available in the group. But this is not the group's only appeal. Persons sincerely looking for spiritual truth can easily be enticed into The Family because of the extremely "Christian" image it presents to the general public. On the surface it appears thoroughly evangelical. Its official *Statement of Beliefs* is carefully worded to sound orthodox:

> We are a Bible-based Christian fellowship. . . . We believe in the one true God. . . . We affirm that "God is a Spirit" (John 4:24) and that "God is love" (1 John 4:8), and that "God so loved the world that He gave His only begotten Son [Jesus Christ]." . . . Salvation is God's free gift to all who will simply confess that they are in need of His mercy and forgiveness, and will believe on and personally receive His Son, Jesus Christ, into their hearts.[79]

This Christian-sounding presentation of The Family has no doubt led unsuspecting young people with little or no biblical training into the group. They are then lured deeper into the organization by constant misinterpretation of the Bible coupled with a living environment that overtly appeals to their carnal nature. An unbeliever or a very young Christian could easily mistake their emotional and physical feelings with spirituality. This in turn could place them on the long road of sin and deception from which they may never return, as was the case with Arnaldo Padilla.

There is also a zealous dedication present in members of The Family. They firmly hold to their convictions, earnestly preach their message, and always offer intense "love" to spiritual truth seekers. All of these traits of The Family make it not only an easy group to fall into, but a very difficult one from which to emerge.

RECOMMENDED READING

Davis, Deborah. *The Children of God: The Inside Story* (Grand Rapids, MI: Zondervan, 1984).

Enroth, Ron. "Children of God: An Interview with Bill and Deborah (Linda Berg) Davis," *Eternity*, July/August 1984, 24–29.

Ericson, Edward E. and Paul MacPherson, "The Deceptions of the Children of God," *Christianity Today*, July 20, 1973, 14-23.

Gordon, Ruth. *Children of Darkness* (Wheaton, IL: Tyndale, 1988).

Hopkins, Joseph M. "The Children of God: Disciples of Deception," *Christianity Today*, February 18, 1977, 18-23.

Kent, Stephen A. "Lustful Prophet: A Psychosexual Historical Study of the Children of God's Leader, David Berg," *Cultic Studies Journal*, vol. 11, no. 2 (1994), 135–188. (Available from AFF, P.O. Box 2265, Bonita Springs, FL 33959.)

Moore, Evan. "Sex in the Name of God," *Houston Chronicle*, February 4, 1990, 1A, 15A.

Muir, Hugh. "Family Values," (London) *Sunday Telegraph Magazine*, January 5, 1997, 15–17.

Pement, Eric. "Built on a Lie," *Cornerstone*, vol. 11, no. 63, 4–6, 8.

Van Zandt, David E. *Living in the Children of God* (Princeton, NJ: Princeton University Press, 1991).

MORMONISM
THROUGH THE LOOKING GLASS

*[The Lord] will make me be god to you in His stead, and the Elders
to be [a] mouth[piece] for me; and if you don't like it, you must
lump it. . . . I have more to boast of than ever any man had. I am
the only man that has ever been able to keep a whole church together
since the days of Adam. . . . Neither Paul, John, Peter, nor Jesus
ever did it. I boast that no man ever did such a work as I.*

JOSEPH SMITH,
FOUNDER OF MORMONISM[1]

Jerald Tanner and Sandra McGee were descended from families that had
held prestigious positions within the Mormon community. Jerald's great-
great-grandfather, John Tanner, had joined Mormonism just two years after
the church's 1830 founding as one of its wealthiest early pioneers. In fact,
it was John's financial contributions to the fledgling sect that enabled first-
generation Mormons to build a temple in Kirtland, Ohio (1836). Sandra's
great-great-grandfather was the famous Brigham Young, the Mormon
prophet who established Salt Lake City after leading thousands of followers from the Midwest to the Great Salt Lake Basin in Utah. Young was also
the second president of the church, successor to Joseph Smith,
Mormonism's founder.

Although Jerald and Sandra had been steeped in Mormonism for many
years, both of them eventually began having serious doubts about their
faith. Jerald was the first to question his beliefs. While still a teenager, he
was presented with *An Address to All Believers in Christ*, an 1887 booklet
written by David Whitmer, an early companion of Joseph Smith. Whitmer
charged Smith with altering the revelations contained in the *Doctrine &*

Covenants—one of the church's books of scripture—so that he and other Mormon leaders could pursue their own selfish desires:

> In the winter of 1834 they [Mormon leaders] saw that some of the revelations in the Book of Commandments *had to be changed*, because the heads of the church had gone too far, and had done things in which they had already gone ahead of some the former revelations. So the book of "Doctrine and Covenants" was printed in 1835, and some of the revelations changed [from when they were first printed in the Book of Commandments in 1833] and added to.[2]

Jerald could not, would not believe Whitmer's charges. He threw the book down in disgust. Later, however, he traveled to Independence, Missouri, to see an original copy of the 1833 *Book of Commandments* for himself. When he compared it to a modern copy of the *Doctrine & Covenants* he realized his worst fears: Whitmer had told the truth; the revelations had indeed been changed. This new information prompted Jerald to embark on an intensive examination of Mormon history. With each passing day he uncovered more and more evidence that the church he firmly believed to be the "only true church" was actually in error. While in Independence, he also met a group of Christians who demonstrated something Jerald had never before experienced:

> They got me thinking about Christianity. Their lives were different than mine. I knew they had something that I didn't have—a reality, a love, a peace in their lives. They all were bearing testimony [about] what the Lord did for them, not what a "church" did. It impressed me.

The Mormon Church had never stressed to Jerald his need for a Savior but instead taught him that gaining eternal life was primarily a result of leading a good life. He was given a great deal of information about good morals and Joseph Smith's life, but precious little about Christ. But thanks to the testimony of Jerald's new Christian friends, he gradually came to realize that he was a sinner in need of forgiveness and responded by accepting Jesus Christ as his personal Lord and Savior.

Meanwhile, Sandra was having her own struggles with Mormonism, especially its positive stand on polygamy as a God-ordained practice and the subtle racism underlying many of its doctrines. Her uncertainties only intensified when she enrolled in the Mormon Institute of Religion after graduating from high school:

> I started asking questions in class to answer my doubts. One day my teacher took me aside and told me to stop asking questions in class. There was a girl attending the class who was thinking of joining the church. I was disturbing her with my questions. My attempt to find answers to my questions had been silenced.

Shortly after this experience Sandra met Jerald, and together they began studying the Bible. Sandra immediately noticed several contradictions between Mormonism and Christianity. Gradually she also started seeing her great-great-grandfather, Brigham Young, in an altogether different light. He was not the holy prophet of God she had always thought him to be but was an adulterous, violent, and dictatorial leader who promoted the doctrine of blood atonement, which teaches that some sins were not dealt with through Christ's death. For these sins, said Young, a person must be executed and have his or her own blood spilled.[3] Sandra was shocked.

Amid such discoveries Sandra and Jerald were married. Not long afterward, Sandra began understanding that everyone was a sinner in need of forgiveness, forgiveness that could only be obtained through faith in the person and work of Jesus Christ. The full realization of this truth did not fill her heart and mind until early one morning when she happened to tune into a Christian radio station:

> A minister was preaching on the great love of God and the mercy offered to us through Jesus Christ. Nothing ever struck me with such force. I opened my heart to God and received Christ as my savior. The Holy Spirit flooded my soul with such joy that I wept for more than an hour.

When they moved to Salt Lake City in 1960, they had no intention of sharing their findings with the predominantly Mormon population of the city. But both of them soon felt obliged to reveal to the public all the information that the Mormon hierarchy had been suppressing for years. High-ranking Mormon official LeGrand Richards warned them, "Don't start anything against this church." Jerald and Sandra knew that they had to obey God rather than man, and they started a full-time ministry—Utah

Lighthouse Ministry—dedicated to spreading the truth about Mormon doctrine and history.

As of 1997, countless Mormons had become Christians because of the Tanners' research. Sandra says that she and Jerald receive letters and phone calls every week from people who have left the church after reading their materials:

> A lot of them are recent converts [to Mormonism] within the last year or two. They go into Mormonism quickly without understanding its doctrine or not knowing its history. Then someone shows them some of our research and the person feels he has been deceived. He has not been given a proper presentation of what he was joining.

Tragically, most of these converts come from nominal Christian backgrounds. This is a trend that the Tanners have dedicated themselves to stopping. "If Christians were more aware of Mormonism and its teachings, it couldn't have the growth rate it does," Jerald says. "We're trying to provide information that will explain Mormonism." The fifty-plus books and pamphlets that the Tanners have produced over the past several decades clearly show that in their goal to spread truth, they have been quite successful.[4]

HOW IT ALL BEGAN

The Church of Jesus Christ of Latter-day Saints (LDS)—commonly referred to as Mormonism—was founded in 1830 by Joseph Smith, Jr. (1805–1844). He established his church on the premise that Christendom had completely fallen away from the true Gospel of Jesus Christ and had substituted the good news of salvation with satanically-inspired doctrines of men. Smith additionally maintained that he had been personally chosen by God to be humanity's latter-day prophet, a chosen vessel divinely ordained to restore the "lost" Gospel to the earth. He alone possessed the pure teachings of Christ, and salvation could only be obtained by becoming one of his followers.

Mormonism's history actually begins ten years earlier, when Smith was fourteen years old and living in Manchester, New York, a small village near the city of Palmyra. According to Smith's memoirs, which still serve as the

LDS church's authoritative account of Mormonism's founding, the year 1820 brought a great religious revival to the area where Smith lived. This "unusual excitement on the subject of religion" led him to retreat to a secluded spot in the woods to pray about which Christian sect he should join. "I kneeled down and began to offer up the desires of my heart to God," Smith would later write. "I had scarcely done so, when immediately I was seized upon by some power . . . . Thick darkness gathered about me, and it seemed to me for a time as if I were doomed to sudden destruction."[5]

Just as Smith was about to abandon himself to "destruction—not to an imaginary ruin, but to the power of some actual being from the unseen world"—a most unexpected event took place: God the Father and Jesus Christ physically appeared and rescued him from the clutches of the dark power.[6] After regaining his composure, Smith asked these "Personages" standing in the air above him to identify the Christian sect that was doctrinally correct so that he would know which one to join. He was told that he "must join none of them, for they were all wrong." The account continues:

> The Personage who addressed me said that all their creeds were an abomination in his sight; that those professors were all corrupt; that: "they draw near to me with their lips, but their hearts are far from me, they teach for doctrines the commandments of men, having a form of godliness, but they deny the power thereof." He again forbade me to join any of them.[7]

For the next three years Smith related his vision and God's message to various townspeople. The local populace allegedly responded with "bitter persecution." This, however, only served to strengthen his testimony. Then, on September 21, 1823, Smith reportedly had a second vision, during which an angel named Moroni appeared to him. The heavenly being of light revealed to Joseph that there was a book of golden plates buried in a hillside located just beyond the city limits of Manchester. Moroni further told Smith that these plates were inscribed with an account of the ancient inhabitants of the Americas. The plates were also said to contain "the fulness of the everlasting gospel," which Jesus Himself had preached to this continent's ancient inhabitants.[8]

During the four years following Moroni's initial visit, Smith claimed that he received even more visitations from the spirit world. Through these encounters he became spiritually seasoned and in 1827 was finally allowed to retrieve the golden plates from their resting place. Upon examining them, he claimed that their etchings were "Reformed Egyptian" characters. He then "translated" them by use of a peep stone, or "seer" stone, that was about the size and shape of an egg, only more flat, and "chocolate" in color. The end result was the *Book of Mormon* (BOM), which is the foundational religious text for the LDS Church. David Whitmer, in *An Address to All Believers in Christ*, described in great detail how Smith produced this text:

> Smith would put the seer stone into a hat, and put his face in the hat, drawing it closely around his face to exclude the light; and in the darkness the spiritual light would shine. A piece of something resembling parchment would appear [to Joseph], and on that appeared the writing [from the plates]. One character at a time would appear, and under it was the interpretation in English. Brother Joseph would read off the English to Oliver Cowdery, who was his principle [sic?] scribe, and when it was written down and repeated to Brother Joseph to see if it was correct, then it would disappear, and another character with the interpretation would appear.[9]

Whitmer's testimony regarding these events are supported by several other witnesses, including Smith's own wife, Emma Hale-Smith, her father, Isaac Hale, and Mormon leader Martin Harris, who served for a short time as Smith's scribe.[10] Moreover, many LDS leaders (e.g., apostles George Q. Cannon, John Widtsoe, and Bruce McConkie)[11] and Mormon scholars (e.g., B. H. Roberts and Arch S. Reynolds)[12] have admitted that Smith did indeed use a seer stone to translate the characters. In fact, in his 1956 book *Doctrines of Salvation* (vol. 3), tenth Mormon president Joseph Fielding Smith (1876–1972)—the grandnephew of Joseph Smith—revealed that this same seer stone "is now in the possession of the Church."[13]

Joseph the Occultist

Using a seer stone to gather otherwise unobtainable information is known as scrying, an occult practice that falls into the broader category of divination, which is clearly condemned in Scripture (Deut. 18:9–12; Jer. 27:9; Ezek. 13:9). Persons using this form of divination gaze at a shiny or polished surface "to induce a trance-state in which scenes, people, words, or images appear as part of a psychic communication."[14] A popular modern-day witch, Doreen Valiente, explains that scrying is named after the word *descry*, which originally meant "to reveal." Although the term is mostly used in reference to crystal ball gazing, scrying "embraces all forms of developing clairvoyance by gazing at or into some object. . . . The practice of scrying is common to magicians of all ages and countries. . . . [I]t is still as popular with contemporary witches as it was long ago."[15]

Like many persons living in rural America during the nineteenth century, Smith regularly practiced scrying and coupled it with working as a "money-digger"—i.e., someone who, for a fee, would use divination to find buried treasure. Such activity was illegal because money-diggers habitually bilked clients out of hard-earned cash by promising to find them large caches of treasure. But anti-money-digging laws were usually ignored because punishment for such activity was mild. Interestingly, Smith was convicted in 1826 for "glass-looking" (yet another term used to describe Smith's chosen form of divination). The following account of his preliminary hearing appeared in an 1873 issue of *Fraser's Magazine*. It includes an admission of guilt by Smith, as well as the sworn statements of witnesses Josiah Stowel, Arad Stowel, and Jonathan Thompson:

STATE OF NEW YORK v. JOSEPH SMITH.

Warrant issued upon written complaint upon oath of Peter G. Bridgeman, who informed that one Joseph Smith of Bainbridge was a disorderly person and an impostor. Prisoner [Smith] brought before Court March 20, 1826. Prisoner examined: says that . . . . he had a certain stone which he had occasionally looked at to determine where hidden treasures in the bowels of the earth were; that he professed to tell in this manner where gold mines were a distance under ground, and had looked for Mr. Stowel several times, and had informed him where he could find these treasures, and Mr. Stowel had been engaged in digging for them. That at Palmyra he pretended to tell by looking at this stone where coined money was buried in Pennsylvania, and while at Palmyra had ascertained in that way where lost property was of various kinds, that he had occasionally been in the habit of looking through this stone to find lost property for three years, but of late had pretty much given it up on account of its injuring his health, especially his eyes, making them sore. . . . [Josiah Stowel] says that prisoner had been at his house something like five months . . . that he pretended to have skill of telling where hidden treasures in the earth were by means of looking through a certain stone; that prisoner had looked for him sometimes; once to tell him about money buried in Bend Mountain in Pennsylvania, once for gold on Monument Hill, and once for a salt spring; and . . . . that prisoner [i.e., Smith] had told by means of this stone where a Mr. Bacon had buried money; that he and prisoner had been in search of it. . . . Arad Stowel says that he went to see whether prisoner could convince him that he possessed the skill he professed to have, upon which prisoner laid a book upon a white cloth, and proposed looking through another stone which was white and transparent, hold the stone to the candle, turn his head to book, and read. The deception appeared so palpable that witness went off disgusted. . . . Prisoner pretended to him that he could discover objects at a distance by holding this white stone to the sun or candle; that prisoner rather declined looking into a hat at his dark coloured stone, as he said that it hurt his eyes. Jonathan Thompson says that prisoner was requested to look for chest of money; did look, and pretended to know where it was. . . . Thompson says that he believes in the prisoner's professed skill.

And therefore the Court find the Defendant guilty. Costs: Warrant, 19c. Complaint upon oath, 25 1/2 c. Seven witnesses, 87 V2 c. Recognisances, 25c.

Mittimus. lc. Recognisances of witnesses, 75c. Supoena, 18c.—$2.68.[16]

For many years Mormons labeled as a fabrication this 1873 reprint of the 1826 court record. LDS apostle John Widtsoe stated: "This alleged court record . . . seems to be a literary attempt of an enemy to ridicule Joseph Smith. . . . There is no existing proof that such a trial was ever held."[17] Mormon scholar Francis Kirkham agreed:

A careful study of all facts regarding this alleged confession of Joseph Smith in a court of law that he had used a seer stone to find hidden treasure for purposes of fraud, must come to the conclusion that no such record was ever made, and therefore, is not in existence. . . . [T]here is no evidence to prove one was ever made in which he confessed in a justice of the peace court that he had used a seer stone to find hidden treasures for purposes of fraud and deception.[18]

For several years such arguments held some degree of merit. After all, the hearing record in *Fraser's Magazine* was published forty-seven years after the fact. But then in 1971, religion researcher Wesley P. Walters made one of the most important LDS-related discoveries of the modern era. He was searching through court records stored in the basement of the old county jail located near Bainbridge, New York (the home of Smith during his glass-looking trial) when he discovered two cardboard boxes that had been shoved against a wall in a darkened corner of the room.

The boxes contained bundles of water-damaged and mildewed court bills dating back to the early 1800s. In the 1826 bundle he found several bills showing the court costs of a Justice Albert Neely. One of the hearings was for "Joseph Smith the Glass Looker." The judge's charges, $2.68, exactly matched the figure given for court costs in *Fraser's Magazine*. The date was also the same: March 20, 1826. This long-forgotten document provided indisputable proof that Joseph Smith was defrauding various persons by telling them that he could find buried treasure via "glass-looking." The relevant section of this invaluable document is herein reproduced:

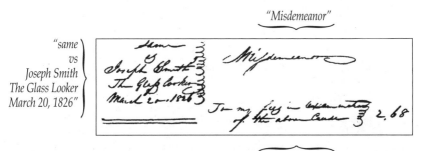

In 1826, when the letter "s" was repeated in a word such as "glass," the two consonants appeared as a "p." This can clearly be seen in the bill for Joseph Smith's trial. As stated in the court record published by Fraser's Magazine, Judge Neely's costs amounted to $2.68.

Mormon authorities were quick to call this document a forgery but were eventually forced to accept it as genuine. LDS Church historian Leonard J. Arrington admitted that the bill was indeed drawn up by the local judge and that it referred "to Smith as a 'glass looker' (one who, by peering through a glass stone, could see things not discernible by the natural eye). The bills class the offense as a misdemeanor and indicate that at least twelve witnesses were served subpoenas."[19]

Before Neely's bill was found, Mormon scholar Dr. Hugh Nibley wrote a significant observation regarding the 1873 *Fraser's Magazine* court record of Smith's glass-looking hearing: "[I]f this court record is authentic it is the most damning evidence in existence against Joseph Smith. [It would be] the most devastating blow to Smith ever delivered."[20] LDS scholar Francis Kirkham made a similar observation:

> If any evidence had been in existence that Joseph Smith had used a seer stone for fraud and deception, and especially had he made this confession in a court of law as early as 1826, or four years before the Book of Mormon was printed, and this confession was in a court record, it would have been impossible for him to have organized the restored Church.[21]

Since the authentication of Walters's find, however, Mormons have become conspicuously silent. LDS authorities have also tried to avoid discussing the 1 9/16 inch in diameter magic medallion made of silver that was found in Smith's pocket after he was murdered. This "Jupiter Talisman" was kept by Joseph's widow and passed down through generations until it was purchased by a private collector and transferred to Utah to be housed in the Wilford C. Wood Collection.

Surprisingly, it was a Mormon scholar—Dr. Reed Durham, director of

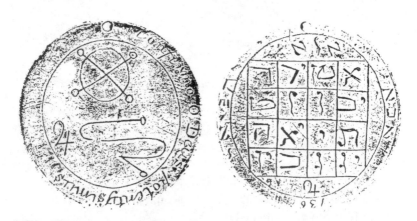

Both sides of Joseph Smith's magical talisman. The Jupiter Table (right) contains Hebrew letters, each of which has a corresponding numerical value. These numerical values, when added together in any direction, give the same total: 34. The total of the four columns is 136, which according to Amulets and Superstitions, written by Egyptologist E. A. Walls Budge, is "the number for the spirit and Demon of the planet" (p. 394). The opposite side (left) contains various magical symbols including the astrological sign for the planet Jupiter, a cross for the spirit of Jupiter, and a symbol that stands for the orbital path of Jupiter.

the LDS Institute of Religion at the University of Utah and president of the Mormon History Association—who correctly identified the talisman. Mormons had previously called the object the "Masonic jewel of the Prophet Joseph Smith." Durham, too, believed it to be Masonic in nature until he found a picture and explanation of it in *The Magus*, an 1801 magic book written by Francis Barrett, a professor of occult philosophy in London.[22] Dr. Durham, not realizing the implications of such a discovery, announced his find during an address to the Mormon History Association on April 20, 1974:

> All available evidence suggests that Joseph Smith the Prophet possessed a magical Masonic medallion, or talisman, which he worked during his lifetime. . . . [It] can now be identified as a Jupiter talisman. . . . The characters on the talisman are primarily Hebrew, but there is one inscription in Latin. . . . [O]n the side over to the right is a Hebrew word which means "Abbah," which means father. . . . [Look at] the other side of the talisman and you will see the Latin phrase, "Cantermo odeus potentisimus" (not at all correctly written). It's lousy Latin, but probably means, perhaps, "Confirm, O God, who is all powerful"; or "Almighty God confirm me, or uphold me, or support me." It is not accurately grammatical, but that is the term on the medallion or talisman. . . . The purpose of the Table of Jupiter in talismanic magic was to be able to call upon celestial intelligences, assigned to the particular talisman, to assist one in all endeavors. . . . When properly invoked, with Jupiter being very powerful and ruling in the heavens, these intelligences—by the power of an ancient magic—guaranteed to the possessor of this talisman the gain of riches, and favor, and power, and love and peace; and to confirm honors, and dignities, and councils. Talismatic magic further declared that any one who works skillfully with this Jupiter Table would obtain the power of stimulating anyone to offer his love to the possessor of the talisman, whether from a friend, brother, relative, or even any female.[23]

Arthur E. Waite, renowned scholar of occultism, explains in *The Occult Sciences* (1891) that the Talisman of Jupiter is kept in order to "attract to the wearer the benevolence and sympathy of everyone. It averts anxieties, favours honourable enterprises, and augments well-being in proportion to social condition. It is [also] a protection against unforeseen accidents, and the perils of a violent death."[24]

Hyrum Smith—Joseph's brother—also practiced magic. His twentieth-century descendants still possess various ceremonial magic items that were owned and used in magic rituals by both Hyrum and Joseph. These include three parchments and a ten-inch dagger, each of which is covered with magical symbols. The dagger, for instance, has the sigil (i.e., seal) of Mars etched on it. According to the *Encyclopedia of Occultism and Parapsychology*, such signs are like "signatures of gods and other supernatural entities, and the inscribing of such sigils evokes the entity which they symbolize."[25] The *Dictionary of Mysticism and the Occult* reveals that Mars, the god of war, was one of the most notable of all Roman gods, along with none other than Jupiter. Mars "was the personification of violent or hostile acts, aggression, and strong willpower."[26]

Hyrum's three parchments are inscribed with numerous sigils, as well as with ceremonial magic symbols and signs associated with witchcraft. Especially interesting is his "Holiness to the Lord" parchment. Among its many inscriptions are two circular "pentacles": one in the upper right-hand corner and one in the lower left-hand corner. These can clearly be seen in the following photographic reproduction.

Both pentacles appear in various books on magic, including Reginald Scot's *The Discoverie of Witchcraft*, first published in 1584 and reprinted in 1971. The full meaning of these two symbols remains unclear. However, insight into their supposed powers can be gleaned from a message that is

One of three magical parchments owned by Hyrum Smith and used in magic rituals he performed with his brother Joseph. the item is referred to as Hyrum's "Holiness to the Lord" parchment because those words are inscribed along its borders.

printed beneath one of the pentacles in Scot's book (p. 401): "Whoso beareth this sign about him, all spirits shall do him homage."[27] Unfortunately, most Mormons do not know about these artifacts and continue to view Smith as God's hand-picked prophet who restored the true Gospel that Christianity had "lost" by the 1800s.

1830–1844

Four years after his Bainbridge hearing, Smith founded the LDS Church. Although his group rapidly grew, it soon came into conflict with neighboring communities due to its many controversial doctrines. For example, Smith and fellow Mormons advocated polygamy, also known as "plural marriage." This was justified through a July 12, 1843 revelation from God. Mormon polygamy continued unabated until 1890, when the U.S. government forced the church to abandon it. Contemporary Mormons still consider polygamy a righteous lifestyle that they foresee themselves resuming in the future.[28]

Smith and his followers also were very militant. In fact, Smith raised a private army with which he tried to forcibly regain property that had been lost in 1838 by Mormon settlers in Missouri. The state militia, however, put down Smith's efforts and exiled the entire Mormon population, which moved to Illinois and founded the city of Nauvoo, where Smith organized the Nauvoo Legion and proclaimed himself Lieutenant-General. As the city grew, so did the Mormon army. In *No Man Knows My History*, Fawn Brodie makes the following observations:

> Few visitors to Nauvoo . . . had any idea of the potentialities of the Mormon movement. But many of them were troubled by the unmistakable military atmosphere that pervaded the city. . . . Every able-bodied man between eighteen and forty-five was compelled to join [the Legion], and heavy fines were imposed for failure to appear at parade. . . . Joseph requested—and received—from Governor Carlin the commission of lieutenant-general and thereafter frequently jested about his outranking every military officer in the United States. . . . His uniform was smartly designed: . . . On his hip he carried a sword and two big horse-pistols. Delighting in the pomp and splendor of parades, he called out the Legion on every possible occasion, marching at the head on his magnificent black stallion, Charlie.[29]

By 1842 Smith's Legion was approximately 2,000 soldiers strong, and Nauvoo had become a fully militarized city where terms such as Colonel and Captain were often used in place of more religious titles such as Brother and Elder. This sizable force of fighting men made non-Mormons living nearby rather nervous. Consider this excerpt from the July 21, 1841 issue of the *Warsaw Signal*, a local newspaper:

> How military these people are becoming! Every thing they say or do seems to breathe the spirit of military tactics. Their prophet appears, on all great occasions, in his splendid regimental dress, signs his name Lieut. General, and more titles are to be found in the Nauvoo Legion, than any one book on military tactics can produce. . . . Truly, fighting must be a part of the creed of these Saints![30]

Mormons were seen as extremely threatening on the frontiers of nineteenth-century America. LDS writer Kenneth W. Godfrey has noted that Americans were for the most part opposed to large standing armies: "Thus, many citizens of Illinois viewed with abhorrence the growing might of the Nauvoo Legion. Each muster, parade, or mock battle caused speculation regarding the ultimate design of its leaders. . . . Citizens living in Missouri were especially fearful that the Mormons would assault their homes and cities in retribution for the losses they had suffered in that state in 1837 and 1838."[31]

The situation was worsened by Smith's reputation as a swindler and con man who had previously been involved in illegal banking and counterfeiting. In 1836 he and other Mormon leaders established a Bank in Kirtland, Ohio—the Kirtland Safety Society—for the purpose of storing money connected with land speculation. Unfortunately, the bank was started without a charter from the state. He went even further by obtaining printing plates and producing worthless bills.

Smith then converted his "bank" into a joint stock operation—the Kirtland Safety Society Anti-Banking Company. He claimed that this firm had been capitalized at four million dollars, when in reality its worth was not quite 4,000 dollars. Smith maintained that God Himself had commanded him through a revelation to set up the institution and that it would "swallow up all other banks . . . and grow and flourish and spread from the rivers to the ends of the earth, and survive when all others would be laid to ruins."[32]

In the end it was discovered that all of Smith's printed bills—about $150,000 worth in circulation—were not backed by either silver or gold. Blame-shifting followed, with Smith pointing the accusatory finger at apostates whom he charged with having stolen the company's wealth out of the vault. Numerous lawsuits were filed, with Smith being fined $1,000 in the first and only case that ever made it to trial. Smith's troubles were further complicated when he attempted to fraudulently transfer his property to others so he would not lose it to persons seeking retribution for having been taken in by his banking scheme.[33]

Tensions between the Mormons and surrounding communities culminated in 1844 when a non-Mormon newspaper—the *Nauvoo Expositor*—exposed the fact that Smith was secretly practicing polygamy. (His 1843 revelation was not made public until several years later.) Smith exploded with rage, declaring that it was all lies. He then ordered his followers to "smash the press and pi [throw into disarray] the type."[34] Smith's command was unquestioningly obeyed since by this time he had actually crowned himself King of the Mormons (1842).[35] Concerning the destruction of the newspaper, Smith made the following entry in his *History of the Church*, under the date June 10, 1844:

> The Council passed an ordinance declaring the Nauvoo Expositor a nuisance, and also issued an order to me to abate the said nuisance. I immediately ordered the Marshal to destroy it without delay, ... About 8 p.m. the Marshal returned and reported that he had removed the press, type, printed paper, and fixtures into the street, and destroyed them.[36]

Perhaps as many as 200 Mormons showed up to demolish the *Expositor*, many of them armed with muskets, swords, pistols, bowie knives, and sledgehammers. The owner of the publication, Charles Foster, as well as several employees fled to Carthage, Illinois, where they lodged a complaint with law enforcement authorities.

This was the last straw. Smith had simply broken too many laws. Arrest warrants were issued for both him and his brother Hyrum. Other Mormon leaders were to be arrested as well. The Smith brothers were taken into custody within days and held at the Carthage, Illinois, jail. Unfortunately, the anger that the Smiths had stirred up over the years boiled over in the form of a lynch mob of about 140 men who gathered around the jail at approximately

5 P.M. on June 27, 1844. Smith's supporters knew trouble was brewing and smuggled two guns to their prophet and his brother. The gunfight that ensued when the mob invaded the jailhouse left both Joseph and Hyrum dead.

Brigham and Beyond

The power struggle after Smith's death placed Brigham Young (1801–1877), a high-ranking Mormon, in control of the struggling sect. Young is best known for leading thousands of Mormons on a treacherous trek (February 1846–June 1847) from Nauvoo to the Great Salt Lake Valley in what is now Utah. It was also during Young's leadership that the infamous Mountain Meadows Massacre took place. The 1857 tragedy left approximately 100 non-Mormon emigrants from Missouri and Arkansas (including women and children) dead. They were murdered by a band of Mormons and Indians after some of the emigrants spoke derisively about Joseph Smith.[37]

Like Smith, Young held Christianity in contempt, stating: "When the light came to me, I saw that all the so-called Christian world was groveling in darkness."[38] He also declared: "The Christian world, so-called, are heathens as to their knowledge of the salvation of God. . . . With regard to true theology, a more ignorant people never lived than the present so-called Christian world."[39] These sentiments have been expressed time and again throughout Mormonism's history by various LDS leaders:

> Christians—those poor miserable priests Brigham was speaking about— some of them are the biggest whoremasters there are on earth.[40]

> What does the Christian world know about God? Nothing. . . . [S]o far as the things of God are concerned, they are the veriest of fools; they know neither God nor the things of God.[41]

> O, blush for modern christianity !—a pious name for Atheism![42]

For nearly 100 years Mormonism remained a controversial organization known for violence, anti-Christian rhetoric, and polygamy. Then, in the 1890s, when the LDS Church was forced to abandon polygamy, a new evangelistic strategy was adopted by the church: present a more positive public image and try to blend in with mainstream Christianity. Compare the previously cited comments by nineteenth-century Mormons with the following comment made by LDS apostle Bruce McConkie (1915–1985): "Mormonism is Christianity; Christianity is Mormonism; they are one and the same, and they are not to be distinguished from each other in the minutest detail."[43]

Since implementing this new approach to gaining converts, the LDS Church has experienced phenomenal growth. It has used Christianity's legitimate standing as a world religion as a guise for their heretical belief system that originated with Joseph Smith. A majority of persons remain unaware of the many blasphemous doctrines taught within the LDS Church. As a result, the year 1997 saw Mormonism post a membership of nearly ten million people worldwide.[44]

A large percentage of these converts have naively accepted the Mormon claim that the LDS Church is Christian. Nothing, however, could be farther from the truth. Unlike Christians, who base their faith solely on the Bible, Mormons build their belief system on four "Standard Works" of scripture: the Bible, the *Book of Mormon* (BOM), *Doctrine & Covenants* (D&C), and the *Pearl of Great Price* (PGP). These are considered "the will, mind, word, and voice of the Lord."[45] They are "the standards, the measuring rods, the gauges by which all things are judged."[46] Also authoritative are the speeches and writings of the current President/Prophet of the church, whose directives are viewed as completely binding on all members.[47]

Although the Bible is listed among the "Standard Works," acceptance of it is "coupled with a reservation that it is true only insofar as translated correctly. . . . The other three [Standard Works], having been revealed in modern times in English, are accepted without qualification."[48] According to McConkie, this is necessary because the various versions of the Bible "do not accurately record or perfectly preserve the words, thoughts, and intents of the original inspired authors."[49] Such a position has enabled Mormon leaders to mold for themselves a religious cult that denies every essential of Christianity, as the next several sections demonstrate.

Heavenly Father and Heavenly Mother

Mormonism teaches that before being born on earth, all of us lived in heaven, where we were "reared to maturity, becoming grown spirit men and women prior to coming upon this earth."[50] McConkie explains: "Every form of life had an existence in a spirit form before being born on this earth."[51] We not only existed before our birth but actually had relationships with one another. We even knew Jesus, who allegedly allowed us to assist Him in creating the earth.[52]

This is not to say that everyone started out as a fully formed spirit being. Mormons assert that all of us proceeded from a vast supply of cosmic spirit matter known as "intelligence" or spirit element, which at some point was divided up and organized into heavenly babies. Again McConkie explains: "[I]ntelligence or spirit element became intelligences after the spirits were born as individual [spirit] entities."[53]

Inextricably linked to such a concept is the Mormon belief that God the Father is a man—"an exalted, glorified, and perfected Man"[54]—but nevertheless a mere man. He is our *literal* Father and as such has a heavenly wife who is our *literal* Mother. McConkie has stated: "Implicit in the Christian verity that all men are the spirit children of an *Eternal Father* is the usually unspoken truth that they are also the offspring of an *Eternal Mother*."[55] Joseph F. Smith (1838–1918)—sixth President of the LDS Church—issued the following statement: "Man, as a spirit, was begotten and born of Heavenly Parents, and reared to maturity in the eternal mansions of the Father prior to coming upon earth in a temporal body to undergo an experience in mortality."[56] This Heavenly Parents doctrine stems not from the Bible but from the mind of Joseph Smith:

> When light burst forth from heaven in revelations to the Prophet Joseph Smith, a more complete understanding of man—especially regarding his personal relationship to Deity—was received than could be found in all of the holy scriptures combined. The stupendous truth of the existence of a Heavenly Mother, as well as a Heavenly Father, became established facts in Mormon theology. A complete realization that we are the offspring of Heavenly Parents—that we were begotten and born into the spirit world and grew to maturity in that realm—became an integral part of Mormon philosophy.[57]

According to Mormonism, it was through sexual relations between God and His celestial wife that every person was organized into existence from eternal spirit matter (i.e., "intelligence"): "Our *spirit bodies* had their beginning . . . when we were born as the spirit children of God our Father.

Through that birth process spirit element was organized into intelligent entities."[58] Brigham Young articulated this doctrine in the clearest of terms: "He [God] created man, as we create our children; for there is no other process of creation in heaven, on the earth, in the earth, or under the earth, or in all the eternities, that is, that were, or that ever will be."[59]

An even more significant aspect of this doctrine claims that God Himself was once a mere mortal with his own set of "heavenly parents" whom he had to worship while on his way to godhood.[60] An oft-quoted speech delivered by Joseph Smith at an LDS conference held in Nauvoo, Illinois, on April 6, 1844 gives perhaps the clearest and most concise explanation possible of the Mormon doctrine of deity:

> God Himself was once as we are now, and is an exalted Man . . . if you were to see him to-day, you would see him like a man in form—like yourselves, in all the person, image, and very form as a man. . . . We have imagined and supposed that God was God from all eternity, I will refute that idea . . . he was once a man like us; yea, that God himself the Father of us all, dwelt on an earth the same as Jesus Christ himself did.[61]

In perfect agreement with Smith, Brigham Young preached the following:

> If our Father and God should be disposed to walk through one of these aisles, we should not know him from one of the congregation. You would see a man, and that is all you would know about him; you would merely know Him as a stranger from some neighboring city or country. This is the character of Him whom we worship and acknowledge as our Father and God.[62]

In *The Gospel Through the Ages*, Mormon apostle Milton R. Hunter reveals exactly what God had to do in order to become God:

> [H]ow did He [God] become glorified and exalted and attain His present status of Godhood? . . . [A]eons ago God undoubtedly took advantage of every opportunity to learn the laws of truth and as He became acquainted with each new verity He righteously obeyed it. . . . He exerted His will vigorously. . . . As he gained more knowledge through persistent effort and continuous industry, as well as through absolute obedience, His understanding of the universal laws continued to become

more complete. Thus He grew in experience and continued to grow until He attained the status of Godhood.[63]

These sentiments are expressed in the Mormon couplet, "As man is, God once was; as God is, man may become."[64] It must be stressed that "God," since he was once a man like us, was literally "born of a woman" and dwelt on an earth[65] where he himself sinned and physically died.[66] Moreover, God's "father" had his own deified Father, who in turn had a father.[67] This chain of gods has supposedly extended back for aeons, making the LDS god nothing more than one god in a long succession of man-gods.

Jesus, Our Elder Brother

Most non-Mormons do not realize that in LDS theology Jesus Christ is little more than our elder brother. He, like everyone else, was organized out of spirit matter and was given a spiritual body by birth to the Heavenly Father and Heavenly Mother.[68] Jesus only differs from us in that he was the very first spirit baby formed from spirit element. Jesus is *literally* our big brother, "the most intelligent, the most faithful, and the most Godlike of all the sons and daughters of our Heavenly Father in the spirit world."[69]

This doctrine, however, is by no means the most controversial aspect of Mormon Christology. That distinction belongs to the LDS view of our Savior's birth. Latter-day Saints believe that Jesus was incarnated—i.e., conceived, received a *physical* body—through sex between God and Mary. The *Encyclopedia of Mormonism* states: "Latter-day Saints recognize Jesus as literally the Only Begotten Son of God the Father in the flesh. . . . This title signifies that Jesus' physical body was the offspring of a mortal mother and the eternal Father."[70] Mormon author Carlfred Broderick comments:

> [L]atter-day prophets have made it clear that despite what it says in Matthew 1:20, the Holy Ghost was not the father of Jesus. . . . [T]he role of the Holy Ghost was to make it possible for the mortal, Mary, to withstand the immediate presence of God. . . . The Savior was fathered by a personage of flesh and bone.[71]

Oddly, Mormons often claim that they believe in the virgin birth. This may seem like a contradiction. But former Mormon Thelma Geer, in her insightful book *Mormonism, Mama, and Me,* explains that when Latter-day Saints talk about the virgin birth, what they are actually saying is that Mary was a virgin when God the Father came to visit her, but she was not a virgin when He left.[72] This explanation is supported by numerous remarks about the virgin birth that have been made by several high-ranking Mormon authorities, including Brigham Young:

> The birth of the Saviour was as natural as are the births of our children. . . . He partook of flesh and blood—was begotten of his father, as we were of our fathers. (Brigham Young)[73]

> Christ was begotten by an Immortal Father in the same way that mortal men are begotten by mortal fathers. (Bruce McConkie)[74]

> I was naturally begotten; so was my father, and also my Saviour Jesus Christ . . . he is the first begotten of his father in the flesh, and there was nothing unnatural about it. (Heber C. Kimball)[75]

These explanations of Jesus' conception are clearly unbiblical. Scripture indicates that Christ was miraculously conceived in the womb of the virgin Mary by the power of the Holy Spirit. The Bible explicitly states: "When as his mother Mary was espoused to Joseph, before they came together, she was found with child of the Holy Ghost. . . . the angel of the Lord appeared unto him [Joseph] in a dream, saying, 'Joseph, thou son of David, fear not to take unto thee Mary thy wife: for that which is conceived in her is of the Holy Ghost'" (Matthew 1:18-20, KJV). Contrast this passage with what was preached by Brigham Young in 1852: "Now, remember from this time forth, and for ever [sic], that Jesus Christ was not begotten by the Holy Ghost."[76]

Pride and Prejudice

Since its earliest days, Mormonism and racism have been synonymous terms to individuals well acquainted with LDS doctrine. Today, however, the prejudicial aspects of the Mormon faith have been virtually obscured thanks to a concerted effort by Mormon leaders to portray their church as an equal-opportunity religion. This new LDS public image began to unfold on June 9, 1978, when blacks were finally given access to the Mormon priesthood in response to mounting social pressures.[77]

Such a politically correct move, however, could hardly eradicate the racism that Mormonism had promoted for nearly 140 years. To date, no LDS authority has ever repudiated the many declarations made by Mormon leaders, including Joseph Smith's 1843 statement, "Had I anything to do with the negro, I would confine them by strict law to their own species."[78]

The racism in Mormonism can be traced to their beliefs concerning our alleged pre-mortal life. LDS president Joseph Fielding Smith explains:

> *There is a reason why one man is born black* and with other disadvantages, while *another is born white* with great advantages. The reason is that we once had an estate before we came here, and were obedient, more or less, to the laws that were given us there. *Those who were faithful in all things there received greater blessings here, and those who were not faithful received less.*[79]

Latter-day Saints assert that our skin color is not just based on general obedience in heaven but is more specifically linked to our conduct in the spiritual realm during a great "rebellion" that culminated in a heavenly war between Lucifer and Christ:

> When . . . Jesus was chosen to be the Redeemer of the world, some rebelled. . . . In this great rebellion in heaven, Lucifer, or Satan. . . . and one-third of the hosts thereof [angels] were cast out. . . . There were no neutrals in the war in heaven. *All took sides either with Christ or with Satan* . . . the Negro, evidently, is receiving the reward he merits.[80]

Here on earth the less "valiant" spirits pay dearly for their less than admirable behavior by being born through the lineage of Cain (the son of Adam and Eve who slew his brother Abel):

> Those who were less valiant in pre-existence . . . are known to us as the *negroes.* Such spirits are sent to earth through the lineage of Cain. . . . are denied the priesthood. . . . are not equal with other races where the receipt of certain spiritual blessings are concerned . . . this inequality is not of man's origin. It is the Lord's doing.[81]

Bruce McConkie penned the above words in 1966 when those of African descent were still not allowed to hold the priesthood. Even today, however, many Mormons continue to view blacks as inferior. Consider the words of Joseph Fielding Smith: "Not only was Cain called upon to suffer, but because of his wickedness he became the father of an inferior race."[82] Brigham Young spoke out even more forcefully:

> You see some classes of the human family that are black, uncouth, uncomely, disagreeable, and low in their habits, wild, and seemingly deprived of nearly all the blessings of the intelligence that is generally bestowed upon mankind. . . . Cain slew his brother . . . and the Lord put a mark on him, which is the flat nose and black skin.[83]

> Shall I tell you the law of God in regard to the African race? If the white man who belongs to the chosen seed mixes his blood with the seed of Cain, the penalty, under the law of God, is death on the spot. This will always be so.[84]

Young's stand against interracial marriage has been echoed on numerous occasions by LDS authorities. Consider, for example, the contents of a 1947 letter written by the First Presidency, which consists of the highest-ranking Mormons—i.e., the president and his two personal counselors:

> [I]t has been the doctrine of the Church . . . that the Negroes are not entitled to the full blessings of the Gospel . . . your ideas, as we understand them, appear to contemplate the intermarriage of the Negro and White races, a concept which has heretofore been most repugnant to most normal-minded people . . . there is a growing tendency . . . toward the breaking down of race barriers in the matter of intermarriage between whites and blacks, but it does not have the sanction of the Church and is contrary to Church doctrine.[85]

Thelma Geer, a fourth-generation Mormon who eventually left the LDS church, remembers exactly what it is like growing up as a Mormon:

> As a white Mormon, I proudly accepted the teaching that my fair skin and Mormon parentage signified that I had been one of God's most intelligent and obedient born-in-heaven spirit children. . . . As a reward for my superior attributes and attitudes, I had been singled out, trained, and

qualified to be born a white Latter-day Saint, deserving of emulation, adulation, and eventual deification. All dark-skinned people, even darker-complexioned Caucasians ... had been inferior spirits in heaven.[86]

In contrast, Scripture plainly tells us that "God is no respecter of persons; but in every nation he that feareth him, and worketh righteousness, is accepted with him" (Acts 10:34–35, KJV). God's Word also informs us that there are absolutely no race distinctions in Christ (Gal. 3:28).

Salvation by Works Alone

Mormons put an especially imaginative twist on Christ's atonement and its merits. They believe that although Jesus did indeed die for everyone, He did not do so in order to cleanse each individual from his or her personal sins. According to LDS teachings, Jesus died so that humanity could be resurrected on judgment day. McConkie writes that if there had been no atonement, "temporal death would have remained forever, and there never would have been a resurrection. The body would have remained forever in the grave."[87] This "redemption from death," which is applicable to everyone—Mormon and non-Mormon alike—is known as "general salvation"[88] It has nothing to do with being forgiven or cleansed of personal sins.

Full salvation, however, does involve being purged of one's own sins. But unlike Christians, Mormons believe that such is accomplished by human works rather than by God's grace. Jesus' death merely opened up the way for Mormons to procure release from the effects of their sins and pursue godhood (see next section):

> **The Individual Effect of the Atonement** makes it possible for any and every soul to obtain absolution from the effect of personal sins, through the mediation of Christ; but such saving intercession is to be invoked by individual effort as manifested through faith, repentance, and continued works of righteousness . . . the blessing of redemption from individual sins, while open for all to attain, is nevertheless conditioned on individual effort.[89]

Latter-day Saints attempt to legitimize blending faith and works for salvation by citing James 2:14–17, which tells us that faith without works is dead. But in declaring that a professed faith without works is a dead faith, James is simply saying that someone who has a genuine faith will produce good works as a consequence of the supernatural working of the Holy Spirit in his or her life. If no good works are being done by an individual, then the faith which that person says he or she possesses is not a genuine faith. It is a false (or dead) faith. Anyone who has truly obtained salvation by "faith" will naturally manifest the kind of good works that are consistent with salvation. In other words, Christians do good works *because* of salvation, not *for* salvation (Rom. 4:5).

To further complicate their erroneous view of salvation, Mormons teach that Jesus completed the act of atonement in the Garden of Gethsemane where He toiled in prayer on the night of his betrayal:

> In one of his books, *Come Unto Christ*, President Benson wrote: "There [in Gethsemane] He suffered the pains of all men. . . . It was in Gethsemane that Jesus took on Himself the sins of the world. . . . His pain was equivalent to the cumulative burden of all men."[90]

In actuality, Jesus bore the sins of the world while on the cross (1 Peter 2:24; Col. 1:20), not while in Gethsemane. Furthermore, not everyone is blessed through Christ's crucifixion. Only those who accept his sacrifice and surrender their life to Him will receive the benefit of Jesus' death and resurrection (Rom. 10:9), which is forgiveness of sins (Acts 10:43) and salvation (Rom. 3:24). Eternal life "in Christ," rather than eternal existence through resurrection, is the free gift offered by God to humanity (Rom. 6:23). This gift is obtainable only by grace through faith (Eph. 2:8–10).

The Crowning Achievement

When Christians discuss salvation with a Latter-day Saint, they often do not realize that "salvation" in Mormonism differs from "salvation" in Christianity. Full salvation for Mormons is nothing less than godhood. It is achieved by traveling along a spiritual path they call "eternal progression." Such a process, according to Mormon theology, has produced an innumerable number of gods throughout the universe. This belief, too, originated with Joseph Smith, who in 1844 revealed that God the Father, Jesus Christ, and the Holy Ghost were "three distinct personages and three Gods."[91]

LDS Apostle Orson Pratt expanded on Smith's view, theorizing, "If we should take a million of worlds like this and number their particles, we should find that there are more Gods than there are particles of matter in those worlds."[92] Brigham Young, much less willing to calculate how many gods exist, would only say, "How many Gods there are, I do not know. But there never was a time when there were not Gods."[93]

If all goes well, each Mormon (male and female) will obtain his or her own exaltation (godhood) and take his or her place among the other gods and goddesses of the universe. It is a "gradually unfolding course of advancement and experience—a course that began in a past eternity [pre-existence] and will continue in ages future."[94] Joseph Smith declared: "[Y]ou have got to learn how to be Gods yourselves . . . the same as all Gods have done before you,—namely, by going from one small degree to another, and from one small degree to another."[95]

Becoming a god is what being a Mormon is all about. According to the popular LDS reference book *Mormon Doctrine*, "That exaltation which the saints of all ages have so devoutly sought is *godhood* itself."[96] Godhood's ultimate reward is definitely appealing:

> Godhood is to have the character, possess the attributes, and enjoy the perfections which the Father has. It is to do what he does, have the powers resident in him, and live as he lives.[97] Those who obtain exaltation will gain all power and thus themselves be omnipotent.[98]

As pleasing as this reward may be, the main benefit of deification is the ability to create spirit babies through celestial sex just like the Heavenly Father has done:

> [E]xaltation consists in the continuation of the family unit in eternity. . . . Those who obtain it . . . have spirit children in the resurrection, in relation to which offspring they stand in the same position that God our Father stands to us.[99]

Clearly, such beliefs do not line up with what has historically been referred to as Christianity. Where, then, do such doctrines originate? Most of them can be found in Joseph Smith's extra-biblical writings, each of which will now be discussed.

The Book of Mormon

The *Book of Mormon* (BOM), *Doctrine & Covenants* (D&C), and *Pearl of Great Price* (PGP) allegedly restore many truths that were either taken out of the Bible or lost from Christianity. Of these texts, the BOM is by far the most well known. Mormons view it as sort of a second Bible that tells of "God's dealings with the people of the American continents from about 2200 [B.C.] . . . to [A.D.] 421."[100] The basic story line is explained in the BOM's introduction:

> The book was written by many ancient prophets by the spirit of prophecy and revelation. Their words, written on gold plates, were quoted and abridged by a prophet-historian named Mormon. The record gives an account of two great civilizations. One came from Jerusalem in 600 B.C., and afterward separated into two nations, known as the Nephites and the Lamanites. The other came much earlier when the Lord confounded the tongues at the Tower of Babel. This group is known as the Jaredites. After thousands of years, all were destroyed except the Lamanites, and they are the principal ancestors of the American Indians. The crowning event recorded in the *Book of Mormon* is the personal ministry of the Lord Jesus Christ among the Nephites soon after his resurrection. It puts forth the doctrines of the gospel, outlines the plan of salvation, and tells men what they must do to gain peace in this life and eternal salvation in the life to come. After Mormon completed his writings, he delivered the account to his son Moroni, who added a few words of his own and hid up the plates in the Hill Cumorah.[101]

One of the most famous passages in the BOM relates directly to Christianity. Smith apparently knew that many Christians would object to another book of scripture, so he cleverly included condemnations of the Bible in the BOM, each of which were written as if it were God Himself speaking:

> [M]any of the Gentiles shall say: A Bible! A Bible! We have got a Bible, and there cannot be any more Bible. But thus saith the Lord God: . . . Thou fool, that shall say: A Bible, we have got a Bible, and we need no more Bible. . . . [M]y work is not yet finished; neither shall it be until the end of man. . . . Wherefore, because that ye have a Bible ye need not suppose that it contains all my words; neither need ye suppose that I have not caused more to be written.[102]

It certainly would have been possible for God to impart extra-biblical scripture to various persons living in the Americas. The question is: Does the *Book of Mormon* reflect divine authorship? Overwhelming evidence would lead any objective investigator to answer no. The BOM is filled with linguistic, historical, cultural, and archaeological inaccuracies that belie its human origin (i.e., Smith). For example, Smith claims that he translated the BOM from Reformed Egyptian characters. But there exists no historical evidence that a "Reformed" Egyptian language ever existed anywhere in the New World (i.e., North and South America). There is also no evidence that the following BOM words are Egyptian or Semitic: Shazar (1 Nephi 16:13-14), Irreantum (1 Neph 17:5), deseret (for "bee," Ether 2:3), and Liahona (Alma 37:38).

It is also noteworthy that the BOM is written entirely in King James English, which is from the sixteenth century. If Smith actually had translated another language into the English of his time period (i.e., the nineteenth century), the BOM would read in a manner more in line with his day. Numerous Mormon critics have theorized that when Smith wrote the BOM, he tried to authenticate it by using King James English. This is a likely scenario since hundreds of verses in the BOM are copied directly from the King James Version of the Bible.[103]

The BOM also contains a number of geographical mistakes. For instance, 1 Nephi 17:5 describes Arabia as being "bountiful because of its much fruit and also wild honey," and 1 Nephi 18:1 indicates that Arabia contained ample timber. But Arabia has never had ample or bountiful supplies of timber, fruit, or honey. The BOM also speaks of a river in Arabia named Laman that flows continually to the Red Sea (1 Nephi 2:6-9). In reality, there has never been any true river in Arabia.[104]

The BOM even contains numerous archaeological inaccuracies. It is asserted in 1 Nephi 18:25, for example, that the New World had cows, oxen, asses, horses, and goats "for the use of man" in 600 B.C. But there were no such animals in the New World until Europeans brought them to the continent several hundred years later.[105] Discrepancies between the BOM and historical fact are so numerous that it would require an entire volume to catalog and explain them. Consequently, I have chosen to simply excerpt an article by biology professor Thomas Key, which appeared in a 1985 issue of the *Journal of the American Scientific Affiliation*. It clearly establishes the enormous problems faced by Mormons who claim that the BOM is God's infallible Word:

Ether 9:18-19 contains several problems. First, it lists domestic cattle, oxen and cows as separate species! Second, these did not exist in the Americas at that time. Third, domestic swine did not exist here then. Fourth, horses, asses and elephants did not exist in America at that time.... There are serious problems in the description of the behavior related to poisonous snakes, etc. in Ether 9:30-34. First, the notion that snakes increase as a drought increases is contradicted by the fact that reptiles are particularly sensitive to heat and lack of water, and would die off faster than other animals. Second, even with the large population of modern America, only about twenty people die yearly by snake bite. It is certainly not realistic for Ether to claim that numerous people and animals were exterminated by snakes.... Satyrs (2 Nephi 23:21) and dragons (2 Nephi 23:22, 8:9) are mentioned as literal creatures and not figurative. Chickens (3 Nephi 10:4-6) and dogs (Alma 16:10, Mosiah 12:2, and 3 Nephi 7:8) were non-existent here at the time. In 3 Nephi 20:16 and 21:12, lions are described as "beasts of the forests." Contrary to popular opinion and the Book of Mormon, lions do not live in forests or jungles. They live in savannahs and veldts (few scattered trees) and lions never inhabited the Americas. Silk is erroneously mentioned as being produced in the Americas at that time (1 Nephi 13 :7, Alma 4:6 and Ether 9:17 and 10:24). . . . Clothes moths are mentioned in 3 Nephi 13:19-20 and 27:32, yet there were no woolen garments for moths to attack as sheep had not yet been introduced [to America]. . . . 2 Nephi 17:15 lists two foods at that time; butter and honey. But Indians had no milk animals nor honey bees. . . . Alma 46:40 attributes "the cause of disease to . . . the nature of the climate," instead of to filth, poor diet, or germs. . . . 3 Nephi 17:7 mentions leprosy in 34 A.D., yet the first known case in the Americas was in 1758. . . . The implied reproduction rate in the Book of Mormon is astronomical! The story starts in 600 B.C. and extends to 421 A.D. It involves a mere handful of people who travel from "the land of Jerusalem" [sic] to the Promised Land of America. Every four or five years or so there are devastating wars that kill many thousands of people (Alma 28:2, etc.), or as Ether 15:2 says, "nearly two millions of mighty men" in addition to their wives and children. For this to be so, it would be necessary for each couple to have scores of children, and for them to reach maturity in three or so years throughout the supposed period.[106]

Some of the errors in the BOM are actually quite humorous. For example, Ether 15:30–31 states that an individual named Shiz was beheaded and goes on to state that *after* he was beheaded he raised up on his hands, fell back to the ground, and then struggled for breath! A number of equally problematic passages can be found:

- Hundreds of years before Christ, a Hebrew is called by a popular nineteenth-century American name, "Sam" (1 Nephi 2:5).
- 1 Nephi 8:4 contains the Old English poetical word "Methought," which can hardly be considered an accurate rendering of any "Reformed Egyptian" character.
- 2 Nephi 25:19 states that the "name" of the Savior would be Jesus Christ. But "Christ" is not Jesus' last name. It is a *title* that actually means "anointed one."
- In Jacob 7:27, a Hebrew uses the French word *adieu* to say farewell.

Throughout the years, LDS Church authorities have tried in vain to correct the countless problems contained in the BOM. In fact, there have been nearly 4,000 substantive changes made to the BOM since it was first published in 1830. Most of these changes were made to eradicate Smith's appalling grammatical errors. The following represents but a small sampling from the 1830 edition (emphasis is added):

"... and also of Adam and Eve, which *was* our first parents" (p. 15).

"[T]his *he done*, that he might overthrow the doctrine of Christ" (p. 140).

"[N]o man can look in them, except he be commanded, lest he should look for that he *had not ought* and he should perish" (p. 173).

"[B]oth Alma and Helam *was* buried in the water" (p. 192).

"[T]he daughters of the Lamanites did gather themselves together *for to sing*" (p. 196).

"As I was *a journeying* to see a very near kindred" (p. 249).

"[W]hen they *had arriven* in the borders of the land" (p. 270).

"[T]he Lamanites saw that Moroni was *a coming* against them" (p. 403).

"And thus ended the record of Alma, which *was wrote* upon the plates of Nephi" (p. 347).

"There were no robbers ... neither were there Lamanites, *nor no manner of Ites*; but they were one, the children of Christ" (p. 515).

Some of the changes that have been made to the BOM amount to drastic revisions in doctrine, especially surrounding the identity of Jesus Christ. In 1830 Smith seemed to think that Jesus was the Father. In other portions of the text, however, Smith spoke of Jesus as if he were God's grandson. These passages were subsequently changed:

BOOK OF MORMON–COMPARISON OF EDITIONS

1830 Edition	*Modern Edition*
"Behold the Lamb of God, yea, even the Eternal Father!" (p. 25).	"Behold the Lamb of God, yea, even the Son of the Eternal Father!" (1 Nephi 11:21).
"I looked and beheld the Lamb of God, that he was taken by the people; yea, the Everlasting God, was judged" (p. 26).	"I looked and beheld the Lamb of God, that he was taken by the people; yea, the Son of the everlasting God was judged" (1 Nephi 11:32).
"[T]he Lamb of God is the Eternal Father, and the Saviour of the world" (p. 32).	"[T]he Lamb of God is the Son of the Eternal Father, and the Savior of the world" (1 Nephi 13:40).
"I know that Jesus Christ shall come; yea, the Son of the Only Begotten of the Father" (p. 236).	"I know that Jesus Christ shall come, yea, the Son, the Only Begotten of the Father" (Alma 5:48).
"[T]hey become High Priests forever, after the order of the Son of the Only Begotten of the Father" (p. 259)	"[T]hey become high priests forever, after the order of the Son, the Only Begotten of the Father" (Alma 13:9).

Doctrine & Covenants

The D&C is a book containing alleged revelations given to Joseph Smith. The volume, originally published in 1833 as the *Book of Commandments* and then printed again in 1835 as the D&C, has been changed numerous times throughout the years. For instance, what was originally a 141-word revelation in Chapter 6 of the 1833 edition ended up being a 252-word revelation in Section 7 in the D&C. When Chapter 4 of the *Book of Commandments* appeared in the D&C as Section 5, it not only had 201 words deleted, but had 269 different words added.

These are not the only changes that were made to Smith's revelations. In fact, very few of the "revelations" contained in current editions of the D&C appear as they first did in the 1833 *Book of Commandments*. It is important to remember that when these revelations came to Smith, he said that they were the very words of God. The first revelation in the 1833 edition reads:

> Search these commandments, for they are true and faithful, and the prophecies and promises which are in them, shall be fulfilled. What I the Lord have spoken, I have spoken, and I excuse not myself, and though the heavens and earth pass away, my word shall not pass away.[107]

Nevertheless, Smith proceeded to drastically change the revelations. He did so for a variety of reasons: to expand his powers, clarify evolving doctrines, create new beliefs, add spice to old beliefs, and conceal church dogma from non-Mormons. This type of dishonesty continues to be perpetrated by current leaders of the Mormon Church. A case in point would be Section 137 of the D&C, which was added to the volume by LDS authorities on April 3, 1976. The revelation/vision—received by Joseph Smith back on January 21, 1836—was approved for inclusion after a positive vote by Church members. But few Mormons realized that their leaders had changed the revelation.

In Joseph Smith's own diary, under the date of January 21, 1836, his handwritten account of the vision reads: "The heavens were opened upon us and I beheld the celestial Kingdom of God. . . . I saw father Adam, and Abraham and Michael and my father and mother, my brother Alvin that has long since slept."[108] But when this revelation appeared in the modern edition of the D&C, the words "and Michael" had been deleted. Why would LDS leaders tamper with a vision transcribed by Joseph Smith himself? Apparently "and Michael" was deleted in order to conceal a glaring contradiction between Smith's 1836 vision and two revelations already contained in the D&C (27:11 and 107:54), each of which teach that Adam *is* Michael![109]

Pearl of Great Price

The *Pearl of Great Price* is a collection of writings that deal with "many significant aspects of the faith and doctrine" of Mormonism.[110] The items, first produced by Joseph Smith and published in periodicals of his day, include the *Book of Moses*, the *Book of Abraham*, various *Writings of Joseph Smith*, and *The Articles of Faith*, which is a statement of faith by Joseph Smith. Of these works, the most influential and controversial are the *Book of Moses* and the *Book of Abraham*.

The *Book of Moses* is a nine-chapter version of the first six chapters of Genesis. Smith asserted that many of the truths originally contained in the first book of the Bible had been removed by either unscrupulous scribes or careless copiers. Smith felt that his job as God's latter-day prophet was to fill in the blanks. He claimed to have succeeded in his goal thanks to direct revelations from God. Predictably, the *Book of Moses* contradicts the Bible in numerous places. For example, Moses 5:10–11 indicates that the fall of Adam and Eve was actually a *blessing!*

This twisted view of man's sinful state is tied to the Mormon belief that all of God's children can themselves become gods. The Fall was necessary so we could experience "mortality," which is a prerequisite of godhood. Mortality is an indispensable part of "eternal progression."[111] Through mortality, people supposedly learn the lessons necessary for achieving divine status. The Bible, of course, teaches that the Fall was the tragic result of sin. Eve was deceived, and Adam deliberately disobeyed the Lord (Gen. 3:13; 1 Tim. 2:14). Furthermore, the Fall did not bring blessings but instead brought the curse of death to all men (Rom. 5:12; 6:23; 8:10).

Even more controversial than the *Book of Moses* is the *Book of Abraham*, which Smith said he translated from papyri taken from the catacombs of Egypt. According to Smith, the papyri (acquired in 1835) were authored in Egypt by Abraham. Mormons believe that Smith's "translation" has imparted to them "priceless information about the gospel, pre-existence, the nature of Deity, the creation, [and] the priesthood . . . which is not otherwise available."[112]

So important was this document to Smith that he made three sketches of the papyri's images. These drawings, which are reproduced in each edition of the *Book of Abraham*, also include Smith's interpretation of what the hieroglyphics represent. All of the characters allegedly relate in some way to various biblical personalities and doctrines that are part of the LDS belief system.

As far back as 1912, Egyptologists and other qualified scholars have been labeling Smith's interpretation of the drawings as fraudulent. Consider these comments:[113]

Dr. A. H. Sayce (Oxford, England): "It is difficult to deal seriously with Joseph Smith's impudent fraud. . . . Smith has turned the Goddess [Isis] into a king and [the god] Osiris into Abraham."

Dr. W. M. Flinders Petrie (London University): "To any one with

According to Smith, Facsimile No. 1 shows an evil priest (1) attempting to sacrifice Abraham (2), who has been fastened upon an altar.

Smith claimed that the characters on Facsimile No. 2 depict numerous Mormon concepts including their belief that God is a man who sits on a literal throne (1). The planet "Kolob," which Mormons believe to be the planet nearest to God's celestial residence, is also said to be shown (2).

In Smith's explanation of Facsimile No. 3, he identifies each of the figures as: (1) Abraham, sitting on King Pharaoh's throne; (2) King Pharaoh; (3) Prince of Pharaoh, King of Egypt; (4) Shulem, one of the king's principal waiters: and (5) Olimah, a slave belonging to the prince.

knowledge of the large class of [Egyptian] funeral documents to which these belong, the attempts to guess a meaning are too absurd to be noticed. It may be safely said that there is not one single word that is true in these explanations."

James H. Breasted, Ph.D. (Haskell Oriental Museum, University of Chicago): "To sum up, then, these three fac-similes of Egyptian documents in the 'Pearl of Great Price' depict the most common objects in the mortuary religion of Egypt. Joseph Smith's interpretations of them as part of a unique revelation through Abraham, therefore, very clearly demonstrates that he was totally unacquainted with the significance of these documents and absolutely ignorant of the simplest facts of Egyptian Writing and civilization."

Dr. Arthur C. Mace (Assistant Curator, Metropolitan Museum of Art, New York, Department of Egyptian Art): "I return herewith, under separate cover, the 'Pearl of Great Price.' The 'Book of Abraham,' it is hardly necessary to say, is a pure fabrication. . . . Joseph Smith's interpretation of these cuts is a farrago [confused mixture] of nonsense from beginning to end."

Professor S. A. B. Mercer, Ph.D. (Western Theological Seminary, Custodian Hibbard Collection, Egyptian Reproductions): "Smith knew neither the Egyptian language nor the meaning of the most commonplace Egyptian figures. . . . the explanatory notes to his fac-similes cannot be taken seriously by any scholar, as they seem to be undoubtedly the work of pure imagination."

Despite such scathing appraisals of Smith's work, Mormons continued to steadfastly support their prophet's rendering of the hieroglyphics, claiming that no scholar had examined the original documents from which Smith made his drawings. Moreover, the drawings represented only a few of the many papyri fragments Smith used to produce the entire *Book of Abraham*. The bulk of his translation was taken from papyri that contained actual writing rather than just pictures.[114]

For many years it seemed that these arguments would indefinitely protect the LDS faith because the original papyri fragments Smith "translated" into the *Book of Abraham* had been destroyed in the great Chicago fire of 1871. The *Book of Abraham*, it seemed, would forever be beyond a thorough scholarly investigation. Then in 1967, to everyone's great surprise, Smith's original papyri fragments were recovered from an old, dusty storage bin located in New York's Metropolitan Museum of Art.

Egyptologists, religion scholars, and other interested parties hailed the discovery as one of the great finds of this century. Unfortunately for Mormons, careful examination of the scrolls revealed them to be nothing but common Egyptian funeral texts belonging to the *Book of Breathings*, written around the first century B.C.—a full 2,000 years *after* Abraham had died. Furthermore, it was discovered that Smith had embellished his drawings with images and hieroglyphics that the originals do not contain.

With regard to the written texts, they bear no resemblance whatsoever to Smith's *Book of Abraham* "translation." In fact, scholars found that Smith invented lengthy paragraphs from simple hieroglyphics that represented little more than one short word. The following chart represents a small sampling of Smith's mistranslation:[115]

In *Mormonism: Shadow or Reality?* Jerald and Sandra Tanner have aptly commented: "That the Utah Mormon leaders would continue to endorse the Book of Abraham in the face of the evidence which has been presented is almost beyond belief."[116]

HIEROGLYPHICS—COMPARISON OF TRANSLATIONS

Correct Translation	*Joseph Smith's Book of Abraham Translation (1:11-15)*
"the, this" 	11. Now, this priest had offered upon this altar three virgins at one time, who were the daughters of Onitah, one of the royal descent directly from the loins of Ham. These virgins were offered up be-cause of their virtue; they would not bow down to worship gods of wood or of stone, therefore they were killed upon this altar.
"pool" 	and it was done after the manner of the Egyptians. 12. And it came to pass that the priests laid violence upon me, that they might slay me also, as they did those virgins upon this altar; and that you may have a knowledge of this altar, I will refer you to the representation at the commencement of this record.
"water" 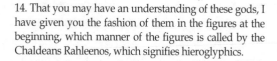	13. It was made after the form of a bedstead, such as was had among the Chaldeans, and it stood before the gods of Elkenah, Libnah, Mahmackrah, Korash, and also a god like unto that of Pharaoh, king of Egypt.
"great"	14. That you may have an understanding of these gods, I have given you the fashion of them in the figures at the beginning, which manner of the figures is called by the Chaldeans Rahleenos, which signifies hieroglyphics.
	15. And as they lifted up their hands upon me, that they might offer me up and take away my life, behold, I lifted up my voice unto my God, and the Lord hearkened and heard, and he filled me with the vision of the Almighty, and the angel of his presence stood by me, and immediately unloosed my bands.

ACCORDING TO THE BIBLE

Latter-day Saints maintain that they are Christians who believe in the Bible and preach the doctrines of Christianity. The truth, however, is that Mormons are not Christians. In fact, Mormonism contradicts Scripture at every turn. For example, the LDS teaching that there exists more than one god is refuted by numerous biblical passages, including Isaiah 44:8 where God declares: "[Y]ou are My witnesses. Is there any God besides Me . . . ? I know of none." The Lord has also stated: "Before me there was no God formed, and there will be none after Me" (Isa. 43:10). Even the demons realize there exists only one God, and they tremble (James 2:19).

Church apostle James Talmage has stated: "We believe in a God . . . who has attained His exalted state by a path which now His children are permitted to follow, whose glory it is their heritage to share."[117] Yet in Isaiah 42:8 and Isaiah 48:10–11, God assures us that He shares His glory with no one. Such verses indicate that the Mormon goal of becoming a god will never be reached.

Regarding our alleged pre-existence, Brigham Young explained that people are "first made spiritual, and afterwards temporal [fleshly]."[118] Paul the apostle, however, taught differently: "[T]hat was *not* first which is spiritual, but that which is natural: and afterward that which is spiritual" (1 Cor. 15:46, KJV, emphasis added). Paul is simply saying here that the natural, or physical, comes first, *then* comes the spiritual. Zechariah 12:1, in agreement with Paul, indicates that God forms the spirit within the body of each man and each woman on earth, rather than in the womb of a celestial Heavenly Mother.

One biblical passage often cited by Mormons to support their pre-mortal doctrine is Jeremiah 1:5: "Before I formed thee in the belly I knew thee; and before thou camest forth out of the womb I sanctified thee, and I ordained thee a prophet" (KJV). This verse, on the surface, does seem to say that God indeed knew us before we were born. Mormons assert, therefore, that for God to have had such knowledge, we must have existed with Him in heaven prior to being born. But in context, Jeremiah is not referring to a pre-earth life with God. The passage is speaking of God's omniscience (compare Ps. 139:11–12; 147:5; 1 John 3:19–20), specifically His *foreknowledge*. The Old Testament prophet is addressing the fact that even before our births, God knows everything about our lives—including our identity. He knows us as if we already existed. As Romans 4:17 puts it, "God . . . calleth those things which be not as though they were" (KJV).

Concerning our identity as God's children, Scripture nowhere says that we were procreated in the heavenly realms as *literal* sons and daughters of a Heavenly Father and his wife. Instead, we are described by the Bible as children of God by adoption (Rom. 8:15). Furthermore, Scripture explicitly states that God is not a man (Num. 23:19; 1 Sam. 15:29; Hos. 11:9). The Bible also tells us that God did not evolve into deity from a mere man who himself had to worship another god—i.e., *his* Heavenly Father. God has always been God (Isa. 41:4; 57:15; Rom. 16:25–26). In the words of Psalms 90:2 and 93:2, God has been God "from everlasting to everlasting." He is unchanging (Mal. 3:6; Heb. 6:17–18; James 1:17). The Mormon concept of God as a man with a body of flesh and bones[119] is also contradicted by Scripture. John 4:24 says, "God is spirit," and Jesus taught in Luke 24:39 that "a spirit does not have flesh and bones."

Clearly, Mormons believe in "another Jesus . . . a different spirit . . . a false gospel" (2 Cor. 11:4). The true Gospel, according to Scripture, is the death, burial, and resurrection of Christ (1 Cor. 15:1–4). Compare this message with the words of LDS authority George Q. Cannon: "Who is there that believes more in true evolution than the Latter-day Saints—The evolution of man until he shall become a God. . . . That is the Gospel of Jesus Christ believed by the Latter-day Saints."[120]

WHAT'S THE ATTRACTION?

Mormons view themselves as being not only morally and ethically superior, but spiritually superior to everyone else. Brigham Young remarked, "[T]his people are the best people that ever lived upon the earth."[121] Joseph Fielding Smith wrote: "SAINTS ARE THE BEST PEOPLE. *We are, notwithstanding our weaknesses, the best people in the world* . . . this truth is evident to all who are willing to observe for themselves. We are morally clean, in every way equal, and in many ways superior to any other people."[122] Mormons also believe that their church is 'the only true and living church upon the face of the whole earth"[123] and that "'the power of God unto salvation' (Rom. 1:16) is absent from all but the Church of Jesus Christ of Latter-day Saints."[124]

It cannot be denied that such teachings would appeal to many individuals searching for emotional comfort, especially persons who may be battling low self-esteem. An appeal to one's pride is perhaps the oldest technique used by cults to gain converts. After all, everyone has an ego and, because of sin, enjoys having that ego stroked. Mormon leaders, as the previous quotations show, excel at making church members feel as if they are in an elite class by themselves.

Another powerful attraction of the LDS Church lies in the traditional values, family togetherness, and morally clean lifestyle promoted by its members. These aspects of Mormonism make the organization one of society's most appealing bastions of conservatism. The public's perception of the Mormon faith as being a wholesome alternative to secularism, coupled with the standard LDS practice of not disclosing controversial doctrines until potential converts are well within the fold, has clearly resulted in a marked membership increase for the church in the 1990s, an increase that Mormon leaders see continuing for many years to come.

Finally, Mormonism has recently become an attractive alternative to other religions because its members have succeeded in passing off their organization as just another Christian denomination. Latter-day Saints have gone so far as to infiltrate mainstream Christian churches in an effort "to convert Christian pastors to Mormonism, and thereby win not only one person, but the entire church to the LDS theology."[125] There are indications that this tactic is working.

According to a March 1991 issue of the official LDS Church newspaper, *Church News*, Mormons have allied themselves with the Free Memorial Baptist Church in Atlanta, Georgia. Additionally, the speakers at a 1991 meeting of eight southeast Christian congregations included Mormon regional president Bryce Gibby and LDS Georgia Atlanta Mission president John Fowler.[126]

Even more disturbing is what took place in Hollister, California, a year earlier. After having a "ministerial meeting" with a neighboring Mormon leader, Southern Baptist pastor Bill Habing ended up inviting the local Mormon Stake Missionary to speak at his San Juan Road Baptist Church once a week.[127] Habing had apparently ignored Jesus' admonition, "Beware of the false prophets, who come to you in sheep's clothing, but inwardly are ravenous wolves" (Matt. 7:15).

RECOMMENDED READING

Abanes, Richard. *Embraced by the Light and the Bible* (Camp Hill, PA: Horizon Books, 1994).

Cares, Mark J. *Speaking the Truth in Love to Mormons* (Milwaukee: Northwestern Publishing House, 1993).

Geer, Thelma "Granny." *Mormonism, Mama, & Me* (Chicago: Moody Press, 1979; 1986 edition).

Larson, Charles M. *By His Own Hand Upon Papyrus* (Grand Rapids, MI: Institute for Religious Research, 1992 edition).

Martin, Walter. *The Maze of Mormonism* (Ventura, CA: Regal Books, 1962; 1978 edition).

McKeever, Bill and Eric Johnson. *Questions to Ask Your Mormon Friend* (Minneapolis: Bethany House, 1994).

McKeever, Bill. *Answering Mormons' Questions* (Minneapolis: Bethany House, 1991).

Scott, Latayne Colvett. *The Mormon Mirage* (Grand Rapids, MI: Zondervan, 1979).

Tanner, Jerald and Sandra Tanner. *Mormonism: Shadow or Reality?* (Salt Lake City: Utah Lighthouse Ministry, 1987 edition).

_____. *The Changing World of Mormonism* (Chicago: Moody Press, 1979).

JEHOVAH'S FALSE WITNESSES

[People] have at hand the Bible, but it is little read or understood. So, does Jehovah have a prophet to help them, to warn them of dangers and to declare things to come? These questions can be answered in the affirmative. . . . This "prophet" was not one man, but was a body of men and women . . . [known] as International Bible Students. Today they are known as Jehovah's Christian witnesses.

THE WATCHTOWER, APRIL 1, 1972[1]

Twenty-year-old Randy Watters was drawn into the kingdom of the cults during the summer of 1972 after discovering two books that his mother had haphazardly stuffed in a drawer: *The Truth That Leads to Eternal Life* and *Then Is Finished the Mystery of God*. Both volumes were published by the Watch Tower Bible & Tract Society, the parent corporation of the Jehovah's Witnesses. The books, which had been purchased from Witnesses canvassing the neighborhood, soon took on a crucial role in Randy's life. He studied them relentlessly and within a few short months was attending religious services at a nearby "Kingdom Hall of the Jehovah's Witnesses." In November he was baptized into the cult and further committed himself to "God's organization" by signing up as a "Pioneer" (i.e., a member who engages in full-time, door-to-door witnessing).

For nearly two years Randy tirelessly worked to distribute Watch Tower literature announcing "Jehovah's Kingdom." His dedication was so impressive that in 1974 he was granted permission to work at Bethel, the international headquarters of the Jehovah's Witnesses located in Brooklyn, New York. Three years later he had reached the prestigious status of an overseer and Bethel elder. This was a major accomplishment for someone so young. As Randy remembers it, he achieved quite a reputation:

I was in charge of the presses that printed their Bibles, and I helped start an offset training school. Later projects involved helping to renovate the entire printing operation. Traveling regularly around New England as a speaker, I made many fine friends and enjoyed my work. I was convinced this was truly "God's organization," and was even zealous to report those who were entertaining thoughts contrary to those of the "faithful slave" [a term that collectively refers to the organization's spiritual elite]. I was known as an "organization man."

Like many cults, the Jehovah's Witnesses present many do's and don'ts that members must obey if they hope to earn salvation. Unique to the Watch Tower, however, is its ban on various activities that are widely accepted in society. The organization does not allow members to observe holidays (e.g., Christmas, Thanksgiving, or Easter), nor can they celebrate birthdays, Mother's Day, Father's Day, or Valentine's Day. Witnesses also cannot vote, salute the American flag, say the Pledge of Allegiance, or sing the "National Anthem." More devastating is the group's ban on blood transfusions, which has led to countless Witness deaths over the years, including many children.[2]

But these were not the doctrines that eventually altered Randy's perspective of the group. His views began changing after a 1979 business trip. He and another factory overseer found themselves agreeing on the fact that when it came to salvation, the Witnesses make one's works far more important than one's faith. In subsequent weeks Randy studied Scripture apart from literature produced by the Watch Tower, paying special attention to Paul's letters to the Romans and Galatians. He also attended a private Bible study being held by some fellow Bethel workers. As they went through the New Testament chapter by chapter, it became increasingly clear that studying Scripture itself was far different from studying Scripture with Watch Tower literature.

Randy eventually found out that there were many such groups at Bethel and that most of them were coming to the same conclusion: the "Governing Body" (i.e., the ruling hierarchy) of the organization was promoting legalism, which Scripture condemns (Gal. 2:21; 3:1–14). But this disturbing discovery would remain unspoken for some time because most of the Witnesses at Bethel were committed believers who did not want to stir up trouble. Trouble, however, was just around the corner.

Word began to spread that some Bethel workers had actually expressed doubts over a long-held Jehovah's Witness doctrine—a foundational doctrine—involving the prophetic significance of the year 1914. It did not take long for the Governing Body to realize that these "independent thinkers"[3] had done much more than just present a few opposing opinions: they had threatened the doctrinal stability of the entire organization. Several high-ranking Witnesses felt that such questioning was a result of too much intellectual freedom within the organization in general. As a result, the Governing Body deemed it necessary to lay down rules to "keep the brothers in line." They felt that a member's love for God could not keep him or her out of trouble. Followers needed even stricter rules and regulations to govern all aspects of life, including their thoughts.

By the end of 1979, no one at Bethel dared admit to having any opinions contrary to those expressed through official Watch Tower publications. Those who did express differences were quickly "disfellowshipped" (i.e., expelled from the organization). Some disfellowshipped members were vocal. But most remained silent, preferring to leave without a fight. Approximately 100 Bethel workers ended up making a quiet exit during 1980. The oppressive atmosphere that descended on Randy and his remaining coworkers was almost unbearable. Bethel leaders went so far as to draw up ten questions that were used to interrogate suspected doubters of God's truths as revealed by the Watch Tower. A popular Bible commentary was even banned from the libraries because some Bethelites who had used it in their studies realized that the Watch Tower's biblical scholarship was terribly flawed and criticized it.

Because of his administrative position, Randy always knew through the grapevine who was going to "get the ax" each day. He could then only watch as junior members of the Governing Body took turns defaming the "apostates" in order to prove their loyalty to the older members of the Governing Body. The insecurity of Watch Tower leaders over their doctrinal foundation was finally revealed in the August 15, 1981 issue of *The Watchtower* (pp. 28-29). The main article attacked those who wanted to study Scripture without the aid of Jehovah's Witnesses literature:

> They say that it is sufficient to read the Bible exclusively, either alone or in small groups at home. But, strangely, through such "Bible reading,"

they have reverted right back to the apostate doctrines that commentaries by Christendom's clergy were teaching 100 years ago.

To rank-and-file Witnesses, the message was clear: they were not allowed to study or interpret God's Word for themselves, but would be expected to rely on the Governing Body to interpret Scripture for them. This was too much for Randy, who decided to take two months off from work to simply read the Bible and discover for himself the way to reach God. He gradually realized that it was God who had already reached out to him through the person and work of Christ. Jesus was the mediator between God and man (1 Tim. 2:5), not some Governing Body comprised of fallible men.

Randy never went back to Bethel. Instead, he sent the Watch Tower a letter of resignation from the Jehovah's Witnesses. He has since become one of America's most respected critics of the Watch Tower Society. His *Free Minds Journal* —a bimonthly periodical that provides up-to-date information on the Jehovah's Witnesses—has become a very enlightening publication to many persons throughout the world.

HOW IT ALL BEGAN

The Watch Tower Bible & Tract Society (WTBTS)—commonly known as the Jehovah's Witnesses (hereafter referred to as JWs)—is easily one of the most deceptive of today's religious cults. Since its inception in the late 1800s, the group's hierarchy has kept rank-and-file members in line with false prophecies, doctrinal flip-flops, scholastic dishonesty, and psychological manipulation via peer pressure, verbal intimidation, and threats of excommunication. Despite countless warnings about the WTBTS that have been issued by counter-cult organizations, the group continues to thrive worldwide. Much of the cult's success can be attributed to the zealous proselytizing efforts of its members. In 1996, for instance, Jehovah's Witnesses spent a total of 1,140,621,714 hours preaching their message in 223 countries.[4]

The group's evangelistic strategy rests on door-to-door witnessing coupled with distribution of two semi-monthly magazines: *Awake!* and *The Watchtower.* The former publication targets non-members and focuses on current events, while the latter periodical is the Society's "chief means of instructing members in doctrine and practice."[5] As of January 1998, circulation for *Awake!* was 18,350,000 in eighty languages, and circulation for *The Watchtower* was 20,980,000 in 126 languages.[6] The WTBTS has also produced a significant number of books throughout its history, and continues to do so at a rate of one or two per year. These books promote basic doctrines, serve as instructional guides for living, and contain Bible studies.

JWs have even produced their own translation of the Bible: *The New World Translation of the Holy Scriptures* (NWT). Numerous scholars have labeled it an obvious propaganda tool filled with deliberate mistranslations of the biblical Greek texts in order to promote the unorthodox doctrines propagated by the Witnesses.[7] Nevertheless, by 1998 over 82,513,571 million copies of the NWT had been published in thirty languages.[8] This does not mean that JWs are avid Bible students. Although many JWs may indeed read their Bibles, they are allowed to do so only in conjunction with other WTBTS publications, which serve to interpret Scripture for them.

According to JWs, the Bible is actually an "organizational book" that is beyond the understanding of all persons except the Governing Body of the WTBTS. Scripture does not belong "to individuals, regardless of how sincerely they may believe that they can interpret the Bible."[9] Consequently, JWs assert: "Only this organization functions for Jehovah's purpose and to his praise. To it alone God's Sacred Word, the Bible, is not a sealed book."[10] This method of keeping members obedient to a predetermined set of beliefs promoted by WTBTS leaders can be traced to the teachings of the organization's founder, Charles Taze Russell, who stated that only by studying his writings could anyone gain a proper understanding of Scripture.[11]

Rise of the Russellites

The roots of the Jehovah's Witnesses go back several years before Charles Taze Russell (1852–1916) was even born, to a time in early nineteenth-century America when apocalyptic expectations were running high. The millennial madness that swept through the U.S. during the early 1800s began with the publication in 1836 of a sixty-four page pamphlet entitled *Evidence from Scripture and History of the Second Coming of Christ About the Year A.D. 1843, and of His Personal Reign of 1,000 Years*. The booklet's author—Baptist preacher William Miller—postulated that according to biblical chronology Jesus' return would occur around 1843.

The prediction spread like wildfire across all denominational lines in the church, and within a few short years a bona fide religious movement was in full swing. It pulled followers from the Methodists, Baptists, Presbyterians, and Congregationalists. Soon these so-called "Millerites" had inadvertently formed a new sect that religion watchers of the day labeled "Adventists." The formation of this new sect was anything but peaceful. As the terminal date of history grew ever closer, Miller's followers became increasingly antagonistic toward fellow Christians who would not join their movement. They finally branded all other churches as "Babylon," the false religious system spoken of in Revelation 14:8; 17:5. Mainline churches responded by expelling and excommunicating from their ranks countless Millerite ministers and laypersons.

Miller eventually refined his date to March 21, 1843-March 21, 1844. Obviously, Jesus did not return in 1844. But this did not dissuade Miller or his followers from believing that the end was near. Miller discovered a slight miscalculation he had made and revised his date to October 22, 1844. Millerite expectations rose once again, only to be dashed when Christ did not return as predicted. That date would come to be known as the "Great Disappointment." Although the Millerite movement was irrevocably shattered, a number of Adventist organizations emerged from his disappointed flock. The Seventh-day Adventists, under the leadership of Ellen G. White, would grow to become the most famous of these groups.

A lesser-known faction that branched out from the Millerites was the Second Adventists. Unlike the Seventh-day Adventists, who eschewed date-setting, the Second Adventists continued to speculate about the timing of Christ's return. They eventually set yet another date for His second advent: 1873/1874. It was into this apocalyptic fold that a young man named Charles Taze Russell was drawn. By the year 1870 he had formed his own home Bible study group in Allegheny, Pennsylvania, focusing primarily on biblical passages dealing with Christ's second coming. The group grew so enamored with Russell that they eventually elected him to be their "pastor."

Needless to say, these Second Adventists were thoroughly disappointed in 1874 when Jesus did not show up as expected. But rather than admitting there had been an error in their time calculations, the Second Adventists came up with a novel explanation for what had transpired. They maintained they had indeed been right about the *date* of Jesus' return but had been wrong about the *manner* of it, concluding that He must have returned *invisibly*, as Russell explained:

> Looking back to 1871, we see that many of our company were what are known as Second Adventists, and the light they held briefly stated, was that there would be a second advent of Jesus. . . . This they claimed would occur in 1873. . . . Well, 1873 came . . . and yet no burning of the world. . . . But prophecies were found which pointed positively to 1874 as the time when Jesus was due to be present. . . . The autumn of 1874, anxiously expected, finally came, but the earth rolled on as ever. . . . Then the prophetic arguments were carefully re-examined. Was an error found? No, they stood the test of all investigation. . . . Dark indeed seemed the outlook; all were discouraged. . . . Just at this time Bro. Keith, (one of our contributors) was used of the Lord to throw another beam of *light* on the subject which brought order out of confusion, and caused all of the former "light" to shine with tenfold brightness. . . . [A] new idea of *a presence* unseen, except by the eye of faith. . . . [W]e realized that when Jesus should come, it would be as unobserved by human eyes as though an angel had come. . . . Here was a new thought: Could it be that the *time prophecies* . . . were really meant to indicate when the Lord would be *invisibly present* to set up his kingdom? . . . [T]he evidences satisfied me.[12]

Such an explanation virtually ignores the biblical passages that describe Jesus' return to earth as a physical event that will be seen by everyone (e.g., Acts 1:9–11; Rev. 1:7). Nevertheless, Russell and his followers clung to their end-time scenario and proceeded to preach their message to the masses through a periodical Russell started in 1879: *Zion's Watch Tower and Herald of Christ's Presence*. It later evolved into what is now known as *The Watchtower*. Then in 1884, Russell founded and installed himself as president of Zion's Watch Tower Tract Society. This organization, which eventually became the Watch Tower Bible & Tract Society, continues to serve as the legal corporation for Russell's spiritual progeny: the Jehovah's Witnesses.

Armageddon, Inc.

Under Russell, the WTBTS experienced tremendous growth. Members, then known collectively as the International Bible Students Association, looked exclusively to Russell for spiritual nourishment. Especially popular was his six-book series called *Studies in the Scriptures*.[13] Through these books, Russell not only taught that Jesus had returned invisibly in 1874 but claimed that His arrival in the heavenly realms marked the beginning of humanity's "Time of Trouble," which would culminate with the Battle of Armageddon in 1914 and the end of the world as we know it.

> [W]e present the Bible evidence proving that the full end of the times of the Gentiles, i.e., the full end of their lease of dominion, will be reached in A.D. 1914; and that that date will be the farthest limit of the rule of imperfect men.... [A]t that date the Kingdom of God, for which our Lord taught us to pray, saying "Thy Kingdom come," will have obtained full, universal control, and that it will then be "set up," or firmly established, in the earth.[14]

> [T]he "battle of the great day of God Almighty" (Rev. 16:14), which will end in A.D. 1914 with the complete overthrow of earth's present rulership, is already commenced.[15]

> [A]ll present governments will be overthrown and dissolved.... [T]he full establishment of the Kingdom of God, will be accomplished by the end of A.D. 1914.[16]

This same prediction was printed in *Zion's Watch Tower & Herald of Christ's Presence*.[17] With the commencement of World War I in 1914, Russell preached his message with even more zeal, declaring: "The present great war in Europe is the beginning of the Armageddon of the scriptures."[18] Russell, however, never lived to see Christ's return. He died on October 31, 1916, still believing that "the end" was imminent. He was wrong. But faithful followers continued to promote the prophetic chronology that their beloved pastor had so painstakingly formulated.

It has since been discovered that many converts to Russell's flock held on to their expectations due in part to a concerted effort made by WTBTS leaders to cover up the various mistakes and false prophecies that had been published by the Watch Tower. Russell himself had initiated the practice as his doomsday date drew nearer. For example, later editions of *Studies in the Scriptures* contained subtle changes in the text where Russell had made explicit declarations regarding the timing of the end. He altered them in an effort to give his predicted "end" more time to unfold. These alterations were made with no footnote indicating that textual changes had been inserted. Compare the following photostatic reproductions of various passages taken from different editions of *Studies in the Scriptures*, volumes 2, 3, and 4. (The alterations have been underlined to assist the reader in locating them.)

COMPARISON OF EDITIONS—STUDIES IN THE SCRIPTURES: VOL. 2, P. 99

1906 Edition

In view of this strong Bible evidence concerning the Times of the Gentiles, we consider it an established truth that the final end of the kingdoms of this world, and the full establishment of the Kingdom of God, will be accomplished by the end of A. D. 1914. Then the prayer of the

1913 Edition

In view of this strong Bible evidence concerning the Times of the Gentiles, we consider it an established truth that the final end of the kingdoms of this world, and the full establishment of the Kingdom of God, will be accomplished by the end of A. D. 1914. Then the prayer of the

---

COMPARISON OF EDITIONS—STUDIES IN THE SCRIPTURES: VOL. 3, P. 228

1908 Edition

That the deliverance of the saints must take place some time before 1914 is manifest, since the deliverance of fleshly Israel, as we shall see, is appointed to take place at that time, and the angry nations will then be authoritatively commanded to be still, and will be made to recognize the power of Jehovah's Anointed. Just how long before 1914 the last living members of the body of Christ will be glorified, we are not directly informed ; but it certainly will not

1916 Edition

That the deliverance of the saints must take place very soon after 1914 is manifest, since the deliverance of fleshly Israel, as we shall see, is appointed to take place at that time, and the angry nations will then be authoritatively commanded to be still, and will be made to recognize the power of Jehovah's Anointed. Just how long after 1914 the last living members of the body of Christ will be glorified, we are not directly informed ; but it certainly will not

---

COMPARISON OF EDITIONS—STUDIES IN THE SCRIPTURES: VOL. 4, P. 604

1897 Edition

date;—the " harvest" or gathering time beginning October 1874; the organization of the Kingdom and the taking by our Lord of his great power as the King in April 1878, and the time of trouble or "day of wrath" which began October 1874 and will end October 1914; and the

1916 Edition

date;—the " harvest" or gathering time beginning October 1874; the organization of the Kingdom and the taking by our Lord of his great power as the King in April 1878, and the time of trouble or "day of wrath" which began October 1874, and will cease about 1915; and the

---

The most fascinating change made to *Studies in the Scriptures* appears in volume 3, where Russell sought to prove his Armageddon timetable through pyramidology, which is an occult system of prophetic speculation "based on various proportions and measurements of the Great Pyramid [of Gizeh], which are held to correlate with important historical events."[19]

Russell taught that the pyramid was "God's Stone Witness" corroborating biblical prophecy. To, Russell, the pyramid's "Descending Passage"—which starts inside the structure's entrance and leads toward its "Subterranean Chamber" (or "Pit")—was a prophetic marker of world events.[20] He believed that the "Pit" designated the "Time of Trouble" (i.e., a period of catastrophe), which he predicted would occur just prior to the 1914 Battle of Armageddon.

Russell further taught that each inch in the passage represented one year and that by taking measurements of the "Descending Passage" and numerous intersecting passages, one could predict exactly when the world's time of trouble was to begin. Predictably, Russell discovered that the measurements pointed to the very year that he himself had already arrived at through computations based on Bible chronology: 1874. It was yet another confirmation to Russell that 1874 marked the beginning of the end, which would culminate in 1914 with the Battle of Armageddon.

But as 1914 drew near, Russell began to worry that perhaps God's "Battle" would not take place. To alleviate his fears, he came up with an ingenious way to buy himself more time. He had volume 3 reprinted and simply stretched the Great Pyramid's passage by forty-one inches. Each extra inch translated into an extra year. Suddenly, the WTBTS was teaching that the *beginning* of the end had not started in 1874 after all! The year 1915 was the landmark date for the beginning of trouble to start.

COMPARISON OF EDITIONS—STUDIES IN THE SCRIPTURES: VOL. 3, P. 342

1897 Edition	1916 Edition
Then measuring *down* the "Entrance Passage" from that point, to find the distance to the entrance of the "Pit," representing the great trouble and destruction with which this age is to close, when evil will be overthrown from power, we find it to be 3416 inches, symbolizing 3416 years from the above date, B. C. 1542. This calculation shows A. D. 1874 as marking the beginning of the period of trouble; for 1542 years B. C. plus 1874 years A. D. equals 3416 years. Thus the Pyramid witnesses that the close of 1874 was the *chronological* beginning of the time of trouble such as was not since there was a nation—no, nor ever shall be afterward.	Then measuring *down* the "Entrance Passage" from that point, to find the distance to the entrance of the "Pit," representing the great trouble and destruction with which this age is to close, when evil will be overthrown from power, we find it to be 3457 inches, symbolizing 3457 years from the above date, B. C. 1542. This calculation shows A. D. 1915 as marking the beginning of the period of trouble; for 1542 years B. C. plus 1915 years A. D. equals 3457 years. Thus the Pyramid witnesses that the close of 1914 will be the beginning of the time of trouble such as was not since there was a nation—no, nor ever shall be afterward.

By the early 1920s, most WTBTS leaders felt that the numerous changes to Russell's writings would buy their organization an adequate amount of extra time for the world's end to occur. So confident were they that the planet's demise was near that Russell's successor—J. F. Rutherford

(1869–1942)—started making his own predictions. The year 1914 had easily replaced 1874 as the *beginning* of troubles. But what year would replace 1914 as the date of the end? Rutherford picked 1925.

Millions Now Living Will Never Die

Joseph Franklin Rutherford became president of the Watch Tower in 1917. He was a charismatic leader who rabidly attacked "Christendom" through radio programs, public speeches, convention lectures, books, pamphlets, and assorted publications. Under his leadership, the size of Russell's organization grew exponentially. In fact, it was Rutherford who instituted the door-to-door preaching for which Witnesses have become so well known. It was also Rutherford who introduced several new doctrines into the group, while at the same time contradicting a number of Russell's teachings.

His administration additionally saw the name "Jehovah's Witnesses" adopted in 1931 as a descriptive term that would forever identify the doctrinally shifting cult of "Bible Students" that Russell had founded. The new name was adopted for two reasons: 1) to separate followers of the Watch Tower from traditional Christian groups; and 2) to delineate Rutherford's followers from those individuals who wanted to remain true to Russell's teachings and who had formed their own Russellite groups.

Perhaps the most infamous period of Rutherford's presidency took place from 1918 to 1925. During this era of JW history, the Watch Tower Society declared with full assurance that 1925 would bring the complete overthrow of all worldly governments, the resurrection of Old Testament saints (e.g., Abraham and Jacob), and the establishment of God's earthly kingdom. In other words, 1925 would mark the end of the world.[21] Rutherford first announced this prophecy during a 1918 lecture that was eventually turned into a 1920 booklet entitled *Millions Now Living Will Never Die*.

Throughout the early 1920s this prediction was consistently reinforced by a nationwide campaign that included speaking engagements, posters, flyers, large billboards, and newspaper advertisements. Books published by the WTBTS during these years also supported the prediction.[22] The most authoritative pronouncements on the subject, however, appeared in *The Watchtower* magazine. Consider the following:

Abraham should enter upon the actual possession of his promised inheritance in the year 1925 A.D. [1917][23]

If any one who has studied the Bible can travel through Europe and not be convinced that the world has ended, that the day of God's vengence is here, and that the Messianic kingdom is at the door, then he has read his Bible in vain. . . . The date 1925 is even more distinctly indicated by the Scriptures because it is fixed by the law God gave Israel. . . . [E]ven before 1925 the great crisis will be reached and probably passed. [1922][24]

[T]he present crisis in the world is caused by the long-looked-for King of Glory, the Lord Jesus, taking unto himself his great power and . . . making way for the era of peace and happiness in the joyous time just over the horizon of 1925, when God's will shall be done on earth as it is in heaven. [1923][25]

Rutherford claimed that his prediction was based on nothing less than "the promises set forth in the divine Word."[26] The certainty with which *The Watchtower* preached the world's soon demise brought many converts into the organization. But as God's day of judgment approached, the Watch Tower started to once more back away from dogmatic assertions it had made about the time of the end. For example, the July 15, 1924 issue of *The Watchtower* stated: "The year 1925 is a date definitely and clearly marked in the Scriptures, even more clearly than that of 1914; but it would be presumptuous on the part of any faithful follower of the Lord to assume just what the Lord is going to do during that year."[27] The most obvious attempt at downplaying prior declarations about doomsday appeared in the January 1, 1925 issue of *The Watchtower*:

The year 1925 is here. With great expectation Christians have looked forward to this year. Many have confidently expected that all members of the body of Christ will be changed to heavenly glory during the year. This may be accomplished. It may not be.[28]

As more of 1925 slipped away, WTBTS leaders seemed to have completely forgotten about their previous statements regarding the year's significance. In one book they published that year, Rutherford declared that faithful followers should expect to see only one thing in 1925: "[E]xpect the people to begin to receive some knowledge concerning God's great plan of restoration."[29] In another 1925 booklet he actually wrote: "Much has heretofore been said about 1925. . . . Many people are looking for something phenomenal to happen. . . . A careful consideration of prophecy will enable you to be fortified against whatsoever comes."[30]

The Watchtower of September 1, 1925 issued what was perhaps the most unbelievable warning: "It is to be expected that Satan will try to inject into the minds of the consecrated the thought that 1925 should see an end of the work [i.e., the end of the world]."[31] What about all of the previous statements in *The Watchtower* concerning 1925? According to WTBTS leaders, rank-and-file members had misunderstood what was printed and erroneously "anticipated that the work [i.e., the world] would end in 1925, but the Lord did not so state."[32] This excuse, however, completely contradicted what WTBTS leaders had declared in the August 15, 1922 edition of *The Watchtower*: "This chronology is not of man but of God . . . of divine origin . . . absolutely and unqualifiedly correct."[33]

To date, the organization's Governing Body is still trying to convince Jehovah's Witnesses that the fiasco of 1925 was the fault of various members who had read far too much into what appeared in official Watch Tower publications. *The 1980 Yearbook of Jehovah's Witnesses*, for instance, explains:

> The book *Millions Now Living Will Never Die* had been widely used . . . and on the basis of its contents, much was expected of 1925. . . . It was stated in the "Millions" book that we might *reasonably* expect them [Abraham, Isaac, and Jacob] to return shortly after 1925, but this was merely an expressed opinion [emphasis added].[34]

But the *Millions* book actually says something quite different. Pages 89–90 read: "[T]he great jubilee cycle is due to begin in 1925. At that time the earthly phase of the kingdom shall be recognized. . . . Therefore we may *confidently* expect that 1925 will mark the return of Abraham, Isaac, Jacob and the faithful prophets of old" [emphasis added].[35] Rutherford's statements on page 97 are even more definitive:

> [T]he old order of things, the old world, is ending . . . and that the new order is coming in, and that 1925 shall mark the resurrection of the faith-

ful worthies of old. . . . [M]illions of people now on the earth will be still on the earth in 1925. Then, based upon the premises set forth in the divine Word, we must reach the positive and indisputable conclusion that millions now living will never die.[36]

Clearly, Rutherford and other WTBTS officials misled members into believing that God's Word pointed to 1925 as the end of the world. In 1929 they were still claiming that Armageddon was near: "It is a special pleasure to announce that the next few years [c. 1930s] will witness the full establishment of that kingdom which is to be the desire of all nations."[37] As we have already seen, this latter prediction was not the first false prophecy to be made by the Watch Tower, nor would it be the last. The next two presidents of the Jehovah's Witnesses—Nathan Knorr and Frederick Franz—would make their own false prophecies.

Armageddon . . . Again

When Nathan Knorr (1905–1977) took over for Rutherford in 1942, one of his first acts as president was the release of a new book entitled *The New World*. This volume continued promoting what had become a standard line of the WTBTS—i.e., that the Old Testament saints were soon to be resurrected in order to assume their roles as earthly rulers in Jehovah's kingdom. *The New World* proclaimed, "[T]hose faithful men of old may be expected back from the dead any day now."[38] A 1942 issue of *Consolation* (eventually renamed *Awake!*) additionally promised: "[T]hat these princes will *shortly* take office upon earth as perfect men is found in the prophecy of Daniel. . . . Proof is now submitted that we are now living at 'the end of the days,' and we may expect to see Daniel and the other mentioned princes any day now!"[39]

Such predictions came as a surprise to no one. The WTBTS had been suggesting for several years that Armageddon would occur in the 1940s as a result of World War II. An earlier *Consolation* article (October 1941) had stated: "[T]he German people are awakening to their horrible predicament. . . . [T]heir faces are . . . filled with forebodings of what the near future will bring and is already hastening to bring to them—Armageddon, the battle of that great day of God Almighty."[40] As far back as May 1940, the *Informant*—a members-only publication—had declared: "The year 1940 is certain to be the most important year yet, because Armageddon is very near."[41]

In September 1940 WTBTS leaders reiterated: "The Kingdom is here, the King is enthroned. Armageddon is just ahead."[42] The September 15, 1941 issue of *The Watchtower* told readers that a recently released book entitled *Children* would be "the Lord's provided instrument for most effective work in the remaining months before Armageddon."[43] Tragically, these false prophecies were coupled with a series of directives that advised JWs to forsake marriage and child-rearing:

> There are now on earth Jonadabs [i.e., Jehovah's Witnesses] devoted to the Lord. . . . Would it be Scripturally proper for them to now marry and begin to rear children? No, is the answer, which is supported by the Scriptures.[44]

> Scriptures appear to clearly show that the survivors of Armageddon will be those Jonadabs who henceforth "seek righteousness" . . . should they marry now? . . . [S]hould the Jonadabs now be encouraged to marry and rear children? No, is the answer supported by the Scriptures.[45]

> [T]he great multitude who survive the battle of Armageddon will be the only ones of the human race to abide on the earth. . . . [S]hould those begin now to marry and bring forth children in fulfillment of the divine mandate? No, is the answer; which the Scriptures fully support.[46]

Countless JWs throughout the world made decisions about their future based on this advice that had appeared in official Watch Tower publications. Many witnesses all lived to regret not having followed through with their original plans to marry and/or bear children because Armageddon never came. Knorr responded by simply ignoring the misleading statements that the WTBTS had published. Then, after twenty more years of continuing to preach the "soon" arrival of Armageddon, Knorr chose yet another date for the end of human history: 1975.

This Time for Sure

Pushing Armageddon all the way up to 1975 took quite a bit of work on the part of WTBTS leaders. They had to completely rewrite Russell's outdated mode of calculating when the end would occur. The 1943 book *The Truth Shall Make You Free* was Knorr's first step to formally erase what Witnesses had been believing since 1879. The volume completely did away with Russell's dating system, replacing it with the one currently being used by the Jehovah's Witnesses. According to the new system, Jesus did not return invisibly in 1874 but returned in 1914![47]

It was further taught that many persons comprising "the generation" that was alive during 1914 would live to see Armageddon and the establishment of God's kingdom. This "1914 generation" timetable continued to be reinforced until 1966, when the book *Life Everlasting in Freedom of the Sons of God* set 1975 as the target date for Armageddon, the alleged end of 6,000 years of history since the creation of Adam.[48] In JW eschatology, this meant that the end of the world would occur within eight years. More importantly, plenty of people from the "1914 generation" would still be alive in 1975:

> [I]t was to our generation that Jesus referred when he added the key thought: "This generation will by no means pass away until all these things occur." (Matt. 24:34) The generation that saw the beginning of woes in 1914 would also see the end of Satan and his entire wicked system of things. Some who were alive then would still be alive when "the end" comes. It is to be carefully noted that the youngest of those who saw with understanding the developing sign of the end of this system of things from its start in 1914 are now well over sixty years of age![49]

By 1968 the WTBTS was boldly pushing 1975 as the completion date of human history.[50] A 1966 issue of *Awake!* promised: "[W]ithin relatively few years we will witness the fulfillment of the remaining prophecies that have to do with the 'time of the end.'"[51] One especially influential article appearing in a 1968 issue of *The Watchtower* was entitled "Why Are You Looking Forward to 1975?" The story continued: "Are we to assume from this study that the battle of Armageddon will be all over by the autumn of 1975, and the long-looked-for thousand-year reign of Christ will begin by then? . . . It may involve only a difference of weeks or months, not years."[52]

It was the 1940s all over again. Witnesses were once more counseled not to get married or have children, and young adults were advised to forego higher education and professional careers in order to devote themselves to the organization in the months remaining before Armageddon:

> [T]he end of this system is so very near! . . . Reports are heard of brothers selling their homes and property and planning to finish out the rest of their days in this old system in the pioneer service. . . . [T]his is a fine way to spend the short time remaining before the wicked world's end.[53]

> Today there is a great crowd of people who are confident that a destruction of even greater magnitude is now imminent. The evidence is that Jesus' prophecy will shortly have a major fulfillment, upon this entire system of things. This has been a major factor in influencing many couples to decide not to have children at this time. They have chosen to remain childless so that they would be less encumbered to carry out the instructions of Jesus Christ to preach the good news of God's kingdom earth wide before the end of this system comes.[54]

> Will you be finishing school soon? If so, what have you decided to do after you graduate? . . . Of course, there may be a tempting offer of higher education or of going into some field of work that promises material rewards. . . . In view of the short time left, a decision to pursue a career in this system of things is not only unwise but extremely dangerous. . . . Many young brothers and sisters were offered scholarships or employment that promised fine pay. However, they turned them down and put spiritual interests first.[55]

Although such statements were clearly reminiscent of what had been said in the 1940s, WTBTS leaders had already taken steps to psychologically prepare JWs to tolerate more talk about "the end." By 1968 the Governing Body—under Knorr's leadership—was actually claiming that JWs during World War II "didn't succomb [sic]" to any expectations about that war leading to Armageddon.[56] This made the new prophecy about 1975 seem more reliable and trustworthy.

Adding considerable credence to the 1975 prediction was Watch Tower vice president Frederick Franz (1893–1992), who would succeed Knorr as president in 1977. In fact, Franz had been the Governing Body member who authored *Life Everlasting in Freedom of the Sons of God*.[57] Franz would also be instrumental in providing the excuse for why 1975 did *not* bring the end as predicted. As in the past, the average Jehovah's Witness was blamed for having "missed the point" of all the WTBTS's statements and erroneously "thinking that Bible chronology reveals the specific date."[58]

The most notable aspect of Franz's term as president was his steadfast adherence to the teaching that persons alive during 1914 (that "generation") would definitely see Armageddon. But when Franz died in 1992 at the age of ninety-nine, it became apparent that there were not many individuals left who had witnessed the events of 1914. This realization placed the Governing Body in a very precarious situation since much of the Watch Tower's doctrine has been based on the belief that the generation of 1914 would see Jehovah's Kingdom established. The problem, however, would be cleverly dealt with by Franz's successor, seventy-two-year-old Milton G. Henschel.

Good-bye 1914

Milton Henschel is the only JW president born after the death of Russell. His primary concern after taking office was figuring out how to rescue the WTBTS from total collapse. Franz's death had made it uncomfortably clear that very few individuals who saw the events of 1914 were still alive. The long-held prophecy that some people of the 1914 generation would see the establishment of Jehovah's Kingdom was set to crumble, and with it, the entire eschatological structure of "God's organization."

The prophecy originally held that persons old enough to see "with understanding" the events of 1914 would also live to see the world's end. Such individuals, according to WTBTS leaders, probably would have been no younger than fifteen years old in 1914.[59] It was taught that this 1914 generation "logically would not apply to babies born during World War I."[60] Then in the 1980s, the Watch Tower contradicted itself by revealing that the term "generation" applied to people who were only *babies* in 1914.[61] By extending "the generation" to babies, WTBTS leaders were able to buy more time for the end to come before that generation passed away.

But this left Henschel with no more ways to redefine the 1914 "generation." Consequently, he simply discarded the entire generation prophecy in the November 1, 1995 issue of *The Watchtower*. This "new light"[62] of truth explained that the "generation" mentioned by Jesus in Matthew 24 has nothing to do with individuals—adults or babies—living in 1914. Now the term simply applied to wicked mankind in general; more specifically, any and all people of the earth in any generation who "see the sign of Christ's appearance but fail to mend their ways."[63]

The all-important "generation" had been relegated to everyone living in today's wicked system, or perhaps in the wicked system of 100 years from now, or 1,000 years from now. All time elements had been completely removed. Although this bold step contradicted the position that had been held by JWs for eighty years, it was a change that *had* to be made. One can only wonder how members of the Watch Tower can psychologically justify God's prophecies changing so arbitrarily:

WATCH TOWER PROPHECY CHANGES

Pre-1995	Post-1995
"[T]he generation alive in 1914, some will see the major fulfillment of Christ Jesus' prophecy and destruction."[64] "What, then, is the 'generation' that 'will by no means pass away until all these things occur'? . . . It is the generation of people who saw the catastrophic events that broke forth in connection with World War I. . . . We can be happy, therefore, for Jesus' assurance that there will be survivors of 'the generation of 1914' . . . when the 'great tribulation' rings down the curtain on this wicked system of things."[65] "[B]efore the 1914 generation completely dies out, God's judgment must be executed."[66]	"Jehovah's people have at times speculated about the time when the 'great tribulation' would break out, even tying this to calculations of what is the lifetime of a generation since 1914. . . . [But] rather than provide a rule for measuring time, the term 'generation' as used by Jesus refers principally to contemporary people of a certain historical period, with their identifying characteristics."[67] "God's servants in modern times have tried to derive from what Jesus said about 'generation' some clear time element calculated from 1914. . . . [T]he recent information in *The Watchtower* about 'this generation' . . . did give us a clearer grasp of Jesus' use of the term 'generation,' helping us see that his usage was no basis for calculating—counting from 1914—how close to the end we are."[68]

The Final Excuse

Despite the many false prophecies that have been made by God's prophet-like organization (see this chapter's opening quote), JWs continue to maintain that they are not a collective false prophet and have never made *any* false prophecies! But the Watch Tower does indeed fall under the condemnation of false prophets found in Deuteronomy 18:20–22: "'How shall we know the word which the LORD has not spoken?' When a prophet speaks in the name of the LORD, if the thing does not come about or come true, that is the thing which the LORD has not spoken. The prophet has spoken it presumptuously; you shall not be afraid of him."

The all-important question that must be asked is quite simple: Has the WTBTS ever claimed to be a collective prophet that has made predictions in the name of the Lord? Put another way, have the Jehovah's Witnesses ever attributed their predictions directly to God? The answer is an easily documentable yes. *The Watchtower* of May 1, 1938 claims that God actually uses angels to supernaturally impart His divine messages to the writers of WTBTS literature. As a result, *everything* published by the WTBTS must be received by faithful Witnesses as God's words:

> The resolutions adopted by conventions of God's anointed people, booklets, magazines, and books published by them, contain the message of God's truth and are from the Almighty God, Jehovah, and provided by him through Christ Jesus and his underofficers [i.e., angels].... The interpretation of prophecy, therefore, is not from man, but is from Jehovah.... It is his truth, and not man's.[69]

As if this statement were not clear enough, a 1943 issue of *The Watchtower* took great pains to explain that representatives of Jehovah's organization are *not* "an earthly tribunal of interpretation, delegated to interpret the Scriptures and its prophecies." According to this issue's article, it is God the Father who interprets prophecies and Jesus Christ who proclaims those prophecies to WTBTS leaders. The organization is then merely used by God "to publish the interpretation after the [spiritual] Supreme Court by Jesus Christ reveals it."[70] Consider, too, the following excerpts from *The Watchtower* that clearly attribute the words of WTBTS publications directly to God:

> Whom has God actually used as his prophet? . . . Jehovah's Witnesses are deeply grateful today that the plain facts show that God has been pleased to use them.[71]

> Those who are convinced that *The Watchtower* is publishing the opinion or expression of a man should not waste time in looking at it at all. . . . Those who believe that God uses *The Watchtower* as a means of communicating to his people, or of calling attention to his prophecies, should study *The Watchtower*.[72]

All this information came not from or by man, but by the Lord God, being given to his people gathered under Christ at the temple, and these things learned by them in the secret place.[73]

The WTBTS has even published statements that specifically label the "1914 generation" prophecy as having come directly from Jehovah God:

> *Jehovah's prophetic word* through Jesus Christ is: "This generation [of 1914] will by no means pass away until all things occur." (Luke 21:32) And Jehovah, who is the source of inspired and unfailing prophecy, will bring about the fulfillment. . . . [P]rophecies regarding "the time of the end" will be fulfilled *within the life span of the generation of 1914*" [emphasis added].[74]

> [T]his magazine builds confidence in *the Creator's promise* of a peaceful and secure new order *before the generation that saw the events of 1914 C.E. passes away*" [emphasis added].[75]

> [T]his magazine builds confidence in the *Creator's promise* of a peaceful and secure new world *before the generation that saw the events of 1914 passes away* [emphasis added].[76]

Ironically, an October 8, 1968 edition of *Awake!* reads: "True, there have been those in times past who predicted an 'end to the world,' even announcing a specific date. . . . The 'end' did not come. They were guilty of false prophesying. Why? What was missing? . . . Missing from such people were God's truths and the evidences that he was guiding and using them."[77]

Doctrinal Flip-Floppers

In vacillating on their prophecies, JWs present nothing new to the study of religion. For thousands of years false prophets have tried to salvage their false prognostications by changing dates and rearranging timetables. The JWs are somewhat unique, however, in that they have regularly contradicted themselves on doctrines that have nothing to do with prophecy. The following represents only a partial sampling of the numerous issues on which JWs have flip-flopped:

THE GREAT PYRAMID

Pre-1928

"THE TESTIMONY OF GOD'S STONE WITNESS AND PROPHET, THE GREAT PYRAMID IN EGYPT. . . . [T]he Great Pyramid . . . acquires new interest to every Christian advanced in the study of God's Word; for it seems in a remarkable manner to teach, in harmony with all the prophets, an outline of the plan of God, past, present and future."[78]

"The great Pyramid of Egypt, standing as a silent and inanimate witness of the Lord, is a messenger; and its testimony speaks with great eloquence concerning the divine plan."[79]

Post-1928

"[N]owhere in the Word of God is the pyramid of Gizeh either directly or indirectly mentioned. . . . [T]o teach it in the church is a waste of time, to say the least of it. It is more than a waste of time. It is diverting the mind away from the Word of God and from his service. If the pyramid is not mentioned in the Bible, then following its teachings is being led by vain philosophy and false science and not following after Christ. . . . [T]he great pyramid of Gizeh, as well as the other pyramids thereabout, also the sphinx, were built by the rulers of Egypt under the direction of Satan the Devil. . . . Satan put his knowledge in dead stone, which may be called Satan's Bible, and not God's stone witness."[80]

COLLEGE EDUCATION

1969

"Many schools now have student counselors who encourage one to pursue higher education. . . . Do not be influenced by them. Do not let them 'brain-wash' you with the Devil's propaganda to get ahead, to make something of yourself in this world. The world has very little time left! Any "future" this world offers is no future! . . . Make pioneer service, the full-time ministry, with the possibility of Bethel or missionary service your goal."[81]

1992-Present

"[T]he general trend in many lands is that the level of schooling required to earn decent wages is now higher than it was a few years ago. . . . So no hard-and-fast rules should be made either for or against extra education. . . . If Christian parents responsibly decide to provide their children with further education after high school, that is their prerogative."[82]

VACCINATIONS

1931-1952

"Vaccination is a direct violation of the everlasting covenant that God made with Noah after the flood."[83]

1952-Present

"Is vaccination a violation of God's law . . . ? The matter of vaccination is one for the individual that has to face it to decide for himself. . . . [I]t does not appear to us to be in violation of the everlasting covenant made with Noah."[84]

ORGAN TRANSPLANTS

1967

"When there is a diseased or defective organ, the usual way health is restored is by taking in nutrients. . . . When men of science conclude that this normal process will no longer work and they suggest removing the organ and replacing it directly with an organ from another human, this is simply a shortcut. Those who submit to such operations are thus living off the flesh of another human. That is cannibalistic. . . . Jehovah God did not grant permission for humans to try to perpetuate their lives by cannibalistically taking into their bodies human flesh, whether chewed or in the form of whole organs or body parts taken from others."[85]

1980-Present

"Regarding the transplantation of human tissue or bone from one human to another, this is a matter for conscientious decision by each one of Jehovah's Witnesses. Some Christians might feel that taking into their bodies any tissue or body part from another human is cannibalistic. . . . Other sincere Christians today may feel that the Bible does not definitely rule out medical transplants of human organs. . . . It may be argued, too, that organ transplants are different from cannibalism since the 'donor' is not killed to supply food. . . . Clearly, personal views and conscientious feelings vary on this issue of transplantation. . . . [T]here is no Biblical command pointedly forbidding the taking in of other human tissue."[86]

On some topics the Watch Tower has actually repudiated itself more than once and in doing so, ended up reverting right back to the position it had held more than 100 years earlier. WTBTS leaders have attempted to justify this back-and-forth manner of dispensing spiritual "truth" by comparing it to how a sailboat zigzags in the wind as it makes forward progress, as illustrated in a December 1, 1981 issue of *The Watchtower* (p.27):

² However, it may have seemed to some as though that path has not always gone straight forward. At times explanations given by Jehovah's visible organization have shown adjustments, seemingly to previous points of view. But this has not actually been the case. This might be compared to what is known in navigational circles as "tacking." By maneuvering the sails the sailors can cause a ship to go from right to left, back and forth, but all the time making progress toward their destination in spite of contrary winds. And that goal in view for Jehovah's servants is the "new heavens and a new earth" of God's promise.—2 Pet. 3:13.

Tacking into the Wind

A cursory examination of the Watch Tower's doctrinal history reveals that it has definitely taken a zigzag course:

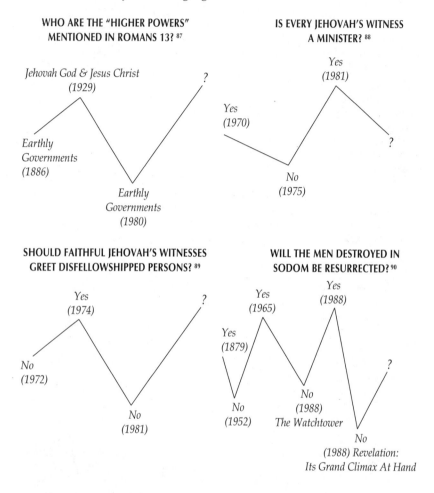

Ironically, an August 1, 1992 issue of *The Watchtower* actually condemned any organization that taught its members doctrine in a zigzag fashion:

> "[T]he way I am running is not uncertainly . . ." (1 Corinthians 9:26). . . . [T]o run "not uncertainly" means that to every observer it should be very evident where the runner is heading. *The Anchor Bible* renders it "not on a zigzag course." If you saw a set of footprints that

meanders up and down the beach, circles around now and then, and even goes backward at times, you would hardly think the person was running at all, let alone that he had any idea where he was heading. But if you saw a set of footprints that form a long, straight line, each footprint ahead of the previous one and all evenly spaced, you would conclude that the footprints belong to one who knows exactly where he is going.[91]

The Watchtower has printed an even more pointed warning that seems to describe exactly what the Watch Tower has been guilty of on numerous occasions:

> It is a serious matter to represent God and Christ in one way, then find that our understanding of the major teachings and fundamental doctrines of the Scriptures was in error, and then after that, to go back to the very doctrines that, by years of study, we had thoroughly determined to be in error. Christians cannot be vacillating—"wishy-washy" about such fundamental teachings. What confidence can one put in the sincerity or judgment of such persons?[92]

These doctrinal flip-flops have caused a considerable amount of embarrassment and frustration for JWs trying to figure out exactly how they are to "'believe all things,' all the things that *The Watchtower* brings out."[93] JWs often claim that any doctrinal flip-flops are a result of Jehovah's "light" of truth simply getting brighter and brighter. Consequently, some changes are to be expected. But according to yet another article appearing in *The Watchtower*, Jehovah's "light" of truth, as it gets brighter, *cannot* contradict former light: "A new view of truth never can contradict a former truth. '*New light*' never extinguishes older '*light*,' but adds to it."[94]

Perhaps the most disturbing aspect of the Watch Tower Society is its tendency to resort to lying in order to cover up embarrassing doctrinal mistakes and prophetic blunders. The attempts by WTBTS leaders to rewrite their organization's history is reflective of the actions taken by Big Brother in George Orwell's futuristic sci-fi thriller *1984*. The following segment will document only a few of the many times Watch Tower leaders have blatantly lied to their trusting followers.

WATCHTOWERGATE: LIES AND COVER-UPS

The Watch Tower Society readily admits that "[a] religion that teaches lies cannot be true."[95] Yet this is precisely what the Watch Tower itself has done on numerous occasions. For example, JW leaders have attempted to cover up its history of date-setting errors. The following charts present recently made statements by the WTBTS with previous declarations. The year each statement was made appears in parentheses:

TIME OF THE END

Actual Statement	*Cover-Up*
"The overthrow of that dominion in 1798 by the French Revolution marked the beginning of the 'time of the end' . . ." (1879). [96]	"Jehovah's Witnesses have consistently shown from the Scriptures that the year 1914 marked the beginning of this world's time of the end . . ." (1993).[99]
"The year 1799 marked the beginning of the 'time of the end,' when various events were to occur" (1914).[97]	
"Twelve hundred and sixty years from A.D. 539 brings us to 1799, which is another proof that 1799 definitely marks the beginning of 'the time of the end'" (1927).[98]	

JESUS' INVISIBLE RETURN

Actual Statement	*Cover-Up*
"[T]he Bridegroom came in the Autumn of 1874, and he appeared to the eyes of faith" (1881).[100]	"The Watchtower has consistently presented evidence to honesthearted students of Bible prophecy that Jesus' presence in heavenly Kingdom power began in 1914. Events since that year testify to Jesus' invisible presence" (1993).[103]
"Our Lord, the appointed King, is now present, since October 1874, A.D." (1897).[101]	
"The Scriptural proof is that the second presence of the Lord Jesus Christ began in 1874 A.D." (1929).[102]	

The WTBTS has also tried to conceal its reversal on vaccinations. At one time JW leaders banned vaccinations as being in "direct violation of the everlasting covenant that God made with Noah after the flood."[104] The

Society also warned: "Oh, yes, serums, vaccines, toxins, inoculations, are all 'harmless,' because the man who is selling them says so. You, my friends, believe this LIE, and continue to submit your body to these violations, then all I can say is, 'God have mercy on your soul.' . . . All vaccination is unphysiological—a crime against nature."[105]

The Governing Body has recently sought to deceive members into believing that they never taught such things about vaccinations. Consider the following comment that appeared in a 1993 edition of *Awake!*: "Previous articles in this journal and its companion, *The Watchtower*, have presented a consistent position: It would be up to the Bible-trained conscience of the individual Christian as to whether he would accept this treatment for himself and his family."[106]

Contrary to this statement, the *Awake!* magazine—formerly known as *Golden Age* and *Consolation* — has indeed printed official statements against vaccinations (see notes #104 and #105). Yet another condemnation of vaccinations appeared in the April 24, 1935 issue of *Golden Age* wherein the court testimony of a faithful JW (Maria Braught) was quoted: "[V]accination is a direct violation of the holy law of Jehovah God. . . . I have no alternative. I must obey Jehovah God's law" (p. 471).

One of the most blatant examples of the Watch Tower's willingness to lie to trusting followers, especially new converts unaware of the Society's history, appeared in a 1988 issue of *The Watchtower*. In one of the magazine's articles an elderly JW named Matsue Ishii gives her testimony, claiming that in 1928/29 she learned that Christ's invisible presence began in 1914, discovering this doctrine from *The Harp of God* (1921) by J. F. Rutherford.[107] But such a claim cannot be true. In 1928 the WTBTS was still teaching that Jesus' invisible presence began in 1874, not 1914! In fact, pages 235–236 of the 1928 edition of *The Harp of God* reads: "This date, therefore, when understood, would certainly fix the time when the Lord is due at his second appearing . . . [it] brings us to 1874 A.D., at which time, according to Biblical chronology, the Lord's second presence is due. . . . The time of the Lord's second presence dates from 1874, as above stated."[108]

A similar lie was reported in the September 1, 1990 issue of *The Watchtower* where a faithful JW, Jack Nathan, claims that shortly after 1920 he learned from a follower of Russell that Jesus had returned invisibly in 1914.[109] Nathan maintains that this was confirmed to him through *Studies in the Scriptures.* But in 1920 *The Watchtower* was still printing articles declaring that Jesus had returned invisibly in 1874. All the way up through 1929, in fact, *The Watchtower,* as well as all of Rutherford's books, presented the 1874 date.[110] Consequently, it would have been impossible for someone involved with the Watch Tower in 1920 to have told Nathan that Jesus had been present since 1914. It would have been equally impossible for Nathan to have gotten his information from Russell's books. *Studies in the Scriptures* always taught that Jesus' invisible presence began in 1874.[111] Even later editions of the books never placed Jesus' invisible presence in 1914. Consider the following excerpts from 1923 editions:

> The date of our Lord's second advent, and the dawn of the Times of Restitution, we have already shown to be A.D. 1874. (*Studies in the Scriptures,* vol. 2, 1889; 1923 edition)[112]

> Our Lord, the appointed King, is now present, since October 1874, A.D., according to the testimony of the prophets, to those who have ears to hear it. (*Studies in the Scriptures,* vol. 4, 1897; 1923 edition)[113]

Finally, this same lie regarding the WTBTS's consistency in teaching Jesus' invisible presence in 1914 was repeated in the September 15, 1990 issue of *The Watchtower.* It misleads readers into thinking that Rutherford taught Jesus' invisible return in 1914 by noting that during a 1922 convention Rutherford told listeners: "Since 1914 the King of Glory has taken his power."[114] But the 1990 issue fails to mention that Rutherford was *not* speaking about Jesus' return. A November 1, 1922 issue of *The Watchtower* fully quotes Rutherford in context as having stated: "Since 1874 the King of glory has been present. . . . Since 1914 the King of Glory has taken his power and reigns. . . . Do you believe it? Do you believe that the King of glory is present, and has been since 1874?"

WTBTS leaders appear quite willing to rewrite history in an effort to present their organization as having consistently taught various doctrines. JWs would do well to heed what the WTBTS itself stated in the 1974 book *Is This Life All There Is?*: "It is obvious that the true God, who is himself 'the God of truth' and who hates lies, will not look with favor on persons who cling to organizations that teach falsehood. . . . And, really, would you want to be even associated with a religion that had not been honest with you?"[115]

ACCORDING TO THE BIBLE

The Jehovah's Witnesses preach a wide range of heretical doctrines that touch upon nearly all aspects of the Christian faith. Although space does not permit an in-depth exploration of exactly how JWs have arrived at their beliefs or how WTBTS leaders use deception to promote their doctrines, a discussion of the main theological positions of JWs will be given. The most significant Christian doctrine undermined by the Watch Tower is clearly the doctrine of the Trinity.

God in Three Persons

The Christian doctrine of the Trinity teaches that there is only one true God who within His eternal nature exists as three co-equal and co-eternal Persons; namely, the Father, Son, and Holy Spirit. Although these three Persons are distinct in function, position, and relationship, they all share the same divine nature (or essence) and in so doing, exist as one divine being. All three Persons are in *full* possession of the divine essence. However, they "cannot be conceived [of] as three separate individuals, but are *in* one another, and form a solidaric unity" [emphasis added].[116] Simply put, the Father, Son, and Holy Spirit *are* the one true God. Each Person, therefore, may properly be called God collectively as well as individually.

JWs commonly argue that neither the word *Trinity*, nor the concept of the Trinity can be found in the Bible. Consequently, they claim, it should not be believed. They further assert that the belief actually originated among various pagan nations that worshiped triads of gods. Such a concept, say WTBTS leaders, was adopted by the apostate Christian churches in the third or fourth centuries.[117] The Trinity, therefore, is a lie from Satan, and anyone who worships the Trinity is in reality worshiping a three-headed demon God.

It must first be noted that rejecting the Trinity because the word *Trinity* does not appear in Scripture is an argument with no merit. The term *Trinity* simply makes it easier to refer to the Bible's teachings about God's nature. A single word is often used to represent a complex idea. Water, for instance, consists of two parts hydrogen and one part oxygen (H_2O), yet one would never say, "May I please have a glass of two parts hydrogen and one part oxygen?" Instead, *water* is used for the sake of convenience. This is how the term *Trinity* is used by Christians. The word *Bible* is not in Scripture either, but JWs have no problem using this designation for God's Word.[118]

Regarding the JW argument about the Trinity not appearing as an official doctrine until the third and fourth centuries, this is only half correct. The Trinity was not *formally* expressed until approximately the fourth century, after the Nicea and Constantinople Councils (A.D. 325 and A.D. 381). But these gatherings were not convened in order to invent new doctrines. They were held in order to set forth in a formal manner the doctrines that Christians were *already* believing and to work out a way of accurately communicating these doctrines throughout the world.

In other words, although the Trinity doctrine had not been officially stated until the Nicea and Constantinople Creeds, it was already being adhered to by Christians. More than 100 years before the Council of Nicea, for example, Christians recognized that God existed in plurality. Note the following quotation from Hippolytus (c. ?–a.d. 235):

> There is, brethren, one God . . . . God, subsisting alone, and having nothing contemporaneous [at the same time with Himself], determined to create the world. . . . [T]here was nothing contemporaneous with God. Beside Him there was nothing; but He, while existing alone, *yet existed in plurality* [emphasis added].[119]

It also must be recognized that any similarities between the Christian Trinity and pagan triads does not make the Trinity untrue. Apparent similarity between two lines of thought does not necessarily mean that those two lines of thought have the same origin. This is especially true when it comes to religion. Most religions have numerous similarities. For example, Buddhism teaches that murder is wrong. So does Christianity. Does this mean that the Christian stand against murder is pagan and therefore should be rejected? Consider, too, the fact that some pagans believe in the existence of at least one God. Does this mean that anyone else who believes in one God is actually borrowing from pagan teachings? Of course not.

Additionally, there is a vast difference between pagan triads of antiquity and the Christian Trinity, which is unique in numerous ways. First, pagan triads usually consisted of three *separate* gods. They did not constitute one god. Second, non-Christian trinities were "always or nearly always merely the three gods at the top of the hierarchy of many gods worshipped in polytheistic religions."[120] Third, pagan deities were not thought of as being co-equal; one of the deities was always greater than the other. Finally, it cannot be proven that Christians borrowed anything from pagan religions to form the Trinity doctrine. Renowned Christian scholar Gleason Archer explains:

> [T]he concept of God as one in essence but three in centers of consciousness—what the Greek church referred to as three *hypostases* and the Latin church as *personae*—is absolutely unique in the history of human thought. No other culture or philosophical movement ever came up with such an idea of God as this—an idea that remains very difficult for our finite minds to grasp.[121]

JWs also insist that the Trinity doctrine is completely incomprehensible and confusing. This, too, is untrue. The Trinity may be difficult to *fully* comprehend, but it is hardly beyond any degree of understanding. Intellectually grasping a concept, while at the same time not being able to fully comprehend exactly *how* that concept can be true, are compatible states of mind. For example, I understand that earth is revolving at several thousands of miles per hour, but I certainly do not *fully comprehend* how that can be. I also understand that the chair on which I am sitting is comprised of millions of molecules moving so fast that they are forming only what looks like a solid object, but I certainly do not *fully comprehend* how that can be.

If we are willing to accept these physical realities without fully comprehending them, it is only fair that we give the same level of consideration to the doctrine of the Trinity despite our inability to fully comprehend it. God has explicitly told us that certain aspects of His nature are unsearchable (Ps. 145:3; Isa. 40:28; Rom. 11:33). The question to ask, therefore, is not, *how* does the Trinity exist? but simply, *Does* the Trinity exist? According to Scripture, the answer to the latter question is yes. For those whose minds cannot let go of the former question, there are several analogies for the Trinity that may be helpful.

Time, for instance, consists of three distinct things: past, present, and future. These three aspects of time correspond well to the Trinity's Father, Son, and Holy Spirit. In both cases the three aspects are entirely distinct from one another. Moreover, all three aspects of time, although distinct, share the same nature of that which they comprise. In other words, the past, present, and future can all be referred to individually as time in somewhat the same fashion as the Father, Son, and Holy Spirit can each be referred to as God. Also, if any of the three elements of time were to be removed, time would no longer exist. In this dimension of reality, there is no such thing as time without a past, a present, or a future. Similarly, God would not be God without a Father, a Son, or a Holy Spirit. All three Persons *are* God, just as all three aspects of time *are* time.

Time is but one of many analogies that have been proposed in an effort to represent the Trinity. Another is the multiplication formula ($1 \times 1 \times 1 = 1$). Of course, no analogy for the Trinity is without its drawbacks. But this is what one would expect since we are dealing with a reality that is far beyond our limits of knowledge and reasoning. "My thoughts are not your thoughts, neither are your ways My ways," declares the Lord in Isaiah 55:8. He goes on to explain, "For as the heavens are higher than the earth, so are My ways higher than your ways, and My thoughts than your thoughts" (v. 9).

It should come as no surprise that human analogies fail to perfectly describe a spiritual being as complex and *non*-human as God. Nevertheless, they can still serve as "reminders that the imprint of the triune God may be found in creation."[122] Ultimately, the Trinity is a divine mystery with regard to *how* it could possibly be a reality. *That* it is a reality, however, has been clearly established by Scripture. In other words, the Trinity may be *beyond* reason, but it certainly is not *contrary* to reason. (For biblical proofs of the Trinity, see Appendix A.)

Jesus Christ

According to the WTBTS, it was actually Michael the Archangel—the first and greatest creation of Jehovah God—who became the "perfect man" Jesus in order to redeem humanity from Adam's curse.[123] He was not always "the Christ" but became Christ at His baptism.[124] Jesus went back to being Michael the Mighty God[125]—a lesser deity than Jehovah—after he was *spiritually* resurrected from the grave.[126] JWs also believe that Yahweh (i.e., Jehovah) is *Almighty* God, whereas Jesus is a second god whom they designate as the *mighty* god (i.e., a lesser god).[127]

In addition to these two deities, there exists a spiritually elite class of JWs known as the "Little Flock," who supposedly have a divine nature that will fully manifest itself when they are resurrected as gods. Members of this flock represent the organization's spiritual cream-of-the-crop and as such are the only JWs who are considered God's children. Together with Jesus, they constitute "the Christ" of Scripture.[128] Although JWs draw a fine distinction between all of these gods by limiting their worship to only Jehovah God,[129] their theological position is rife with unbiblical concepts.

First, the JW belief system—which reserves worship for just one God while recognizing the existence of more than one God—is known as henotheism. Scripture, however, teaches strict monotheism (i.e., belief in the existence of only one God). Jesus cannot be just another "god" who is lesser in power than Jehovah God because many biblical verses pointedly contradict the notion that there exists more than one God (Deut. 4:35, 39; 32:39; 2 Kings 19:19; Ps. 86:10; Mark 12:29).

According to Scripture, there exists only one true God (2 Chron. 15:3; Jer. 10:10; John 17:3). All other "gods" are false gods that can take the form of physical idols made by men's hands (Lev. 19:4; Deut. 27:15), persons who think they are gods (Ps. 82:2–7; Ezek. 28:2, 9), or any spiritual entity other than God that someone follows (2 Cor. 4:4). *Anything* can be made into a god: sex, drugs, money, beauty, food. But these gods are not *true* gods or gods by nature (Gal. 4:8). They are false idols of worship, also referenced in the Bible as "so-called gods" (1 Cor. 8:4-6).

Second, the JW contention that "Christ was first of God's creations [Col. 1:15; Rev. 3:14]."[130] is an erroneous interpretation of the verses cited. In fact, the arguments perfectly illustrate how cults rely on poor scholarship to justify their beliefs. When one carefully examines the passages mentioned, it becomes obvious that the biblical authors are communicating a message vastly different than "Jesus is a created being."

In Colossians 1:15-17, the Greek text indicates that Jesus is an heir, or the one who is first in rank and is superior over all creation as Lord. The passage includes the word *prototokos* ("firstborn" or "first-bearer") rather than *protoktistos* ("first-created"). One example of "firstborn" being used in this way can be found in Jeremiah. 31:9 where Ephraim is called God's firstborn. Genesis 41:51–52, however, states that Manasseh was *literally* the firstborn, not Ephraim. Ephraim was the preeminent son of the family.

Obviously, "firstborn" does not always have to mean the first one born or the first created.

In Revelation 3:14, the Greek word translated "beginning" (*arche*) also does not necessarily refer to a literal beginning. It often connotes the idea of something being "the origin" or the "active cause" of something. In this passage, then, Jesus is being referred to as the source or origin of all creation. In other words, Jesus is the one from whom all creation springs. *Arche* is the same word from which we get our English word *architect*. Nowhere in the Bible is Jesus spoken of as being a creation of God. He is, in fact, described as the Creator of all that exists (John 1:3; Col. 1:16).

And nowhere does the Bible call Jesus Michael the archangel. An especially interesting passage relating to this is Jude 9 where Michael, in his own authority, was unable to rebuke Satan. However, in Mark 9:25 and elsewhere Jesus Himself, while in a form lower than the angels (i.e., the form of man), rebuked Satan without hesitation. Furthermore, Hebrews 2:5 says an angel cannot rule the world, and yet Luke 1:32- 33 and Revelation 19:16 portray Christ as reigning supreme. Jesus and Michael are obviously not the same being. Moreover, Christ is consistently referred to as God (John 20:28; Heb. 1:8-9).

Regarding Jesus' resurrection, the Bible affirms that He did indeed rise *bodily* from the grave. He was not raised as a "spirit creature," as JWs teach.[131] Colossians 2:9 states that in Christ "all the fulness of Deity dwells [present tense] in bodily form." This is a fulfillment of the prophecy Christ spoke in John 2:19 to hostile crowds: "Destroy this temple, and in three days I will raise it up." The Jews failed to grasp the meaning behind Jesus' words, but John tells us in subsequent verses exactly what Jesus meant:

> But He was speaking of the temple of His body. When therefore He was raised from the dead, His disciples remembered that He said this; and they believed the Scripture, and the word which Jesus had spoken (vv. 21-22).

Notice that Jesus said, "Destroy *this* temple [meaning the body He then had], and . . . I will raise *it* [the same body] up." He did not say, "Destroy this temple, and in three days I will raise up another spiritual, non-fleshly body in its place." Either Jesus did what He said He would do or He did not. Moreover, the Greek word used by John to clarify Christ's comment about

His "body" (*soma*, v. 21) indicates that a fleshly body would be raised from the dead. The noun *soma* is always used in the NT for the physical body.

Additional verses relating to Jesus' physical body include those in which the gospel writers speak of Jesus being touched and handled (Matt. 28:9; John 20:17, 27; 1 John 1:1). Our Lord Himself said that he had "flesh and bones" (Luke 24:39). JWs usually dismiss these biblical references to Jesus' material body by stating that He temporarily "materialized or took on a fleshly body, as angels had done in the past."[132] It is said that He even manufactured wounds in this fake body in order to convince the disciples of His identity.[133] But this creates a dilemma involving the moral character of Christ since He indicated to His disciples that the body He was showing them was the *very same* body that went from the cross to the grave: "See My hands and My feet, that it is I Myself; touch Me and see, for a spirit does not have flesh and bones as you see that I have" (Luke 24:39). Was Jesus telling the truth or not? A sincere seeker of truth will accept at face value Christ's words regarding the nature of His resurrected body.

The Holy Spirit—God's Active Force?

The WTBTS claims that the Holy Spirit is not a person but is an impersonal "active force" very similar to electricity. It is nothing more than the "power" by which Jehovah accomplishes his purposes.[134] In addressing these heretical positions, one must first show biblically that the Holy Spirit is indeed a person. This is fairly easy to accomplish. Numerous Old and New Testament passages ascribe to the Holy Spirit characteristics consistent with personhood: He feels emotion (Isa. 63:10; Rom. 15:30; Eph. 4:30), possesses knowledge (1 Cor. 2:11), and has a mind (Rom. 8:27).

Additionally, the Spirit acts in ways that only a person can act: He teaches (Neh. 9:20; Luke 12:12; John 14:26), bears witness (John 15:26; Acts 5:32; Rom. 8:16), leads and guides (John 16:13; Rom. 8:14), hears (John 16:13), glorifies Christ (John 16:14), convicts unbelievers' hearts (John 16:8), intercedes for believers (Rom. 8:27), speaks and gives commands (Acts 8:29; 10:19–20; 11:12; Rev. 22:17), calls Christians into service (Acts 13:2), appoints individuals to church offices (Acts 20:28), makes decisions (Acts 15:28), works according to His own will (1 Cor. 12:11), and exhibits self-control by not acting "on his own initiative" when doing so would conflict with the will of the Father and Son (John 16:13).

Interestingly, the Watch Tower printed a story in the December 8, 1973 issue of *Awake!* that supported the personhood—or personality—of Satan with the following argument: "[C]an an unintelligent force carry on a conversation with a person? Also, the Bible calls Satan a manslayer, a liar, a father . . . and a ruler. Only an intelligent person could fit all those descriptions."[135] This criteria used by the Watch Tower regarding the significance of personal attributes is the same criteria used by Christians to establish the personality of the Holy Spirit. If WTBTS leaders were to be consistent in applying this criteria to the Holy Spirit, they would have to acknowledge the Spirit as a person just as they acknowledge Satan as a person. But this they refuse to do.

The question remains: Is the Holy Spirit God? Yes, the Scripture clearly claims. In Acts 5, Ananias and his wife Sapphira sold their property but were dishonest about how much they had received from the purchase. Peter confronted Ananias: "Ananias, why has Satan filled your heart to lie to the Holy Spirit, and to keep back some of the price of the land?" (v. 3). Peter goes on to tell Ananias that in lying to the Holy Spirit, he had actually lied "to God" (v. 4). It should also be mentioned here that a person can only lie to another person. This passage, therefore, gives further proof that the Spirit is not an "active force" or an impersonal power.

In addition to this powerful passage, a number of verses attribute divine characteristics and actions to the Holy Spirit. For example, Luke 1:68–70 records John the Baptist declaring, "Blessed be the Lord God of Israel. . . . He spoke by the mouth of His holy prophets from of old." Compare this statement with the words of Paul the apostle: "The Holy Spirit rightly spoke through Isaiah the prophet to your fathers" (Acts 28:25). Consider, too, 1 Corinthians 3:16 and 6:19, which state, "[T]he Spirit of God dwells in you . . . your body is the temple of the Holy Spirit." Compare these two verses with 2 Corinthians 6:16: "We are the temple of the living God; just as God said, 'I will dwell in them.'" Finally, God is eternal (Ps. 90:2), as is the Spirit (Heb. 9:14).

Salvation

Unlike Christians, JWs have not been forgiven for their personal sins. In their view, Jesus' death on the cross only took care of the sin of Adam. They are left to clear away their own sins by their good works, which they hope will be enough to earn the reward of salvation. Each JW must prove himself or herself worthy of everlasting life. These conditions placed upon salvation are clearly unbiblical, as the following chart explains:

SALVATION

Watch Tower	*Scripture*
"[God] could not set aside the judgment that he had entered against Adam. He could, however, be consistent . . . by permitting another to pay the debt of Adam and thereby to open the way for Adam and his offspring to be released from sin and death."[136]	Jesus' death not only paid for Adam's sin, but also paid for our sins (1 Cor. 15:3; Gal. 1:4; Heb. 9:28; 1 Peter 2:24).
"It is for the reward of eternal life that every last person on earth should now be working. Are you?"[137] "To get one's name written in that book of life will depend upon one's works, whether they are in fulfillment of God's will and approved by his Judge and King."[138]	Salvation is a gift, not a reward (Rom. 5:15-16; 6:23; Eph 2:8). Works do not produce salvation (Rom. 4:1-4). They are a by-product of salvation that a person has already received (James 2:14-18).
"Jesus Christ identified a first requirement when he said in prayer . . . 'This means everlasting life, their taking in knowledge of you.' . . . Many have found the second requirement more difficult. It is to obey God's laws. . . . A third requirement is that we be associated with God's channel, his organization. . . . To receive everlasting life in the earthly Paradise we must identify that organization and serve God as part of it. The fourth requirement . . . requires that prospective subjects of his Kingdom support his government by loyally advocating his Kingdom rule to others [i.e., preaching door-to-door]."[139]	The Watch Tower has misquoted Jesus' words in John 17:3. He actually stated that eternal life is simply knowing God. In other words, salvation comes when one realizes who God is. Nowhere does Jesus equate salvation with an ongoing process of taking in knowledge. Concerning one's need to obey God's law, this is only half true. We are indeed told to keep Jesus' commandments (John 14:15, 21; 15:10; 1 John 2:3; 3:22-24; 2 John 1:6). But at the same time, we know that because of sin and the weakness of our flesh, no one can keep the whole law (James 2:10). Consequently, although it is in and of itself holy (Rom. 7:12; 1 Tim. 1:8), the law is also a curse to man because it points out sin (Gal. 3:13). Fortunately, Christ kept the law perfectly (Matt. 5:17), and His righteousness is imputed to us apart from the law (Rom. 3:28). In this way the law is fulfilled in us (Rom. 8: 3-4). No one is justified by works (Rom. 3:20; Gal. 2:16; 3:11), and those who seek justification through works will be severed from Christ (Gal. 5:3-4). Jesus is the end of the law (Rom. 10:4). We live under grace (Rom. 6:14).
"Jehovah God will justify, declare righteous, on the basis of their own merit all perfected humans who have withstood that final, decisive test of mankind [the release of Satan from bondage after the 1000-year reign of Christ]."[140]	

The Bible

As previously mentioned, the Watch Tower claims that anyone who seeks to understand the Bible through a course of personal study will soon find themselves in spiritual darkness. According to one recent issue of *The Watchtower*, people who read the Bible apart from WTBTS literature "will not progress along the road of life" no matter how much Bible reading they do.[141] JWs must receive all of their spiritual "nourishment" from the books and magazines published by the WTBTS, the primary source of truth being *The Watchtower*.[142]

But Scripture does not promote such beliefs. In 1 Corinthians 12:8-10—a passage about spiritual gifts—there is no mention of spiritually-elite individuals or special organizations having authoritative insights into Scripture. One would think that if such gifts existed, they would be mentioned as spiritual gifts in the Bible. The importance of such gifts would be tremendous. It can only be assumed that there exists no such thing as a divinely chosen person or group of persons commissioned by God to be His unique channel of biblical understanding to humanity.

Moreover, there are passages that state that the Gospel itself contains what is needed for salvation and that everything necessary for eternal life is given to each believer personally (for example, Rom. 1:16; 2 Peter 1:3). Acts 17:11 additionally reveals that persons who use the Bible to question the teachings of a religious leader are to be commended for their careful consideration, not condemned. Jesus Himself gave a sobering message in John 12:47-48 that directly relates to the whole issue of whether Christians need to have the Bible interpreted for them by an organization:

> *If anyone hears my sayings, and does not keep them, I do not judge him; for I did not come to judge the world, but to save the world. He who rejects me, and does not receive my sayings, has one who judges him; the word I spoke will judge him at the last day.*

In other words, people will be judged according to the manner in which they followed Jesus' words, not in the way they followed the words of some self-proclaimed "prophet" group or organization claiming a special understanding of Scripture. According to our Lord, we may personally learn of Him with the aid of the Holy Spirit, who imparts understanding to our hearts. In fact, Scripture gives us marvelous promises regarding God's desire and willingness to reveal Himself to us through His Word: "He leads the humble in justice, and He teaches the humble His way" (Ps. 25:9). We are also told that God will help us understand the Bible. Ephesians 1:17-18 states that the Spirit will provide wisdom and illumination of Scripture so that we may be enlightened by God's truth. First Corinthians 2:12 tells us that the Spirit of God assists us so that we may "know the things freely given to us by God." Jesus assured His disciples that the Holy Spirit would be sent to personally teach and guide God's followers (John 16:13–15). He who wrote Scripture helps us understand it.

This is not to say that the Lord has not called some Christians to be teachers, having gifted them to serve in the church (Eph. 4:11; 1 Tim 3:2; 2 Tim. 2:2). Such individuals are able to help fellow believers learn about God and grow in Christ. But these teachers are never above Scripture itself (James 3:1). They are never to become mediators between God and His children (1 Tim. 2:5), as the WTBTS leaders have done.

WHAT'S THE ATTRACTION?

Most people would agree that life in this world is very troubling. Crime is on the rise, wars continue unabated, famines strike yearly, and corruption in government only seems to be getting worse. Everyone not only discusses these issues but often can agree on numerous points concerning them. After all, who would not say that war is terrible? JWs consistently exploit these issues as common ground that is inevitably used as springboards to evangelism. WTBTS publications are literally packed with stories on the horrors of current society: plagues, crime, drug use, youth problems, wars. Each article ends with penetrating questions: Wouldn't you like to know when the horror will end? Is there a way to escape the destruction humanity now faces?

The answers in WTBTS literature invariably involve coming to God's one true organization for relief and "biblical" solutions to life's many problems. For some, just seeing JWs speak out forcefully against such controversial issues as wars, corrupt government, and crime is enough to get them involved in the organization. Once inside the cult, many persons find it extremely satisfying to have every aspect of their life ordered by clear do's and don'ts, especially young people with no living skills or older persons tired of making decisions about life in an ever-increasingly complex world of alternatives. Other individuals—who may be disillusioned with mainstream Christianity, yet at the same time want to rediscover their Christian roots—may be drawn to the JWs because the Watch Tower not only quotes the Bible but pronounces scathing condemnations on mainstream churches (i.e., Christendom).

There is also the attraction of prophecy. For thousands of years people have wanted to know the future and have been drawn to persons/organizations that claim to hold the key to unlocking the secrets of the future. Obviously, the Watch Tower is one such organization. WTBTS leaders are forever telling gullible followers and new converts that they alone can truly make accurate predictions about the end of the world. This claim, however, has been proven untrue over and over again. The desire many people have to find *somebody* who is able to tell them the future in an uncertain world often overshadows common sense. As a result, they continue to stay in the group, hoping that maybe next time the prophecy will prove true.

RECOMMENDED READING

Bowman, Robert M. *Understanding Jehovah's Witnesses* (Grand Rapids, MI: Baker, 1991).

_____. *Why You Should Believe in the Trinity* (Grand Rapids, MI: Baker, 1989).

Magnani, Duane. *The Watchtower Files* (Minneapolis: Bethany House, 1983).

Reed, David. *Index of Watchtower Errors* (Grand Rapids, MI: Baker, 1990).

_____. *Blood on the Altar* (Amherst, NY: Prometheus, 1996).

_____. *How to Rescue Your Loved Ones from the Watchtower* (Grand Rapids, MI: Baker, 1989).

_____. *Jehovah's Witness Literature* (Grand Rapids, MI: Baker, 1993).

Rhodes, Ron. *Reasoning from the Scriptures with the Jehovah's Witnesses* (Eugene, OR: Harvest House, 1993).

Watters, Randall. *Thus Saith the Governing Body of Jehovah's Witnesses* (Manhattan Beach, CA: Free Minds, Inc., 1987). Available from Free Minds, Inc., Box 3818, Manhattan Beach, CA 90266.

APPENDIX A

"BLESSED TRINITY"

The significance of the Trinity doctrine in orthodox Christianity cannot be overstated. It has been described as "the heart of the Christian conception of God . . . central to our faith,"[1] "one of the most important doctrines of the Christian faith,"[2] and a doctrine without which some of the most basic Bible teachings about God would remain "nearly incomprehensible."[3] It is also one of the doctrines that is almost always distorted by cults. Consequently, Christians must be able not only to define and explain the Trinity but to biblically support it.

A good starting point for any study of the Trinity begins with Deuteronomy 6:4, which may be the most important Hebrew passage relating to God's nature: "Hear, O Israel! The LORD [Yahweh] our God, the LORD [Yahweh] is one." This verse, known as the *Shema*, served as the cornerstone of Old Testament (OT) Jewish thought concerning the God of Israel; i.e., there exists only one true God, Yahweh. By taking such a theological position, the Jews forever separated themselves from the surrounding polytheistic cultures (e.g., the Egyptians, Philistines, Babylonians, Canaanites, and Moabites).

The reality of the existence of only one true God is stressed time and again throughout the OT (see, for example, 2 Sam. 7:22), especially in the pronouncements of God Himself (see Isa. 45:21–22; 46:8–9). One of the main purposes of the OT prophets was to continually call Jews back from idolatry to the worship of the one true God (see 1 Kings 18:18ff.). The prophets "strengthened monotheistic doctrine by constantly reminding Israel of the vast gulf that separated the Lord from pagan idols and the so-called gods that they represented (Hos. 4:12; Isa. 2:8, 20; 17:8; 31:7; Jer. 10:5, 10)."[4]

Although there are no OT passages that explicitly describe God as a triune being, there are many OT verses that at the very least suggest a plurality within God's nature. For example, in Genesis 1:26 God says, "Let Us [plural] make man in Our [plural] image [plural], according to Our [plural] likeness." The use here of plural pronouns is most interesting. Renowned biblical scholar and linguistic expert Gleason Archer comments:

> This first person plural can hardly be a mere editorial or royal plural that refers to the speaker alone, for no such usage is demonstrable anywhere else in biblical Hebrew. Therefore we must face the question of who are included in this "us" and "our." It could hardly include the angels in consultation with God, for nowhere is it ever stated that man was created in the image of angels, only of God.[5]

Even more thought-provoking is verse 27: "God created man in His own [singular] image, in the image of God He [singular] created him; male and female He [singular] created them." A striking and deliberate switch to singular pronouns is made here. According to Archer, the verse is implying that "the plural equals the singular. This can only be understood in terms of the Trinitarian nature of God. The one God subsists in three Persons, Persons who are able to confer with one another and carry their plans into action together—without ceasing to be one God."[6]

Some theologians maintain that the use of plural pronouns in Genesis suggests a plurality of majesty, a form of speech a king would use—i.e., "We are pleased to grant your request." But this is highly unlikely according to many other linguistic experts and Bible scholars. Wayne Grudem, professor of biblical and systematic theology at Trinity Evangelical Divinity School, observes that in Old Testament Hebrew, "there are no other examples of a monarch using plural verbs or plural pronouns of himself . . . so this suggestion has no evidence to support it."[7]

The OT also contains verses wherein one Person called God (or Lord) is interacting in some way with another Person called God (or Lord).

Consider Psalm 45:6–7: "Thy throne, O God, is forever and ever . . . . Thou hast loved righteousness, and hated wickedness; therefore God, Thy God, has anointed Thee." Consider, too, Genesis 19:24, which refers to Sodom and Gomorrah's fate: "Then the LORD [YHWH] rained on Sodom and Gomorrah brimstone and fire from the LORD [YHWH] out of heaven." Especially interesting is Isaiah 44:6: "Thus says the LORD [yhwh], the King of Israel and his Redeemer, the LORD [YHWH] of hosts."

A few verses even mention all three of the Persons resident within the nature of the one true God. An outstanding occurrence of this is found in Isaiah 48:12–16. The verse begins with Yahweh speaking: "Listen to Me, O Jacob, even Israel whom I called; I am He, I am the first, I am also the last"[i.e., the Son, cf. Rev. 22:12–13]. The passage continues: "Come near to Me, listen to this: From the first I have not spoken in secret, from the time it took place [i.e., Israel's deliverance], I was there" (v. 16a). Finally, God declares, "And now the LORD GOD [YHWH] has sent Me, and His Spirit."

None of these verses conclusively prove the Trinity. They do, however, serve as a theological doorway through which an understanding of God's triunity can be accessed from the New Testament. Berkhof writes: "The Old Testament does not contain a full revelation of the Trinitarian existence of God, but does contain several indications of it. And this is exactly what might be expected."[8] Robert Lightner, professor of systematic theology at Dallas Theological Seminary, remarks: "Throughout the Old Testament there are hints of the Trinity, but God's unity is stressed. The revelation is much clearer and more complete in the New Testament. We need the teaching from both testaments for the full picture."[9]

Like the OT, the NT consistently affirms the existence of only one God (Gal. 3:20; 1 Tim. 2:5). Additionally, however, the NT presents numerous passages that identify three distinct persons—the Father (1 John 3:1), the Son (1 John 1:3), and the Holy Spirit (John 14:16, 26; 15:26; 16:13-14)—each of whom are referred to as God (*the Father*, John 6:27; Rom. 1:7; 1 Thess. 1:1; *the Son*, John 20:28; Heb. 1:8-9; *the Holy Spirit*, Acts 5:3-4).

The importance of each of these verses is intensified by the many other NT passages that not only designate the Father, Son, and Holy Spirit as God, but also ascribe to them the same attributes and divine acts. All three are said to dwell in believers (John 14:17, 20, 23). Each one is said to have been active in the resurrection of Christ (*the Father*, Gal. 1:1; *the Son*, John 2:19–20; 10:17; *the Holy Spirit*, Rom 8:11), while at the same time we are told that it was God who raised Jesus from the dead (1 Cor. 6:14). All three possess and impart eternal life (*the Father*, John 5:26; *the Son*, John 1:4; 5:21, 26; 10:28; 11:25; *the Holy Spirit*, 2 Cor. 3:6; Gal. 6:8).

The NT also presents the Father, Son, and Holy Spirit as having an unusually close union. All are specifically mentioned in the Great Commission (Matt. 28:19), Paul's benediction to the Corinthian church (2 Cor. 13:14), and Peter's salutation to Christians living in Asia Minor (1 Peter 1:2). Jesus' baptism provides an exceptionally vivid illustration of the triune God (Matt 3:16–17). Furthermore, the NT applies numerous OT titles and actions reserved for God to Jesus and the Holy Spirit.

Only the Trinity doctrine is able to reconcile these biblical passages with those Scriptures that teach there is only one God.

APPENDIX B
RECOMMENDED MINISTRIES

GENERAL CULTS

Religious Information Center
President/Founder—Richard Abanes
P.O. Box 80961
Rancho Santa Margarita, CA 92688
714-858-8936 (phone/fax)
raric@aol.com

Watchman Fellowship
National Director—James Walker
P.O. Box 13340
Arlington, TX 76094
817-277-0023 / 817-277-8098 (fax)
http://www.watchman.org

Answers In Action
Founders/Directors—Bob & Gretchen
    Passantino
P.O. Box 2067
Costa Mesa, CA 92628
714-646-9024
http://answers.org/

Christian Research Institute
President—Hank Hanegraaff
30162 Tomas
Rancho Santa Margarita, CA 92688
714-858-6100
http://www.equip.org/

Personal Freedom Outreach
President—Kurt Goedelman
P.O. Box 26062
Saint Louis, MO 63136
314-388-2648

Jude 3 Missions
Founder/Director—Kurt Van Gorden
P.O. Box 1901
Orange, CA 92668
714-247-1850

Gospel Truths Ministries
Executive Director—Luke Wilson
1340 Monroe Avenue, N. W.
Grand Rapids, MI 49505
616-451-4562 / 616-451-8907 (fax)

JEHOVAH'S WITNESSES

Comments from the Friends
Founder/Director—David Reed
Box 819
Assonet, MA 02702
508-763-8050
http://www.ultranet.com/~comments

Free Minds, Inc.
Founder/Director—Randall Watters
P.O. Box 3818
Manhattan Beach, CA 90266
310-545-7831 / 310-545-0068 (fax)
http://www.freeminds.org/rwatters.htm

Witness, Inc.
National Director—Duane Magnani
P.O. Box 597
Clayton, CA 94517
510-672-5979

Equippers, Inc.
Director—Peter Barnes
4621 Soria Dr.
San Diego, CA 92115
619-270-2991

MORMONISM

Utah Lighthouse Ministry
Founders/Directors—Jerald & Sandra
Tanner
P.O. Box 1884
Salt Lake City, UT 84110
801-485-8894 / 801-485-0312 (fax)
http://www.alphamin.org/catalog.html
E-mail: ulm@utah-inter.net

Mormonism Researched
Founder/Director—Bill McKeever
P.O. Box 20705
El Cajon, CA 92021
619-447-3873 (phone/fax)
http://www.mrm.org

Utah Missions, Inc.
Director—Michael Reynolds
P.O. Box 348
Marlow, OK 73055
405-658-5631
800-654-3992 (orders)

NOTES

Introduction

1. Joan Carol Ross and Michael D. Langone, *Cults: What Parents Should Know* (New York: Carol Publishing, 1988), 29.
2. Walter Martin, *The Kingdom of the Cults* (Minneapolis: Bethany House, 1965; 1985 edition), 11.
3. Gordon Lewis, *Confronting the Cults* (Grand Rapids, MI: Baker, 1975), 4.
4. Walter Martin, *The Rise of the Cults* (Grand Rapids, MI: Zondervan, 1955), 11–12. Quoted in Irvine Robertson, *What the Cults Believe* (Chicago: Moody Press, 1966; 1991 edition), 13.
5. Alan W. Gomes, *Unmasking the Cults* (Grand Rapids, MI: Zondervan, 1995), 7.
6. Christian Research Institute, "Cults and Aberrational Groups," Statement DC-920.

Chapter 1
Behind the New Age Craze

1. Daniel Jacob, Internet posting. Quoted in Ted Daniels, "An Internet Miscellany," *Millennial Prophecy Report*, vol. 4, no. 2, July 1995. Internet edition at http://www.channel1.com/mpr/netmisc.htm.
2. Ron Rhodes, *The Counterfeit Christ of the New Age Movement* (Grand Rapids, MI: Baker, 1990; 1991 edition), 226.
3. Story based on author's January 14, 1997 interview with Brad Scott.
4. Elliot Miller, *A Crash Course on the New Age Movement* (Grand Rapids, MI: Baker, 1989), 15.
5. Russell Chandler, *Understanding the New Age* (Grand Rapids, MI: Zondervan, 1991; 1992 edition), 17.
6. J. Gordon Melton, Jerome Clark, and Aidan A. Kelly, *New Age Encyclopedia* (Detroit: Gale Research, Inc., 1990), p. xiii.
7. David Spangler, *Revelation: The Birth of a New Age* (San Francisco: The Rainbow Bridge, 1976), 19.
8. From last source cited, 105.
9. Marilyn Ferguson, *The Aquarian Conspiracy* (Los Angeles: J. P. Tarcher, 1980), 29.
10. Otto Friedrich, "New Age Harmonies," *Time*, December 7, 1987, 62.
11. Robert Burrows, in *New Age Rage*, ed. Karen Hoyt (Old Tappan: NJ: Fleming H. Revell, 1987), 31.
12. Leslie A. Shepard, ed., *Encyclopedia of Occultism & Parapsychology*, vol. 2 (Detroit: Gale Research Inc., 1991), 1086; cf. Melton, Clark, and Kelly, xxiii.
13. Rhodes, 147–164, 247.

14. J. Gordon Melton, *Encyclopedic Handbook of Cults in America* (New York: Garland Publishing, 1986; 1992 edition), 165–166.

15. Shepard, 1582.

16. Leslie A. Shepard, ed., *Encyclopedia of Occultism & Parapsychology*, vol. 1 (Detroit: Gale Research Inc., 1991), 612.

17. Shepard, vol. 1, 611.

18. Shepard, vol. 2, 1588.

19. Gordon Stein, ed., *The Encyclopedia of the Paranormal* (Amherst, NY: Prometheus Books, 1996), 576.

20. Melton, Clark and Kelly, xxv.

21. J. Gordon Melton, Jerome Clark, and Aidan A. Kelly, *New Age Almanac* (New York: Visible Ink Press, 1991), 7.

22. Walter Martin, *The New Age Cult* (Minneapolis: Bethany House, 1989), 133.

23. J. Gordon Melton, "New Thought and the New Age," in James R. Lewis and J. Gordon Melton, *Perspectives on the New Age* (Albany, NY: State University of New York Press, 1992), 16.

24. Melton, "New Thought," 26.

25. Shepard, vol. 1, 151.

26. Melton, Clark, and Kelly, *New Age Encyclopedia*, xxvi.

27. Aldous Huxley, *The Perennial Philosophy* (New York: Harper & Row, 1944; 1970 edition), vii.

28. David Clark, *The Pantheism of Alan Watts* (Downers Grove, IL: InterVarsity Press, 1978), 14.

29. Alan W. Watts, *The Way of Zen* (New York: Pantheon Books, 1957), front cover.

30. J. Isamu Yamamoto, "Zest for Zen," *Christian Research Journal,* Winter 1995, 14.

31. From last source cited, 14.

32. D. T. Suzuki. Quoted in Stephen Batchelor, *The Awakening of the West* (Berkeley, CA: Parallax Press, 1994), 213.

33. From last source cited. Quoted in Batchelor, 362.

34. David K. Clark and Norman L. Geisler, *Apologetics in the New Age* (Grand Rapids, MI: Baker, 1990; 1992 edition), 59.

35. Swami Muktananda, *Sidha Meditation: Commentaries on the Shiva Sutras and Other Sacred Texts* (Oakland, CA: Siddha Yoga Dham of America, 1975), 98–99. Quoted in John Ankerberg and John Weldon, *Encyclopedia of New Age Beliefs* (Eugene, OR: Harvest House, 1996), 225.

36. Swami Muktananda, *Mukteshwari*, Part 2 (Ganeshpuri, India: Shree Gurudev Ashram, 1973), 158. Quoted in Ankerberg and Weldon, 225.

37. Swami Muktananda. Quoted in Chandler, 61.

38. Maharishi Mahesh Yogi, *The Science of Being and the Art of Living* (London: International SRM Publications, 1966), 26–27. Quoted in Vishal Mangalwadi, *The World of Gurus* (Chicago: Cornerstone Press, 1992), 78.

39. Sai Baba, *Sathyam-shivam Sundaram,* Part 3 (Bangalore, India: Sri Sathya Sai Publication and Education Foundation, 1973), 112. Quoted in Ankerberg and Weldon, 225.

40. Sai Baba, *Sathya Sai Speaks*, vol. 9 (Bangalore, India: Sri Sathya Sai Publication and Education Foundation, n.d.), 68. Quoted in Ankerberg and Weldon, 225.

41. Baba, *Sathya Sai Speaks,* 184. Quoted in Ankerberg and Weldon, 225.

42. Ferguson, 382.

43. Chandler, 341.

44. Spangler, 194.
45. Benjamin Creme, *The Reappearance of the Christ and the Masters of Wisdom* (Los Angeles: Tara Center, 1980), 110–111.
46. Eldon K. Winker, *The New Age Is Lying to You* (St. Louis: Concordia, 1994), 191.
47. Two Disciples, *The Rainbow Bridge* (Escondido, CA: The Triune Foundation, 1981), 13.
48. RAMTHA, with Douglas James Mahr, *Voyage to the New World* (Friday Harbor, WA: Masterworks, Inc., 1985), 36.
49. From last source cited, 61.
50. David Spangler, *Emergence: Rebirth of the Sacred* (Forres, Scotland: Findhorn Publications, n.d.), 144. Quoted in Chandler, 266.
51. Ferguson, 29.
52. RAMTHA, 176.
53. John Dunphy, "A Religion for the New Age," *The Humanist* (January/February 1983), 26.
54. Douglas R. Groothuis, *Unmasking the New Age* (Downers Grove, IL: InterVarsity Press, 1986), 24.
55. Shirley MacLaine. Quoted in William Goldstein, "Life on the Astral Plane," *Publishers Weekly* March 18, 1983, 46. Cited in Groothuis, 26.
56. Julius J. Finegold and William M. Thetford, eds., *Choose Once Again: Selections from a Course in Miracles* (Millbrae, CA: Celestial Arts, 1981), 2–3.
57. Martin, 133.
58. From last source cited, 129.
59. Groothuis, 150.
60. Spangler, *Revelation*, 75.
61. Creme, 120.
62. Benjamin Creme, *Maitreya's Mission* (London: Share International Foundation, 1986), 68.
63. Levi Dowling, *The Aquarian Gospel of Jesus the Christ* (Marina Del Rey, CA: DeVorss & Co., 1978), 13.
64. Creme, *The Reappearance*, 28.
65. John White, "Jesus and the Idea of a New Age," *The Quest*, Summer 1989, 14. Quoted in Doug Groothuis, *Revealing the New Age Jesus* (Downers Grove, IL: InterVarsity Press, 1990), 15.
66. Creme, *The Reappearance*, 119–120.
67. Dowling, 110.
68. *Tulsa World*, April 23, 1994, 7. Quoted in *EMFJ Update*, January 1995, 5.
69. Bob and Gretchen Passantino, "When Christians Meet New-Agers," *Christian Herald*, February 1988, 51.
70. Douglas Groothuis, "New Age or Ancient Error," *Moody Monthly*, February 1985, 20–22.
71. Martin E. Marty, "An Old New Age in Publishing," *Christian Century*, November 18, 1987, 1019.

Chapter 2
World of the Occult

1. Aleister Crowley, *Magick in Theory and Practice* (New York: Dover Publications, 1976), 12.
2. Story based on author's January 26, 1997 interview with Karen Winterburn; cf. Karen

Winterburn, "Delivered from Twelve Years of Occult Bondage," *Christian Research Newsletter*, vol. 3, no. 2, 1–2.

3. *The Steinerbooks Dictionary of the Psychic, Mystic, Occult* (Blauvelt, NY: Rudolf Steiner Publications, 1973), 148.

4. Leslie A. Shepard, ed., *Encyclopedia of Occultism & Parapsychology*, vol. 2 (Detroit: Gale Research Inc., 1991), 1207.

5. Julien Tondriau, *The Occult: Secrets of the Hidden World* (New York: Pyramid Communications, 1972), 5. Originally published in France as *L'OCCULTISME* (Verviers, France: Gerard & Co., 1964).

6. Tondriau, 5.

7. Clifford Wilson and John Weldon, *Psychic Forces and Occult Shock* (Chattanooga: Global Publishers, 1987), 104.

8. Carol McGraw, "Seekers of Self Now Herald the New Age," *Los Angeles Times*, February 17, 1987, part 1, 3.

9. George H. Gallup and Frank Newport, "Belief in Paranormal Phenomena Among Adult Americans," *Skeptical Inquirer*, vol. 15, no. 2 (Winter 1995), 137.

10. Richard Morin, "A Revival of Faith in Religion," *The Sacramento Bee*, July 4, 1993, 1.

11. "Current Research: Recent Findings on Religious Attitudes and Behavior," *Religion Watch*, February 1993, 3.

12. Wade Clark Roof, "The Four Spiritual Styles of Baby Boomers," *Denver Post*, March 21, 1993, 4.

13. *U.S. News & World Report*, October 24, 1994, 17.

14. According to the online service of *Magill's Survey of Cinemas*, more than 200 horror movies were released between 1980 and the first part of 1991.

15. Dion Warwick's involvement with psychic hot lines is well-known due to her many info-mercials for such services. Billy Dee Williams advertised his own psychic hot line in the July 1996 issue of *McCall's*, 139.

16. Jeffrey Kluger, "CIA ESP," *Discover*, April 1996, 34.

17. Arthur C. Lehmann and James E. Myers, *Magic, Witchcraft, and Religion* (Mountain View, CA: Mayfield Publishing Co., 1993), 369–370.

18. Will Bradbury, ed., *Into the Unknown* (Pleasantville, NY: The Reader's Digest Association, 1981), 203.

19. From last source cited.

20. Shepard, 1207.

21. Nevill Drury, *Dictionary of Mysticism and the Occult* (New York: Harper & Row, 1985), 161.

22. Elliot Miller, *A Crash Course on the New Age Movement* (Grand Rapids, MI: Baker, 1989), 36.

23. Robert Monroe, *Journeys Out of the Body* (New York: Doubleday, 1971; New York: Anchor Books edition, 1977), 138–139.

24. Adapted from W. Elwyn Davies, *Principalities and Powers* (Minneapolis: Bethany House, 1976), 303–304; cf. Josh McDowell and Don Stewart, *Handbook of Today's Religions* (San Bernardino, CA: Here's Life Publishers, Inc., 1983; 1992 edition), 153.

25. Russ Parker, *Battling the Occult* (Downers Grove, IL: InterVarsity Press, 1990), 53–60.

26. Ken Myers. Quoted in Julia Duin, "Wizards and Witches Go Mainstream," *Christian Research Journal*, Fall 1996, 45.

27. Duin, 45.

Chapter 3
The Devil Made Me Do It

1. Anton LaVey, *The Satanic Bible* (New York: Avon Books, 1969), 33–34, 45.

2. Sean Sellers. Quoted in Jerry Johnston, *The Edge of Evil* (Dallas: Word, 1989), 18.

3. Sellers. Quoted in Johnston, 18.

4. Arthur Lyons, *Satan Wants You* (New York: Mysterious Press, 1988), 11.

5. Sellers. Quoted in Johnston, 20–21. For the sake of clarity, the order in which Sellers's statements appear has been slightly altered. The quotations themselves, however, are entirely accurate.

6. Quoted in Johnston, 18.

7. Sean Sellers. Quoted in John Trott, "About the Devil's Business," *Cornerstone*, vol. 19, issue 93, 10.

8. Bob Passantino and Gretchen Passantino, *When the Devil Dares Your Kids* (Ann Arbor, MI: Servant Publications, 1991), 159.

9. Sellers. Quoted in Johnston, 19.

10. Craig Hawkins, "The Many Faces of Satanism," *Forward*, Fall 1986, 17.

11. Bob Passantino and Gretchen Passantino, *Satanism* (Grand Rapids, MI: Zondervan, 1995), 7.

12. Lyons, 9.

13. Passantino, *When the Devil*, 34.

14. J. Gordon Melton, *Encyclopedia of American Religions* (Detroit: Gale Research, Inc., 1996), 165.

15. Anton LaVey, *The Devil's Notebook* (Portland, OR: Feral House, 1992), 93.

16. Melton, 165.

17. Lyons, 9.

18. From last source cited, 9–11.

19. Jill Neimark, "It's Magical, It's Malleable, It's Memory," *Psychology Today*, January/February 1995, 45.

20. Neimark, 45.

21. A number of articles—secular and Christian—have dealt with this issue. Christian articles include: Bob Passantino and Gretchen Passantino, "The Hard Facts About Satanic Ritual Abuse," *Christian Research Journal*, Winter 1992, 21–23, 32–34; Gretchen Passantino, Bob Passantino, and John Trott, "Satan's Sideshow," *Cornerstone*, vol. 18, issue 90, 24–28; Gretchen Passantino, "Innocence Lost in Landmark Daycare Case," *Cornerstone*, vol. 23, issue 104, 14, 16–17; Mark Pendergrast, "Sorcerer's Apprentice: A Christian Therapist Renounces Memory Repression," *Cornerstone*, vol. 24, issue 107, 34–37, 42; and Daniel Brailey, "The Prosecution of a False Memory: An Update on the Paul Ingram Case," *Cornerstone*, vol. 25, issue 109, 23–24. Secular articles include: Eric Felton, "Ritual Child Sex Abuse: Much Ado About Nothing," *Insight on the News*, October 7, 1991, 27–29; Debbie Nathan, "The Ritual Sex Abuse Hoax," *Village Voice*, June 12, 1990, 36–44; Martin Gardner, "The Tragedies of False Memories," *Skeptical Inquirer*, vol. 18, no. 5 (Fall 1994), 464–470; Dr. John Hochman, "Recovered Memory Therapy and False Memory Syndrome," *Skeptic*, vol. 2, no. 3 (1994), 58–61; Laura Pasley, "Misplaced Trust," *Skeptic*, vol. 2, no. 3 (1994), 62–67; Margaret Carlson, "The Sex-Crime Capital," *Time*, November 13, 1995. Books dealing with SRA include: Mark Pendergrast, *Victims of Memory* (Hinesburg, VT: Upper Access, Inc., 1995) and Debbie Nathan and Michael Snedeker, *Satan's Silence* (New York: Basic Books, 1995).

22. LaVey, *Devil's Notebook*, 9.

23. From last source cited, 64.

24. From last source cited, 63.

25. From last source cited, 10.

26. From last source cited, 9.

27. LaVey, *Satanic Bible*, 52–54.

28. LaVey, *Devil's Notebook*, 32.

29. LaVey, *Satanic Bible*, 25.

30. Simon Dwyer, "The Plague Yard," in *Rapid Eye*, vol. 2, ed. Simon Dwyer (London: Creation Books, 1992; 1995 edition), 170.

31. LaVey, *Devil's Notebook*, 22.

32. From last source cited, 27.

33. Passantino, *When the Devil*, 42.

34. Anton LaVey. Quoted in Blanche Barton, *The Secret Life of a Satanist* (Los Angeles: Feral House, 1990), 205.

35. Aleister Crowley, *Magick in Theory and Practice* (New York: Dover Publications, 1976), 12.

36. LaVey, *Satanic Bible*, 110.

37. Marcello Truzzi, "The Occult Revival As Popular Culture: Some Observations on the Old and the Nouveau Witch," *Sociological Quarterly*, vol. 13 (Winter 1972). Reprinted in Arthur C. Lehmann and James E. Myers, eds., *Magic, Witchcraft, and Religion* (Mountain View, CA: Mayfield Publishing, 1993), 404.

38. Truzzi, 404.

39. Leslie A. Shepard, ed., *Encyclopedia of Occultism and Parapsychology*, vol. 2 (Detroit: Gale Research, Inc., 1991), 1569.

40. From last source cited, 1569.

41. Vicki L. Dawkins and Nina Downey Higgins, *Devil Child* (New York: St. Martin's Press, 1989), 58. Quoted in Passantino, *When the Devil*, 44–45.

42. Dwyer, 169.

43. John Cooper, *The Black Mask: Satanism in America Today* (Old Tappan, NJ: Fleming H. Revell, 1990), 107–108.

44. Hawkins, 20.

45. Crowley, 96.

46. From last source cited, 98.

47. Robert J. Jamra, *The Church of Satan* (Los Angeles: Church of Satan, n.d.), 3. Quoted in Lawrence C. Trostle, *The Stoners: Drugs, Demons, and Delinquency* (New York: Garland Publishing, 1992), 64.

48. LaVey, *Satanic Bible*, 89.

49. From last source cited, 88.

50. From last source cited, 51.

51. Deborah Hastings, "Rape, Torture Also Charged in Stabbing Death of Teen," *Orange County Register*, May, 4, 1996, 26 (news section).

52. Deborah Hastings, "Teens Accused of Girl's Murder to Please Satan," *Orange County Register*, May 3, 1996, 6 (metro section).

53. Hastings, "Rape, Torture," 26.

54. Anton LaVey. Quoted in John Fritscher, "Straight from the Witch's Mouth," in *Magic, Witchcraft, and Religion*, 389.

55. LaVey, *Satanic Bible*, 39.

56. Burton H. Wolfe, *The Devil's Avenger* (New York: Pyramid Books, 1974), 35.

57. LaVey, *Satanic Bible*, 40.

58. LaVey. Quoted in Fritscher, 389.

59. LaVey, *Satanic Bible*, 30, 33.

60. Burton H. Wolfe, introduction to *Satanic Bible*, 15.

61. LaVey. Quoted in Fritscher, 388.

62. LaVey, *Satanic Bible*, 31, 33.

63. Sean Sellers. Letter to John Trott, July 15, 1990. Quoted in Trott, 10.

64. James. Quoted in Larry Kahaner, *Cults That Kill* (New York: Warner Books, 1988), 90.

65. Phil. Quoted in Kahaner, 85.

66. LaVey, *Devil's Notebook*, 105.

67. From last source cited, 117.

68. From last source cited, 62.

69. From last source cited, 97.

70. Dwyer, 170.

Chapter 4
Hollywood's Favorite Religion

1. L. Ron Hubbard, "Keeping Scientology Working," *HCO Policy Letter* (Hubbard Communications Office), February 7, 1965, 9. Quoted in Craig Branch, "Hubbard's Religion," *Watchman Expositor*, vol. 13 no. 2 (1996), 10, Internet edition available at http://rampages.on ramp.net/~watchman/hubrel103,htm. This same statement appears in a slightly different form in Bent Corydon and L. Ron Hubbard Jr., *L. Ron Hubbard: Messiah or Madman?* (Secaucus, NJ: Lyle Stuart, Inc., 1987), 57: "Your next endless trillions of years and the whole agonized future of every man, woman, and child on this planet depend on what you do here and now, with and in Scientology."

2. This account is an adaptation of the Scotts' story as written by Anna Waterhouse, "Escape from Scientology," *Christian Research Newsletter*, vol. 1, issue 1, 1–2. Information from a published Christian Research Institute interview with the Scotts was also used (see "An Insider's View of Scientology," *Christian Research Newsletter*, vol. 3, issue 5, 1–2).

3. Church of Scientology, "The Creed of The Church of Scientology," *Freedom*, September 1994, 35.

4. J. Gordon Melton, *Encyclopedia of American Religions* (Detroit: Gale Research, Inc., 1996), 696.

5. The Public Relations Office of L. Ron Hubbard, *L. Ron Hubbard: The Current Scene—Volume 1: 1983–1984* (Los Angeles: The Public Relations Office of L. Ron Hubbard, 1984), 4.

6. Friends of L. Ron Hubbard, *L. Ron Hubbard: A Profile* (Los Angeles: CSI, 1995), 118.

7. Richard Behar, "Scientology: The Cult of Greed," *Time*, May 6, 1991, 51.

8. Richard Kyle, *The Religious Fringe* (Downers Grove, IL: InterVarsity Press, 1993), 305; cf. Joseph M. Hopkins, "Scientology: Religion or Racket? Part 1," *Christianity Today*, vol. 14 no. 3 (1969), 6 and Harriet Whitehead, "Reasonably Fantastic: Some Perspectives on Scientology, Science Fiction, and Occultism," in *Religious Movements in Contemporary America*, eds., Irving I. Zaretsky and Mark P. Leone (Princeton, NJ: Princeton University Press, 1974), 549.

9. Joel Sappell and Robert W. Welkos, "The Making of L. Ron Hubbard: Creating the Mystique," *Los Angeles Times,* June 24, 1990. Internet edition available at http://homepage.cistron.nl/~davel/la/la90-1a2.html. This is taken from part 1 of a six-part investigative series on Scientology by the *Los Angeles Times*. The series appeared between June 24 and June 29, 1990. It is one of the most accurate, in-depth exposés on Hubbard and Scientology to be printed by a newspaper. The entire six part series is available on the Internet at http://homepage.cistron.nl/~davel/la/la90.html.

10. Friends of L. Ron Hubbard, 54.

11. Hubbard married his second wife—Sara Northrup—in late 1946, almost a full year and a half *before* he was divorced from Louise Grubb. His divorce from Grubb was not granted in Port Orchard, Oregon, until December 24, 1947. He married Northrup in Chestertown, Maryland, on August 10, 1946. In fact, Hubbard married Northrup eight months before Grubb had even *filed* for divorce (Jesus People U.S.A., *Pandora's Box: Cult of the Month*, 2).

12. L. Ron Hubbard. Quoted in Sappell and Welkos, "The Making of L. Ron Hubbard: The Mind Behind the Religion," *Lost Angeles Times*, June 24, 1990. Internet edition available at http://homepage.cistron.nl/~davel/la/la90-1a1.html.

13. L. Ron Hubbard. quoted in Sapell and Welkos. "The Making of L. Ron Hubbard: The Mind Behind the Religion."

14. Leslie A. Shepard, ed., *Encyclopedia of Occultism & Parapsychology*, vol. 1 (Detroit: Gale Research, Inc., 1991), 359-360.

15. Sappell and Welkos, "The Making of L. Ron Hubbard: The Mind Behind the Religion."

16. L. Ron Hubbard, *Conditions of Space/Time/Energy*, Philadelphia Doctorate Course (PDC), Lecture 18, 1952. Quoted in Jon Atack, *A Piece of Blue Sky* (New York: Lyle Stuart, 1990), 89; cf. 91.

17. L. Sprague de Camp. Quoted in Sappell and Welkos, "The Making of L. Ron Hubbard: The Mind Behind the Religion."

18. Paul Rydeen, "Jack Parsons: The Magickal Scientist and His Circle," *The Excluded Middle*, no. 6, 40–42, 62, 65–66.

19. Adam Rostoker, "Whence Came the Stranger," in *Rapid Eye 3*, ed. Simon Dwyer (London: Creation Books, 1995), 233.

20. Rostoker, 229.

21. From last source cited, 233.

22. Aleister Crowley, *Book of the Law*. Quoted in Russell Miller, *Bare-Faced Messiah* (London: Michael Joseph, 1987), 119.

23. Bent Corydon and L. Ron Hubbard, Jr., *L. Ron Hubbard: Messiah or Madman?* (New York: Lyle Stuart, 1987), 256; cf. Miller, 119.

24. Miller, 119–124; cf. Corydon and Hubbard, 256–257.

25. Parsons. Quoted in Atack, 97.

26. Jack Parsons, *The Collected Works of Jack Parsons* (New York: OTO). Quoted in Atack, 96-97.

27. The Church of Scientology claims that Hubbard never got involved with black magick as an occultic believer and maintains that he was acutally working for the Navel Intelligence in order to break up black magick in America (see Sappell and Welkos, "The Making of L. Ron Hubbard: The Mind Behind the Religion.")

28. L. Ron Hubbard, *The Fundamentals of Thought* (Los Angeles: Church of Scientology of California, 1956; 1976 edition), 15.

29. L. Ron Hubbard, *Dianetics and Scientology: Technical Dictionary* (Los Angeles: Bridge Publications, 1975; 1987 edition), 9.

30. Hubbard, *The Fundamentals*, 58–60. Hubbard also teaches that there is a third part of the mind—the somatic mind—that is subject to both the analytical and reactive mind, as well as to the thetan. But the somatic mind is not here discussed since it seems to play a significantly lesser role in Scientology, at least from an outsider's point of view.

31. Hubbard, *Dianetics and Scientology*, 336.

32. L. Ron Hubbard, *The Creation of Human Ability* (Los Angeles: Church of Scientology, 1954; 1976 edition), 279; cf. Friends of L. Ron Hubbard, 82.

33. Friends of L. Ron Hubbard, 82; cf. L. Ron Hubbard, *Dianetics Today* (Los Angeles: Church of Scientology, 1975), iv.

34. L. Ron Hubbard, *Dianetics: The Evolution of a Science* (Los Angeles: Church of Scientology of California, 1950; 1977 edition), 109.

35. L. Ron Hubbard, *Dianetics: The Modern Science of Mental Health* (New York: Hermitage House, 1950), 130–131.

36. Hubbard, *Dianetics: The Modern Science*, 156; cf. 131–132.

37. From last source cited, 132–133.

38. Hubbard, *The Creation*, 251.

39. Hubbard, *Dianetics: The Evolution*, 70.

40. The word *memory* is used loosely here. In Scientology, an "engram" is not really a "memory" per se because memories are received through the analytical mind, whereas engrams are "recorded" irrespective of sight and sound in the reactive mind.

41. Hubbard, *Dianetics: The Modern Science*, 158.

42. From last source cited, 160.

43. From last source cited.

44. Church of Scientology Information Service, *Scientology: A World Religion Emerges in the Space Age* (Los Angeles: Church of Scientology, 1973), 28–29. Christian scholar John Weldon provides yet another example of an engram in his article "Scientology: From Science Fiction to Space-Age Religion," which appeared in the *Christian Research Journal* (Summer 1993, p. 22): "A boy falls out of a tree just as a red car passes by and is knocked unconscious. Later, even as a man, red cars (even red things) may restimulate the episode in various ways and cause irrational reactions. This man may thus refuse to ride in a red car and may even get ill or dizzy when confronted with the possibility."

45. L. Ron Hubbard, *Volunteer Ministers Handbook* (Los Angeles: Church of Scientology, 1976), 551–552.

46. Friends of L. Ron Hubbard, 87.

47. L. Ron Hubbard, *E-Meter Essentials* (Los Angeles: Bridge Publications, 1961; 1988 edition), 33.

48. From last source cited, 31.

49. Church of Scientology Information Service, *Scientology: A World Religion*, 40–41; cf. Church of Scientology, *The Scientology Handbook* (Los Angeles: Bridge Publications, 1994), xi–xii.

50. J. Gordon Melton, *Encyclopedia*, 745

51. Church of Scientology, *What Is Scientology?* (Los Angeles: Church of Scientology, 1978; 1979 edition), 146.

52. Hubbard, *The Fundamentals*, 87.

53. Melton, *Encyclopedia*, 745.

54. L. Ron Hubbard, *Science of Survival* (Wichita, KS: Hubbard Dianetics Foundation, 1951), 255.

55. Hubbard, *The Fundamentals*, 17.

56. From last source cited, 14.

57. *Dianetics*, 92; cf. Roy Wallis, "'Poor Man's Psychoanalysis?': Observations On Dianetics," *Zetetic*, vol. 1, no. 1 (Fall/Winter 1976), 13.

58. Hubbard, *Dianetics: The Evolution*, 94.

59. L. Ron Hubbard, *Dianetics and Scientology: Technical Dictionary* (Los Angeles: Bridge Publications, 1975; 1987 edition), 75.

60. Hubbard, *The Creation*, 68–70.

61. Hubbard, *Dianetics and Scientology*, 75.

62. Hubbard, *What Is Scientology?*, 461.

63. Leisa Goodman, "Lawbreakers Are Thieves and Liars, Not 'Critics': Church of Scientology Responds," *Skeptic*, vol. 4, no. 1 (1996), 19.

64. L. Ron Hubbard. Quoted in Joel Sappell and Robert W. Welkos, "The Selling of a Church: Church Markets Its Gospel With High-Pressure Sales," *Los Angeles Times*, June 25, 1990, http://homepage.cistron.nl/~davel/la/la90-2a.html.

65. Friends of L. Ron Hubbard, 91.

66. Joel Sappell and Robert W. Welkos, "The Making of L. Ron Hubbard: Defining the Theology," *Los Angeles Times*, June 24, 1990, Internet edition available at http://homepage.cistron.nl/~davel/la/la90-1b.html.

67. Church of Scientology, *The Scientology Handbook*, xxv.

68. Church of Scientology, *What Is Scientology?*, 275.

69. Hubbard, *The Creation*, 248.

70. Hubbard, *What Is Scientology?*, 566; cf. *Scientology Catechism*, 213, 215. Quoted in Craig Branch, "Hubbard's Religion," *The Watchman Expositor*, vol. 13, no. 2, 10.

71. Christopher Evans, *Cults of Unreason* (New York: Dell, 1973), 17; cf. Harriet Whitehead, "Reasonably Fantastic: Some Perspectives on Scientology, Science Fiction, and Occultism," in Irving I. Zaretsky and Mark P. Leone, eds., *Religious Movements in Contemporary America* (Princeton, NJ: Princeton University Press, 1974), 547–548, and David G. Bromley and Anson D. Shupe, *Strange Gods* (Boston: Beacon Press, 1981), 48.

72. Church of Scientology, *Scientology: A World Religion*, 23; cf. Hubbard, *Fundamentals*, 44, 69, 70 and Hubbard, *The Creation*, 113, 248.

73. Church of Scientology Information Service, Department of Archives, *Scientology: A World Religion*, 21; cf. Hubbard, *The Fundamentals*, 54.

74. J. Gordon Melton, *Encyclopedic Handbook of Cults in America* (New York: Garland, 1986; 1992 edition), 193.

75. Melton, *Encyclopedic Handbook*, 193–196.

76. L. Ron Hubbard. Quoted in Sappell and Welkos, "The Making of L. Ron Hubbard: Defining the Theology."

77. L. Ron Hubbard, *Saint Hill Special Briefing Course* (taped lecture), July 23, 1963. Transcript availabe on the Internet at http://login.eunet.no/~ingar/clambake/archive/lec-bli.html. This teaching of Hubbard's has been verified by several former members. One such individual, who has transcripts of the *Saint Hill Special Briefing Course*, has posted relevant information about Hubbard's July 23, 1963 statements on the Internet at http://home.sol.no/~spirious/CoS/archive/lectures.html; cf. Sappell and Welkos, "The Making of L. Ron Hubbard: Defining the Theology."

78. Hubbard. Quoted in Sappell and Welkos, "The Making of L. Ron Hubbard: Defining the Theology."

79. L. Ron Hubbard, *Scientology: A History of Man* (Denmark: Scientology Publications Organization, 1952; 1980 edition), 116.

80. Hubbard, *Scientology: A History of Man*, 99–100, 104–105.

81. Church of Scientology. Quoted in Sappell and Welkos, "The Making of L. Ron Hubbard: Defining the Theology."

82. Hubbard, *The Fundamentals*, 66.

83. This synopsis of teh OT-3 session is built from two accounts. 1) Sappell and Welkos, "The Making of L. Ron Hubbard: Defining the Theology": and 2) "Urgent-Important," *L. A. Reader*, June 7, 1985, 27; cf. Atak, 31-33. Hubbard may have first revealed this story to followers during an October 3, 1968 lecture that he gave aboard his sailing vessel, the *Apollo*. Transcripted excerpts of this lecture, including the parts where he talks about Xenu, can be found in several places (e.g., on the Internet at http://wpxx02.toxi.uni-wuerzburg.de/~cowen/essays /marcabs.html). This same lecture about Xenu and body-thetans is also referenced in the legal declaration of Hana (Eltringham) Whitfield, April 4, 1994, in the case of the *Church of Scientology International vs. Steven Fishman and Uwe Geertz*. Document is on file at the United States District Court—Central District of California and is available on the Internet at http://wpxx02.toxi.uni-wuerzburg.de/~krasel/CoS/aff/aff_hw94a.html.

84. Church of Scientology, *What Is Scientology?*, 544-545.

85. From last source cited, 544.

86. Walter Martin, *The Kingdom of the Cults* (Minneapolis: Bethany House, 1965; 1985 edition), 345.

87. Kurt Van Gorden, "Scientology," in *Evangelizing the Cults,* ed.Ronald Enroth (Ann Arbor, MI: Servant Publications, 1990), 161.

88. John Ankerberg and John Weldon, *Encyclopedia of New Age Beliefs* (Eugene, OR: Harvest House, 1996), 524.

89. Church of Scientology, *Scientology: A World Religion*, 11.

90. Church of Scientology, *L Ron Hubbard: Founder of Dianetics and Scientology*, 1. Quoted in Branch, 10.

91. Church of Scientology. Quoted in Ann-Mary Currier, "Religion: Scientologists Do Well in Hub," *Boston Globe*, October 7, 1972, n.p. Reprinted in Church of Scientology, *Scientology: A World Religion*, 33.

92. Church of Scientology, *Scientology: A World Religion*, 17; cf. Church of Scientology, *What Is Scientology?*, 200.

93. Church of Scientology, *Scientology: A World Religion*, 17; cf. Church of Scientology, *What Is Scientology?*, 200.

94. Church of Scientology. Quoted in Currier, n.p. Reprinted in Church of Scientology, *Scientology: A World Religion*, 33.

95. L. Ron Hubbard, *Scientology 8-8008*, 72. Quoted in Branch, 11.

96. Philadelphia Doctorate Course #9. Text available on the Internet at http://student.uq.edu.au /~py101663/sci/hubbardo.htm.

97. L. Ron Hubbard, *The Phoenix Lectures* (Los Angeles: Church of Scientology, 1968; 1979 edition), 27.

98. Walter A. Elwell, *Evangelical Dictionary of Theology* (Grand Rapids, Baker, 1984; 1996 edition), 710–711.

99. This statement by Hubbard appears in two Scientology documents; 1) *Certainty Magazine*, Vol. 5, No. 10. Quoted in Kevin Victor Anderson, *The Anderson Report: Scientology and Religion: Report of the Board of Enquiry into Scientology*, published in 1965 by the State of Victoria,

Australia. Internet edition available at http://www.demon.co.uk/castle/audit/ar27.html (main page for entire report starts at http://www.demon.co.uk/castle/audit/andrhome.html); and 2) *Ability* #81 (c. 1959), 31. Quoted in Roy Wallis, *The Road to Total Freedom: A Sociological Analysis of Scientology* (New York: Columbia University Press, 1977), 104; cf. Ankerberg and Weldon, 530.

100. L. Ron Hubbard, Class 8 Course (lecture 10), tape recorded on the ship *Apollo*, October 3, 1968. Quoted in Jim Bianchi, "Scientology FAQ: A skeptic's view, v. 1.9," December 21, 1996, Internet edition available at http://www.rpi.net.au/~marina/faq/jimbol.htm; cf. Branch, 28, Internet editiona available at http://rampages.onramp.net/~watchman/hubrel03.htm; also see Corydon and Hubbard Jr., 362. Hubbard made this statement during the same lecture in which he discussed the Xenu episode, which is also known ans the R6 incident.

101. L. Ron Hubbard, "Resistive Cases Former Therapy," *HCO Policy Letter* (Hubbard Communications Office), September 23, 1968, Class VIII. Quoted in Branch, 28, Internet edition available at http://rampages.onramp.net/~watchman/hubre103.htm. This teaching by Hubbard is also discussed in the legal declaration of Gerald Armstrong, January 26, 1997, in the cases of *Gerald Armstrong v. Grady Ward, Religious Technology Center v. H. Keith Henson,* and *Religious Technology Center v. Dennis Elrich.* Documentation is on file at the United States District Court—Northern District of California and is available on the Internet at http://wpxx02.toxi.uni-wuerzburg.de/~krasel/CoS/aff/aff_ga97.html.

102. L. Ron Hubbard, "Duplication," *PAB (Professional Auditors Bulletins)*, #31, vol. 2, July 23, 1954, 26. Quoted in Branch; cf. Anderson..

103. L. Ron Hubbard, "Routine 3," *HCO Bulletin* (Hubbard Commucations Office), May 11, 1963, 1-3. Quoted in Anderson; cf. Sappell and Welkos, "The Making of L. Ron Hubbard: Defining the Theology." As of November 1997, the full text of this particular bulletin was available at http://www.primenet.com/~lippard/bfm/heaven.htm.

104. Church of Scientology, *Volunteer Ministers Handbook*, 348–349.

105. Church of Scientology, *What Is Scientology?*, 546.

106. Church of Scientology, *Scientology: A World Religion*, 23.

107. L. Ron Hubbard, *Axiom 188*. Quoted in Church of Scientology, *Dianetics Today*, 984.

108. Church of Scientology, *Volunteer Ministers Handbook*, 349; cf. L. Ron Hubbard, *HCO Bulletin* (Hubbard Communications Office), January 2, 1960. L. Ron Hubbard. Quoted in Branch, 11.

109. Hubbard, *PAB (Professional Auditors Bulletin)*, #31. Quoted in Branch, 11; cf. Anderson.

110. Church of Scientology, *What Is Scientology?*, 545.

111. Church of Scientology, *Scientology: A World Religion*, 8.

112. Church of Scientology, *A Description of the Scientology Religion*, 57. Quoted in Branch, 11.

113. Friends of L. Ron Hubbard, 7.

114. Hubbard, *The Creation*, 180; cf. L. Ron Hubbard, *Have You Lived Before This Life?* (Los Angeles: Church of Scientology, 1977), 1, 31, 45.

115. L. Ron Hubbard. *HCO Bulletin* (Hubbard Communications Office), July 18, 1959. Quoted in Branch, 11; cf. Greg Loren Durand, "The Dangers of Dianetics: Scientology's Roadmap to Mental Bondage," Internet edition available at http://204.97.103.50/members/f4bs/dia-netic.htm.

116. Hubbard, *The Creation*, 180.

117. Church of Scientology, *Scientology: A World Religion*, 15–16, 35.

118. From last source cited, 15.

119. Hubbard, *Have You Lived Before?*, 284.

120. Joseph P. Gudel, Robert M. Bowman, and Dan Schlesinger, "Reincarnation: Did the Church Suppress It?," *Christian Research Journal* (Summer 1987), 9–12.
121. J. D. Douglas, ed., *The New International Dictionary of the Christian Church* (Grand Rapids, MI: Zondervan, 1978), 257
122. Gudel, Bowman, and Schlesinger, 12.
123. John Travolta. Quoted in Behar, 50.
124. Kirstie Alley. Quoted in Behar, 50.
125. Reuters, January 5, 1997, America Online.
126. "Lisa Marie Leans on MTV Brass." *Denver Post,* June 19, 1995. Reference to this incident can also be found in Mark Ebner, "Do You Want to Buy a Bridge?," *Spy Magazine,* February 1996, Internet edition available at http://miso.wwa.com/~vickie/cos/spy.html.
127. Joel Sappell and Robert W. Welkos, "The Selling of a Church: The Courting of Celebrities," *Los Angeles Times,* June 25, 1990, Internet edition available at http://homepage.cistron.nl/~davel/la/la90-2c.html.
128. Mary Williams Walsch, "German Leaders, U.S. Stars Clash On Scientology, *Los Angeles Times,* January 11, 1997, A8.
129. Erik Kirschbaum (Reuters), "Hollywood Stars Accuse Germany," January 9, 1997, America Online.
130. Terrence Petty (AP), "Germany Lashes Out at Hollywood," January 10, 1997, America Online.
131. AP, "Germany, Scientologists Rebuked," January 16, 1997, America Online.
132. Joel Sappell and Robert W. Welkos, "The Selling of a Church: Church Markets Its Gospel with High-Pressure Sales."

Chapter 5
Christian Identity: White Makes Right

1. Thomas E. O'Brien, *Verboten* (Metairie, LA: New Christian Crusade Church, 1974; 1987 reprint entitled *Proof: God's Chosen Are White Adamic Christians, "Verboten"*), 76.
2. Charles Conley. Quoted in James Ridgeway, *Blood in the Face* (New York: Thunder's Mouth Press, 1990), 70. This comment was made at a Klan rally during the 1960s in response to public outrage over the KKK bombing of the Sixteenth Street Baptist Church in Birmingham, where four young black girls where killed. Conley argued that nobody should be upset because black children were not really human children.
3. Clary's story is taken from information obtained from author's November 20, 1995 interview with Clary and Clary's book *Boys in the Hood* (Bakersfield, CA: Pneuma Life Publishing, 1995).
4. The Hebrew nation was a united group of twelve distinct tribes distinguished along familial lines stemming from ten of Jacob's sons (Reuben, Simeon, Judah, Dan, Naphtali, Gad, Asher, Issachar, Zebulun, and Benjamin) and two of Joseph's sons (Manasseh and Ephraim). The descendants of Levi were put in a separate category because they served as holy priests.
5. J. D. Douglas and Merrill C. Tenney, eds., *The New International Dictionary of the Bible* (Grand Rapids, MI: Zondervan, 1987), 194–195.
6. Several tribes and nations throughout the world claim to be descended from the "lost" ten tribes of Israel. Interestingly, each group does seem to have numerous religious traditions/beliefs and social customs indicating that at some point in their history they may have, at the very least, been influenced by Israelites. Among the many groups of people who trace their lineage back to Israel are: the black Lembas people of South Africa,

Zimbabwe, and Mozambique; the Mountain Jews of the Caucasia region in Daghestan, Azerbaijan, and Armenia; the Pathans of Afghanistan; the Ben Menashe (Manasseh) of North East India; and the Chiang-Min population who live in the mountain ranges on the Chinese-Tibetan border. Even some Japanese people claim that residents of Japan are descended from Israel (see *Beyond the Sambatyon: The Myth of the Ten Lost Tribes of Israel* [Creative Multi-Media, 1994]).

7. Pete Peters, "Frequently Asked Questions and Answers on Israel-Identity," Internet posting at Scriptures for America, http://ra.nilenet.com/!tmw/, to Library, to Israel-Identity F.A.Q., to Question 5.

8. James E. Wise, *The Seed of the Serpent* (Harrison, AK: Kingdom Identity Ministries, n.d.), 7-8.

9. *1995 Sons of Liberty Book and Video Cassette List*, 33.

10. Charles Lee Mange, *The Two Seeds of Genesis 3:15* (Nevada, MO: Wake Up America, n.d.), 6.

11. "Seed of the Serpent," *Morning Watch Chapel*, n.d., 7.

12. Robert Miles, "Cain and Abel," *Beyond the Bars . . . . The Stars*, July-August 1985, C.

13. The "Serpent Seed" doctrine does not assert that Eve had intercourse with a snake. Identity teaches that the term "serpent" is figurative language for a physical manifestation of Satan in the form of a man-like being (see Bertrand Comparet, *Adam Was Not the First "Man"* [flyer]), 2.

14. Richard Butler. Quoted in Brad Knickerbocker, "Followers See Validation for Their Views in the Bible," *Christian Science Monitor*, April 20, 1995, 10.

15. Michael L. Hansen, "The Aryan Art of War," *Calling Our Nation*, no. 34, 8.

16. *Doctrinal Statement of Beliefs* (Harrison, AK: Kingdom Identity Ministries, n.d.), 6.

17. Richard Butler, *Who, What, Why, When, Where: Aryan Nations* (tract), 3.

18. Pete Peters, "Frequently Asked Questions and Answers on Israel-Identity," Internet posting at Scriptures for America, http://ra.nilenet.com/!tmw/, to Library, to Israel-Identity F.A.Q., to Question 11.

19. *Aryan Nations Newsletter*, no. 35, 1.

20. Comparet, 2.

21. Bertrand Comparet, *The Cain-Satanic Seed Line* (Hayden Lake, ID: Aryan Nations, n.d.), 5.

22. The American Institute of Theology, *Correspondence Bible Course* (Newhall, CA: The American Institute of Theology, 1970; 1981 edition), 16, and O'Brien, 3.

23. Butler, *Who, What, Why*, 3.

24. Pete Peters, "Concerning the Oklahoma Bombing," *Scriptures for America*, vol. II (1995), 2; available from Internet posting at Scriptures for America, http://ra.nilenet.com/!tmw/.

25. Weisman, *Who Is Esau-Edom* (Burnsville, MN: Weisman Publications, 1991), 26.

26. James Combs, *Tolerance: Jewry's War on Whites* (Boring, OR: Christian Patriot Association, n.d.), 10-11.

27. Combs, 14–17.

28. "Why Oppose the Jews," *Calling Our Nation*, no. 15, 6.

29. Weisman, 108–109.

30. "Last Days of ZOG," *Calling Our Nation*, no. 59, 25; Cf. Thomas Robb, *Interracial* (Harrison, AK: Message of Old Publications, n.d.), 7.

31. Robb, 5.

32. Combs, 3.

33. Jack Mohr, "Kingdom Identity: Part I," *Christian Patriot Crusader*, vol. 7, no. 4 (December 1991), 4-5.

34. Pete Peters, *A Scriptural Understanding of the Race Issue* (LaPorte, CO: Scriptures for America, 1990), 15.

35. Jack Mohr, *Seed of Satan: Literal or Figurative?* (tract); Cf. *Who Are You and Why Are You Here* (Bay St. Louis, MS: America Awake, n.d.), 5, and letter from Jack Mohr to *Apologetics*, May, 28, 1990, 8. See Pete Peters, "Frequently Asked Questions," Question 5. The Khazars have nothing at all to do with either the northern or southern kingdoms of Israel, let alone modern-day Jews. They were a distinct people who converted to Judaism centuries ago.

36. Pete Peters, "Inter-Racial Marriage," part 1, cassette 170 (La Porte, CO: Scriptures for America). Quoted in Viola Larson, "Identity: A Christian Religion for White Racists," *Christian Research Journal* (Fall 1992), 25; Cf. Pete Peters, *A Scriptural Understanding*, 15.

37. Louis Beam, "Letter to Editor," *Aryan Nations*, no. 25, 17.

38. David Tate, "Why?," *Aryan Nations*, no. 25, 12. Tate is currently serving a life sentence for machine-gunning to death thirty-one-year-old Missouri State Trooper Jimmie Linegar in 1985.

39. Roy B. Mansker, "The Jews Have a Plan," *Calling Our Nation*, no. 33, 4.

40. Richard Butler, letter to an Aryan Kinsman, *Aryan Nations*, no. 25, 20.

41. William Gayley Simpson, "The Everlasting Truth About Race," *Christian Patriot Crusader*, vol. 7, no. 4 (December 1991), 19–20.

42. Louis Beam, *The Seditionist*, issue 1 (Winter 1988), 4.

43. Jack Mohr, *I Believe* (tract), 6.

44. Richard Butler. Quoted in Doug Vaughan, "Terror on the Right: The Nazi and Klan Resurgence," *Utne Reader*, August/September 1985, 48. Butler believes that "Ameri" means "heavenly" and "rica" stands for "reich," meaning kingdom; hence, his belief that "America" is God's "heavenly kingdom" (Cf. "America" [Lake Hayden, ID: Aryan Nations, n.d., 1]).

45. David Tate, "Spring Cleaning," *The Way*, May-July 1989, 10.

46. Robb, 7.

47. Thom Robb. Quoted in Bill Walker, "Warriors in the Fight Against Racial Equality," *Minneapolis Star-Tribune*, July 22, 1986, 9A. Cf. Coates, 80–81.

48. Butler, *Who, What, Why*, 4.

49. Butler. Quoted in "Terror on the Right," 47.

50. Butler. Quoted in Knickerbocker, 10.

51. L. "Dale" Chesson, "To All Aryan Brothers and Sisters," *Calling Our Nation*, no. 34, 9.

52. Beam, *Seditionist*, 2. Cf. Butler, letter to an Aryan Kinsman, 20.

53. Butler, *Who, What, Why*, 4.

54. "Why Oppose the Jews," *Calling Our Nation*, no. 15, 6.

55. Cheryl Hoffman (pseudonym). Quoted in Verne Becker, "The Counterfeit Christianity of the Ku Klux Klan," *Christianity Today*, April 20, 1984, 32.

56. John Perkins, "He's My Brother," *Cornerstone*, vol. 25, issue 108, 43. John Perkins is an African-American Christian who was a leader in the civil rights movement of the 1960s. His moving story about being nearly beaten to death by Mississippi highway patrolmen appears in this 1995 issue of *Cornerstone*. To request a copy of the article or magazine, write to: *Cornerstone*, 939 W. Wilson Ave., Chicago, IL 60640, 312-561-2450.

Chapter 6
Black Muslims: Allah's Black Supremacists

1. Louis Farrakhan, *The Announcement: A Final Warning to the U.S. Government* (Chicago: Final Call, 1989). Quoted in Mattias Gardell, *In the Name of Elijah Muhammad: Louis Farrakhan and the Nation of Islam* (Durham, NC: Duke University Press, 1996), 148.

2. Elijah Muhammad, *Muhammad Speaks*, February 11, 1972. Quoted in C. Eric Lincoln, *The Black Muslims in America* (Grand Rapids, MI: William B. Eerdmans, 1994), 69.

3. Elijah Muhammad, *The Supreme Wisdom: Solution to the So-called Negroes' Problem* (Chicago: University of Islam, 1957), 13. Quoted Lincoln, 74.

4. Bernard's story has been adapted from Herbert Toler, "Marching to a Different Drum," *Charisma*, May 1996, 29–31.

5. Arthur J. Magida, *Prophet of Rage* (New York: Basic Books, 1996), 44.

6. Erdmann D. Beynon, "The Voodoo Cult Among Negro Migrants in Detroit," *American Journal of Sociology* 43 (July 1937–May 1938): 896; cf. Lincoln, 12–13.

7. Gardell, 51.

8. Magida, 47–48.

9. From last source cited, 48.

10. From last source cited, 48–49.

11. Denke Majied. Quoted in Beynon, 895.

12. Majied. Quoted in Beynon, 895.

13. Magida, 53–54. Elijah Muhammad, Fard's successor, explained the origins of the white race as follows: "Who are the white race? . . . . 'Why are they white-skinned?' Answer: Allah (God) said this is due to being grafted from the Original Black Nation, as the Black Man has two germs (two people) in him. One is black and the other brown. The brown germ is weaker than the black germ. The brown germ can be grafted into its last stage, and the last stage is white. A scientist by the name of Yakub discovered this knowledge . . . 6,645 years ago, and was successful in doing this job of grafting after 600 years of following a strict and rigid birth control law" (Elijah Muhammad, "Mr. Muhammad Speaks," *Pittsburgh Courier*, July 4, 1959. Quoted in Lincoln, 72.

14. Gardell, 163–165.

15. Magida, 54.

16. Henry J. Young, *Major Black Religious Leaders Since 1940* (Nashville: Abingdon, n.d.), 67. Quoted in Joseph P. Gudel and Larry Duckworth, "Hate Begotten of Hate," *Forward* (Fall 1986), 9. Published by the Christian Research Institute.

17. Gardell, 59.

18. From last source cited, 171.

19. Clifton E. Marsh, *From Black Muslims to Muslims* (Metuchen, NJ: Scarecrow Press, 1984), 53. Quoted in Magida, 42; cf. Gardell, 50.

20. W. D. Fard, "Lost-Found Muslim Lesson No. 2." Reprinted in Khalid S. Lateef, *The Holy Quran's Condemnation of the Racist and Un-Islamic Ideology of "The Lessons" of W. D. Fard and the Teachings of Minister Louis Farrakhan's "Nation of Islam"* (Wheatley Heights, NY: Americans for Justice and Positive Change, n.d.), 12–13; cf. Magida, 50.

21. Beynon, 899; cf. Gardell, 57.

22. Magida, 51.

23. From last source cited, 51.

24. Martha F. Lee, *History of the Nation of Islam* (Lewiston, NY: Edwin Mellon Press, 1988), 35. Cited in Magida, 47.

25. Magida, 46.

26. Elijah Muhammad, *Message to the Black Man in America* (Chicago: Muhammad Mosque of Islam No. 2, 1965), 164. Quoted in Gudel and Duckworth, 10.

27. Magida, 54.

28. From last source cited, 77.

29. Malcolm X, *The Autobiography of Malcolm X, As Told to Alex Haley* (New York: Ballantine Books, 1965; 1973 edition), 299.

30. Magida, 76.

31. From last source cited, 74.

32. From last source cited, xxi.

33. Haman Cross, Jr. and Donna E. Scott, *What's Up with Malcolm* (Chicago: Moody Press, 1993), 15.

34. Magida, 4.

35. *Biography: Malcolm X* (New York: ABC News Production/A&E Television Networks, 1995).

36. Magida, 34.

37. Elma Lewis. Quoted in Magida, 9.

38. Louis Farrakhan, speech before Christian clergy, St. Louis, September 13, 1995. Quoted in Magida, 9.

39. Louis Farrakhan, interview in Steven Barboza, *American Jihad: Islam After Malcolm X* (New York: Doubleday, 1994), 148.

40. Farrakhan, in *American Jihad*, 149; cf. Magida, 32.

41. Magida, 78.

42. From last source cited, 79.

43. Farrakhan, in *American Jihad*, 146–147.

44. Magida, 79.

45. See "Malcolm Rejects Racist Doctrine," *New York Times*, October 4, 1964, in FBI file on Malcolm X, October 4, 1964. Cited in Magida, 82.

46. Louis Farrakhan, "Boston Minister Tells of Malcolm—Muhammad's Biggest Hypocrite," *Muhammad Speaks*, December 4, 1964, 11–15; cf. Magida, 83.

47. Farrakhan, "Boston Minister."

48. Malcolm X, "There Is a World Wide Revolution Going On," in *Malcolm X: The Last Speeches*, ed. Bruce Perry (New York: Pathfinder, 1989), 356; cf. Magida, 88.

49. *Biography: Malcolm X.*

50. Lincoln, 269.

51. Louis Farrakhan. Quoted in Herbert Toler, "Louis Farrakhan: What Does He Stand for?," *Charisma*, May 1996, 31.

52. Louis Farrakhan. Quoted in "Love Ya or Libya," *Time*, October 28, 1996, 30.

53. Louis Farrakhan. Quoted in *Kayhan* (Iranian newspaper), February 1996. Quoted in Toler, "Louis Farrakhan," 31.

54. Louis Farrakhan, speech on February 22, 1981. Quoted in Magida, 132.

55. Gardell, 129.

56. Farrakhan, *The Announcement*. Quoted in Gardell, 129.

57. Jabril Muhammad, *Farrakhan, the Traveler* (Phoenix: Phoenix and Co., 1985), 59. Quoted in Gardell, 129.

58. Magida, 141.

59. Louis Farrakhan, *The Final Call*, May 4, 1992. Quoted in Toler, "Louis Farrakhan," 31.

60. Magida, 159.

61. From last source cited, 159.

62. Khallid Abdul Muhammad, speech at Kean College, November 29, 1993. Quoted in Magida, 174–175.

63. Muhammad. Quoted in Magida, 174–176.

64. Louis Farrakhan, "The Divine Destruction of America: Can She Avert It?," speech delivered at Mosque Maryam (Chicago), June 9, 1996. Reprinted in *The Final Call*, online edition at http://www.noi.org/finalcall/MLFspeaks/destruction.html.

65. Farrakhan, "The Divine Destruction."

66. "Update: Farrakhan Decodes ID4," *Skeptic*, vol. 4, no. 3 (1996), 39.

67. Gardell, 131–133; cf. Tynetta Muhammad, "When the Saints Go Marching in," *The Final Call*, September 27, 1995, 31 and "Update: Farrakhan Decodes ID4," *Skeptic*, vol. 4, no. 3 (1996), 39.

68. Farrakhan, *The Announcement*. Quoted in Gardell, 133.

69. Gardell, 135.

70. Louis Farrakhan, unrecorded dinner conversation with Mattias Gardell, May 21, 1989. Quoted in Gardell, 135.

71. Elijah Muhammad. Quoted in *New York Herald Tribune*, April 3, 1963, as cited in Walter Martin, *The Kingdom of the Cults* (Minneapolis: Bethany House, 1965), 262.

72. Elijah Muhammad, "I Want to Teach You," *The Final Call*, online edition at http://www.noi.org/finalcall/columns/hemspks.html. Reprinted from Elijah Muhammad, *Our Savior Has Arrived* (Chicago: Muhammad's Temple of Islam No. 2, 1974).

73. Elijah Muhammad, *Message to the Black Man*, 7; cf. Gardell, 171.

74. Elijah Muhammad, "I Want to Teach You."

75. Gardell, 144–145.

76. Elijah Muhammad, "Mr. Muhammad Speaks," *Pittsburgh Courier*, May 2, 1959. Quoted in Lincoln, 70.

77. From last source cited.

78. Louis Farrakhan, "Jesus Saves," Savior's Day speech, February 26, 1995. Reprinted in *The Final Call*, vol. 14, no. 10, Internet edition at http://www.noi.org/FCN/MLFspeaks/jesussaves.html.

79. Elijah Muhammad, "Mr. Muhammad Speaks," May 2. Quoted in Lincoln, 116.

80. From last source cited.

81. Farrakhan, "Jesus Saves."

82. Elijah Muhammad. Quoted in Lincoln, 70.

83. Farrakhan, "Jesus Saves."

84. Hassain, *Muhammad Speaks*, October 29, 1971. Quoted in Lincoln, 30.

85. Malcolm X, interview on "The Hate That Hate Produced," *Newsbeat*, presented by Mike Wallace and Louis Lomax, WNTA-TV, July 10, 1959. Quoted in Lincoln, 71.

86. Jabril Muhammad, *Farrakhan the Traveler*. Quoted in Gardell, 144.

87. Elijah Muhammad, *The Supreme Wisdom*, 38. Quoted in Lincoln, 71.

88. Elijah Muhammad, "Mr. Muhammad Speaks," *Pittsburgh Courier,* August 15, 1959. Quoted in Lincoln, 66.

89. Louis Farrakhan. Quoted in Magida, 131.

90. Jabril Muhammad, *Farrakhan, the Traveler,* 59. Quoted in Gardell, 129.

91. Louis Farrakhan, speech of February 26, 1983. Quoted in Magida, 135.

92. Farrakhan, unrecorded dinner conversation. Quoted in Gardell, 129.

93. Malcolm X, in Elijah Muhammad, *The Supreme Wisdom,* 6–7.

94. Elijah Muhammad, "Mr. Muhammad Speaks," *Pittsburgh Courier,* July 18, 1959. Quoted in Lincoln, 73.

95. Elijah Muhammad, "Mr. Muhammad Speaks," *Pittsburgh Courier,* December 13, 1958. Quoted in Lincoln, 73

96. Malcolm X. Martin, 266.

97. From last source cited.

98. Louis Farrakhan, speech of April 20, 1985. Quoted in Toler, "Louis Farrakhan," 31.

99. "Perspectives," *Newsweek,* October 30, 1995, 27.

100. Toler, "Louis Farrakhan," 31.

101. Anthony M. Platt, "Born in the USA," *Los Angeles Times Book Review,* March 2, 1997, 8.

102. Howard Fineman and Vern E. Smith, "An Angry 'Charmer,'" *Newsweek,* October 30, 1995, 33.

103. Sylvester Monroe, "The Mirage of Farrakhan," *Time,* October 30, 1995, 52.

104. Lincoln, 17.

105. Magida, xxiii.

106. Norm R. Allen, "Farrakhan and the Million Man March," *Free Inquiry,* vol. 16, no. 1 (Winter 1995/96), 28.

107. Allen, 28.

108. Mark Whitaker, "And Now What?," *Newsweek,* October 30, 1995, 30.

109. Ben White. Quoted in Whitaker, 30.

110. Martin, 274.

Chapter 7
Moon's Moonies

1. Sun Myung Moon, *Master Speaks.* Quoted in Frederick Sontag, *Sun Myung Moon and the Unification Church* (Nashville: Abingdon, 1977), 116–117.

2. Sun Myung Moon, *Master Speaks,* January 30, 1973. Quoted in Sontag, 121.

3. Sun Myung Moon, *Master Speaks,* 1974 (Rowlane Farmhouse). Quoted in Ingo Michehl, Public Statement, available on Internet at http://trancenet.org.

4. This story is an adaptation of Ingo's public statement about his life in the Unification Church. It can be accessed on the Internet at http://trancenet.org.

5. Joon Ho Seuk, "Unificationism" (lecture), delivered at the Madison, Wisconsin Civic Center, April 17, 1983. Transcript printed as *Unificationism & Martial Arts* (Madison, WI: University of Wisconsin CARP, 1983), 7–8. Reprinted in Michael L. Mickler, ed., *The Unification Church II: Inner Life* (New York: Garland Publishing, 1990), 205–206.

6. See Steve Kemperman, *Lord of the Second Advent* (Ventura, CA: Regal Books, 1981).

7. J. Gordon Melton, *Encyclopedic Handbook of Cults in America* (New York: Garland Publishing, 1992), 296.

8. The Unified Family, *Sun Myung Moon* (The Unified Family: New York, n.d.), 1.

9. From last source cited, 2.

10. I believe this observation to be accurate, though I do not have specific examples.

11. The Unified Family, 2.

12. Marc Gallanter, *Cults: Faith, Healing, and Coercion* (New York: Oxford University Press, 1989), 130.

13. The Unified Family, 2–4.

14. From last source cited, 4.

15. From last source cited.

16. From last source cited, 6.

17. From last source cited, 7–9.

18. Gallanter, 130.

19. From last source cited, 131–132.

20. From last source cited, 133.

21. From last source cited.

22. Don Lattin, "Rev. Moon Tries to Go Mainstream," *San Francisco Chronicle*, October 31, 1996, A1.

23. Religion News Service. August 2, 1996. America Online. It must be noted that none of these Christians in any way endorse Moon's doctrinal beliefs. Their presence at Unification-sponsored events reflects their desire to back the sociopolitical views often promoted at Moon's various rallies and conferences. Participation in such events by Christians is an issue that has sparked a great deal of controversy. Some born-again believers see no reason why Christians should not lend their support to sociopolitical movements that involve unbelievers and cultists. Other Christians, however, feel that the involvement in such activities not only blurs the line between believers and unbelievers, but also serves to legitimize decidedly unbiblical religious groups whose hidden agenda is to use mainstream Christians to further their goals.

24. "The Unification Church Seeks Influence, Acceptance Among the Political ('Christian') Right," *Christian Research Journal*, vol. 11, no. 1 (Summer 1988), 5.

25. Meredith Ferguson, "On the Rebound," *Los Angeles Times*, September 10, 1996, E8.

26. Ronald Enroth. Quoted in Ferguson.

27. "Is Christian Involvement in the Unification Church Wise?," *Cornerstone* , vol. 26, issue 3 (1997), 19.

28. Lattin, A1.

29. William Heath, Associated Press, November 23, 1996, America Online.

30. Bob Waldrep, "Unification Church Influence in America," *Watchman Expositor*, vol. 13, no. 5 (1996), 8–9.

31. From last source cited, 9.

32. From last source cited.

33. Roger A. Dean, *Moonies: A Psychological Analysis of the Unification Church* (New York: Garland, 1992), 52–53.

34. Sun Myung Moon, *Master Speaks*, March 24, 1974. Quoted in Dean, 54.

35. Calvin Sims, "Moon's Unification Church Gains Respect in Latin America," *New York Times*, November 24, 1996, America Online.

36. Sontag, 122.

37. Waldrep, 8.

38. Sun Myung Moon, *Master Speaks*, May 17, 1973. Quoted in Sontag, 122.

39. Sun Myung Moon, interview with Frederick Sontag, February 3, 1977. Quoted in Sontag, 147.

40. Sun Myung Moon, *Exposition of the Divine Principle* (New York: The Holy Spirit Association for the Unification of World Christianity, 1996), xxii.

41. James R. Lewis, Introduction to J. Gordon Melton, ed., *Cults and New Religions: The Unification Church III* (New York: Garland Publishing, 1990), second page of introduction, no page number.

42. Moon, *Exposition*, 16.

43. Sontag, 123.

44. Moon, *Exposition*, 119.

45. From last source cited, 120.

46. From last source cited, 121.

47. Sun Myung Moon, *Divine Principle: Two Hour Lecture* (New York: HSA-UWC, 1977), 2.

48. Moon, *Exposition*, 136.

49. Moon, *Divine Principle: Two Hour*, 3.

50. Moon, *Exposition*, 156, 59, 60, 63–64.

51. From last source cited, 165; cf. 68.

52. Sun Myung Moon, 5B.

53. Moon, *Exposition*, 392.

54. From last source cited.

55. From last source cited, 166–167.

56. From last source cited, 280.

57. From last source cited, 171.

58. From last source cited, 141.

59. Sun Myung Moon, "A Special Message for the Age" (lecture), delivered in Buenos Aires, November 23, 1996. Reprinted in *Las Vegas Review-Journal*, February 3, 1997, 5B.

60. Sontag, 143; cf. Moon. Quoted in Sontag, 119.

61. Tyler O. Hendricks, *Unification News*, December 1995, 29. Quoted in Waldrep.

62. Moon, *Exposition*, 399–411.

63. From last source cited, 119.

64. Lewis, introduction.

65. Moon, *Exposition*, 411.

66. From last source cited, 404–405.

67. Sontag, 105.

68. Moon, *Exposition*, 49.

69. From last source cited, 140–141.

70. From last source cited, 49, 140.

71. From last source cited, 399–400, 410.

72. From last source cited, 401.

73. Moon, *Las Vegas Review-Journal*, 4B.

74. From last source cited.

75. From last source cited, 5B.

76. Lattin, A1.

77. Sun Myung Moon, speech delivered on True Parent's Day, April 18, 1996. Reprinted in *Unification News*, June 1996, 3. Quoted in Waldrep.

78. *Victory of Love* (New York: The Holy Spirit Association for the Unification of World Christianity, 1992), 63, 65–66.

79. Sontag, 123.

80. From last source cited, 131–132.

81. Moon, *Exposition*, 405.

82. Moon, *Las Vegas Review-Journal*, 5B.

83. Sontag 135.

84. From last source cited.

85. From last source cited, 125.

86. Young Oon Kim, *Unification Theology* (New York: The Holy Spirit Association for the Unification of World Christianity, 1980), 197.

87. Moon, *Exposition*, 122.

88. From last source cited, 117.

89. Kim, 65.

90. From last source cited, 163.

91. Moon, *Exposition*, 279.

92. Kim, 172.

93. Walter Martin, *The Kingdom of the Cults* (Minneapolis: Bethany House, 1965; 1985 edition), 344.

94. Moon, *Exposition*, 400.

95. Sontag, 130.

96. Dean, 98.

97. From last source cited, 98–99.

98. Anonymous. Quoted in From last source cited, 62.

99. Enroth, *The Lure of the Cults* (Downers Grove, IL: InterVarsity Press, 1979; 1987 edition), 50.

100. From last source cited, 51.

101. From last source cited, 52.

Chapter 8
All in "The Family"

1. David Berg, *"C'mon Ma, Burn Your Bra!": GP 286* (London: The Children of God, 1973), December 22, 1973, 286:32. Berg's letters were divided into numbered verses so that his followers could more easily refer to a particular passage. Consequently, the following notes refer to the letter number and verse of the document cited rather than the page number. For example, this quotation is taken from *Mo Letter 286*, verse 32.

2. This story is based on the author's March 9, 1997 interview with Sylvia Padilla.

3. Stephen Kent, "Lustful Prophet: A Psychosexual Historical Study of the Children of God's Leader, David Berg," *Cultic Studies Journal*, vol. 11, no. 2 (1994), 135.

4. This is the current position of The Family as taught by Berg: "[W]hy couldn't God have used the angel Gabriel to [sexual obscenity deleted] Mary. . . . Gabriel supplied the sperm, Mary supplied the egg & God supplied the Spirit. Why not? It sure sounds like that to me . . . 'HE CAME IN UNTO HER', & that expression's only used in having sex throughout the Bible" (David Berg, *Answers to Your Questions!—No. 8: DFO 1566*, 1566:6). "Gabriel was a spirit, an angel of God. He is already, in a sense, a part of God, or a representation of God. . . . [T]he angel came 'in unto her' is a term, a phrase used in the Bible only for sexual intercourse . . . since the wording is so specific that He did come 'in unto her,' He in other words had sexual intercourse with her. . . . It was the Angel Gabriel that 'came in unto' her. . . . I did that this morning with you [Maria]. I came in unto you when we had sexual intercourse, we [sexual obscenity deleted]!" (David Berg, *More on TM & the Unified Field!: DO 1854*, 1854:42, 43, 45, 48). Prior to making these statements, Berg taught that it was God Himself who had intercourse with Mary: "Which was the more remarkable . . . the more intimate experience for Mary?— When Gabriel stood there merely making an announcement to her, or when the Lord Himself came in unto her, & had intercourse with her . . . [and] produced His Own Son!" (David Berg, *Listen!: DO 998*, February 12, 1976, 998:18). "GOD HIMSELF HAD SEX WITH MARY TO HAVE JESUS! . . . God Himself took human form & literally [sexual obscenity deleted] Mary to make her pregnant with Jesus!" (David Berg, *The Devil Hates Sex: DFO 999*, May 20, 1990, 999:111).

5. Berg claims to have learned about Jesus' sexual encounters through a vision he had of Christ: "THAT'S THE ONLY TIME I EVER HAD A VISION OF CHRIST. . . . [S]ex is no sin! why should Jesus have been considered sinful to have enjoyed sex with Mary & Martha?—Which He did according to what I saw in my vision" (David Berg, *Houris of Heaven: DFO 1237*, May 30, 1975, 1237:30, 46). "JESUS AND MARY WERE ENJOYING SEX WITHOUT SIN!" (David Berg, *Little Nuggets: DFO 651*, 651:45). "JESUS KNEW WHAT IT WAS LIKE TO BE SICK. . . . HE MAY HAVE EVEN CONTRACTED A DISEASE FROM MARY MAGDALENE, WHO HAD BEEN A KNOWN PROSTITUTE, and several other women that were prostitutes that followed Him, or Mary and Martha. . . . IF HE'D NEVER SUFFERED THEIR SEXUAL DIS-EASES HE COULD NEVER REALLY HAVE FULL COMPASSION ON THEIR SUFFER-INGS. . . . [T]he Lord had sex with Mary and Martha and probably Mary Magdalene the harlot!" (David Berg, *Afflictions: DO 569*, November 25, 1976, 569:28, 29, 33, 48, 51, 52, 55, 183).

6. "[T]he Lord says . . . thou shalt be as one that is drunken with Me and one that doth **revel in My love**. (Mo sees a wine-drinking sex orgy with the Lord and others and laughs)." (David Berg, *A Psalm of David: GP 152*, 152:16).

7. The Family, "Baby, Remember My Name!," Internet document at The Family Web Page, http://www.deltanet.com/family/founder/trib_44.htm.

8. Alex Constantine, "Family Ties," in *Psychic Dictatorship in the U.S.A.* (Portland: Feral House, 1995), 132; Jerry Cooper, "A Wolf Among the Flock," *Alliance Life Magazine*, May 13, 1992, 12; Sylvia Padilla. Quoted in Hugh Muir, "Family Values," *(London) Sunday Telegraph Magazine*, January 5, 1997, 17.

9. David Berg, *"My Love Legend"* (London: The Children of God, 1973; a special publication), 8.

10. Berg, "My Love," 8.

11. David Berg, *Women in Love: GP 292*, December 20, 1973, 292:84.

12. Kent, 177; cf. David E. Van Zandt, *Living in the Children of God* (Princeton, NJ: Princeton University Press, 1991), 32–33.

13. Deborah (Linda Berg) Davis, *The Children of God* (Grand Rapids, MI: Zondervan, 1984), 26.

14. No Longer Children Ministry, *Urgent Warning* (tract), 2. This ministry to former COG members may be reached by writing to: No Longer Children, Box 415-8155 Park Rd., Richmond, B.C. Canada V6Y 3C9.

15. Muir, 16; cf. Davis, 28–29. Berg's granddaughters—Joyanne Treadwell and Merry Berg—ended up being sexually molested by Berg as well. In a 1992 interview, Merry stated that "she experienced dozens of intrusive sexual encounters with her grandfather. . . . She was not yet twelve when the first incident allegedly took place" (see Kent, 159).

16. Davis, 36–37.

17. From last source cited, 38.

18. David Berg. Quoted in Davis, 40.

19. Davis, 40.

20. Van Zandt, 34.

21. Many of Berg's followers received prophecies that California would sink into the Pacific on April 15, 1969 (see Van Zandt, 34).

22. David Berg, *The Old Church and the New Church: No. A*, August 26, 1969. Cited in Davis, 54–56.

23. Kent, 135.

24. Joe Maxwell, "Children of God Revamp Image, Face Renewed Opposition," *Christian Research Journal*, Fall 1993, 5.

25. Maria, *Loving Jesus—Part 5*: GN663 00, January 1996, 663: 130, 132..

26. Gideon. Quoted in Muir, 17.

27. Maxwell, 6.

28. Joseph Hopkins, "The Children of God: Disciples of Deception," *Christianity Today*, ?????? ??, 1977, ???.

29. David Berg, *Suggestions*, "for leaders only," November 1, 1971, 1.

30. David Berg, *Sex Jewels: DO 919*, May 1980, 919:22, 45.

31. David Berg, *Gypsy Joys: DFO 1125*, April 30, 1976, 1125:15, 16.

32. Kent, 160–161.

33. From last source cited, 148–151.

34. David Berg, *Revolutionary Sex: DO 258*, March 27, 1973. Quoted in Kent, 153–154.

35. David Berg, *Sex in Heaven: GP 818*, July 1970, 818:3–4.

36. David Berg, *The Test of Faith (Good News, No. 9): DFO 1281*, 1982, 1281:9.

37. Sodomy/homosexuality is about the only Christian taboo that the group does not break: "We don't have very many No-No's . . . (sodomy) is about the only sexual one we have" (David Berg, *Excommunication Rules & Procedures: DO 1323*, 1323:3).

38. Berg, *Sex Jewels*, 919:37.

39. David Berg, *Nuns of Love: DFO 570*, February 19, 1977, 570:50.

40. Berg, *Sex Jewels*, 919:29.

41. David Berg, *One Wife: DO 249*, October 28, 1973. Quoted in Kent, 166.

42. David Berg, *Family News International No. 50*, March 1, 1982, 34.

43. David Berg, *Child Brides: DO 902*, April 4, 1977, 902:1, 5–6.

44. Berg, *The Devil Hates Sex*, 999:20–21, 110.

45. World Services Family, *The Pubs Purge!*, 1991, 1.

46. David Berg, *Mugshots!: DO 979*, March 1981, 979:16, 18–19, 62.

47. Berg, *The Devil Hates Sex*, 999:126, 133.

48. Berg also taught that when women were having intercourse with strangers, they were actually having sex with Jesus (David Berg, *The FFing Revolution: DO 575*, August 7, 1976, 575:96–97).

49. David Berg, *Afflictions: DO 569*, November 25, 1976. Quoted in Kent, 181.

50. The Family, "Flirty Fishing," Internet document at The Family Web Site, http://www.thefamily.org /ourfounder/tribute/trib_21.htm.

51. The Family, http://www.thefamily.org/ ourfounder/tribute/trib_21.htm.

52. Gideon. Quoted in Muir, 17.

53. The Family, "The Fall of Man," *Our Statement of Faith*, 1 (sec. 4); cf. "Born Again—Are You?," in *Growing in Love*, 10.

54. David Berg, *God's Only Law of Love: DFO 592*, July 29, 1977, 592:29-30.

55. David Berg, *Is Love Against the Law: GP 648*, 648:7–8, 9.

56. David Berg, *Desertion: DFO 1022*, 1022:8.

57. David Berg, *Grace vs. Law: DFO 635*, 635:67.

58. David Berg, *Aphrodite!—Goddess of Love!: DO 1412*, January 13, 1972, 1412:2.

59. *The Mo Letters*, Volume V, credits page.

60. David Berg, *Old Bottles: DO 242*, 242:38.

61. Berg, *Grace vs. Law*, 635:70.

62. David Berg, *The Word—New and Old (MT 13:52): GP 329*, September 1974, 329:22, 24.

63. Berg, *Grace vs. Law*, 635:70.

64. David Berg, *The One That Got Away Part II: Jesus & Sex!: LTO 525*, November 3, 1974, 525:54.

65. David Berg, *The Mystery of Otano! DFO 769*, November 13, 1977, 796:8.

66. Berg, *Grace vs. Law*, 635:55, 57.

67. Berg, *More on TM & the Unified Field*, 1854:14; cf. David Berg, *The Constellation of Daniel: DFO 1308 (Good News no. 15)*, October 1982, 1308:69.

68. David Berg, *The Goddess of Love: DFO 723*, June 27, 1978, front page caption.

69. David Berg, *Islam: DFO 631*, 631:130.

70. David Berg, *Here & Now for There & Then: DFO 1092*, January 11, 1981, 1092:50.

71. Berg, *C'mon Ma*, 286:23, 32.

72. Berg, *The Goddess of Love*, 723:3, 6, 11, 14.

73. David Berg, *Our Audience with the King of Kings!: DO 2115*, 2115:25, 26.

74. David Berg, *Where Do Babies Come from?: DFO 794*, March 5, 1979, 794:1.

75. David Berg, *More Holy Ghosts: DO 621*, 621:26.

76. David Berg, *The Goddesses: LTA 224*, April 1973, 224:3.

77. Berg, *Houris of Heaven*, 1237:14, 16, 22.

78. Nevill Drury, *Dictionary of Mysticism and the Occult* (San Francisco: Harper & Row, 1985), 129.

79. The Family, *Our Statement of Faith*.

Chapter 9
Mormonism Through the Looking Glass

1. Joseph Smith, *History of the Church* (Salt Lake City: Deseret Book Co., 1980 edition), 6:319–320, 408–409.

2. David Whitmer, *An Address to All Believers in Christ* (Richmond, MO: David Whitmer, 1887), 56–57.

3. The doctrine of "Blood Atonement" is well documented in the writings and speeches of numerous Mormon leaders. Brigham Young stated: "Suppose you found your brother in bed with your wife, and put a javelin through both of them, you would be justified, and they would atone for their sins, and be received into the kingdom of God. I would at once do so in such a case. . . . There is not a man or woman, who violates the covenants made with their God, that will not be required to pay the debt. The blood of Christ will never wipe that out, your own blood must atone for it" (Brigham Young, "A Discourse by President Brigham Young, Delivered in the Tabernacle, Great Salt Lake City, March 16, 1856," as reported by G. D. Watt, *Journal of Discourses* [Liverpool, England: Orson Pratt for the Church of Jesus Christ of Latter-day Saints, 1856; modern 1966 lithographed edition], 3:247). Young also declared: "There are sins that men commit for which they cannot receive forgiveness in this world, or in that which is to come, and if they had their eyes open to see their true condition, they would be perfectly willing to have their blood spilt upon the ground, that the smoke thereof might ascend to heaven as an offering for their sins; and the smoking incense would atone for their sins, whereas, if such is not the case, they will stick to them and remain upon them in the spirit world. . . . And furthermore, I know that there are transgressors, who, if they knew themselves, and the only condition upon which they can obtain forgiveness, would beg of their brethren to shed their blood, that the smoke thereof might ascend to God as an offering to appease the wrath that is kindled against them, and that the law might have its course. I will say further; I have had men come to me and offer their lives to atone for their sins. It is true that the blood of the Son of God was shed for sins through the fall and those committed by men, yet men can commit sins which it can never remit. . . . There are sins that can be atoned for by an offering upon an altar, as in ancient days; and there are sins that the blood of a lamb, of a calf, or of turtle doves, cannot remit, but they must be atoned for by the blood of the man. That is the reason why men talk to you as they do from this stand; they understand the doctrine and throw out a few words about it. You have been taught that doctrine. but you do not understand it" (Brigham Young, "A Discourse by President Brigham Young, Delivered in the Bowery, Great Salt Lake City," September 21, 1856, as reported by G. D. Watt, *Journal of Discourses* [Liverpool, England: S. W. Richards for the Church of Jesus Christ of Latter-day Saints, 1857; modern 1966 lithographed edition], 4:53–54).

4. This story is taken primarily from personal conversations with Sandra Tanner as well as from an article about the Tanners by Chris Vlachos, "Why the Tanners Challenge the Mormon Establishment: 'We Left the Mormon Church,'" *Moody*, June 1980, 35–36.

5. Joseph Smith, *History of the Church* (Salt Lake City: Deseret Book Co., 1980 edition), 1:5.

6. From last source cited, 1:5–6.

7. From last source cited, 1:6.

8. Church of Jesus Christ of Latter-day Saints, Introduction to *The Book of Mormon* (Salt lake City: Church of Jesus Christ of Latter-day Saints, 1990 edition).

9. Whitmer, 12.

10. In the May 19, 1888 edition of *The Saints' Herald*, Emma Hale-Smith related the following information to her son, via a published letter: "In writing for your father I frequently wrote day after day, after sitting by the table, close to him, he sitting with his face buried in his hat, with the stone in it, and dictating hour after hour with nothing between us" (p. 310). Quoted in Gerald and Sandra Tanner, *Mormonism: Shadow or Reality?* (Salt Lake City: Utah Lighthouse Ministry, 1987), 41. Isaac Hale's signed affidavit regarding Joseph Smith's method of pro-

ducing the *Book of Mormon* was originally published in *The Susquehanna Register*, May 1, 1834. Quoted in Tanner and Tanner, 41. Martin Harris, during a speech delivered in Salt Lake City, September 4, 1870, confirmed that Smith produced the *Book of Mormon* by use of a peep stone in a hat. Quoted in Andrew Jenson, "The Three Witnesses," *The Historical Record*, vol. 6, May 1887, 216.

11. George Q. Cannon, *Life of Joseph Smith*, 56. Quoted in Tanner and Tanner, 40. John Widtsoe, *Joseph Smith: Seeker After Truth*, 267. Quoted in Tanner and Tanner, 40; Bruce McConkie, *Mormon Doctrine* (Salt Lake City: Bookcraft, 1966; 1977 edition), 818.

12. B. H. Roberts, *A Comprehensive History of the Church of Jesus Christ of Latter-day Saints* (Salt Lake City: Church of Jesus Christ of Latter-day Saints, 1930 edition), 1:129, 6:230; cf. B. H. Roberts, *A Comprehensive History of the Church of Jesus Christ of Latter-day Saints*, vol. 6 (Salt Lake City: Church of Jesus Christ of Latter-day Saints, 1930 edition), 230; Arch S. Reynolds, *How Did Joseph Smith Translate?* (Springville, UT: Arch S. Reynolds, 1952); 5; and *The Urim and Thummim* (Springville, UT: Arch S. Reynolds, 1953), 18–20.

13. Joseph Fielding Smith, *Doctrines of Salvation*, vol. 3 (Salt Lake City: Bookcraft, 1956), 225.

14. Nevill Drury, *Dictionary of Mysticism and the Occult* (San Francisco: Harper & Row, 1985), 241.

15. Doreen Valiente, *An ABC of Witchcraft Past & Present* (New York: St. Martin's Press, 1973), 343–344.

16. *Fraser's Magazine*, February 1873, 229-230. Quoted in Tanner and Tanner, 32.

17. John Widtsoe, *Joseph Smith—Seeker After Truth*, 78. Quoted in Tanner and Tanner, 34.

18. Francis Kirkham, *A New Witness for Christ in America*, vol. 1 (Salt lake City: Utah Printing Co., 1942; 1960 edition), 385–386, 391.

19. Leonard J. Arrington and David Bitton, *The Mormon Experience* (Champaign, IL: University of Illinois Press, 1992), 10–11. Quoted in Tanner and Tanner, 49-A.

20. Hugh Nibley, *The Myth Makers*, 142. Quoted in Tanner and Tanner, 49-A.

21. Kirkham, 387.

22. Kurt Seligman, *Magic, Supernaturalism, and Religion* (New York: Pantheon, 1948; 1971 edition), 161.

23. Reed Durham, address to Mormon History Association, April 20, 1974. Reprinted in David C. Martin, "Reed C. Durham, Jr.'s Astounding Research On the Masonic Influence On Mormonism," *Mormon Miscellaneous*, October 1975, 14–15.

24. Arthur E. Waite, *The Occult Sciences* (Mokelumne Hill, CA: Mokelumne Hill Press, 1972 edition); cf. Arthur E. Waite, *The Occult Sciences* (Kila, MT: Kessinger Publishing Co., 1993 edition). Quoted in Lewis Spence, *The Encyclopedia of the Occult* (London: Bracken, 1994 edition), 401.

25. Leslie A. Shepard, ed., *Encyclopedia of Occultism and Parapsychology*, vol. 2 (Detroit: Gale Research, Inc., 1991), 1521.

26. Drury, 172.

27. Reginald Scot, *The Discoverie of Witchcraft*, 401. Quoted in Jerald Tanner and Sandra Tanner, "Mormonism & Magic," *Salt Lake City Messenger*, issue no. 49 (December 1982), 3.

28. Mormons believe they will again practice polygamy during the earthly millennial reign of Christ: "[T]he restoration of the Church and Gospel of Jesus Christ, is to prepare for the second coming of the Savior, which is nigh at hand; to help usher in His great millennial reign, when the Gospel in its fulness, including plural marriage, will be lived by worthy members of the Church" (John J. Stewart, *Brigham Young and His Wives*, 73). Quoted in Tanner and Tanner, *Mormonism: Shadow or Reality?*, 244.

29. Fawn Brodie, *No Man Knows My History* (New York: Knopf, 1971), 270-271. Quoted in Tanner and Tanner, *Mormonism: Shadow or Reality?*, 253–254.

30. *Warsaw Signal*, July 21, 1841. Quoted in Tanner and Tanner, *Mormonism: Shadow or Reality?*, 254.

31. Kenneth W. Godfrey, *Brigham Young University Studies*, Winter 1968, 206–207.

32. Warren Parrish, *Painesville Republican*, February 22, 1838, as quoted in Max Parkin, *Conflict at Kirtland*, 297. Cited in Tanner and Tanner, *Mormonism: Shadow or Reality?*, 531.

33. Letter by J. Butterfield, U.S. Attorney for the District of Illinois, to C. B. Penrose, Solicitor of the Treasury, October 13, 1842, National Archives of the United States, Records of the Solicitor of the Treasury, Record Group 206, microfilm copy. Quoted in Tanner and Tanner, *Mormonism: Shadow or Reality?*, 535.

34. Smith, 6:445.

35. Thomas Ford, *History of Illinois*, as quoted in Klaus J. Hansen, *Quest for Empire*, 155. Cited by Tanner and Tanner, *Mormonism: Shadow or Reality?*, 415; cf. Godfrey, 212–213 and Smith, 6:568–569.

36. Smith, 6:432.

37. Juanita Brooks, *The Mountain Meadows Massacre* (Oklahoma City: University of Oklahoma Press, 1950; 1972 edition).

38. Brigham Young, "Remarks by President Brigham Young, made in the Bowery, Great Salt Lake City," July 26, 1857, as reported by G. D. Watt, J. V. Long, and others, *Journal of Discourses* (Liverpool, England: Asa Calkin for the Church of Jesus Christ of Latter-day Saints, 1858; modern 1966 lithographed edition), 5:73).

39. Brigham Young, "Remarks by President Brigham Young, made in the Bowery, Great Salt Lake City," September 16, 1860, as reported by G. D. Watt and J. V. Long, *Journal of Discourses* (Liverpool, England: George Q. Cannon for the Church of Jesus Christ of Latter-day Saints, 1861; modern 1966 lithographed edition), 8:171 and Brigham Young, "Remarks made by President Brigham Young, made in the Tabernacle, Great Salt Lake City," October 7, 1860, 8:199.

40. Heber C. Kimball, "Remarks by President Heber C. Kimball, made in the Bowery, Great Salt Lake City," July 26, 1857, as reported by G. D. Watt, J. V. Long, and others, *Journal of Discourses* (Liverpool, England: Asa Calkin for the Church of Jesus Christ of Latter-day Saints, 1861; modern 1966 lithographed edition), 5:89.

41. John Taylor, "Discourse by Elder John Taylor, Delivered in the New Tabernacle, Salt Lake City," May 6, 1870, as reported by D. W. Evans and John Grimshaw, *Journal of Discourses* (Liverpool, England: Horace S. Eldredge for the Church of Jesus Christ of Latter-day Saints, 1871), 13:225.

42. Orson Pratt, *The Kingdom of God*, no. 2, pt. 1, October 31, 1848, 3. Reprinted in Orson Pratt, *Orson Pratt's Works*, vol. 2 (Orem, UT: Grandin Book Co., 1990).

43. McConkie, 513.

44. The Church of Jesus Christ of Latter-day Saints, *1997-98 Church Almanac* (Salt Lake City: Deseret News, 1996), 524.

45. McConkie, 764–765.

46. From last source cited, 764–765.

47. From last source cited, 765.

48. From last source cited, 764.

49. From last source cited, 383; cf. 83.

50. Milton R. Hunter, *The Gospel Through the Ages* (Salt Lake City: Deseret Book Co., 1958), 127.

51. McConkie, 590.

52. From last source cited, 169.

53. From last source cited, 387; cf. 751.

54. From last source cited, 751.

55. From last source cited, 516.

56. Joseph F. Smith, John R. Winder, and Anthon H. Lund (First Presidency), *Improvement Era*, vol. 13, 80. Quoted in Hunter, 99.

57. Hunter, 98–99.

58. McConkie, 750.

59. Brigham Young, "Remarks by President Brigham Young, delivered in the Bowery, Great Salt Lake," June 18, 1865, as reported by G. D. Watt, E. L. Sloan, and D. W. Evans, *Journal of Discourses* (Liverpool, England: Brigham Young, Jr., for the Church of Jesus Christ of Latter-day Saints, 1867), 11:122.

60. Church of Jesus Christ of Latter-day Saints, *Achieving a Celestial Marriage* (Salt Lake City: Church of Jesus Christ of Latter-day Saints, 1976), 132.

61. Joseph Smith, "A Discourse, by President Joseph Smith, delivered at the Conference held near the Temple in Nauvoo," April 6, 1844, as reported by G. D. Watt, J. V. Long, and others, *Journal of Discourses* (Liverpool, England: Asa Calkin for the Church of Jesus Christ of latter-day Saints, 1859), 6:3–4.

62. Brigham Young, "Remarks by President Brigham Young, Delivered in the Tabernacle, Great Salt Lake City," January 8, 1865, as reported by G. D. Watt, E. L. Sloan, and D. W. Evans, *Journal of Discourses* (Liverpool, England: Brigham Young, Jr., for the Church of Jesus Christ of Latter-day Saints, 1867), 11:40.

63. Hunter, 114–115.

64. Lorenzo Snow, *Millennial Star*, vol. 54, 404; cf. Hunter, 105–106.

65. Church of Jesus Christ of Latter-day Saints, *Search the Commandments Melchizedek Priesthood Personal Study Guide* (Salt Lake City: Church of Jesus Christ of Latter-day Saints), 152.

66. *Achieving a Celestial Marriage*, 132.

67. *Search the Commandments Melchizedek Priesthood Personal Study Guide*, 152; cf. Joseph Fielding Smith, *Doctrines of Salvation*, 2:47.

68. McConkie, 278.

69. Hunter, 21.

70. Daniel H. Ludlow, ed., *Encyclopedia of Mormonism* (New York: Macmillan, 1992), 729.

71. Carlfred Broderick, "Three Philosophies of Sex, Plus One," *Dialogue: A Journal of Mormon Thought*, vol. 2, no. 3 (Autumn 1967), 100–101.

72. Thelma "Granny" Geer, *Mormonism, Mama, & Me* (Chicago: Moody, 1979; 1986 edition), 91–92.

73. Brigham Young, "Remarks by President Brigham Young, Made in the Bowery, Great Salt Lake City, July 8, 1860," as reported by G. D. Watt and J. V. Long, *Journal of Discourses* (Liverpool, England: George Q. Cannon for the Church of Jesus Christ of Latter-day Saints, 1861; modern 1966 lithographed edition), 8:115.

74. McConkie, 547.

75. Heber C. Kimball, "Remarks by President Heber C. Kimball, Made in the Bowery, Great Salt Lake City, September 2, 1860," as reported by G. D. Watt and J. V. Long, *Journal of Discourses*

(Liverpool, England: George Q. Cannon for the Church of Jesus Christ of Latter-day Saints, 1861; modern 1966 lithographed edition), 8:211.

76. Brigham Young, "A Sermon Delivered by President Brigham Young, in the Tabernacle, Great Salt Lake City, April 9, 1852," as reported by G. D. Watt, *Journal of Discourses* (Liverpool, England: F. D. Richards for the Church of Jesus Christ of Latter-day Saints, 1855), 1:51.

77. For an in-depth discussion of the events surrounding the opening of the Mormon priesthood to blacks, see Chapter 21—"The Negro in Mormon Theology"—in *Mormonism: Shadow or Reality?* by the Tanners.

78. Smith, *History of the Church*, 5:217–218.

79. Joseph Fielding Smith, *Doctrines of Salvation*, vol. 1 (Salt Lake City: Bookcraft, 1954), 61.

80. From last source cited, 64–65.

81. McConkie, 527.

82. Joseph Fielding Smith, *The Way to Perfection* (Salt Lake City: Genealogical Society of Utah, 1931), 101.

83. Brigham Young, "Remarks by President Brigham Young, Delivered in the Tabernacle, Great Salt Lake City," October 9, 1859, as reported by G. D. Watt, J. V. Long, and others, *Journal of Discourses* (Liverpool, England: Amasa Lyman for the Church of Jesus Christ of Latter-day Saints, 1860), 7:290.

84. Brigham Young, "Remarks by President Brigham Young, Made in the Tabernacle, Great Salt Lake City, March 8, 1863," as reported by G. D. Watt and J. V. Long, *Journal of Discourses* (Liverpool, England: Daniel H. Wells for the Church of Jesus Christ of Latter-day Saints, 1865), 10:110.

85. LDS First Presidency, July 17, 1947 letter from LDS First Presidency to Dr. Lowery Nelson. Quoted in John J. Stewart, *Mormonism and the Negro* (Orem, UT: Book Mark, 1960; 1964 edition), 47.

86. Geer, 24–25.

87. McConkie, 63.

88. From last source cited, 65.

89. James Talmage, *A Study of the Articles of Faith* (Salt Lake City: The Church of Jesus Christ of Latter-day Saints, 1890; 1948 edition), 89.

90. Ezra Taft Benson, *Teachings of Ezra Taft Benson*. Quoted in "Gethsemane Was Site of 'Greatest Single Act,'" *Church News*, June 1, 1991, 14.

91. Smith, *History of the Church*, 6:474.

92. Orson Pratt, "A Discourse by Elder Orson Pratt, Delivered in the open air, on the Temple Block, Great Salt Lake City, February 18, 1855," as reported by G. D. Watt, *Journal of Discourses* (Liverpool, England: F. D. Richards for The Church of Jesus Christ of Latter-day Saints, 1855) 2:345.

93. Brigham Young, "Remarks by President Brigham Young, Delivered in the Tabernacle, Great Salt Lake City, October 8, 1859," as reported by G. D. Watt, J. V. Long, and Others, *Journal of Discourses* (Liverpool, England: Amasa Lyman for the Church of Jesus Christ of Latter-day Saints, 1860), 7:333.

94. McConkie, 238.

95. Joseph Smith, "A Discourse, by President Joseph Smith, Delivered at the Conference held near the Temple, in Nauvoo," April 6, 1844, as reported by G. D. Watt, J. V. Long, and others, *Journal of Discourses* (Liverpool, England: Asa Calkin for the Church of Jesus Christ of latter-day Saints, 1859), 6:4.

96. McConkie, 321.

97. From last source cited, 321.

98. From last source cited, 44.

99. From last source cited, 257.

100. The Church of Jesus Christ of Latter-day Saints, *Gospel Principles* (Salt Lake City: The Church of Jesus Christ of Latter-day Saints), 351.

101. Introduction to *The Book of Mormon*.

102. *The Book of Mormon*, 2 Ne. 29:3, 6, 9–10.

103. See table below.

COMPARISON—BOOK OF MORMON VS. SCRIPTURE

Book of Mormon	*Scripture (KJV)*
"I say unto thee, woman, there has not been such great faith among all the people of the Nephites" (Alma 19:10).	"I say unto you, I have not found so great faith, no, not in Israel" (Luke 7:9).
"[T]he axe is laid at the root of the tree, therefore every tree that bringeth not forth good fruit shall be hewn down and cast into the fire" (Alma 5:52).	"[T]he axe is laid unto the root of the trees, therefore every tree which bringeth not forth good fruit is hewn down and cast into the fire" (Matt. 3:10).
"O wretched man that I am" (2 Nephi 4:17).	"O wretched man that I am" (Rom. 7:24).
"[B]e stedfast and immoveable, always abounding in good works" (Mosiah 5:15).	"[B]e stedfast, unmoveable, always abounding in the work of the Lord" (1 Cor. 15:58).
"[S]tand fast in this liberty wherewith ye have been made free" (Mosiah 23:13).	"Stand fast therefore in the liberty wherewith Christ hath made us free" (Gal. 5:1).
"... the gall of bitterness and bonds of iniquity" (Mosiah 27:29).	"... the gall of bitterness, and in the bond of iniquity" (Acts 8:23).

104. Geoffrey W. Bromiley, gen. ed., *The International Standard Bible Encyclopedia*, vol. 1 (Grand Rapids, MI: William B. Eerdmans, 1979; 1989 edition), 222.

105. Key, 4.

106. From last source cited, 4–5.

107. Joseph Smith, *Book of Commandments* (Independence, MO: W. W. Phelps & Co., 1833), Chapter 1, verse 7, p. 6. Reprinted in Wilford C. Wood, *Joseph Smith Begins His Work*, vol. 2 (CITY?: Wilford C. Wood, 1962).

108. Joseph Smith, *1835-1836 Diary*, January 21, 1836. Reprinted in Dean C. Jessee, ed., *The Papers of Joseph Smith*, vol. 2 (Salt Lake City: Deseret Book Co., 1992), 156–157.

109. *Doctrine & Covenants*, sec. 107:54.

110. The Church of Jesus Christ of Latter-day Saints, Introduction to *Pearl of Great Price* (Salt Lake City: The Church of Jesus-Christ of Latter-day Saints, 1990 edition).

111. Joseph Fielding Smith, vol. 1, 113–115.

112. McConkie, 564.

113. All quotations are taken from F. S. Spalding, *Joseph Smith, Jr., As a Translator* (1912), 23, 24, 26–27, 29. Quoted in Tanner and Tanner, *Mormonism: Shadow or Reality?*, 299–300.

114. *Improvement Era*, vol. 16, 343. Quoted in Tanner and Tanner, *Mormonism: Shadow or Reality?*, 322.

115. This chart is taken from Charles M. Larson, *By His Own Hand Upon Papyrus* (Grand Rapids, MI: Institute for Religious Research, 1985; 1992 edition), 97.

116. Tanner and Tanner, *Mormonism: Shadow or Reality?*, 369.

117. Talmage, 430.

118. Young, *Journal of Discourses*, 1:50.

119. *Doctrine & Covenants*, sec. 130:22.

120. George Q. Cannon, *Gospel Truth*, ed. Jerreld L. Newquist, vol. 1 (Salt Lake City: Deseret Book Co., 1974), 9.

121. Brigham Young, "A Discourse by President Brigham Young, Delivered in the Bowery, Great Salt Lake City," March 8, 1857, as reported by G. D. Watt, *Journal of Discourses*, (Liverpool, England: S. W. Richards for the Church of Jesus Christ of Latter-day Saints, 1857; modern 1966 lithographed edition), 4:269.

122. Joseph Fielding Smith, *Doctrines of Salvation*, vol. 1, 236.

123. McConkie, 136.

124. Kent P. Jackson, "Early Signs of the Apostasy," *Ensign*, December, 1984, 9.

125. Rick Branch, "Mormon Church Infiltrates Christianity," *Watchman Expositor*, vol. 9, no. 3 (1992), 7.

126. Branch, 7.

127. Will Schmidt, "Mormons Teach in a Baptist Church," *Watchman Expositor*, vol. 7, no. 3 (1990), 2.

Chapter 10
Jehovah's False Witnesses

1. *The Watchtower* (Brooklyn: Watchtower Bible & Tract Society), April 1, 1972, 197.

2. The tragic consequences of the Jehovah's Witnesses' ban on blood transfusions has been reported numerous times in various newspapers. American Red Cross figures published in 1980 reveal that approximately 100 people per 1,000 need a blood transfusion every year. The JWs 1996 membership totaled 5,413,769, which means that every year, using the 1980 Red Cross statistics, approximately 541,376 JWs need blood. No one has kept statistics on JW deaths due to the Watch Tower's ban on blood, but the numbers must be staggering. Even if only one out of every 10 JWs who needs a transfusion dies, this would add up to 54,137 deaths a year. Consider the following news story headlines: "Boy Dies As Family Refuses Medical Aid" (1961), "Pregnant Woman Dies After Refusing Transfusion" (1986), "J.W. Woman Dies Refusing Transfusion" (1989), "Man Refuses Blood for 4 Days, Dies" (1989), "Witness Wins in Court, Dies in Hospital" (1990). These headlines were taken from David Reed, *Comments from the Friends*, Fall 1991 and Duane Magnani, *Danger at Your Door* (Clayton, CA: Witness, Inc., 1987).

3. *The Watchtower*, January 15, 1983, 27.

4. *The Watchtower*, January 1, 1997.

5. David A. Reed, *Jehovah's Witness Literature* (Grand Rapids, MI: Baker, 1993), 155.

6. *Awake!*, October 22, 1997, 2.

7. *The Watchtower*, November 1, 2.

8. Greta Hawkins (Public Affairs Representative for the Watch Tower), author's October 29, 1997 interview with Hawkins.

9. *The Watchtower*, October 1, 1967, 587.

10. *The Watchtower*, July 1, 1973, 402.

11. In reference to Russell's *Studies in the Scriptures* series of books, the September 15, 1910 issue of *The Watchtower* stated: "[N]ot only do we find that people cannot see the divine plan in studying the Bible by itself, but we see, also, that if anyone lays the Scripture Studies aside, even after he has used them, after he has become familiar with them, after he has read them for ten years—if he then lays them aside and ignores them and goes to the Bible alone, though he has understood his Bible for ten years, our experience shows that within two years he goes into darkness. On the other hand, if he had merely read the Scripture Studies with their references, and had not read a page of the Bible, as such, he would be in the light at the end of two years, because he would have the light of the Scriptures" (*The Watch Tower & Herald of Christ's Presence*, September 15, 1910, 298-299. As reprinted in the Watch Tower reprints, vol. 5 [Pittsburgh: Watch Tower Bible & Tract Society, 1919], 4685).

12. *Zion's Watch Tower & Herald of Christ's Presence*, February 1881, 3. As reprinted in the Watch Tower reprints, vol. 1 (Pittsburgh: Watch Tower Bible & Tract Society, 1919), 188; *Zion's Watch Tower & Herald of Christ's Presence*, August 1883, 1. As reprinted in the Watch Tower reprints, vol. 1 (Pittsburgh: Watchtower Bible & Tract Society, 1919), 513; *Zion's Watch Tower & Herald of Christ's Presence*, July 15, 1906, 230–231, as reprinted in the Watch Tower reprints, vol. 5 (Pittsburgh: Watch Tower Bible & Tract Society, 1919), 3822.

13. After Russell's death, the WTBTS released a seventh volume of *Studies in the Scriptures* (1917), which was purportedly a "posthumous work of Pastor Russell." In reality, it was written by Clayton J. Woodworth and George Fisher, two loyal followers of Russell's successor, J. F. Rutherford.

14. Charles Taze Russell, *The Time Is at Hand*, vol. 2 of *Studies in the Scriptures* (Allegheny, PA: Watch Tower Bible & Tract Society, 1889; 1906 edition), 76–77.

15. From last source cited, 101.

16. From last source cited, 98–99; cf. Charles Taze Russell, *Thy Kingdom Come*, vol. 3 of *Studies in the Scriptures* (Allegheny, PA: Watch Tower Bible & Tract Society, 1891; 1908 edition), 126.

17. "The date of the close of that 'battle' [of Armageddon] is definitely marked in Scripture as October, 1914. It is already in progress, its beginning dating from October, 1874." *Zion's Watchtower & Herald of Christ's Presence*, January 15, 1892, 21–23. As reprinted in the Watch Tower reprints, vol. 2 (Pittsburgh: Watch Tower Bible & Tract Society, 1919), 1355. "We see no reason for changing the figures. . . . They are, we believe, God's dates, not ours. But bear in mind that the end of 1914 is not the date for the *beginning*, but for the *end* of the time of trouble." *Zion's Watchtower & Herald of Christ's Presence*, July 15, 1894, 226–231. As reprinted in the Watch Tower reprints, vol. 2, 1677.

18. Charles Taze Russell, *Pastor Russell's Sermons* (Brooklyn: People's Pulpit Association, 1917), 676.

19. Rudolf Steiner, *The Steinerbooks Dictionary of the Psychic, Mystic, Occult* (Blauvelt, NY: Rudolf Steiner Publications, 1973), 173.

20. Russell, *Thy Kingdom Come*, 341.

21. J. F. Rutherford, *Millions Now Living Will Never Die* (Brooklyn: Watch Tower Bible & Tract Society, 1920), 89–90, 97.

22. Even before Rutherford had made his 1918 speech, the Watch Tower was advocating 1925 as a probable date for the world's end. *The Finished Mystery* (Brooklyn: Watch Tower Bible & Tract Society, 1917) stated: "[T]here is evidence that the establishment of the Kingdom in Palestine will probably be in 1925, ten years later than we once calculated" (p. 128). Even into 1925, the Society was printing literature declaring that the establishment of God's kingdom on earth would occur near 1925. The following excerpt is taken from *The Way to Paradise* (Brooklyn: Watch Tower Bible & Tract Society, 1925), written by W. E. Van Amburgh, the Society's cor-

porate secretary and treasurer: "We should, therefore, expect shortly after 1925 to see the awakening of Abel, Enoch, Noah, Abraham, Isaac, Jacob. . . . These will form the nucleus of the new kingdom on earth. . . . No doubt many boys and girls who read this book will live to see Abraham . . . and those other fanciful men of old. . . . Of course, it will take some time to get things in smoothly running order after the great stress between now and 1926" (pp. 224–228).

23. *The Watchtower*, October 15, 1917, 317–318. As reprinted in the Watch Tower reprints, vol. 7 (Brooklyn: Watch Tower Bible & Tract Society, 1919), 6157.

24. *The Watchtower*, September 1, 1922, 262.

25. *The Watchtower*, March 15, 1923, 86.

26. Rutherford, 97.

27. *The Watchtower*, July 15, 1924, 211.

28. *The Watchtower*, January 1, 1925, 3.

29. J. F. Rutherford, *Comfort for the Jews* (Brooklyn: Watch Tower Bible & Tract Society, 1925), 86, 88.

30. J. F. Rutherford, *Comfort for the People* (Brooklyn: Watch Tower Bible & Tract Society, 1925), 9.

31. *The Watchtower*, September 1, 1925, 262.

32. *The Watchtower*, August 1, 1926, 232.

33. *The Watchtower*, July 15, 1922, 217.

34. *The 1980 Yearbook of Jehovah's Witnesses* (Brooklyn: Watch Tower Bible & Tract Society, 1979), 62.

35. Rutherford, *Millions*, 89–90.

36. From last source cited, 97.

37. *The Watchtower*, October 1, 1929, 302.

38. *The New World* (Brooklyn: Watch Tower Bible & Tract Society, 1942), 104.

39. *Consolation*, May 27, 1942, 13.

40. *Consolation*, October 29, 1941, 11.

41. *Informant*, May 1940, 1.

42. *The Messenger*, September 1, 1940, 6.

43. *The Watchtower*, September 15, 1941, 288.

44. J. F. Rutherford, *Face Facts* (Brooklyn: Watch Tower Bible & Tract Society, 1938), 46.

45. *The Watchtower*, November 1, 1938, 323.

46. J. F. Rutherford, *Salvation* (Brooklyn: Watch Tower Bible & Tract Society, 1939), 325.

47. *God's Kingdom of a Thousand Years Has Approached* (Brooklyn: Watch Tower Bible & Tract Society, 1973), 209–210. In reality, the date 1874 quietly replaced the 1914 date in a 1930 *Golden Age* magazine, which read in part: "In Matthew 24, Jesus gives His disciples some proofs that He would be present. . . . If it is true that Jesus has been present since the year 1914, then it must be admitted that nobody has seen Him with natural eyes" (*Golden Age*, 1930, 503).

48. *Life Everlasting—In Freedom of the Sons of God* (Brooklyn: Watch Tower Bible & Tract Society, 1966), 29, 35; cf. *The Watchtower*, May 1, 68, 271.

49. *Awake!*, October 8, 1966, 18.

50. The October 8, 1966 issue of *Awake!* reads: "In what year, then, would the first 6,000 years of man's existence and also the first 6,000 years of God's rest day come to an end? The year 1975" (p. 19).

51. *Awake!*, October 8, 1966, 20.

52. *The Watchtower*, August 15, 1968, 494, 499.

53. *Kingdom Ministry*, May 1974, 3.

54. *Awake!*, November 8, 1974, 11.

55. *Kingdom Ministry*, June 1969, 3.

56. *Kingdom Ministry*, January 1968, 5.

57. Raymond Franz, *Crisis of Conscience* (Atlanta: Commentary Press, 1983), 199.

58. *The Watchtower*, July 16, 1976, 440.

59. *Awake!*, October 8, 1968, 13.

60. *The Watchtower*, October 1, 1978, 31.

61. "[T]he babies of that generation are now 70 years old or older. And others alive in 1914 are in their 80's or 90's, a few even having reached a hundred. There are still many millions of that generation alive. Some of them 'will by no mean pass away until all things occur'" (*The Watchtower*, May 15, 1984, 5).

62. Jehovah's Witnesses use the term "New Light" to describe the various changes that are continually made to the set of doctrines they must believe.

63. *The Watchtower*, November 1, 1995, 19.

64. *Awake!*, October 8, 1973, 19.

65. *The Watchtower*, October 15, 1980, 31.

66. *The Watchtower*, May 1, 1985, 4.

67. *The Watchtower*, November 1, 1995, 17.

68. *The Watchtower*, June, 1, 1997, 28.

69. *The Watchtower*, May 1, 1938, 143.

70. *The Watchtower*, July 1, 1943, 203.

71. *The Watchtower*, January 15, 1959, 40–41.

72. *The Watchtower*, January 1, 1942, 5.

73. *The Watchtower*, February 1, 1938, 35.

74. *The Watchtower*, May 15, 1984, 6–7.

75. *Awake!*, January 8, 1982, 2.

76. *Awake!*, March 8, 1988, 2.

77. *Awake!*, October 8, 1968, 23.

78. Russell, *Thy Kingdom Come*, 313–314.

79. *The Watchtower*, May 15, 1925, 148.

80. *The Watchtower*, November 15, 1928, 341, 344.

81. *Awake!*, March 15, 1969, 171.

82. *The Watchtower*, November 1, 1992, 18–20.

83. *Golden Age*, February 4, 1931, 293.

84. *The Watchtower*, December 15, 1952, 764.

85. *The Watchtower*, November 15, 1967, 702; cf. *Awake!*, June 8, 1968: "There are those, such as the Christian witnesses of Jehovah, who consider *all* transplants between humans as cannibalism" (p. 21).

86. *The Watchtower*, March 15, 1980, 31.

87. **Earthly Governments**: "Evil as these Gentile governments have been, they were permitted or 'ordained of God' for a wise purpose. (Rom. 13:1.). . . . God permits them, in the main, to

carry out their own purposes as they may be able, overruling them only when they would interfere with his plans" (Charles Taze Russell, *The Divine Plan of the Ages*, vol. 1 of *Studies in the Scriptures* [Allegheny, PA: Watch Tower Bible & Tract Society, 1886; 1908 edition], 250; cf. *Zion's Watch Tower & Herald of Christ's Presence*, July 1 and 15, 1893, 214–216. As reprinted in the Watch Tower reprints, vol. 1 [Pittsburgh: Watch Tower Bible & Tract Society, 1919], 1555). **Jehovah God & Jesus Christ**: "the higher powers—Rom. 13:1. . . . These scriptures prove that Christ Jesus is the 'higher power' and that Jehovah is the highest or supreme power. 'The higher powers' may therefore be applied to both Jehovah and Jesus, because Christ Jesus always carries out the order of his Father" (*The Watchtower*, June 1, 1929, 163, 165; cf. *Let God Be True* [Brooklyn: Watch Tower Bible & Tract Society, 1946], 248 and *Jehovah's Witnesses in the Divine Purpose* [Brooklyn: Watch Tower Bible & Tract Society, 1959], 91). **Earthly Governments**: "At Romans 13:1 we read: 'Let every soul be in subjection to the superior authorities,' that is, to governments" (*The Watchtower*, May 15, 1980, 4).

88. **Yes** (*The Watchtower*, April 15, 1970, 250); **No** (*The Watchtower*, December 1, 1975, 733); **Yes** (*The Watchtower*, March 15, 1981, 14–17).

89. **No** (*Organization for Kingdom-Preaching and Disciple-Making* [Brooklyn: Watch Tower Bible & Tract Society, 1972], 172); **Yes** (*The Watchtower*, August 1, 1974, 464–465; **No** (*The Watchtower*, September 15, 1981, 24–26).

90. **Yes** (*The Watchtower*, July 1879, 7–8. As reprinted in the Watch Tower reprints, vol. 1 [Pittsburgh: Watch Tower Bible & Tract Society, 1919], 7); **No** (*The Watchtower*, June 1, 1952, 338); **Yes** (*The Watchtower*, August 1, 1965, 479); **No** (*The Watchtower*, June 1, 1988, 31); **Yes** (*Insight on the Scriptures*, vol. 2 [Brooklyn: Watch Tower Bible & Tract Society, 1988], 985); **No** (*Revelation: Its Grand Climax At Hand* [Brooklyn: Watch Tower Bible & Tract Society, 1988], 273).

91. *The Watchtower*, August 1, 1992, 17.

92. *The Watchtower*, May 15, 1976, 298.

93. *Qualified to Be Ministers* (Brooklyn: Watch Tower Bible & Tract Society, 1955), 156.

94. *Zion's Watch Tower & Herald of Christ's Presence*, February 1881, 3. As reprinted in the Watch Tower reprints, vol. 1 (Pittsburgh: Watch Tower Bible & Tract Society, 1919), 188.

95. *The Watchtower*, December 1, 1991, 7.

96. *Zion's Watch Tower & Herald of Christ's Presence*, August 1879, 5. As reprinted in the Watch Tower reprints. vol. 1 (Pittsburgh: Watch Tower Bible & Tract Society, 1919), 24.

97. *Zion's Watch Tower & Herald of Christ's Presence*, November 1, 1914, 325–326. As reprinted in the Watch Tower reprints, vol. 6 (Pittsburgh: Watch Tower Bible & Tract Society, 1919), 5565.

98. J. F. Rutherford, *Creation* (Brooklyn: Watch Tower Bible & Tract Society, 1927), 315.

99. *The Watchtower*, August 15, 1993, 9.

100. *Zion's Watch Tower & Herald of Christ's Presence*, October/November 1881, 3. As reprinted in the Watch Tower reprints, vol. 1 (Pittsburgh: Watch Tower Bible & Tract Society, 1919), 289.

101. Charles Taze Russell, *The Battle of Armageddon*, vol. 4 of *Studies in the Scriptures* (Allegheny, PA: Watch Tower Bible & Tract Society, 1897; 1913 edition), 621.

102. J. F. Rutherford, *Prophecy* (Brooklyn: Watch Tower Bible & Tract Society, 1929), 65.

103. *The Watchtower*, January 15, 1993, 5.

104. *Golden Age*, February 4, 1931, 293.

105. *Consolation* (a former name of *Awake!*), May 31, 1939, 8.

106. *Awake!*, August 8, 1993, 25

107. **Ishii's Testimony**: "[A]t the back of our house on Tojo-cho, Osaka, there was a house with a sign: 'Osaka Branch of the International Bible Students Association' . . . I visited the house.

'Do you believe in the second advent of our Lord?' I asked the young man who answered the door. 'Christ's second advent was realized in 1914,' he answered. In astonishment, I told him that was impossible. 'You should read this book,' he said, handing me *The Harp of God*. . . . Eventually, my husband found out I was reading a Christian book . . . he began wondering whether something very important was involved and so read *The Harp of God* himself. I was baptized the following year, March 23, 1929" (*The Watchtower*, May 1, 1988, 22).

108. J. F. Rutherford, *The Harp of God* (Brooklyn: Watch Tower Bible & Tract Society, 1921; 1928 edition), 235–236.

109. **Nathan's Testimony**: "After the war ended in 1918 . . . I rejoined the army and went off to India. . . . In May 1920 the malaria flared up again, and I was sent up into the foothills to recuperate. . . . Months later, down in Kanpur, I started a Bible study group hoping to learn more about the Lord's return. It was there that I met Frederick James . . . a zealous Bible student. He explained to me that Jesus had been present since 1914, invisible to man. . . . I read *Studies in the Scriptures*, by Charles Taze Russell, and became even more convinced than ever that I should respond to the call to preach" (*The Watchtower*, September 1, 1990, 11).

110. See Rutherford, *Creation*, 289, 306 and *Prophecy*, 65.

111. Russell, *Thy Kingdom Come*, vol. 3, 234-235.

112. Russell, *The Time Is at Hand*, 211.

113. Russell, *The Battle of Armageddon*, 621.

114. *The Watchtower*, September 15, 1990, 17.

115. *Is This Life All There Is?* (Brooklyn: Watch Tower Bible & Tract Society, 1974), 46.

116. Philip Schaff, *Nicene and Post-Nicene Christianity*, vol. 3 of *History of the Church* (Grand Rapids, MI: William B. Eerdmans, 1950 edition), 673.

117. *You Can Live Forever in Paradise on Earth* (Brooklyn: Watch Tower Bible & Tract Society, 1982), pages 40–41 states: "[T]he Trinity is not a Bible teaching. . . . [L]ong before Jesus walked the earth gods were worshipped in groups of three, or trinities, in places such as ancient Egypt and Babylon." Also see *Let God Be True*, which declares: "The origin of the trinity doctrine is traced back to the ancient Babylonians and Egyptians and other ancient mythologists" (p. 101).

118. Robert Bowman, *Why You Should Believe in the Trinity* (Grand Rapids, MI: Baker, 1989), 22.

119. Hippolytus, *Against the Heresy of One Noetus*, vol. 5 of *The Ante-Nicene Fathers*, eds. Alexander Roberts and James Donaldson; rev. ed. A. Cleveland Coxe (Grand Rapids, MI: Eerdmans, 1994 edition), 227.

120. Bowman, 45.

121. Gleason Archer, *Encyclopedia of Bible Difficulties* (Grand Rapids, MI: William B. Eerdmans, 1982), 361.

122. Stanley Grenz, *Theology for the Community of God* (Nashville: Broadman & Holman, 1994), 92.

123. *Should You Believe in the Trinity?* (Brooklyn: Watch Tower Bible and Tract Society, 1989), 15.

124. *You Can Live Forever in Paradise on Earth*, 138.

125. From last source cited, 40.

126. From last source cited, 172.

127. *The Watchtower*, September 15, 1961, 551.

128. "[T]he saints of this Gospel age are an anointed company—anointed to be kings and priests unto God . . . and together with Jesus, their chief and Lord, they constitute Jehovah's Anointed—the Christ" (Russell, *The Plan of the Ages*, 81–82); cf. "[T]he titles, Mighty God, and Everlasting Father, are titles which fully understood, are very appropriate to Our Lord Jesus. . . . [T]he same titles are applicable to the Church his body" (*Zion's Watch Tower & Herald*

of Christ's Presence, October/November 1881, 10, as reprinted in the Watch Tower reprints, vol. 1 [Allegheny, PA: Watchtower Bible & Tract Society, 1919], 297–298) and "Our high calling is so great, so much above comprehension of men, that they feel that we are guilty of blasphemy when we speak of being 'new creatures'—not any longer human. . . . [W]e are divine beings—hence all such are Gods. . . . Now we appear like men, and all die naturally like men, but in the resurrection we will rise in our true character as Gods" (*Zion's Watch Tower & Herald of Christ's Presence*, December 1881, 3, as reprinted in the Watch Tower reprints, vol. 1 Allegheny, PA: Watchtower Bible & Tract Society, 1919], 301).

129. *Listening to the Great Teacher* (Brooklyn: Watchtower Bible & Tract Society, 1971), 139.

130. *Jehovah's Witnesses in the 20th Century* (Brooklyn: Watch Tower Bible and Tract Society, 1979; 1989 edition), 13; Cf. *You Can Live Forever in Paradise on Earth*, 58.

131. *Let God Be True*, 122, 272; cf. *You Can Live Forever in Paradise on Earth*, 143.

132. *You Can Live Forever in Paradise On Earth*, 144–145; cf. *The Kingdom Is at Hand* (Brooklyn: Watch Tower Bible and Tract Society, 1944), 259 and Russell, *The Time Is at Hand*, 127.

133. *You Can Live Forever in Paradise on Earth*, 145.

134. *Holy Spirit* (Brooklyn: Watch Tower Bible and Tract Society, 1976), 11.

135. *Awake!*, December 8, 1973, 27.

136. J. F. Rutherford, *Life* (Brooklyn: Watch Tower Bible and Tract Society, 1929), 199, 206.

137. *The Watchtower*, August 15, 1972, 492.

138. *The Watchtower*, July 1, 1947, 204.

139. *The Watchtower*, February 15, 1983, 12–13.

140. *Life Everlasting*, 400.

141. *The Watchtower*, December 1, 1981, 27.

142. *Theocratic Aid to Kingdom Publishers* (Brooklyn: Watch Tower Bible & Tract Society, 1945), 249–250; cf. *Our Kingdom Service*, April 1981, 1.

Appendix A

1. Stanley Grenz, *Theology for the Community of God* (Nashville: Broadman & Holman, 1994), 99.

2. Wayne Grudem, *Systematic Theology* (Grand Rapids, MI: Zondervan, 1994), 226.

3. Gleason Archer, *Encyclopedia of Bible Difficulties* (Grand Rapids, MI: William B. Eerdmans, 1982), 357.

4. Walter A. Elwell, ed., *Evangelical Dictionary of Theology* (Grand Rapids, MI: Baker, 1984; 1996 edition), 732; cf. Walter A. Elwell, ed., *Baker Encyclopedia of the Bible*, vol. 2 (Grand Rapids, MI: Baker, 1988; 1995 edition), 1485.

5. Archer, 359.

6. From last source cited.

7. Grudem, 227. Grudem's argument is supported by many sources including E. Kautzsch's 1910 edition of *Gesenius' Hebrew Grammar*, which in reference to the plurality of majesty explanation states, "The plural used by God in Genesis 1:26 . . . has been incorrectly explained in this way." E. Kautzsch, ed., *Gesenius' Hebrew Grammar* (Oxford: Clarendon Press, 1910), Section 124g, n. 2.

8. Louis Berkhof, *Systematic Theology* (Grand Rapids, MI: William B. Eerdmans, 1938; 1995 edition), 85.

9. Robert P. Lightner, *Handbook of Evangelical Theology* (Grand Rapids, MI: Kregel Publications, 1995), 47.

INDEX

Abanes, Richard, 269
*Address to All Believers in Christ,
  An* (Whitmer), 185, 190
Age of Aquarius, 16
Alchemy, 37
Alley, Kirstie, 89
Altered states of consciousness
  (ASC), 42
American Family Foundation, The,
  9
America Online, 39
Anglo-Israelism, 96, 100
Ankerberg, John, 83
Answers in Action, 269
Answers to Cultists at Your Door
  (Passantino), 10
Anti-Semitism, hatred of Jews, 93,
  96, 97, 98, 99, 100, 101, 103,
  120, 121
*Aquarian Gospel of Jesus Christ,
  The* (Dowling), 14
Arcane School, 22
Archer, Gleason, 255, 266
Armageddon, 96, 101, 112, 233,
  234, 238, 239, 240, 241, 242
Arrington, Leonard J., 193
Aryan Nations, 94, 97, 100, 101,
  102, 103
Astral projection, 37
Astrology, 37, 38, 40, 41, 42, 43
Augustine, 89

Autobiography of a Yogi
  (Yogananda), 25
Automatic writing, 37

Baba, Meher, 25
Baba, Sai, 14, 25
Baba, Sathya Sai, 25
Bailey, Alice, 22
*Bare-Faced Messiah: The True Story
  of L. Ron Hubbard* (Miller), 71
Barnes, Peter, 270
Barrett, Francis, 195
Bauer, Gary, 143, 144
Beam, Louis, 100, 101
Beatles, the, 25
Berg, Hjalmer and Virginia, 165
Berg, Jane (Miller), 165, 171
Berg, Linda 166, 167
Berg, "Moses" David, 161 (Chapter
  8 *passim*)
Berkhof, 267
Bernard, Alphonso, 107 and fol-
  lowing
Besant, Annie, 20
Bhagwan Shree Rajneesh, 25
Bhaktivedanta Prabhupada, A.
  C., 25
Black, Karen, 89
Black Muslims, 107
Black supremacy, 107 (Chapter 6
  passim)

Blavatsky, Helena Petrovna, 20, 22
Bono, Sonny, 89
Boone, Pat, 144
Book of Babalon (Parsons), 72
Book of Mormon (BOM), 190,
   201, 211, 212, 213, 214
Book of the Law (Crowley), 72
Bouchard, Dan, 61
Breasted, James H., 218
Bridwell, Norman, 45
Broderick, Carlfred, 204
Brodie, Fawn, 197
Brooks, Nona, 21
Brown, Jerry, 25
Buddhism, 20, 146 see also *Zen
   Buddhism*
Bush, George and Barbara, 144,
   145, 169
Butler, Richard, 94, 97, 100, 102,
   103

Cameron, Marjorie, 72
Cannon, George Q., 190, 222
Cartwright, Nancy, 89
Casey, Royce, 61
Cayce, Edgar, 13
Central Council of Jews in
   Germany, 90
Chandler, Russell, 16
Channeling, 12, 20, 22, 37, 154
Chesson, "Dale," 102
Children, 239
Children of God, 161 (Chapter 8
   passim)
Christ Consciousness, 22, 32
Christian Coalition, 143
Christian Identity, 93 (Chapter 5
   passim)
Christian Research Institute, 269
Christian Science, 20, 21
Church of Jesus Christ of Latter-
   day Saints, The, 185 (Chapter 9
   passim)
Church of Satan, 56

Church Universal and Triumphant,
   The (C.U.T.), 36
Clairvoyance, 38, 40, 191
Clark, David, 23
Clary, Johnny Lee, 93 and following
Clement of Alexandria, 89
Combs, James, 99
Come Unto Christ (Benson), 209
Comments from the Friends, 270
Comparet, Bertrand, 98
Concerned Women for America,
   143
Confucianism, 146
Conley, Charles, 93
Cooper, John, 59
Copeland, Kenneth, 22
Corea, Chick, 89
Cosby, Bill, 144
Costa-Gavras, Constantin, 90
Council on American-Islamic
   Relations, 131
Course in Miracles, A, 30
Craft, The, 39
Creation of Human Ability, The
   (Hubbard), 77
Creme, Benjamin, 27, 31
Cross and the Switchblade, The,
   108
Crowley, Aleister, 35, 37, 57, 60,
   71, 72
Cruise, Tom, 89
Cruz, Nicky, 108
Crystal Cathedral, the, 143
Crystal gazing, crystal balls, 37,
   191
Cults, general characteristics, see
   esp. 10, 11, 69, 139
Cults Awareness Ministry, 68-69

Daniel, 42
Davies, W. Elwyn, 44
de Camp, L. Sprague, 71
Delashmutt, Jacob, 61
Demonic influence, 41, 42, 44, 182
Denver, John, 25

Dianetics: The Modern Science of Mental Health (Hubbard), 73, 74
Dictionary of Mysticism and the Occult, 182, 196
Discoverie of Witchcraft, The (Scot), 196
Disney films, 45
Divination, 41, 190, 191
Divine Principle of Sun Myung Moon, 141, 143, 146, 151, 155, 157, 158
Divine Science, 21
Doctrinal Statement of Beliefs, 97
Doctrine and Covenants (D&C), 185-186, 201, 211, 215, 216
Doctrines of Salvation (Smith), 190
Dowling, Levi, 14
Dowsing, 37
Dreams and the interpretation of, 37
Duke, David, 94
Dungeons & Dragons (D&D), 47, 48
Durham, Reed, 194, 195

Eastern mysticism, religion, spirituality, 14, 17, 18, 20, 24
Eddy, Mary Baker, 20, 21
Emerson, Ralph Waldo, 18
Encyclopedia of Mormonism, 204
Encyclopedia of Occultism and Parapsychology, 196
End-times, the, 101, 179
Enroth, Ronald, 144, 158
Equippers, Inc., 270
Evangelizing the Cults (Van Gorden), 83
Evidence from Scripture and History of the Second Coming of Christ About the Year A.D. 1843, and of His Personal Reign of 1,000 Years, 229
Exorcist, The, 39
Extrasensory perception (ESP), 37, 38, 40

Falwell, Jerry, 143, 144
"Family, The", 161 (Chapter 8 *passim*)
Family Research Council, 143
Fard, Wallace D., 108, 109, 110, 111, 112, 113, 114, 119, 126
Farrakhan, Louis, 107, 114, 115, 117, 118, 119, 120, 122, 123, 124, 125, 126, 131, 132
Farrow, Mia, 25
Feinberg, John, 37
Ferguson, Marilyn, 17, 27
Fillmore, Myrtle and Charles, 21
Fiorella, Joseph, 61
Flirty Fishing (FFing), 163, 174, 175, 176
Fortune-telling, 37, 38, 41
Fowler, John, 223
Fox, John, Margaret, Kate, Margaretta, 19
Franz, Frederick, 238, 241, 242
Free Memorial Baptist Church, 223
Free Minds, Inc., 270
Free Minds Journal, 228
Friedman, Michael, 90
Furhman, Mark, 131

Gaddafi, Muammar, 120
Gardell, Mattias, 112
Geer, Thelma, 204, 207
Ghost, 39
Gibby, Bryce, 223
Godfrey, Kenneth W., 198
Goedelman, Kurt, 269
Goodman, Leisa, 78
Gospel Through the Ages, The (Hunter), 203
Gospel Truths Ministries, 269
Groothuis, Doug, 29, 30, 33
Grubb, Louise, 70
Grudem, Wayne, 266

Habing, Bill, 223
Hagin, Kenneth, 22
Hale, Isaac, 190

Hanegraff, Hank, 269
Harp of God, The (Rutherford),
  251
Harris, Martin, 190
Hauntings, 38
Hawn, Goldie, 90
Healing, psychic and otherwise, 20,
  21, 37
Heath, Sir Edward, 144
Hendricks, Tyler O., 151
Henschel, Milton G., 242
Hinduism, 18, 20, 24, 25
Hippolytus, 254
History of the Church (Smith), 199
Hoffman, Dustin, 90
Holmes, Ernest, 21
Hooper, Ibrahim, 131
Hopkins, Emma Curtis, 21
Hubbard, L. Ron (pseudonyms
  Winchester Remington Colt and
  Rene Lafayette), 67, 70, 71, 72,
  73, 74, 75, 77, 78, 79, 80, 81. 83,
  89
Hubbard, L. Ron, Jr., 71
Humbard, Rex, 22
Hunter, Milton R., 203
Hussey, Olivia, 25
Huxley, Aldous, 22, 23

"I Am" sects, 22
Identity see Christian Identity
Independence Day, 123-124
International Bible Students
  (Jehovah's Witnesses),
  International Bible Students
  Association, 225, 232
International Federation of
  Religions and Philosophical
  Minorities, 169
Interracial marriage, 98, 99, 100,
  207
In the Name of Elijah Muhammad
  (Gardell), 112
Irenaeus, 89
Ishii, Matsue, 251

Islam, 109
Is This Life All There Is?, 252

Jack Parsons and the Fall of
  Babylon (Rydeen), 71
Jackson, Jesse, 119
Jacob, Daniel, 13
Jansen, Dan, 144
Jarreau, Al, 89
Jehovah's Witnesses, 169, 225
  (Chapter 10 passim)
Jerome, 89
Jordan, Fred, 165
Jude 3 Missions, 269

Karma, 30
Karriem, Robert, 113
Kelly, Steve (King Peter), 169
Kemp, Jack, 144
Kent, Stephen, 168
Key, Thomas, 212
Kim, Young Oon, 156, 157
Kimball, Heber C., 205
King, Coretta Scott, 144
King, Larry, 90
King, Martin Luther, 119, 120, 144
Kingdom Identity Ministries, 97
Kingdom of the Cults, The
  (Martin), 83
Kirkham, Francis, 192, 194
Klein, Calvin, 25
Knorr, Nathan, 238, 239, 240, 241
Kohl, Helmut, 90
Ku Klux Klan, 94, 96, 104

LaHaye, Beverly, 143, 144
Langone, Michael D., 9
Lark, Hedda, 33
LaVey, Anton, 52, 53, 55, 56, 60,
  63, 64, 65
Life Everlasting in Freedom of the
  Sons of God (Franz), 240, 241
Lightner, Robert, 267
Little, Malcolm, 115 see Malcolm
  X

Loftus, Elizabeth, 54
Lost tribes of Israel, 95, 96
Louis X, 114, 115, 117, 118 see
     Louis Farrakhan
L. *Ron Hubbard: Messiah or
     Madman?* (Hubbard, Jr.), 71
Lyons, Arthur, 51, 52, 53

Mace, Arthur C., 219
MacLaine, Shirley, 33
Magick, magic, 35, 37, 40, 42, 53,
     57, 58, 60, 71, 72, 195, 196
Magick in Theory and Practice
     (Crowley), 60
Magida, Arthur, 117
Magnani, Duane, 270
Magus, The (Barrett), 195
Maharaj Ji, 25
Malcolm X, 114, 115, 116, 117,
     118, 119, 130
Mansker, Roy B., 100
Mars Hills Productions, 45
Martin, Walter, 10, 83, 133
Martyr, Justin, 89
Mason, Marsha, 25
McConkie, Bruce, 190, 201, 202,
     205, 207, 208
McGee, Sandra, 185 and following
McKeever, Bill, 270
Meditation, 15
Mediums, 13, 18, 19, 41
Melton, J. Gordon, 16, 21, 52
Mercer, S. A. B., 219
Mesmer, Franz Anton, 18, 20
*Message to the Black Man in
     America* (Muhammad), 113
Metzger, Tom, 94
Michehl, Ingo, 135 and following
Millennium, 39
Miller, Elliot, 16
Miller, William, Millerites, 230
Million Man March, 119, 121,
     131, 132
*Millions Now Living Will Never
     Die*, 235, 237

Mohr, Jack, 99, 100
Mo Letters, 169, 171, 174, 180
Monism, 16, 27
Monroe, Robert, 42
Montgomery, Ruth, 13
Moon, Sun Myung, 135 (Chapter 7
     passim) see *Unification Church*
Moonies, 135 (Chapter 7 *passim*),
     169 see *Unification Church*
Mormon Doctrine, 210
Mormon History Association, 195
Mormonism, 185 (Chapter 9 *pas-
     sim*)
Mormonism Researched, 270
Mormonism, Mama, and Me
     (Geer), 205
Mormonism: Shadow or Reality?
     (Tanners), 220
Mt. Carmel Outreach, 37
Muhammad, Elijah, 107, 113, 114,
     115, 116, 117, 118, 119, 120,
     122, 124-125, 132
Muhammad, Khallid Abdul, 121
Muhammad, Wallace, 119
Muslim Mosque, Inc., 117
Myers, Ken, 45
My Little Fish, 173, 174
Mysticism, 16, 18

Namath, Joe, 25
Nathan, Jack, 252
National Association of
     Evangelicals (NAE), 143
National Spiritualist Association of
     the United States of America, 19
Nation of Islam (NOI), 107
     (Chapter 6 *passim*)
Nature's Finer Forces (Prasad), 20
Necromancy, 19, 37, 41 see also
     Seances
Neely, Albert, 193
New Age Encyclopedia, 22
New Age Is Lying to You, The
     (Winker), 27

New Age Movement, the, 13
(Chapter 1 *passim*)
New Christian (Identity) Crusade
Church, 93
New Cults, The (Martin), 10
New Thought, 18, 21, 22
New World, The, 238
*New World Translation of the Holy
Scriptures, The* (NWT), 229
Nibley, Hugh, 193
Nirvana, 31
Nolte, Claudia, 91
No Man Knows My History
(Brodie), 197
Numerology, 37, 40

O'Brien, Thomas, 93
Occult, the, occultism, 11, 17, 35
(Chapter 2 *passim*), 51, 52, 146,
181, 182, 190, 195, 233
Occult Sciences, The (Waite), 195
*Occult Secrets of the Hidden
World, The* (Tondriau), 38
Omen, The, 39
Ouija boards, 37
Out-of-body experiences, 37, 42 see
also *Astral projection*
Organization of Afro-American
Unity (OAAU), 119

Padilla, Sylvia and Arnaldo, 161
and following
Paganism, 51
Pahler, Elyse, 61
Palm-reading, palmistry, 37, 43
Pantheism of Alan Watts, The
(Clark), 23
Paramahansa, Swami Muktananda,
25
Paranormal, the, 38
Parapsychology, 40
Parker, Russ, 44
Parsons, John Whiteside, 71, 72, 73
Passantino, Bob and Gretchen, 10,
51, 269

Peale, Norman Vincent, 22
Pearl of Great Price, 201, 211, 216
Perennial Philosophy, the, 22, 23
Perennial Philosophy, The
(Huxley), 22
Perkins, John, 105
Personal Freedom Outreach, 269
Peters, Pete, 98, 99, 100
Petrie, W. M. Flinders, 217
Phenomenon, 39
Piece of Blue Sky, A, 71
Poltergeist: The Legacy, 39
Poole, Elijah, 113 see *Elijah
Muhammad*
Positive thinking, 21, 22
Powell, Colin, 131
Prasad, Rama, 20
Pratt, Orson, 210
Precognition, 40
Presley, Lisa Marie, 89, 90
Presley, Priscilla, 89
Preston, Kelly, 89
Price, Frederick, 22
Principalities and Powers (Davies),
44
Profiler, The, 39
Prophet, Elizabeth Clare, 36
Prophet of Rage (Magida), 117
*PSI Factor: Chronicles of the
Paranormal*, 39
Psychic healing, powers, phenom-
ena, 37, 38, 39, 44, 191
Psychokinesis, 37, 40
Puzo, Mario, 90
Pyramidology, 37, 233, 234

Quayle, Marilyn, 144
Quimby, Phineas P., 18, 20, 21

Racism, racists, 95, 104, 130, 131,
205, 206, 207
Rangel, Charles, 131
Rapid Eye, 71
Recovered memories, 54
Reed, Daniel, 270

Reed, Ralph, 143, 144
Reeves, Christopher, 144
Reincarnation, 20, 30, 31, 88, 89
Religious Information Center, 269
Religious movements, general characteristics, see *Cults*
Religious Science, 21
Reynolds, Arch S., 190
Reynolds, Michael, 270
Rhine, Joseph Banks, 40
Richards, LeGrand, 187
Robb, Thomas, 101
Roberts, B. H., 190
Rosemary's Baby, 39
Ross, Diana, 25
Ross, Joan, 9
Russell, Charles Taze, 229, 230, 231, 232, 233, 234, 235, 239, 240, 242, 252
Rutherford, J. F. (Joseph Franklin), 234, 235, 236, 237, 238, 251, 252
Rydeen, Paul, 71

Sabrina, the Teenage Witch, 39
Saint Germain Press, 22
San Juan Road Baptist Church, 223
Satanic Bible, The, 47, 53, 56
Satanic ritual abuse (SRA), 54
Satanism, 37, 40, 45, 47 (Chapter 3 *passim*)
Satan Wants You (Lyons), 52
Sayce, A. H., 217
Schuller, Robert, 22, 143
Scientology, 67 (Chapter 4 *passim*), 169
Scientology: A World Religion Emerges in the Space Age, 76
Scot, Reginald, 196, 197
Scott, Brad, 13 and following
Scott, Keith and Shawn, 67 and following
Scrying, 190, 191
Seances, 19 see also *Necromancy*

Second Adventists, 230, 231
Secret Relationship Between Blacks and Jews, The, 121
Sellers, Sean, 47 and following, 58, 63
Serpent Seed theory or doctrine, 96, 100
Seventh-day Adventists, 230
Shamanism, 37, 146, 157
Shining, The, 39
Smith, Emma-Hale, 190
Smith, Hyrum, 195, 196, 199, 200
Smith, John, 113
Smith, Joseph, 185, 188, 189, 190, 191, 192, 193, 194, 195, 196, 197, 198, 199, 200, 202, 203, 206, 209, 210, 212, 215, 216, 217, 219
Smith, Joseph F., 202
Smith, Joseph Fielding, 190, 206, 207, 220
Smith, Rodney, 116
Sorcery, 41
Spangler, David, 17, 27, 31
Spells and incantations, casting, 58
Spiritualism, spiritualists, spiritism, 19, 20, 41, 157
Sri Chinmoy, 25
Steiner, Rudolf, 14
St. Germain Foundation, 22
Stone, Oliver, 90
Studies in the Scriptures (Russell), 232, 233, 252
Sun Myung Moon (pamphlet), 139
Supreme Wisdom, The (Muhammad), 107
Suzuki, D. T., 23, 24
Shraddhananda, Swami, 14, 15

Tanner, Jerald and Sandra, 185 and following, 220, 270
Tanner, John, 185
Taoism, 146, 147
Tarot cards, 37, 39, 43

Tate, David, 100
Taylor, Elizabeth, 25
Teen Challenge, 166
Teilhard de Chardin, Pierre, 14
Telekinesis, 37
Telepathy, 40
Tertullian, 89
Then Is Finished the Mystery of God, 225
Theosophical Society, The, 20
Theosophy, 20, 22
Thoreau, Henry David, 18
Tondriau, Julien, 38
Transcendentalism, 18, 19, 20
Transcendental Meditation, 25
Travolta, John, 89
Trinity, the, 253, 254, 255, 256, 265 (Appendix A *passim*)
Truth Shall Make You Free, The, 240
Truth That Leads to Eternal Life, The, 225

UFOs, UFO abductions, 38, 130
Unification Church, the, 135 (Chapter 7 *passim*), 169
Unity School of Christianity, 21
Utah Lighthouse Ministry, 187-188, 270
Utah Missions, Inc., 270

Valiente, Doreen, 191
Van Gorden, Kurt, 83, 269
Victory of Love, 154
Vivekenanda, Swami, 24
Voodoo, 37

Waite, Arthur E., 195
Walcott, Louis Eugene, 115, 116 see *Louis X* and *Louis Farrakhan*
Walker, James, 269
Walters, Barbara, 144
Walters, Wesley P., 193, 194
War of the Wizards, The (Wylie), 45

Warwick, Dion, 39
Watchman Fellowship, 146, 269
Watch Tower Bible & Tract Society, the (WTBTS), 225 (Chapter 10 *passim*)
Watters, Randy, 225 and following, 270
Watts, Alan, 23
Way International, The, 10, 11
Way of Zen, The (Watts), 23
Weldon, John, 83
White Aryan Resistance (WAR), 94
White, Ben, 132
White, Ellen G., 230
White supremacy, 93 (Chapter 5 *passim*)
Whitman, Walt, 18
Whitmer, David, 185, 186, 190
Who, What, Why, When, Where: Aryan Nations (Butler), 102
Widstoe, John, 190, 192
Wierville, Victor Paul, 10
Wilkerson, David, 166
Williams, Billy Dee, 39
Wilson, Luke, 269
Winterburn, Karen, 35 and following
Winker, Eldon, 27
Witchcraft, 37, 40, 41, 45, 51, 58, 191, 196
Witches' Christmas, The (Bridwell), 45
Witches of Eastwick, The, 39
Witness, Inc., 270
Wizard's Hall (Yolen), 45
Wylie, Stephen, 45

X-Files, The, 39

Yamamoto, J. Isamu, 24
Yogananda, Swami Paramahansa, 24
Yogi, Maharishi Mahesh, 25
Yolen, Jane, 45

Young, Brigham, 185, 200, 203, 205, 207, 210

Zen Buddhism, 23, 24
Zerby, Karen (Maria), 167, 169
Zion's Watch Tower Tract Society, 231

BL 2525 .A33 1998
Richard Abanes
Cults, New Religious
Movements, and Your Family

DATE DUE

10/5/09			